The
REAL PROPHET OF DOOM

(KISMET) - INTRODUCTION - PENDULUM FLOW - II

Dwayne W. Anderson

THE REAL PROPHET OF DOOM (KISMET) -
INTRODUCTION - PENDULUM FLOW – II –

iUniverse books may be ordered through booksellers or by contacting:

iUniverse
1663 Liberty Drive
Bloomington, IN 47403
www.iuniverse.com
1-800-Authors (1-800-288-4677)

ISBN: 978-1-4917-9178-3 (sc)
ISBN: 978-1-4917-9180-6 (hc)
ISBN: 978-1-4917-9179-0 (e)

Library of Congress Control Number: 2016904206

Print information available on the last page.

iUniverse rev. date: 03/28/2016

`"- The REAL PROPHET of DOOM (Kismet) - INTRODUCTION - `-PENDULUM `-FLOW - II -"`

Written By: The `"PROPHET"!~ =

`-Dwayne W. Anderson (...) ~

BULLET POINTS FOR: "The Real Prophet of DOOM (Kismet) – Introduction – Pendulum Flow – II "-'

- *ASSASSINATION OF PRESIDENT ABRAHAM LINCOLN*
- *ASSASSINATION OF PRESIDENT JOHN F. KENNEDY*
- *THE PRESIDENCY OF PRESIDENT LYNDON B. JOHNSON*
- *THE LIFE; AND, DEATH OF FIRST LADY MARY TODD LINCOLN*
- *THE LIFE; AND, DEATH OF FIRST LADY LADY BIRD JOHNSON*
- *THE LIFE; AND, DEATH OF FIRST LADY JACQUELINE LEE KENNEDY*
- *THE PRESIDENCY OF PRESIDENT FRANKLIN DELANO ROOSEVELT*
- *THE LIFE; AND, DEATH OF FIRST LADY ELEANOR ROOSEVELT*
- *THE PRESIDENCY OF PRESIDENT THEODORE ROOSEVELT*
- *THE LIFE; AND, DEATH OF FIRST LADY EDITH ROOSEVELT*
- *THE LIFE; AND, DEATH OF PRESIDENT GEORGE WASHINGTON*
- *THE LIFE; AND, DEATH OF FIRST LADY MARTHA WASHINGTON*
- *THE LIFE; AND, DEATH OF PRESIDENT WOODROW WILSON*
- *THE LIFE; AND, DEATH OF PRESIDENT GERALD FORD*
- *THE LIFE; AND, DEATH OF PRESIDENT RONALD REAGAN*
- *THE LIFE; AND, DEATH OF PRESIDENT RICHARD M. NIXON*
- *THE LIFE; AND, DEATH OF PRESIDENT DWIGHT D. EISENHOWER*
- *THE LIFE; AND, DEATH OF PRESIDENT HARRY S. TRUMAN*
- *THE LIFE; AND, DEATH OF U.S. PRESIDENTS of the WHITEHOUSE*
- *THE LIFE; AND, DEATH OF U.S. FIRST LADYS of the WHITEHOUSE*

- *THE LIFE; AND, DEATH OF SOME U.S. VICE-PRESIDENTS of the WHITEHOUSE*
- *THE LIFE AND DEATH OF SCIENTISTS -*
- *THE LIFE AND DEATH OF CELEBRITIES –*
- *THE LIFE, TIMES; and, DEATHS of BIBLICAL CHARACTERS*
- *`-GOD'S `-NAME `-REVEALED-*
- *THE AMERICAN-ENGLISH ALPHABET utilized in `-PROPHECY-*
- *READING the BIBLE in FOCUS of Reciprocal-Sequencing-Numerology-RSN-*

I've `-CREATED a NEW TYPE of PHILOSOPHY (Reciprocal-Sequencing-Numerology) that `-PROVES without `-QUESTION the `-PRESENCE of GOD'S EXISTENCE in our DAILY AFFAIRS!!!!!~'

--------- Forwarded message ----------
From: **Dwayne Anderson** <contacttheprophet@therealprophetofdoom.com>
Date: Sun, Aug 9, 2015 at 2:49 PM
Subject: `-Extraterrestrials & `-Presidents: The Real Prophet Of Doom (Kismet) - Introduction - Pendulum Flow - / Author: Dwayne W. Anderson!!!!!~'
To: Email Cloaked!~'

`-STEVEN; and, `-LUCY HAWKING:

`-The MOVIE `-NATIONAL `-TREASURE (Nicolas Cage)!!!!!~' LIFE `-CIPHERS!!!!!~'

I have `-DISCOVERED a `-NEW; and, `-SCIENTIFIC FORM of `-NUMEROLOGY; that is at its source, `-BOTH `-REAL; and, Undeniably; a `-CREATION of `-GOD'S!!!!!!~'

IT'S; like `-DISCOVERING, a `-NEW `-MATHEMATICAL `-FORMULA!!!!!~' If the `-NEXT `-PERSON ELECTED, is `-WHO I `-SAY; then, `-WE can MAKE `-PROPHECY; through, MY `-NEW `-TYPE of `-NUMEROLOGY called "PENDULUM FLOW"!!!!!~' IT'S a `-MARTIAL `-ART; just as `-WELL, -of my `-OWN `-CREATION!!!!!~' Do `-YOU; want to `-LEARN!!!!!~'

Who's the next `-PRESIDENT?????~'

Jeb Bush, Hillary Clinton; or, Donald Trump?????~' / READ `-BELOW!!!!!~'

`-Extraterrestrials: $100,000,000.00 PRIZE `-AWARD!!!!!~'

Subject Title: `-TARGETS for `-EXTRATERRESTRIALS!!!!!~'

Send `-THIS `-ON; to `-ANYONE, that `-MAY be `-INTERESTED!!!!!~'

Look for LIFE on other PLANETS in the following CONSTELLATIONS: (**13**) Canes Venatici, (**23**) Circinus; and, (**32**) Delphinus!!!!!~ For the `-FOLLOWING: (**12**) Cancer, (**33**) Dorado; and, (**#1**) Andromeda; `-THEY, are giving me a FUNNY FEELING; TOO!!!!!!~' Why don't `-YOU; Check them OUT; just as well!!!!!~'

If The COSMOS could be divided into QUADRANTS of CONSTELLATIONS, look for LIFE on OTHER PLANETS; in, QUADRANTS `-**23**, `-**32**; and, `-**13**!!!!!~'

A "NEW" `-KIND OF "NUMEROLOGY"; CALLED "PENDULUM FLOW", that I've `-CREATED!!!!!~'

Regards, Author/Prophet/Dwayne W. Anderson.../ "The Real Prophet Of Doom!!!!!~'(…)-'

`-PRESIDENTS:

Dr. John P. Holdren, The White House; I have found the `-FORMULAS; and, `-EQUATIONS; of; and, to; `-LIFE & `-DEATH!!!!!~' Anyone's `-AGE of `-DEATH can be clearly `-CALCULATED!!!!!~' View the `-PRESIDENTS `-NUMBERS listed `-BELOW just for an `-EXAMPLE!!!!!~' I have already `-ANALYZED my `-OWN personal family `-HISTORIES; and, the `-WORLD `-HISTORY as a `-WHOLE!!!!!~' Show `-THIS to the `-PRESIDENT – BARACK H. OBAMA, `-PLEASE!!!!!~' My `-NEW `-BOOK is now being `-UPDATED with `-96 brand new PAGES just right `-NOW as I `-SPEAK as I've just been `-INSPIRED to `-WRITE; `-Again!!!!!~' Wait `-One MONTH for `-IT to be `-UPDATED before `-YOU buy a `-COPY of `-IT; entitled: "The Real Prophet of Doom (Kismet) – Introduction – Pendulum Flow –"!!!!!~'

The Presidents with the `-NUMBER `-53+_!!!!!~' Russia's Vladimir Lenin died at the `-AGE of `-53; and, Russia's Joseph Stalin died in `-1953 on its `-RECIPROCAL `-DAY / 03/05/1953 / `-35 = RECIPROCAL = `-53_!!!!!~'

3

'-**44**ᵗʰ President Barack H. Obama ('-**53** years of age in '-**2014**); was born, '-**9** days before the Berlin Wall had begun construction (the '-**13**ᵗʰ of August)!!!!!~ The Berlin Wall was opened in '-1**989** /**RSN** acknowledging '-**53** years since started!!!!!~ Vladimir V. Putin (born '-**85** days before '-19**53**) '-**85** = 8 + 5 = '-**13** = '-**9** years older than President Barack H. Obama!!!!!~ The Days '-**85** (Minus) The Age/Year '-**53** = The Number '-**32**!!!!!~ President Barack H. Obama was born in '-19**61**!!!!!~ President Vladimir V. Putin; in '-2014, at the time of this original writing; was, '-**61**years of age!!!!!~ President Barack H. Obama is **6' 1**" in height!!!!!~ President Vladimir V. Putin; and, President Barack H. Obama; are, '-**RECIPROCALS**!!!!!~ There are some '-**63** days (President John F. Kennedy died in '-19**63** / took office in '-19**61**) for this interaction in between their birthdays!!!!!~' Dwight David ("IKE") Eisenhower was the '-**34**ᵗʰ President of the United States from '-19**53** until '-19**61**!!!!!~' **34** = RECIPROCAL = **43** / George W. Bush.

President George Washington was '-BORN on **2/22/1732**!!!!!~' At the '-AGE of his being '-**44** years of '-AGE the Declaration of Independence came into existence in '-17**76**!!!!!~' '-**23** Years later; the President George Washington had died at the tender '-AGE of '-**67**!!!!!~' '-**32** = RECIPROCAL = '-**23** / '-**76** = RECIPROCAL = '-**67** !!!!!~ With President Woodrow Wilson - there were '-**123** years lying in between both of their births; and, both of their deaths (George Washington's)!!!!!~' President Wilson lived to be '-**67** years of '-AGE; '-too!!!!!~' President Woodrow Wilson in leaving the '-AGE of '-**44**; there were '-**222** days (**Washington's Birthday**) that lie in between his '-DEATH '-DAY (**2/3**/1901)-(19+2+3-1)=('-**23**); and, with the President Theodore Roosevelt taking on the Presidency of the United States of America!!!!!~'President Theodore Roosevelt was married to his '-WIFE; EDITH, for '-**32** YEARS!!!!!~' President Woodrow Wilson at the '-AGE of '-**44** would equal '-**1** Year / '-**222** Days; until, Theodore!!!!!~' '-**1** Year / '-**222** Days = (365 + 222) = '-**587** = (58 + 7) = '-**65** = '-**YEAR** President Abraham Lincoln was '-**SHOT** being married to his wife Mary Todd Lincoln for '-**23** YEARS!!!!!~'

President John F. Kennedy's '-BIRTH equals **5/29/1917**!!!!!~' President Franklin Delano Roosevelt's '-BIRTH equals **1/30/1882**!!!!!~' '-1917 (-) '-1882 = '-**35** YEARS!!!!!~' President John F. Kennedy's '-YEAR of '-DEATH equals **11/22/1963**!!!!!~' President Franklin Delano Roosevelt's '-YEAR of '-DEATH equals **4/12/1945**!!!!!~' '-1963 (-) '-1945 = '-**18**!!!!!~' '-35 + '-18 = '-**53** / '-**35** = **RECIPROCAL** = '-**53** = "**WAR of the '-WORLDS**"!!!!!~'

4

President Lyndon B. Johnson's `-BIRTH equals **8/27/1908!!!!!~**' President Franklin Delano Roosevelt's `-BIRTH in `-DIFFERENCE equals `-**26** YEARS!!!!!~ `-1908 (-) `-1882 = `-**26!!!!!~** President Lyndon B. Johnson's `-YEAR of `-DEATH equals **1/22/1973!!!!!~**' President Franklin Delano Roosevelt's `-DEATH in `-DIFFERENCE equals `-**27** YEARS!!!!!~' `-1972 (-) `-1945 = `-**27!!!!!~**' `-26 + `-27 = `-**53** = **"WAR of the `-WORLDS"!!!!!~**'

President Dwight D. Eisenhower's `-BIRTH equals **10/14/1890!!!!!~**' President Franklin Delano Roosevelt's `-BIRTH in `-DIFFERENCE equals `-**8** YEARS!!!!!~ `-1**890** (-) `-1882 = `-**8!!!!!~** President Dwight D. Eisenhower's `-YEAR of `-DEATH equals **3/28/1969!!!!!~**' President Franklin Delano Roosevelt's `-DEATH in `-DIFFERENCE equals `-**23** YEARS!!!!!~' `-1968 (-) `-1945 = `-**23!!!!!~**' `-8 + `-23 = `-**31** = **RECIPROCAL** = `-**13** = **"A VERY PIVOTAL NUMBER"!!!!!~**' `-**13** + `-**31** = `-**44** = **"MOM"!!!!!~**' `-1969 (-) `-1945 = `-**24!!!!!~**' `-24 (+) `-8 = `-**32** = -a Prophetic Number!!!!!~' Dwight D. Eisenhower became the `-34th President in `-19**53**.

Dwight D. Eisenhower's `-BIRTH **10/14/1890** = (10 + 14 + 18 + 90) = `-**132**
Dwight D. Eisenhower's `-DEATH **03/28/1969** = (03 + 28 + 19 + 69) = `-**119**
`-132 + `-119 = `-**251** = (2 + 51) = `-**53** = **"War of the Worlds"!!!!!~**'
`-53 + `-34 = `-**87** = **RECIPROCAL** = `-**78** = **"AGE of `-DEATH"!!!!!~**'

Harry S. Truman's `-BIRTH **05/08/1884** = (05 + 08 + 18 + 84) = `-**115**
Harry S. Truman's `-DEATH **12/26/1972** = (12 + 26 + 19 + 72) = `-**129**
`-115 + `-129 = `-**244** = (24 x 4) = `-**96** = **RECIPROCAL** = `-**69** = **"The CYCLE of `-LIFE"!!!!!~**' `-**244** = (2 x 44) = `-**88** = **RECIPROCAL** = `-**88** = **"AGE of `-DEATH"!!!!!~**'
`-**53** = **RECIPROCAL** = `-**35** / `-**35** + `-**53** = `-**88** = **"AGE of `-DEATH"!!!!!~**'
`-8472 (-) `-1819 (-) `-826 (-) `-512 = `-**5315** = `-**53**.15 = **ROUNDED DOWN** = `-**53**'!!!!!~'
`-**31.5** = **ROUNDED UP** = `-**32** = -a Prophetic Number!!!!!~'
`-**1972** = `-72 (-) `-19 = `-**53** = **"War of the Worlds"!!!!!~**'

President Abraham Lincoln's `-BIRTH equals **2/12/1809!!!!!~**' President Franklin Delano Roosevelt's `-BIRTH in `-DIFFERENCE equals `-**73** YEARS!!!!!~ `-1882 (-) `-1**809** = `-**73!!!!!~** President Abraham Lincoln's `-YEAR of `-DEATH equals **4/15/1865!!!!!~**' President Franklin Delano Roosevelt's `-DEATH in `-DIFFERENCE equals `-**20** YEARS; and, `-**3** DAYS = (20 + 3) = `-**23!!!!!~**' `-65 (-) `-45 = `-**20!!!!!~**' `-73 (-) `-20 = `-**53** =**"WAR of the `-WORLDS"!!!!!~**'

President Richard Nixon's `-BIRTH equals **1/09/1913!!!!!~**' `-19 + `-13 = `-**32**!!!!!~' President Franklin Delano Roosevelt's `-BIRTH in `-DIFFERENCE equals `-**31** YEARS!!!!!~ `-1913 (-) `-1882 = `-**31**!!!!!~ President Richard Nixon's `-YEAR of `-DEATH equals **4/22/1994!!!!!~**'President Franklin Delano Roosevelt's `-DEATH in `-DIFFERENCE equals `-**39** YEARS; and, `-**10** DAYS = (39 + 10) = `-**49**!!!!!~' `-**49** =**RECIPROCAL** = `-**94** (-) `-45 = `-**49**!!!!!~' `-94 (+) `-45 = `-**139**!!!!!~' `-**31** = **RECIPROCAL** = `-**13** / `-139 (+) `-13 = `-**152** = (1 + 52) = `-**53** =**"WAR of the `-WORLDS"!!!!!~'**

President Gerald Ford's `-BIRTH equals **7/14/1913!!!!!~**' `-19 + `-13 = `-**32**!!!!!~' President Franklin Delano Roosevelt's `-BIRTH in `-DIFFERENCE equals `-**31** YEARS!!!!!~ `-1913 (-) `-1882 = `-**31**!!!!!~ President Gerald Ford's `-YEAR of `-DEATH equals **12/26/2006!!!!!~**'President Franklin Delano Roosevelt's `-DEATH in `-DIFFERENCE equals `-**39** YEARS!!!!!~' `-45 (-) `-6 = `-**39**!!!!!~' `-31 = (3 + 1) = `-**4** / `-39 (-) `-4 = `-**35** = RECIPROCAL = `-**53** = **"WAR of the `-WORLDS"!!!!!~'**

President Ronald Reagan's `-BIRTH equals **2/06/1911!!!!!~**' President Franklin Delano Roosevelt's `-BIRTH in `-DIFFERENCE equals `-**29** YEARS!!!!!~ `-1911 (-) `-1882 = `-**29**!!!!!~ President Ronald Reagan's `-YEAR of `-DEATH equals **6/05/2004!!!!!~**' President Franklin Delano Roosevelt's `-DEATH in `-DIFFERENCE equals `-**41** YEARS; and, `-**53** DAYS = (41 + 53) = `-**94**!!!!!~'!!!!!~' `-45 (-) `-4 = `-**41**!!!!!~' `-29 = (2 + 9) = `-**11** / `-41 (+) `-11 = `-**52** = +1 = `-**53** = **"WAR of the `-WORLDS"!!!!!~'**

President Woodrow Wilson's `-BIRTH equals **12/28/1856!!!!!~**' President Franklin Delano Roosevelt's `-BIRTH in `-DIFFERENCE equals `-**26** YEARS!!!!!~ `-1882 (-) `-1856 = `-**26**!!!!!~ President Woodrow Wilson's `-YEAR of `-DEATH equals **2/03/1924!!!!!~**' President Franklin Delano Roosevelt's `-DEATH in `-DIFFERENCE equals `-**21** YEARS; and, `-**67** DAYS = (67 (-) 21) = `-**46** = `-**23** x `-**2** = `-**232** = **Reciprocal-Sequenced-Numerology**!!!!!~' `-**45** + `-**24** = `-**69** = **"Yin/Yang"** = **"The Cycle of `-LIFE"**!!!!!~' `-45 (-) `-24 = `-**21**!!!!!~' `-26 = (2 + 6) = `-**8** / `-46 (+) `-8 = `-**54**= -1 = `-**53** = **"WAR of the `-WORLDS"!!!!!~'**

President George Washington's `-BIRTH equals **2/22/1732!!!!!~**' President Franklin Delano Roosevelt's `-BIRTH in `-DIFFERENCE equals `-**150** YEARS!!!!!~ `-1882 (-) `-1732 = `-**150**!!!!!~ President George Washington's `-YEAR of `-DEATH equals **12/14/1799!!!!!~**' President Franklin Delano Roosevelt's `-DEATH in `-DIFFERENCE equals `-**54** YEARS!!!!!~' `-**99** +

`-45 = `-144 = "MOM"!!!!!-' `-99 (-) `-45 = `-54 = -1 = `-53 ="WAR of the `-WORLDS"!!!!!-'

`-CONTACT `-ME; for if, `-YOU so `-DESIRE!!!!!-' From: Author: Dwayne W. Anderson!!!!!-'

Live `-PRESIDENTS!!!!!-' (I haven't `-DONE the `-FORMULA `-NUMBERS on `-THEM; `-Yet)!!!!!-'

`-REMEMBER; the Presidents with the `-NUMBER `-53+_!!!!!-' Russia's Vladimir Lenin died at the `-AGE of `-53; and, Russia's Joseph Stalin died in `-1953 on its `-RECIPROCAL `-DAY / 03/05/1953 / `-35 = RECIPROCAL = `-53/|\ !!!!!-'

`-44th President Barack H. Obama (`-53 years of age in `-2014); was born, `-9 days before the Berlin Wall had begun construction (the `-13th of August)!!!!!- The Berlin Wall was opened in `-1989 /RSN acknowledging `-53 years since started!!!!!- Vladimir V. Putin (born `-85 days before `-1953) `-85 = 8 + 5 = `-13 = `-9 years older than President Barack H. Obama!!!!!- The Days `-85 (Minus) The Age/Year `-53 = The Number `-32!!!!!- President Barack H. Obama was born in `-1961!!!!!- President Vladimir V. Putin; in `-2014, at the time of this original writing; was, `-61 years of age!!!!!- President Barack H. Obama is 6' 1" in height!!!!!- President Vladimir V. Putin; and, President Barack H. Obama; are, `-RECIPROCALS!!!!!- There are some `-63 days (President John F. Kennedy died in `-1963 / took office in `-1961) for this interaction in between their birthdays!!!!!-' Dwight David ("IKE") Eisenhower was the `-34th President of the United States from `-1953 until `-1961!!!!!-' 34 = RECIPROCAL = 43 / George W. Bush.

President Jimmy Carter was `-BORN on 10/01/1924 = `-BIRTHDAY `# = `-54 = -1 = `-53

President George H. W. Bush was `-BORN on 06/12/1924 = `-BIRTHDAY `# = `-61

There are `-111 days that `-SEPARATE their `-BIRTHS!!!!!-'

`-111 = "Yin/Yang" = "The Cycle of `-LIFE"!!!!!-'

Same `-BIRTH `-YEAR; and, the Same `-AGE!!!!!-'

7

According to `-**HISTORY**; and, <u>R</u>eciprocal-<u>S</u>equencing-<u>N</u>umerology; `-**93 for `-BOTH (Reagan & Ford); or, the same `-YEAR of `-EXPIRATION; pretty much, for `-BOTH!!!!!~'**

President Bill Clinton was `-BORN on **08/19/1946** = `-BIRTHDAY `# = `-**92**

8 + 19 + 19 = `-**46** = `-23 x `-2 = `-**232** = <u>R</u>eciprocal-<u>S</u>equenced-<u>N</u>umerology!!!!!~'

46 + 46 = `-**92** = BIRTHDAY #!!!!!~'

President George W. Bush was `-BORN on **07/06/1946** = `-BIRTHDAY `# = `-**78**

`-**46** = `-23 x `-2 = `-**232** = <u>R</u>eciprocal-<u>S</u>equenced-<u>N</u>umerology!!!!!~'

There are `-**44 days** that `-**SEPARATE their `-BIRTHS!!!!!~'**

`-**44** = `-4 x `-11 = *Multiple of* `-11 = **"Yin/Yang"** = **"The Cycle of `-LIFE"!!!!!~'**

Same `-BIRTH `-YEAR; and, the Same `-AGE!!!!!~'

`-54 + `-61 + `-92 + `-78 = `-**285** = (28 x 5) = `-**140** = (14 + 0) = `-**14**

`-61 (-) `-54 = `-**7** / `-92 (-) `-78 = `-**14** (Multiple of `-**7**)!!!!!~'

`-7 x `-7 = `-**49** = <u>**RECIPROCAL**</u> = `-**94** = **The `-DEATH `-NUMBERS `-#'S!!!!!~'**

`-<u>**RECIPROCALS**</u>-'

`-**45** + `-**16** + `-**29** + `-**87** = `-**177** = (1 x 77) = `-**77** = `-7 x `-11 = *Multiple of `-11* = **"Yin/Yang"** = **"The Cycle of `-LIFE"!!!!!~'**

My `-UNCLE MICHAEL that I performed the `-FUNERAL `-SERVICES for died on his mother's `-BIRTHDAY (My `-Grandmother)!!!!!~' He was `-BORN on 0**6**/0**5**/19**56**!!!!!~'

`-**65** = <u>**RECIPROCAL**</u> = `-**56** = His `-BIRTH `-YEAR is a `-<u>**RECIPROCAL**</u> of his very own `-**BIRTHDAY**; and, `-BIRTH `-MONTH!!!!!~'

In his `-BURIAL `-TOMB; he is buried with his older `-BROTHER, that `-DIED; at the exact `-AGE of his `-BIRTH = `-**56**!!!!!~'

Uncle Michael was `-BORN on the `-EXACT `-SAME `-DAY; and, `-MONTH; as the `-DEATH `-DAY; and, `-MONTH; for **President Ronald Reagan!!!!!~'**

`-**48** years from `-**BIRTH to `-DEATH between the `-TWO!!!!!~'**

`-**48** = **RECIPROCAL** = `-**84**

`-48 + `-84 = `-**132** = (1 x 32) = `-**32** = -a Prophetic Number!!!!!~'

President RONALD REAGAN'S `-DEATH `-DAY # = the `-NUMBER `-**35!!!!!~'**

06/05/2004!!!!!~' / 06 + 05 + 20 + 04 = `-**35 = RECIPROCAL = `-53!!!!!~'**

The "PROPHET'S" UNCLE `-MICHAEL has a `-BIRTHDAY `-NUMBER of (06/05/1956) = `-**86** = `-AGE of `-DEATH of In-Law's Father – the "PROPHET'S" MOTHER'S FATHER!!!!!~'

The "PROPHET'S" BROTHER has a `-CALCULATION from within his `-BIRTHDAY `-NUMBER of (09/25/1967) = (19 + 67) = `-**86** = `-AGE of `-DEATH of `-GRANDFATHER – the "PROPHET'S" MOTHER'S FATHER!!!!!~'

The "PROPHET'S" UNCLE `-MICHAEL had `-DIED at the tender `-AGE of `-47; while, the `-PROPHET'S BROTHER in `-NOW; `-47 years of `-AGE; at the `-TIME, of this `-REVELATION!!!!!~'

Hillary Rodham Clinton is the `-**Reciprocal** of the "Prophet's" Brother this year of `-**2014/2015!!!!!~** She was Born in `-19**47** while at the Age of `-**67** / The "Prophet's" Brother is at Age `-**47** being born in `-19**67!!!!!~'**

`-47 + `-47 = `-**94** = **RECIPROCAL** = `-**49** = The `-DEATH `-NUMBERS `-#'S!!!!!~'

`-**47** = **RECIPROCAL** = `-**74**

`-47 + `-74 = `-**121** = **R**eciprocal-**S**equenced-**N**umerology!!!!!~'

`-**67** (-) `-56 = `-**11** = **"Yin/Yang" = "The Cycle of `-LIFE"!!!!!~'**

Jeb Bush was `-BORN in `-19**53!!!!!~'** `-Peculiar, **don't** `-you `-**think!!!!!~'**

Jeb Bush is `-**62 YEARS of** `-**AGE!!!!!**~' `-62 (-) `-1 = `-**61!!!!!**~'

APPLE on `-TRACK to make $**52.5** = ROUNDED UP = `-$**53** BILLION DOLLARS by the `-END of `-SEPTEMBER!!!!!~' The `-MOST made by `-ANY other `-BUSINESS/COMPANY `-**EVER!!!!!**~'

North Fire in Southern California Grows to **3,5**00 **Acres!!!!!**~'

`-**3500** = **RECIPROCAL** = `-**5300** / `-**35** = **RECIPROCAL** = `-**53**

Ivan the Terrible, Wladyslaw IV Vasa, Vladislav I of Wallachia; and, Peter the Great `-all `-DIED within their `-**53**rd **YEAR of** `-**LIVING!!!!!**~'

The `-17th President of the United States Andrew Johnson (succeeding President Abraham Lincoln) died at the tender `-AGE of `-**66** in `-HIS `-**67**th `-YEAR of `-LIVING (A Plate `-ENGRAVED at his `-FUNERAL had said that `-HE had `-DIED at the `-AGE of `-**67**); and, the `-1st President of the United States George Washington `-**DIED** at the tender `-**AGE of** `-**67!!!!!**~' There were `-**54** days that lie in between their `-BIRTHDAYS (`-**54** (-**1**) = `-**53**)!!!!!~' From their `-DEATH `-DAYS to `-DEATH `-DAYS; there are/they are `-**230** days `-**APART!!!!!**~' (`-**230** = (23 + 0) = `-**23** = -a **Prophetic Number!!!!!**~' `-**67** = **RECIPROCAL** = `-**76** / **There are** `-**76 years in between their** `-**DEATHS!!!!!**~'

With President **Andrew** Johnson; and, President Abraham Lincoln (`-**BIRTH to** `-**BIRTH**) = `-**46 DAYS** = `-**23** x `-**2** = `-**232** = **Reciprocal-Sequenced-Numerology!!!!!**~'

With President **Andrew** Jackson; and, President Abraham Lincoln (`-**BIRTH to** `-**BIRTH**) = `-**32 DAYS** = -a **Prophetic Number!!!!!**~'

President **Andrew** Johnson's `-WIFE, First Lady – Eliza McCardle Johnson (**A Civil War Woman**) `-DIED in `-18**76**; at the tender `-AGE of `-**65**, in `-HER `-**66**th `-YEAR of `-LIVING surviving President Johnson; her husband, only by `-6 months; and, she was buried next to her husband - the President!!!!!~' `-**76** =**RECIPROCAL** = `-**67!!!!!**~' President **Andrew** Jackson was `-BORN in `-1**767!!!!!**~ `-**32 years later; President George Washington,** `-**DIED!!!!!**~'

Presidents: 1 (George Washington) (-) 7 (Andrew Jackson) = `-**6** / 7 (Andrew Jackson) (-) 16 (Abraham Lincoln) = `-**9** / `-**69** = **"The Cycle of** `-**LIFE"!!!!!**~'

'-Both Ulysses S. Grant; and, Robert E. Lee; died, at the tender '-AGE of '-**63!!!!!**-' **From** '-**DEATH** '-**DAY to** '-**DEATH** '-**DAY; they died** '-**82days** '-**APART!!!!!**-' Jefferson Davis '-**DIED** at the '-AGE of '-**81** = +1 = '-**82!!!!!**-' Abraham Lincoln; and, Jefferson Davis; **their** '-**DEATH** '-**DATES**, '-are; '-**130** days '-**APART!!!!!**-' Mary Todd Lincoln's '-BIRTHDAY; and, Ulysses S. Grant's '-BIRTHDAY ('-BIRTH to '-BIRTH) are '-1**36** days '-**APART!!!!!**- '-**36** = **RECIPROCAL** = '-**63** / Mary Todd Lincoln, Franklin Delano Roosevelt; and, the "PROPHET'S" MOTHER '-Ethelyn; '-all '-DIED at the tender '-AGE of '-**63!!!!!**-'

Uncle CAL shares a '-**BIRTHDAY** with Jennifer Lopez on the '-**24**th **of JULY!!!!!**-' Jennifer Lopez is **5' 5"** (1.**64** m) = **2** x '-**32** = **Reciprocal-Sequenced-Numerology!!!!!**-' She was '-BORN in '-19**69**!!!!!-' '-**69** = "**Yin/Yang**" = "**The Cycle of LIFE**"!!!!!-' Her middle '-**NAME** is '-**LYNN!!!!!**-' She played '-**SELENA** in the '-**MOVIES!!!!!**-' '-**SELENA** was born on 04/1**6** = (1(46)) = '-**46!!!!!**-' Jennifer Lopez just turned '-**46!!!!**-' '-**46** = '-**23** x **2** = **Reciprocal-Sequenced-Numerology!!!!!**-' '-**SELENA** was killed at the tender '-**AGE** of '-**23!!!!!**-'

Selena Gomez was '-**NAMED** after '-**SELENA!!!!!**-' Selena Gomez is **5' 5"** (1.**64** m) = **2** x '-**32** = **Reciprocal-Sequenced-Numerology!!!!!**-' Selena Gomez' '-**BIRTHDAY** was on the **22**nd **of** '-**JULY!!!!!**-' She turned '-**23** years of '-**AGE!!!!!**-'

Uncle CAL/Jennifer Lopez '-**24**th **of** '-**JULY!!!!!**-' *Selena Gomez* '-**22**nd **of** '-**JULY!!!!!**-'

'-*24* + '-*22* = '-**46** / '-*2* = '-**23** = **-a Prophetic Number!!!!!**-'

Bobbi Kristina Brown '-DEAD at the tender '-AGE of '-**22!!!!!**-' (**+1**) = '-**23** = **-a Prophetic Number!!!!!**-'

Modern Day '-**PRESIDENTS** with their **Modern Day** '-**NUMBERS!!!!!**-'

Did '-YOU '-NOTICE; that there are '-**23** days that lie in between the '-BIRTHDAYS of President George H. W. Bush; and, his '-SON President George W. Bush!!!!!-' During this '-TIME of '-**23** days, they are '-**23** years apart in '-LIVING!!!!!-'

There are '-**67** days that lie in between the births of President Bill Clinton; and, President George H. W. Bush!!!!!-'

11

`-**111** (Jimmy Carter/George H. W. Bush) (-) `-**44** (Bill Clinton/George W. Bush) = `-**67**!!!!!~'

Hillary Rodham Clinton is the `-**Reciprocal** of the "Prophet's" Brother this year of `-**2014/2015**!!!!!~ She was Born in `-19**47** while at the Age of `-**67**/ The "Prophet's" Brother is at Age `-**47** being born in `-19**67**!!!!!~'

There are `-**86** days that lie in between; and, `-**88** days from birth to birth that exists between President George W. Bush; and, President Jimmy Carter!!!!!~'

There are `-**42** days that lie in between; and, `-**44** days from birth to birth that exists between President Bill Clinton; and, President Jimmy Carter!!!!!~'

Considering `-DAYS; President Bill Clinton is right in the `-**MIDDLE** of President Jimmy Carter; and, President George W. Bush!!!!!~'

President Jimmy Carter TO President Bill Clinton = `-**22**

President Jimmy Carter TO President George W. Bush = `-**22**

`-22 + `-22 = `-**44** = "BirthYear" of the "PROPHET'S" MOTHER (**Lynn**) (`-19**44**)!!!!!~'

President Jimmy Carter being married to his wife Rosa**lynn** Carter for some `-**69** years standing as equals to the lives of both President George W. Bush; and, President Bill Clinton!!!!!~'

President Jimmy Carter was `-BORN on **10/01/1924** = `-BIRTHDAY `# = `-**54** = -1 = `-**53**

President George H. W. Bush was `-BORN on **06/12/1924** = `-BIRTHDAY `# = `-**61**

There are `-**111 days** that `-SEPARATE their `-BIRTHS!!!!!~'

`-**111** = "Yin/Yang" = "The Cycle of `-LIFE"!!!!!~'

Same `-BIRTH `-YEAR; and, the Same `-AGE!!!!!~'

According to `-HISTORY; and, Reciprocal-Sequencing-Numerology; `-**93 for** `-BOTH (Reagan & Ford); or, the same `-YEAR of `-EXPIRATION; pretty much, for `-BOTH!!!!!~'

President Bill Clinton was '-BORN on **08/19/1946** = '-BIRTHDAY '# = '-**92**

8 + 19 + 19 = '-**46** = '-23 x '-2 = '-**232** = **R**eciprocal-**S**equenced-**N**umerology!!!!!~'

46 + 46 = '-**92** = BIRTHDAY #!!!!!~'

President George W. Bush was '-BORN on **07/06/1946** = '-BIRTHDAY '# = '-**78**

'-**46** = '-23 x '-2 = '-**232** = **R**eciprocal-**S**equenced-**N**umerology!!!!!~'

There are '-**44 days** that '-**SEPARATE their** '-**BIRTHS!!!!!~**'

'-**44** = '-4 x '-11 = *Multiple of* '-11 = **"Yin/Yang"** = **"The Cycle of** '-LIFE"!!!!!~'

Same '-BIRTH '-**YEAR; and, the Same** '-**AGE!!!!!~**'

President RONALD REAGAN'S '-DEATH '-DAY **#** = the '-NUMBER '-**35!!!!!~**'

06/05/2004!!!!!~'

06 + 05 + 20 + 04 = '-**35** = **RECIPROCAL** = '-**53** = **"WAR of the WORLDS"!!!!!~**'

The "PROPHET'S" UNCLE '-MICHAEL has a '-BIRTHDAY '-NUMBER of (06/05/1956) = '-**86** = '-AGE of '-DEATH of In-Law's Father - the "PROPHET'S" MOTHER'S FATHER!!!!!~'

The "PROPHET'S" BROTHER has a '-CALCULATION from within his '-BIRTHDAY '-NUMBER of (09/25/1967) = (19 + 67) = '-**86** = '-AGE of '-DEATH of '-GRANDFATHER - the "PROPHET'S" MOTHER'S FATHER!!!!!~'

The "PROPHET'S" UNCLE '-MICHAEL had '-DIED at the tender '-AGE of '-47; while, the '-PROPHET'S BROTHER in '-NOW; '-47 years of '-AGE; at the '-TIME, of this '-REVELATION!!!!!~'

Hillary Rodham Clinton is the '-**Reciprocal** of the "Prophet's" Brother this year of '-**2014/2015!!!!!~** She was Born in '-19**47** while at the Age of '-**67**/ The "Prophet's" Brother is at Age '-**47** being born in '-19**67**!!!!!~'

`-61 (-) `-54 = `-**7** **/** -92 (-) `-78 = `-**14** **/** `-67 (Hillary Clinton) (-) `-53 (Jeb Bush) = `-**14**

`-14 + `-14 + `-7 = `-**35** = **RECIPROCAL** = `-**53** = "**WAR of the WORLDS**"!!!!!~'

So will **HILLARY CLINTON** be the very `-**NEXT PRESIDENT** (`-**67**); or, will **JEB BUSH** (`-**53**); or, will; `-**HE come** `-**LATER!!!!!~'**

The "**PROPHET**" (**Dwayne W. Anderson**) was `-**BORN** on (0**3**/2**0**/19**70**)!!!!!~'

`-53 + `-67 = `-1**20** = (`-1 x `-20) = `-**20** = Day of `-BIRTH of the `-"**PROPHET**"!!!!!~'

`-53 + `-67 = `-1**20** = The "**PROPHET'S**" BROTHER'S `-BIRTHDAY `-NUMBER!!!!!~'

`-53 + `-70 = `-**123** = PROPHETIC-LINEAR-PROGRESSION!!!!!~'

`-BOOK will be `-AVAILABLE; in, `-ONE (`-1) `-MONTH!!!!!~'

Title: "The Real Prophet Of Doom (Kismet) – Introduction – Pendulum Flow –"

---------- Forwarded message ----------
From: **Dwayne Anderson** <contacttheprophet@therealprophetofdoom.com>
Date: Mon, Aug 10, 2015 at 4:44 AM
Subject: Fwd: `-Extraterrestrials & `-Presidents: The Real Prophet Of Doom (Kismet) - Introduction - Pendulum Flow - / Author: Dwayne W. Anderson!!!!!~'
To: Email Cloaked!~'

Sir Isaac Newton & Mr. Albert Einstein (Comparison/Reciprocals)!!!!!~'

Sir Isaac Newton `-PUBLISHED his `-THEORY of `-GRAVITY in `-1687!!!!!~'
The `-NUMBER is `-EXACTLY (`-2**3**0) = "**The Number** `-**23**" = `-Years from `-1917 to `-1687, that for the `-STUDY of `-FUNDAMENTAL PHYSICS RESEARCH Albert Einstein had a `-1917 `-PAPER on the quantum theory of radiation `-PUBLISHED!!!!!~' Mr. Albert Einstein first brought to the table the possibility of stimulated emission in this `-1917 `-PAPER!!!!!~' In `-1917, Einstein made the applications of the general theory of relativity to model;

and, exemplify the large scale structure of `-OUR `-HEAVENLY `-GOD'S `-UNIVERSE as a `-WHOLE!!!!!~'

Sir Isaac Newton `-BIRTH = **December 25th `-1642** / Mr. Albert Einstein `-BIRTH = **March 15th `-1879**
Sir Isaac Newton `-DEATH = **March 20th `-1727** / Mr. Albert Einstein `-DEATH = **April 18th `-1955**

`-1955 (-) `-1642 = `-**313** = **FATAL SHOT of PRESIDENT JOHN F. KENNEDY!!!!!~'**
`-1879 (-) `-1727 = `-**152** = (1 + 52) = `-**53** = **"WAR of the WORLDS"!!!!!~'**
`-1955 (-) `-1727 = `-**228** = +2 (Rounded Up) = `-**230** = **"The Number `-23"!!!!!~'**
`-1879 (-) `-1642 = `-**237** = -7 (Rounded Down) = `-**230** = **"The Number `-23"!!!!!~'**
`-237 + `-228 = `-**465** = /`-2 = `-**232.5** = (Rounded Down) = `-**232** = **Reciprocal-Sequenced-Numerology!!!!!~'**
`-**32** = **RECIPROCAL** = `-**23**

12/25 to 03/15 = `-**79** days that lie in between these `-BIRTH `-DAYS!!!!!~'
`-**79** = (7 x 9) = `-**63** = **YEAR PRESIDENT JOHN F. KENNEDY was ASSASSINATED!!!!!~'**
12/25 to 04/18 = `-**113** days that lie in between the `-BIRTH of Sir Isaac Newton; and, the `-Death of Mr. Albert Einstein!!!!!~' `-**113** = (1 x 13) = `-**13** = **"A VERY PIVOTAL NUMBER"!!!!!~'**
03/20 to 03/15 = `-**4** days that lie in between the `-DEATH of Sir Isaac Newton; and, the `-BIRTH of Mr. Albert Einstein!!!!!~' **The `-MONTH of `-MARCH = "Equals `-3!!!!!~' (313)-'**
03/20 to 04/18 = `-**28** days that lie in between the `-DEATH of Sir Isaac Newton; and, the `-DEATH of Mr. Albert Einstein!!!!!~' `-**28** + `-**4** = `-**32** = **-a PROPHETIC NUMBER!!!!!~'**

`-79 + `-113 + `-4 + `-28 = `-**224** = -1 = `-**223** = **"The Number `-23"!!!!!~'**
`-79 + `-113 + `-4 + `-28 = `-**224** = +6 (Rounded Up) = `-**230** = **"The Number `-23"!!!!!~'**
`-7 (-) `-2 = `-**5** / `-6 (-) `-1 = `-**5** / Equals = `-**55** = **"SAVES LIVES"!!!!!~'** = `-**55** = **32** + **23!!!!!~'**

`-12 + `-12 + `-03 + `-03 = `-**30**
`-25 + `-25 + `-20 + `-20 = `-**90**
`-03 + `-04 + `-03 + `-04 = `-**14**

15

`-15 + `-18 + `-15 + `-18 = `-**66** / `-30 + `-90 + `-14 + `-66 = `-**200**

`-12 + `-25 + `-03 + `-15 = `-**55**
`-12 + `-25 + `-04 + `-18 = `-**59**
`-03 + `-20 + `-03 + `-15 = `-**41**
`-03 + `-20 + `-04 + `-18 = `-**45** / `-55 + `-59 + `-41 + `-45 = `-**200**

Sir Isaac Newton `-**DIED at the `-AGE of `-84!!!!!~**'
Mr. Albert Einstein `-**DIED at the `-AGE of `-76!!!!!~**'

`-**84** = **RECIPROCAL** = `-**48**
`-**76** = **RECIPROCAL** = `-**67**

`-48 + `-76 = `-**124** = -1 = `-**123** = "**PROPHETIC LINEAR PROGRESSION**" = "**The Number `-23**"!!!!!~'
`-84 + `-76 = `-**160**
`-84 + `-67 = `-**151** / `-**160** + `-**151** = `-**311** = (31 + 1) = `-**32** = **-a PROPHETIC NUMBER!!!!!~**'
`-48 + `-67 = `-**115** = (11.5) = (Rounded Down) = `-**11** = "**Yin/Yang**" = "**The Cycle of LIFE**"!!!!!~'

`-124 + `-160 + `-151 + `-115 = `-**550** = (55 + 0) = `-**55** = **32** + **23** = "**THE PROPHET SAVES LIVES**"!!!!!~'
--
The Prophet!~'
Mediator/Arbitrator: Dwayne W. Anderson
(((Www.TheRealProphetOfDoom.Com)))
- The REAL Prophet of DOOM (Kismet) - Introduction - Pendulum Flow - BOOK –

---------- Forwarded message ----------
From: **Dwayne Anderson** <contacttheprophet@therealprophetofdoom.com>
Date: Sat, Aug 15, 2015 at 4:13 PM
Subject: `-Extraterrestrials & `-Presidents: The Real Prophet Of Doom (Kismet) - Introduction - Pendulum Flow - / Author: Dwayne W. Anderson!!!!!~'
To: fozel@Email Cloaked!~'

James Chadwick (an English Physicist) awarded the `-1935 Nobel Prize in Physics for his `-1932 discovery of the atomic neutron!!!!!~'

The Neutron was `-DISCOVERED in `-1932!!!!!~'

`-35 = **RECIPROCAL** = `-53 = "Atomic Bomb" = "WAR of the WORLDS"!!!!!~'

`-23 = **RECIPROCAL** = `-32 / `-31 = **RECIPROCAL** = `-13

Neutrons, Protons, Electrons, Quarks, `-WHAT'S beneath; `-THEM `-ALL!!!!!~' Protons; and, Neutrons are composed of two types: up `-QUARKS; and, down `-QUARKS!!!!!~' The `-UP `-QUARKS have a `-(+2/3) positive charge; and, the `-DOWN `-QUARKS have a `-(-1/3) negative charge!!!!!~' The `-SUM of the `-CHARGES of the `-QUARKS that are making up the nuclear particle determines its electrical charge!!!!!!~' Likened to the `-GRAVITON (massless), there are `-SPIRITUAL `-PARTICLES (`-FORCES) at `-WORK!!!!!~'

`-YOU `-GALS; and, `-GUYS (`-PHYSICISTS) have some `-FANTASTICAL `-STORIES!!!!!~'

Would `-YOU like to `-KNOW a `-SECRET?????~' Examine your `-WORLD `-HISTORY!!!!!~'

March 20ᵗʰ to July 20ᵗʰ - From the "PROPHET'S" -Dwayne W. Anderson's- BIRTHDAY to the DEATHDAY of Martial Artist Bruce Lee, there are `-**EXACTLY** `-123 DAYS!!!!!~'

Currently, there are `-DISCOVERED some `-23 "MAGNETARS" in the Milky Way Galaxy!!!!~'

Liquid Nitrogen is `-FOUND to be at Negative (-)230 degrees Fahrenheit!!!!!~'

There are some `-320 million cubic miles of `-WATER on the `-EARTH; covering `-IT (the EARTH), by a percentage of `-70% percent!!!!!~' How do `-I remember `-THIS!!!!!~' **It's my `-BIRTHDAY!!!!!~'** `-BIRTHDAY = `-3/20/1970!!!!!~'

From the `-DAY after his `-Death (Martial Artist Bruce Lee) to the `-BIRTHDAY of the "PROPHET'S" BROTHER, there are `-67 **DAYS**!!!!!~' The "PROPHET'S" BROTHER was `-BORN on September 25ᵗʰ in `-1967!!!!!~'

Ernest Rutherford (British Physicist in Nuclear Physics) lived to be `-**66** `-YEARS of `-AGE!!!!!~' Death `-AGE of the "PROPHET'S" FATHER!!!!!~' James Chadwick lived to be `-**82** `-YEARS of `-AGE!!!!!~' Death `-AGE of the "PROPHET'S" FATHER'S MOTHER (GRANDMOTHER)!!!!!~'

Marie Curie (Physicist; and, Chemist that pioneered research in radioactivity) was born on **November 7ᵗʰ** in `-18**67**!!!!!~' She died in her `-**67ᵗʰ** `-YEAR of `-LIVING at the tender `-AGE of `-**66** on **July 4ᵗʰ** in `-19**34**!!!!!~'

`-67 (-) `-34 = `-**33** = **-1** = `-**32** = **-a Prophetic Number!!!!!~'**

11/7 = (11 x 7) = `-**77**

`-77 + `-67 = `-**144** = (1 x 44) = `-**44** = `-YEAR of the "PROPHET'S" MOTHER'S BIRTH YEAR `-19**44**!!!!!~'

Expedition `-**44** on the Space Station in preparation to a trip to `-MARS!!!!!~'

Hugh Hammond Bennett (Soil Surveyor that testified before Congress) at `-AGE `-**53** was the spokesman for the people suffering from the Dust Bowl (`-19**32**) right after **"Black Sunday"** on (04/1**4**/19**35**)!!!!!~'

04/14 = 0414 = (0 + 4) / (1 x 4) = `-44 = `-**44** = `-YEAR of the "PROPHET'S" MOTHER'S BIRTH YEAR `-19**44**!!!!!~'

`-35 = RECIPROCAL = `-53 = "Atomic Bomb" = "WAR of the WORLDS"!!!!!~'

Pierre Curie (Physicist that was a pioneer in piezoelectricity, crystallography, radioactivity; and, magnetism) was `-BORN on May 15ᵗʰ `-1859; and, `-DIED on April 19ᵗʰ in `-1906!!!!!~' Pierre Curie `-DIED at the `-AGE of `-**46** = `-**23** x `-**2** = `-**232** = **Reciprocal-Sequenced-Numerology!!!!!~'**

May 15ᵗʰ = 5/15 = `-**515** = **Reciprocal-Sequenced-Numerology!!!!!~'**

April 19ᵗʰ = (**4** + 1**9**) = `-**23** = **-a Prophetic Number!!!!!~'**

Pierre Curie's `-DEATH `-DATE (`-19ᵗʰ of `-1906) is a `-**RECIPROCAL** of the "PROPHET'S" MOTHER'S FATHER'S (GRANDFATHER'S) `-BIRTHDATE (9/1 of `-1906)!!!!!~'

Bruce Lee `-DIED in `-1973!!!!!~' The "PROPHET" was `-BORN in `-1970!!!!!~'

`-1973 (-) `-1970 = `-**3** / `-1973 (-) `-1967 = `-**6**

`-**36** = **RECIPROCAL** = `-**63** = **AGE of `-DEATH of the "PROPHET'S" MOTHER!!!!!~'**

Johannes Kepler (German Mathematician, Astronomer; and, Astrologer) `-DIED on **NOVEMBER** `-**15**th in `-1**630**!!!!!~' Johannes Kepler died on the `-BIRTHDAY of the "PROPHET'S" MOTHER; and, in the `-YEAR of her `-DEATH!!!!!~' (`-1**630**) = (1 x 63 + 0) = `-**63** = `-**AGE of `-DEATH of the "PROPHET'S" MOTHER!!!!!~'** Galileo Galilei was `-BORN on **February** `-**15**th in `-**1564**; and, `-DIED on **January 8**th in `-**1642**!!!!~ Galileo Galilei (Astronomer, Physicist, Engineer, Philosopher; and, Mathematician) had died `-**351** days from the `-BIRTH of Sir Isaac Newton (English Physicist; and, Mathematician)!!!!!~' Galileo Galilei had `-**DIED** at the `-**AGE** of `-**77**!!!!!~' Nicolaus Copernicus `-**DIED** at the `-**AGE** of `-**70** = "BIRTHYEAR" of the "PROPHET" (19**70**)!!!!!~'

`-**351** = (35 x 1) = `-**35** = **RECIPROCAL** = `-**53** = **"WAR of the WORLDS"!!!!!~'**

(2/15/15/64) + (1/8/16/42) = `-**163** = (**1 x 63**) = `-**63** = `-**AGE of `-DEATH of the "PROPHET'S" MOTHER!!!!!~'**

(2 + 15 + 15 + 64) = `-**96** / (1 + 8 + 16 + 42) = `-**67** / `-96 + `-67 = `-**163!!!!!~'**

Augustus Caesar (The Founder of the Roman Empire; and, its first `-EMPEROR) was `-BORN **September** `-**23**rd in `-**63**BC (The `-YEAR of the "PROPHET'S" MOTHER)!!!!!~' September `-**23**rd Equals (**9 + 23**) = `-**32**!!!!!~' Augustus Caesar died on **August** `-**19**th in `-**14**AD!!!!!~' (`-**14**) is (**2 x 7**) = **2**(**7's**) = `-**77** = `-**YEAR of the `-AGE of `-DEATH of Augustus Caesar!!!!!~'** Augustus Caesar `-**DIED** at the `-**AGE** of `-**75**!!!!!~' `-**75** = **RECIPROCAL** = `-**57** / `-**75** + `-**57** = `-**132!!!!!~'**

Julius Caesar `-DIED within the IDES of MARCH on **March** `-**15**th of `-**44**BC!!!!!~' Five `-DAYS from the "PROPHET'S" `-BIRTH; and, in the `-BIRTHYEAR of the "PROPHET'S" MOTHER (`-19**44**)!!!!!~' (**03/15/44**) = (**3 + 15 + 44**) = `-**62** = +1 = `-**63** = `-**AGE of `-DEATH of the "PROPHET'S" MOTHER!!!!!~'** `-384BC (-) `-322BC = **Aristotle** `-**DIED** at the **tender** `-**AGE** of `-**62**!!!!!~' Encapsulated by the `-NUMBER `-**63**!!!!!~' Julius Caesar `-**DIED** at the tender `-**AGE** of `-**56**!!!!!~' The `-SAME `-AGE as President Abraham Lincoln; and, Leader Adolf Hitler!!!!!~'

19

Take `-EVERY `-PRESIDENT of the UNITED STATES of AMERICA; and, take their `-BIRTHDATE `-YEAR; and, add/subtract `-IT, with the `-BIRTHDATE `-YEAR of the `-32ⁿᵈ PRESIDENT of the UNITED STATES of AMERICA / President Franklin Delano Roosevelt!!!!!~' Now `-TAKE the `-DEATH `-YEAR of President Franklin Delano Roosevelt (`-**45**) of the `-YEAR – (`-19**45**); and, subtract/add this `-NUMBER to `-ANY other `-PRESIDENT'S DEATHDATE `-YEAR `-NUMBER that you are comparing of the UNITED STATES of AMERICA; and, you'll come up, with; and, to; the `-NUMBER `-**35** = **RECIPROCAL** = `-**53**; which `-**EQUALS**, The **"WAR of the WORLDS"!!!!!~'**

The ROMAN EMPIRE was founded in **27** B.C.; and, dissolved in 14**53**C.E.!!!!!~' `-**14** = `-7 (+) `-2 = `-**72** = **RECIPROCAL** = `-**27**!!!!!~' Another `-**53**, the United States of America!!!!!~' `-**1453** + `-**27** = `-**1480**!!!!!~' `-**48** = **RECIPROCAL** = `-**84** / `-**84** + `-**48** = `-**132** = (1 x 32) = `-**32** = -a **Prophetic Number**!!!!!~' The Roman Empire = 1.062 million square miles!!!!!~' `-1.062 = (1 + 62) = `-**63**!!!!!~' Now; The Roman Republic dated from 509B.C. to 27 B.C. = 509B.C. (-) 26B.C. = `-**483B.C.!!!!!~'**

`-27 to `-1453 –

`-**14** = (7 x 2) = `-**72** / `-**27** = **RECIPROCAL** = `-**72**

`-14 + `-53 = `-**67** / `-**67** = (6 + 7) = `-**13**

1480 + 483 = `-**1963** = "The Year U.S. President John F. Kennedy was Assassinated"!!!!!~'

The Founding of ROME was around; and, in; `-800BC = 800BC (-) 508BC = `-**292B.C.**

`-29 (-) 2 = `-**27**

`-805 = RECIPROCAL = `-508 = "Was the FOUNDING of `-ROME in the `-YEAR `-805B.C."!!!!!~'

`-805 (+) `-508 = `-**1313**

`-1963 (+) `-292 = `-**2255** = `-**22.55** = **ROUNDED** = `-**23** = -a **Prophetic Number**!!!!!~'

`-22 + `-55 = `-**77** / `-55 (-) `-22 = `-**33**

`-77 (-) `-33 = `-**44** = "The YEAR the "PROPHET'S" Mother was `-BORN – (`-19**44**)!!!!!~'

`-77 (+) `-77 = `-**154** = 1(**54**) = **"An `-EARTHQUAKE"!!!!!~'**

John F. Kennedy = JFK = `-**INSIGNIA/MONOGRAM**-!!!!!~'

J = `-10 / **F** = `-6 / **K** = `-11

10/6/11 = 10 (+) 6 (+) 11 = `-**27** = 2(7's) = `-**77** = **Death `-AGE of Edward "TED" KENNEDY!!!!!~'**

`-**313**C.E. = the Date of EMPEROR CONSTANTINE'S so-called CONVERSION to "Christianity"; however, he wasn't `-BAPTIZED until some `-**23** years later just prior to his `-DEATH!!!!!~' The official STATE `-RELIGION became `-CHRISTIAN via EMPEROR CONSTANTINE's Devotion at this `-DATE!!!!!~' `-**313** is the `-SIGN (INSIGNIA/ MONOGRAM) of President John F. Kennedy's `-ASSASSINATION of which he was a ROMAN CATHOLIC; and, working within his FAITH!!!!!~' EMPEROR CONSTANTINE was `-EMPEROR for within `-**32** YEARS by `-**ONE**!!!!!~' EMPEROR CONSTANTINE was `-BORN on **2/27/272**; and, `-DIED on **5/22** which `-EQUALS = `-**5** (+) `-**22** = `-**27** within 3**37**AD!!!!!~' `-3**37**AD = 33AD (+) 37AD = `-**70**AD = The `-YEAR the "PROPHET" was `-BORN in (`-19**70**); and, JERUSALEM was ABSOLUTELY `-DESTROYED by the `-ROMAN `-EMPIRE!!!!!~' See the `-NUMBERS!!!!!~' EMPEROR CONSTANTINE `-DIED at the tender `-AGE of `-**65**!!!!!~' `-65 (-) `-2 = `-**63**!!!!!~' `-**63** = **RECIPROCAL** = `-**36**!!!!!~' In `-**306**C.E.; CONSTANTINE succeeded his `-FATHER; and, eventually, with LICINIUS, became a co-ruler of the ROMAN EMPIRE!!!!!~' He; EMPEROR CONSTANTINE, was `-INFLUENCED; by his MOTHER'S Devotion, to `-CHRISTIANITY!!!!!~ The "PROPHET'S" - CHRISTIAN `-MOTHER; died at the tender `-AGE of `-**63**!!!!!~' The "PROPHET'S" `-FATHER `-DIED at the tender `-AGE of `-**66**!!!!!~' `-**66** + `-**70** (**The "PROPHET'S" `-BIRTH**) = `-**136** = (**1 x 36**) = `-**36** = **RECIPROCAL** = `-**63**!!!!!~'

New FORMULATION of `-ARRIVING at the `-DEATH `-AGE of `-PARENTS = `-1 of the `-CHILDREN'S BIRTHDAY `-YEARS added to `-1 PARENT'S `-AGE of `-DEATH to `-ARRIVE (`-**RECIPROCALLY**-`) at the `-AGE of `-DEATH of the other `-PARENT'S (`-SPOUSE'S) `-AGE of `-DEATH!!!!!~'

ABOVE (EXAMPLE) = `-AGE of `-**66**!!!!!~' `-**66** (`-**AGE of FATHER'S `-DEATH**) + `-**70** (**The "PROPHET'S" `-BIRTH `-YEAR**) = `-**136** = (1 x 36) = `-**36** = **RECIPROCAL** = `-**63** (`-**AGE of MOTHER'S `-DEATH**)!!!!!~'

NEW (EXAMPLE) = AUNT SANDRA from the `-BOOK – "The Real Prophet of Doom (Kismet) – Introduction – Pendulum Flow –" `-AGE of `-**68**!!!!!~' `-**68** (`-**AGE of FATHER'S `-DEATH**) + `-**55** (**AUNT SANDRA'S `-BIRTH `-YEAR**) = `-**123** = (1 x 23) = `-**23** = **RECIPROCAL** = `-**32** / (**1 x 32**) = {(32 x 2) + 1} = `-**65** = (`-**AGE of MOTHER'S `-DEATH**)!!!!!~'

NEW (EXAMPLE) = The "PROPHET'S" FATHER from the `-BOOK – "The Real Prophet of Doom (Kismet) – Introduction – Pendulum Flow –" `-AGE of `-**88**!!!!!~' `-**88** (`-**AGE of FATHER'S `-FATHER/The "PROPHET'S" GRANDFATHER'S `-AGE of `-DEATH**) + `-**41** (**The "PROPHET'S" FATHER'S `-BIRTH `-YEAR**) = `-**129** = / **29** = **RECIPROCAL** = 92 = (`-**192**) = {(1 (-) 9) **attached to the Number** `-**2**} = `-**82** = (`-**AGE of MOTHER'S `-DEATH / The "PROPHET'S" GRANDMOTHER'S `-AGE of `-DEATH**)!!!!!~'

(`-19**41**) / `-**41** (**The "PROPHET'S" FATHER'S `-BIRTH `-YEAR**) **x** `-**2** = `-**82** = (`-**AGE of MOTHER'S `-DEATH / The "PROPHET'S" GRANDMOTHER'S `-AGE of `-DEATH**)!!!!!~'

NEW (EXAMPLE) = The "PROPHET'S" FATHER from the `-BOOK – "The Real Prophet of Doom (Kismet) – Introduction – Pendulum Flow –" `-AGE of `-**82**!!!!!~' `-**82** (`-**AGE of FATHER'S `-MOTHER/The "PROPHET'S" GRANDMOTHER'S `-AGE of `-DEATH**) + `-**41** (**The "PROPHET'S" FATHER'S `-BIRTH `-YEAR**) = `-**123** = / **23** = **RECIPROCAL** = 32 / **12** = **RECIPROCAL** = 21 / (23 + 32 + 12 + 21) = `-**88** = (`-**AGE of FATHER'S `-DEATH / The "PROPHET'S" GRANDFATHER'S `-AGE of `-DEATH**)!!!!!~'

(`-19**41**) / `-**41** (**The "PROPHET'S" FATHER'S `-BIRTH `-YEAR**) + `-**47** (`-**AGE of BROTHER MICHAEL'S `-DEATH / from the `-BOOK – "The Real Prophet of Doom (Kismet) – Introduction – Pendulum Flow –" / The "PROPHET'S" UNCLE `-AGE of `-DEATH**) = `-**88** = (`-**AGE of their FATHER'S `-DEATH / The "PROPHET'S" GRANDFATHER'S `-AGE of `-DEATH**)!!!!!~'!!!!!~'

Martin Luther who was a German Friar, a Priest, a Professor of Theology; and, a Key FIGURE of the PROTESTANT REFORMATION was `-INCLUDED within the `-NUMBERS!!!!!~' Martin Luther was `-BORN on **11/10/1483** / 11 + 10 + 14 = `-**35** = **RECIPROCAL** = `-**53**; and, `-DIED on **2/18/1546** / 2 + 18 + 15 = `-**35** = **RECIPROCAL** = `-**53**!!!!!~' `-**83** (-) `-**46** = `-**37** = **3(7's)** = `-**777**!!!!!~' He; Martin Luther, `-DIED within his `-**63**rd YEAR of –LIVING/`-EXISTING!!!!!~'

`-**36** = **RECIPROCAL** = `-**63** / `-**6** = **RECIPROCAL** = `-**9**

`-**69** = **RECIPROCAL** = `-**96** = **"Yin/Yang"**!!!!!~'

`-96 (+) `-69 = `-**165** = 1(**65**) = `-**-AGE-`** of EMPEROR CONSTANTINE of `-ROME-'!!!!!~'

`-96 (-) `-69 = `-**27**

Martin Luther King, Jr. who was an American Baptist Minister, an Activist, a Humanitarian; and, a Leader of the African-American Civil Rights Movement was `-INCLUDED within the `-NUMBERS!!!!!~' Martin Luther King, Jr. was `-BORN on **1/15/1929** / 1 + 15 + 19 = `-**35** = **RECIPROCAL** = `-**53** / `-1 (-) `-15 = `-**14** = (2 x 7) = `-**27**; and, `-DIED on **4/4/1968** / 4 + 4 + 19 = `-**27** =

RECIPROCAL = `-**72** / `-**72** (-) `-**27** = `-**45** (-) `-1 = `-**44** = "The YEAR that the "PROPHET'S" Mother was `-BORN in (`-19**44**)!!!!!~'

`-**1929** = **1**(**929**) = `-**29** = **RECIPROCAL** = `-**92** / `-**92** (-) `-**29** = `-**63**!!!!!~

`-**1968** = `-**68** = **RECIPROCAL** = `-**86** / `-**68** (+) `-**86** = `-**154** = 1(**54**) = "An `-EARTHQUAKE"!!!!!~'

`-**1968** = 1(96)/68 = `-**96** (+) `-**68** = `-**164** = (1 - 64) = `-**63**

`-**1968** = 1(96)/68 = `-**96** (-) `-**68** = `-**28** = (-) `-1 = `-**27**

Martin Luther King, Jr. `-DIED at the tender `-**AGE** of `-**39** / `-**9** = **RECIPROCAL** = `-**6** / **=** \`-**36** = **RECIPROCAL** = `-**63** = Martin Luther (Protestant) = **RECIPROCAL** = Martin Luther King, Jr. (American Baptist)**!!!!!~'** Martin Luther King, Jr. married his `-WIFE in `-19**53**!!!!!~' Martin Luther was married to his `-WIFE Katharina von Bora for `-**21** `-YEARS!!!!!~' Martin Luther King, Jr. was married to his wife Coretta Scott King for `-**15** `-YEARS!!!!!~' `-**21** (+) `-**15** = `-**36** = **RECIPROCAL** = `-**63**!!!!!~'

Martin Luther King, Jr. = MLK = `-**INSIGNIA/MONOGRAM**-!!!!!~'

M = `-13 / **L** = `-12 / **K** = `-11

11, 12, 13 = **Prophetic-Linear-Progression!!!!!~'**

`-11 (+) `-12 (+) `-13 = `-**36** = **RECIPROCAL** = `-**63**

FAITH - ISLAM/MUSLIMS - Qur'an (Koran) the "PROPHET" Muhammad took some `-**23** years to `-RECEIVE his `-REVELATIONS!!!!!~' `-**23** = **RECIPROCAL** = `-**32**!!!!!~' The "PROPHET" Muhammad `-DIED in `-**632**C.E.!!!!!~' The "PROPHET" Muhammad `-DIED at the tender `-AGE of `-**63**!!!!!~'

From the "PROPHET" Dwayne W. Anderson-!!!!!~'

Queen Victoria served for `-63 Years; and, `-7 Months!!!!!~' `-63 + `-7 = `-70 = "BIRTHYEAR of The PROPHET"!!!!!~' Queen Elizabeth II (09.09.2015) has served for `-23,226 Days about `-63 Years; and, `-7 Months!!!!!~' Queen Elizabeth II at 5:30 pm became the longest reigning monarch in Britain's History!!!!!~' Queen Elizabeth II is currently `-89 Years of `-AGE!!!!!~' She came to the `-THROWN in `-1952 at the `-AGE

of `-25!!!!!~' `-52 = <u>RECIPROCAL</u> = `-25!!!!!~' `-52 + `-1 = `-53 = "WAR of the `-WORLDS"!!!!!~'

July <u>20</u>ᵗʰ (Martial Artist Bruce Lee's `-DAY of `-DEATH) = "The Flooding of the `-NILE" = "The Egyptian `-NEW `-YEAR" = "The `-RETURN of `-ISIS" = "The `-WIFE of `-OSIRIS"!!!!!~'

OSIRIS `-Equals = `-"GOD of the `-AFTERLIFE, `-DEATH, `-LIFE; and, the `-RESURRECTION!!!!!~'

`-ATOMIC/`-SUBATOMIC `-DNA?????~'

Again; this is the `-QUESTION with the `-EXACT `-ATOMIC `-STRUCTURE!!!!!~'

A - ADENINE ($C_5H_5N_5$), C - CYTOSINE ($C_4H_5N_3O$), G - GUANINE ($C_5H_5N_5O$); and, T - THYMINE ($C_5H_6N_2O_2$) make up `-DNA (DeoxyriboNucleic Acid)!!!!!!~' What hidden `-MECHANISM is there within the `-ATOMIC/SUBATOMIC `-LAYERS that `-ACTS as a `-DNA for the `-ATOMIC MAKEUP of `-SPECIFIC `-ORDERS; and, `-COHERENT `-STRUCTURES; of the `-ATOMS-' `-THEMSELVES (QUANTUM PHYSICS)?????~ And; what `-TELLS the `-ATOMS `-THEMSELVES the `-ORDER of the `-COHESIVE `-STRUCTURES of `-DNA??????~'

Thanks in Advance!!!!!~'

Author: Dwayne W. Anderson!!!!!~'

I would like to `-FIND someone with a Ph.D. to `-GIVE me the `-ANSWER; for `-IF indeed `-SCIENCE has an `-ANSWER for it `-YET!!!!!~' I've never `-HEARD of it `-QUESTIONED before; but, it's a valid `-QUESTION!!!!!~' I believe `-SCIENTISTS will `-TRY to `-EXPLAIN it `-OFF as a mere `-PHENOMENON!!!!!~' Ultimately; `-WE know the `-ANSWER for `-IT; and, to `-IT -(JEHOVAH)-!!!!!~'

NEOTERIC - modern or recent in origin!!!!!~'

BLOOD MOON - SUPER MOON LUNAR ECLIPSE – SEPTEMBER <u>27</u>ᵗʰ/<u>28</u>ᵗʰ, 20<u>15</u>!!!!!~'

`-27ᵗʰ (-) SEPTEMBER (`-9ᵗʰ) = `-<u>18</u>

PREVIOUS BLOOD MOON - SUPER MOON LUNAR ECLIPSE occurred in `-19**28**!!!!!~'

`-**28** = **RECIPROCAL** = `-**82**

A RARE BLOOD MOON - TOTAL LUNAR ECLIPSE of a SUPER FULL MOON will be visible from most of North America, South America, Europe, West Asia; and, Parts of Africa tonight!!!!!~'

The Last BLOOD MOON - SUPER MOON LUNAR ECLIPSE was in `-19**82**!!!!!~'

Current BLOOD MOON - SUPER MOON LUNAR ECLIPSE is now tonight within `-20**15**!!!!!~'

Future BLOOD MOON - SUPER MOON LUNAR ECLIPSE to be within `-20**33**!!!!!~'

PREVIOUS BLOOD MOONS - SUPER MOON LUNAR ECLIPSES were in `-19**46** & `-19**64**!!!!!~' `-(**RECIPROCALS**)!!!!!~'

`-**46** = **RECIPROCAL** = `-**64**

`-2015 (-) `-1982 = `-**33** Years / SINCE / Next ECLIPSE in `-20**33**!!!!!~' `-**33**/`-**33**!!!!!~' `-1/`-1!!!!!~'

`-2033 (-) `-2015 = `-**18 YEARS** = the `-DIFFERENCE is `-TODAY'S `-DATE of the `-MONTH of `-SEPTEMBER!!!!!~'

`-33 (-) `-18 = `-**15** = CURRENT BLOOD MOON tonight is within the Calendar Year of `-20**15**!!!!!~'

`-**51** = **RECIPROCAL** = `-**15** / `-33 (+) `-18 = `-**51** / `-**18** = **RECIPROCAL** = `-**81**

`-**81** + `-**1** = `-**82** = The Last BLOOD MOON - SUPERMOON LUNAR ECLIPSE which was in `-19**82**!!!!!~' `-**82**/`-**82**!!!!!~' `-1/`-1!!!!!~'

"A blood moon occurs when there's a full moon in close proximity to the Earth — a so-called super moon — in combination with an eclipse of the moon, which happens when the Earth passes between the sun and moon."

"The two events will produce a reddish glow around the somewhat darkened moon for about an hour Sunday night. The last blood moon occurred in 1982 and the next one won't occur until 2033." Quoted Excerpt from: USA TODAY / REPORTER: Brian J. Tumulty !...-'

Shannon & I are `-BOTH (`-EQUINOX-`) `-BABIES!!!!!~' I was `-ONE `-DAY `-BEFORE; and, He was `-TWO `-DAYS `-AFTER this `-YEAR!!!!!~' `-ONE/`-TWO = `-**12** = Our `-BIRTHDAY `-NUMBERS!!!!!~'

Dwayne W. Anderson = 03/2̲0/1970 = SPRING EQUINOX of the `-**21**ˢᵗ of `-MARCH this `-YEAR!!!!!~' EQUINOX = Usually the 20ᵗʰ; or, 21ˢᵗ of the Month of `-MARCH to where the `-SUN is closest to the `-EQUATOR; and, there are `-EQUAL `-DAYS of `-**12** HOURS of `-DAYLIGHT; and, `-**12** HOURS of `-NIGHTTIME!!!!!~'

03 + 20 + 19 + 70 = `-**112** = (1 x 12) = `-**12** = **RECIPROCAL** of the `-**EQUINOX-**`!!!!!~' At the `-TIME of the `-1982 BLOOD MOON; I (Dwayne W. Anderson), was `-12 YEARS of `-AGE!!!!!~'

`-**12** = **RECIPROCAL** = `-**21**

Shannon L. Anderson (My `-BROTHER) = 09/25/1967 = AUTUMNAL EQUINOX of the `-**23**ʳᵈ of `-SEPTEMBER for this `-YEAR!!!!!~' EQUINOX = Usually the 22ⁿᵈ, 23ʳᵈ; or, the 24ᵗʰ of the Month of `-SEPTEMBER to where the `-SUN is closest to the `-EQUATOR; and, there are `-EQUAL `-DAYS of `-**12** HOURS of `-DAYLIGHT; and, `-**12** HOURS of `-NIGHTTIME!!!!!~'

09 + 25 + 19 + 67 = `-**120** = (12 + 0) = `-**12** = **RECIPROCAL** of the `-**SPRING** `-**EQUINOX-**`!!!!!~' At the `-TIME of the `-1982 BLOOD MOON; my `-BROTHER (Shannon L. Anderson), was `-15 YEARS of AGE - (2015) the `-NEXT TIME of the BLOOD MOON `-33 years `-LATER!!!!!~'

09 + 25 + 19 + 67 = `-**120** = (1 + 20) = `-**21** = **The** `-**SPRING** `-**EQUINOX-**` **for this** `-**YEAR**!!!!!~'

AUTUMNAL EQUINOX of the `-**23**ʳᵈ of `-SEPTEMBER for this `-YEAR is a `-**RECIPROCAL** of my very `-BIRTHDAY (03/2̲0) = `-**32**!!!!!~'

FOOD for `-THOUGHT; on, these `-RECIPROCALS / Reciprocal-Sequencing-Numerology – RSN!-` – My INVENTION; and, CREATION of `-DISCOVERY!!!!!~' These `-RECIPROCALS `-MAP `-US ALL throughout `-TIME; and, `-HISTORY for our `-LIFE; and, `-DEATH;

and `-NOW, as `-WE can see `-IT; `-in the `-CELESTIAL `-BODIES, `-Too; or, `-Just as `-WELL!!!!!~' Author of `-DISCOVERY: Dwayne W. Anderson!!!!!~'

TONIGHT'S BLOOD MOON - SUPER MOON LUNAR ECLIPSE – SEPTEMBER 27th/28th, 2015!!!!!~'

In the 20th `-CENTURY, the BLOOD MOON - SUPER MOON LUNAR ECLIPSES occurred `-EVERY `-18 years; EXCEPT, for the `-YEAR of `-2000 for when it didn't `-OCCUR!!!!!~' Why is `-THIS?????~' What `-ACCOUNTS for this `-COSMIC `-HICCUP?????~' Why the `-33 year difference `-NOW; and, then back to the `-NUMBER of `-18 years in between ECLIPSES?????~' Thanks in Advance for your `-RESPONSES!!!!!~' Author: Dwayne W. Anderson!!!!!~'

`-1910 (BLOOD MOON ECLIPSE) - `-1928 (BLOOD MOON ECLIPSE) - `-1946 (BLOOD MOON ECLIPSE) - `-1964 (BLOOD MOON ECLIPSE) - `-1982 (BLOOD MOON ECLIPSE) - `-2000 (NO BLOOD MOON ECLIPSE) - WHAT HAPPENED?????~'

FOOD for `-THOUGHT: Within this `-MAGICAL `-18 YEARS `-SPAN in `-TIME to the `-NEXT BLOOD MOON ECLIPSE that will be in the `-CALENDAR `-YEAR of `-20**33**!!!!!~' At this `-TIME; I (Dwayne W. Anderson) will be `-**63** YEARS of AGE (the AGE of DEATH of `-OUR `-MOTHER); and, my brother (Shannon L. Anderson); will be `-**66** YEARS of AGE (the AGE of DEATH of `-OUR `-FATHER)!!!!!~' Just some `-DEEP `-BLOOD `-LINE / `-"FOOD for `-THOUGHT"~'!!!!!~' Author: Dwayne W. Anderson!!!!!~'

In the `-HUMAN `-BODY, Normally in `-EACH `-CELL there are some `-**23** Chromosomes!!!!!~' The `-**23**rd `-PAIR of `-CHROMOSOMES that `-DIFFER between `-MALE; and, `-FEMALE; are the `-SEX `-CHROMOSOMES!!!!!~' The **23**rd PAIR (XX; or, XY)!!!!!~' The `-NUMBER `-**23**!!!!!~'

There are Some `-**23**,000 `-SPECIES of `-MOSS; that currently `-EXISTS!!!!!!~'

We `-HUMANS breath `-IN; and, `-OUT; approximately, some `-<u>**23**</u>,000 times per day!!!!!~'

Dark Charisma - The `-EVOLUTION of Adolf Hitler from a `-NOBODY in `-19**13** to German Chancellor in `-19**33**!!!!!~'

`-13 = <u>RECIPROCAL</u> = `-31 = <u>RECIPROCAL</u> = `-13 = "A VERY PIVOTAL NUMBER"!!!!!~'

The `-NUMBER `-32; is, `-RIGHT; `-in the `-MIDDLE!!!!!~'

`-23 = <u>RECIPROCAL</u> = `-32 / `-19<u>33</u>!!!!!~'

The `-19**38** radio broadcast of the H. G. Wells' "WAR of the WORLDS" by Orson Welles and his "Mercury Theater on the Air" Crew presented their "MARTIAN like INVASION" on the "DAY" of Mischief Night!!!!!~' Some "People" in the "WORLD" had believed that this radio tale of a story had in fact been "TRUE"!!!!!~'

The "MOVIE" FOR "WAR of the WORLDS" came out in `-19**53**!!!!!~'

`-53 (-) `-38 = `-15 / `-**15** = <u>RECIPROCAL</u> = `-**51** / `-51 (+) `-15 = `-**66** = "AGE of DEATH of the "PROPHET'S" FATHER who was `-BORN in `-19**41** = **"WAR of the WORLDS for the UNITED STATES of AMERICA!!!!!~'**

`-53 + `-38 = `-**91** / `-**91** = <u>RECIPROCAL</u> = `-19

`-91 (-) `-19 = `-**72** / `-**72** = <u>RECIPROCAL</u> = `-**27** = "The ROMAN EMPIRE"!!!!!~'

`-1938 (+) `-1953 = `-**3891**

`-3891 = `-91 (-) `-38 = `-**53** = **"WAR of the WORLDS"!!!!!~'**

`-1938 (-) `-1914 (WWI) = `-**24** / `-1953 (-) `-1941 (WWII) = `-**12**

`-24 (+) `-12 = `-**36** = <u>RECIPROCAL</u> = `-**63** = "AGE of DEATH of the "PROPHET'S" MOTHER!!!!!~'

29

`-24 (-) `-1 = `-**23** = -a Prophetic Number!!!!!~'

`-12 (+) `-1 = `-**13** = "A VERY PIVOTAL NUMBER"!!!!!~'

`-23 (+) `-13 = `-**36** = **RECIPROCAL** = `-**63** = "AGE of DEATH of the "PROPHET'S" MOTHER!!!!!~'

`-1941 (-) `-1914 = `-**27** = "The ROMAN EMPIRE"!!!!!~' / `-**14** = **RECIPROCAL** = `-**41**

THESE `-RECIPROCALS = the **"WAR of the WORLDS"!!!!!!~'**

June `-28th, `-1914 – Gavrilo Princip (`-**23** years of `-AGE) `-**ASSASSINATES** Archduke Franz Ferdinand of `-AUSTRIA who was `-BORN in `-18**63**; and, `-DIED at the `-AGE of `-**50**!!!!!~'

`-50 (-) `-23 = `-**27** = **"The ROMAN EMPIRE"!!!!!~'**

July `-28th, `-1914 – Austria-Hungary `-DECLARES `-WAR on `-SERBIA!!!!!~

June = `-6 / July = `-7 / = `-67!!!!!~'

June `-28th / `-1914 = (6 + 28 + 19 + 14) = `-67 = "The `-YEAR the "PROPHET'S" BROTHER was `-BORN"!!!!!~'

June `-28th / `-1914 = (6 + 28 + 19) = `-53 = "WAR of the WORLDS"!!!!!~'

August 2nd, `-1914 – Ottoman Empire (Turkey); and, Germany sign a **"SECRET" Treaty of Alliance!!!!!~**

August 2nd = `-**82**!!!!!~ / `-**28** = **RECIPROCAL** = `-**82**

`-82 = "The `-AGE of `-DEATH of the "PROPHET'S" GRANDMOTHER!!!!!~'

June `-28th to August 2nd = `-35 `-DAYS!!!!!~' `-35 = RECIPROCAL = `-53 = "WAR of the WORLDS"!!!!!~'

August 3rd, `-1914 – **Germany `-DECLARES `-WAR on `-FRANCE!!!!!~'**

August 3rd = `-**83**!!!!!~

`-83 = **RECIPROCAL** = `-**38** = The Radio Show of the **"WAR of the WORLDS"!!!!!~'**

DECEMBER 7ᵗʰ of `-19**41** = US in the **"WAR"** = 12 + 7 + 19 = `-**38**!!!!!~'

`-12 + `-41 = `-**53** = **"WAR of the WORLDS"!!!!!~'**

The "PROPHET'S" FATHER was BORN on `-**09/01/1941!!!!!~'**

The `-START of the "WAR" in EUROPE (World War II) has generally been held to be at the **1ˢᵗ of** `-**SEPTEMBER in** `-**1939,** beginning with the German invasion of Poland with Britain; and, France soon `-DECLARING `-WAR on Germany some two days later!!!!!~

The "PROPHET'S" MOTHER was `-BORN in `-19**44**!!!!!~'

`-**44** + `-19 = `-**63** = **"AGE of `-DEATH of the "PROPHET'S" MOTHER!!!!!~'**

`-**63** = **RECIPROCAL** = `-**36** / `-**36** = `-**18** * 2

When the "PROPHET" was `-**18** years of `-AGE, the "PROPHET'S" MOTHER was `-**44** years of `-AGE!!!!!~'

When the "PROPHET'S" BROTHER was `-**18** years of `-AGE, the "PROPHET'S" MOTHER was `-**41** years of `-AGE!!!!!~'

`-63 (-) `-36 = `-**27** = **"The ROMAN EMPIRE"!!!!!~'**

`-63 (+) `-36 = `-**99** = **RECIPROCAL** = `-**66** = **"AGE of `-DEATH of the "PROPHET'S" FATHER!!!!!~'**

H. G. WELLS was `-BORN on SEPTEMBER **21**ˢᵗ in `-18**66**; and, `-DIED on `-AUGUST `-**13**ᵗʰ in `-19**46**!!!!!~'

09/21/18/66 (+) 08/13/19/46 = `-**200** = (0 + 20) = `-**20** = The **"PROPHET'S" DAY of `-BIRTH!!!!!~'**

09/21/18/66 (+) 08/13 = `-**135** = (1 x 35) = `-**35** = **RECIPROCAL** = `-**53** = **"WAR of the WORLDS"!!!!!~'**

`-**46** = `-**23** x `-**2** = `-**232** = **Reciprocal-Sequencing-Numerology-RSN**!!!!!~'

31

H. G. WELLS `-DIED at the `-AGE of `-**79**!!!!!~' He forecast the `-ATOMIC `-AGE in a `-**1914** Novel!!!!!~'

`-**79** = **RECIPROCAL** = `-**97**

`-97 (+) `-79 = `-**176** = 1(76) = `-**76** = **RECIPROCAL** = `-**67** = **The "PROPHET'S" BROTHER'S `-YEAR of `-BIRTH!!!!!~'**

`-**35** = **RECIPROCAL** = `-**53** = "WAR of the WORLDS"!!!!!~'

`-79 (-) `-35 = `-**44** = The `-**YEAR** the "**PROPHET'S" MOTHER** was `-**BORN** (`-19**44**)!!!!!~'

`-79 + `-53 = `-**132** = (1 x 32) = `-**32** = -a Prophetic Number!!!!!~'

The `-MOVIE **"WAR of the WORLDS"** was `-RELEASED on <u>July</u> `-**29** in `-19**53**!!!!!~

07/29 = 2(79) = An EMPHATIC WITNESS to the `-Number `-79!!!!!~'

`-**2** x `-**79** = `-**158** = (15 + 8) = `-**23** = -a Prophetic Number!!!!!~'

07/29/19/53 = (7 + 19 + 53) = `-79 = "AGE of `-DEATH of Mr. H. G. WELLS!!!!!~'

08/13 (-) 09/21 = There are some `-**38** days that lie in between the `-**BIRTHDAY**; and, `-**DEATHDAY**; of **Mr. H. G. WELLS!!!!!~'**

`-**38** = (**19** x **2**) = `-**19** as an EMPHATIC WITNESS to the Number = `-**38** = `-**1938** = The `-19**38** radio broadcast of the H. G. Wells' story "WAR of the WORLDS" by the Mr. George Orson Welles!!!!!~'

George Orson Welles was `-BORN on May 6[th] in `-1915; and, `-DIED on October 10[th] of `-1985!!!!!~' Mr. George Orson Welles `-DIED at the tender `-AGE of `-**70** = The "YEAR" the "PROPHET" was `-BORN in `-19**70**!!!!!~'

Birthday `-NUMBER - George Orson Welles = 05/06/19/15 = (05 + 06 + 19 + 15) = `-**45**

Deathday `-Number - George Orson Welles = 10/10/19/85 = (10 + 10 + 19 + 85) = `-**124**

`-**124** (-) `-**45** = `-**79** = **"AGE of `-DEATH of Mr. H. G. WELLS!!!!!~'**

05/06/19/15 (+) 10/10/19/85 = `-**169** = (1 x 69) = `-**69** = **"The `-CYCLE of `-LIFE"!!!!!~'**

`-**45** (-) `-1 = `-**44** = The `-**YEAR** the **"PROPHET'S" MOTHER** was `-**BORN** (`-19**44**)!!!!!~'

`-**124** (-) `-1 = `-**123** = (1 x 23) = `-**23** = -a **Prophetic Number!!!!!~'**

`-45 (+) `-124 = `-**169** = (1 + 69) = `-**70** = The **"YEAR"** the **"PROPHET"** was `-**BORN** in `-19**70**!!!!!~'

The MONGOL EMPIRE - !!!!!~'

The `-MONGOL `-EMPIRE had existed during the `-**13**th; and, `-**14**th Centuries; and, was the largest; and, entirely contiguous land mass `-EMPIRE in our `-WORLD `-HISTORY!!!!!~'

13 + 14 = `-**27** = **"The ROMAN EMPIRE"!!!!!~'**

The Mongol Empire was `-FOUNDED in `-1**206**!!!!!~'

The Mongol Empire was `-DISSOLVED in `-1**368**!!!!!~'

`-1368 (-) `-1206 = `-**162**

The Mongol Empire lasted for `-**162** `-YEARS!!!!!~'

`-1**206** (Founded) = **RECIPROCAL** = (Ended) `-**162** (Years `-LATER)!!!!!~'

`-**26** = **RECIPROCAL** = `-**62**

`-**162** = (1 + 62) = `-**63** = **"AGE of `-DEATH of the "PROPHET'S" MOTHER!!!!!~'**

`-1206 = (12 + 6) = `-**18** / `-1368 = (13 + 68) = `-**81**

`-**18** = **RECIPROCAL** = `-**81**

`-**81** (-) `-**18** = `-**63** = **"AGE of `-DEATH of the "PROPHET'S" MOTHER!!!!!~'**

33

`-The `-NEXT `-NOSTRADAMUS; <u>is</u>, The "PROPHET"; – Mr. Dwayne W. Anderson…(…)…-!!!!!~'

WINTER GARDEN THEATRE on `-BROADWAY…' (In the `-CALENDAR `-YEAR of `-1864)!!!!!~'

BOOTH BENEFIT

For the SHAKESPEARE STATUE FUND…'

The `-PLAY – JULIUS CAESAR – November 25th EVENING; `-OPENED!!!!!~'

Starring in the `-MAJOR `-ROLES!!!!!~'

Junius Brutus Booth as … Cassius!!!!!~'

Edwin Booth as … Brutus!!!!!~'

John Wilkes Booth as … Marc Anthony!!!!!~' (Assassinator of Abraham Lincoln)!!!!!~'

John <u>W</u>ilkes <u>B</u>ooth = <u>JWB</u> = `-<u>INSIGNIA/MONOGRAM</u>-!!!!!~'

<u>J</u> = `-10 / <u>W</u> = `-23 / <u>B</u> = `-2

(10 + 23 + 2) = `-<u>35</u> = <u>RECIPROCAL</u> = `-<u>53</u> = "WAR of the WORLDS"!!!!!~'

…(…)…

<u>E</u>dwin <u>B</u>ooth = <u>EB</u> = `-<u>INSIGNIA/MONOGRAM</u>-!!!!!~'

<u>E</u> = `-5 / <u>B</u> = `-2

`-<u>52</u> = <u>RECIPROCAL</u> = `-<u>25</u>

`-52 (-) `-25 = `-<u>27</u> = "The ROMAN EMPIRE"!!!!!~'

(52 + 1) = `-<u>53</u> = "WAR of the WORLDS"!!!!!~'

…(…)…

Junius Brutus Booth = JBB = `-INSIGNIA/MONOGRAM-!!!!!~'

J = `-10 / **B** = `-2 / **B** = `-2

(10 + 2 + 2) = `-**14** = **RECIPROCAL** = `-**41** = "WAR of the WORLDS"!!!!!~'

`-41 (-) `-14 = `-**27** = "The ROMAN EMPIRE"!!!!!~'

…(…)…

John F. Kennedy = JFK = `-INSIGNIA/MONOGRAM-!!!!!~'

J = `-10 / **F** = `-6 / **K** = `-11

(10 + 6 + 11) = `-**27** = "The ROMAN EMPIRE"!!!!!~'

…(…)…

Abraham Lincoln = AL = `-INSIGNIA/MONOGRAM-!!!!!~'

A = `-1 / **L** = `-12

(1 + 12) = `-**13** = "A VERY PIVOTAL NUMBER"!!!!!~' / `-**13** = **RECIPROCAL** = `-**31**

`-31 + `-13 = `-**44** = "The `-YEAR of the "PROPHET'S" MOTHER'S `-BIRTH (`-19**44**)!!!!!~'

`-31 (-) `-13 = `-**18** = **RECIPROCAL** = `-**81**

`-81 (-) `-18 = `-**63** = "AGE of `-DEATH of the "PROPHET'S" MOTHER!!!!!~'

…(…)…

Martin Luther King, Jr. = MLK = `-INSIGNIA/MONOGRAM-!!!!!~'

M = `-13 / **L** = `-12 / **K** = `-11

11, 12, 13 = **Prophetic-Linear-Progression!!!!!~'**

`-11 (+) `-12 (+) `-13 = `-**36** = **RECIPROCAL** = `-**63**

M = `-13 / **L** = `-12 / **K** = `-11 / **J** = `-10

(13 + 12 + 11 + 10) = `-**46** = "AGE that JOHN F. KENNEDY was `-ASSASSINATED"!!!!!~'

`-**46** = **RECIPROCAL** = `-**64** / `-64 (-) `-46 = `-**18** = **RECIPROCAL** = `-**81**

`-81 (-) `-18 = `-**63** = "AGE of `-DEATH of the "PROPHET'S" MOTHER & `-YEAR that the `-PRESIDENT JOHN F. KENNEDY was `-ASSASSINATED!!!!!~'

...(...)...

Dwayne **W**. **A**nderson = **DWA** = `-**INSIGNIA/MONOGRAM**-!!!!!~'

D = `-4 / **W** = `-23 / **A** = `-1

(4 + 23 + 1) = `-**28** = **RECIPROCAL** = `-**82** = "AGE of `-DEATH of the "PROPHET'S" FATHER'S MOTHER/`-GRANDMOTHER"!!!!!~'

`-82 (-) `-28 = `-**54** = "EARTHQUAKES"!!!!!~'

(54 - 1) = `-**53** = "WAR of the WORLDS"!!!!!~'

(23 - 4 - 1) = `-**18** = **RECIPROCAL** = `-**81**

`-81 (-) `-18 = `-**63** = "AGE of `-DEATH of the "PROPHET'S" MOTHER!!!!!~'

D = `-4 / **A** = `-1

(1/4) = `-**14** = **RECIPROCAL** = `-**41** = "The `-YEAR the "PROPHET'S" FATHER was `-BORN (`-19**41**)" = "WAR of the WORLDS"!!!!!~'

`-41 (-) `-14 = `-**27** = "The ROMAN EMPIRE"!!!!!~'

...(...)...

JESUS **C**HRIST = **JC** = `-**INSIGNIA/MONOGRAM**-!!!!!~'

J = `-10 / **C** = `-3

(10 + 3) = `-**13** = "A VERY PIVOTAL NUMBER"!!!!!~'

`-**13** = **RECIPROCAL** = `-**31**

`-31 + `-13 = `-**44** = "The `-YEAR of the "PROPHET'S" MOTHER'S `-BIRTH (`-19**44**)!!!!!~'

`-**35** = RECIPROCAL = `-**53** = "WAR of the WORLDS"!!!!!~'

`-44 + `-35 = `-**79** = "AGE of `-DEATH of `-H. G. WELLS!!!!!~'

`-**79** = RECIPROCAL = `-**97**

`-44 + `-53 = `-**97** / `-97 (-) `-79 = `-**18** / `-18 + `-18 = `-**36** = RECIPROCAL = `-**63**

`-31 (-) `-13 = `-**18** = RECIPROCAL = `-**81**

`-81 (-) `-18 = `-**63** = "AGE of `-DEATH of the "PROPHET'S" MOTHER!!!!!~'

`-**36** = RECIPROCAL = `-**63** / `-63 (-) `-36 = `-**27** = "The ROMAN EMPIRE"!!!!!~'

`-44 x `-35 = `-**1540** = (15 + 40) = `-**55** = (`-**23** + `-**32**) = "The "PROPHET" & "JESUS" `-SAVES LIVES"!!!!!~'

`-44 x `-53 = `-**2332**

`-**23** = RECIPROCAL = `-**32** = "Two PROPHETIC `-NUMBERS"!!!!!~'

BIBLE BOOK of `-MARK: `-**6**:**3** - ...(-English Revised Edition-1885)...

"Is not this the carpenter, the son of Mary, and brother of James, and Joses, and Judas, and Simon? And are not his sisters here with us? And they were offended in him. (-**English Revised Edition-1885**)...

JESUS CHRIST'S MOTHER `-MARY `-DIED in the `-YEAR `-**48** A.D./C.E.!!!!!~'

`-**48** = RECIPROCAL = `-**84**

`-**84** + `-**48** = `-**132** = (1 x 32) = `-**32** = -a Prophetic Number!!!!!~'

`-**84** (-) `-**48** = `-**36** = RECIPROCAL = `-**63**

MARY `-DIED at the TENDER `-AGE of `-**59**!!!!!~'

`-**59** = **RECIPROCAL** = `-**95** / `-95 (-) `-59 = `-**36** = **RECIPROCAL** = `-**63**

`-95 + `-59 = `-**154** = (1 x 54) = `-**54** = "EARTHQUAKES"!!!!!~'

The "PROPHET'S" MOTHER (`-**44**); and, CHRIST'S MOTHER `-MARY-' (`-**59**)...

`-59 + `-44 = `-**103** = (0 + 13) = `-**13** = "A VERY PIVOTAL NUMBER"!!!!!~'

`-**27** + `-**32** = `-**59** = "AGE of `-DEATH of `-MARY!!!!!~'

...(-English Revised Edition-1885)... = `-85 + `-18 = `-**103**...(...)...-'-'

`-**85** = (8 + 5) = `-**13** = "A VERY PIVOTAL NUMBER"!!!!!~'

`-**85** = **RECIPROCAL** = `-**58**

`-85 (-) `-58 = `-**27** = "The ROMAN EMPIRE"!!!!!~'

`-59 (-) `-44 = `-**15** / `-**15** = **RECIPROCAL** = `-**51**

`-51 (-) `-15 = `-**36** = **RECIPROCAL** = `-**63**...(...)...-'-'

`-51 + `-15 = `-**66** = "AGE of `-DEATH of the "PROPHET'S" FATHER!!!!!~'

The "PROPHET'S" MOTHER (`-**44**); and, CHRIST'S MOTHER `-MARY-' (`-**48**)...

`-48 + `-44 = `-**92** / `-**92** = **RECIPROCAL** = `-**29**

`-92 (-) `-29 = `-**63** = "AGE of `-DEATH of the "PROPHET'S" MOTHER!!!!!~'

If `-**CHRIST** `-**DIED** at the tender `-**AGE** of `-**32**; then,:

`-59 (-) `-32 = `-**27** = "The ROMAN EMPIRE"!!!!!~'

`-**32** = **RECIPROCAL** = `-**23** / `-59 (-) `-23 = `-**36** = **RECIPROCAL** = `-**63**...(...)...-'-'

`-84 + `-95 = `-**179** = (1 x 79) = `-**79** = "AGE of `-DEATH of H. G. WELLS"!!!!!~'

`-48 (-) `-44 = `-**4** / `-63 (-) `-59 = `-**4** / (`-4 /|\ `-4) = `-**44** = "The `-YEAR of the "PROPHET'S" MOTHER'S `-BIRTH (`-19**44**)!!!!!~'

`-79 (-) `-44 = `-**35** = RECIPROCAL = `-**53** = "WAR of the WORLDS"!!!!!~'

Julius **C**aesar = **JC** = `-INSIGNIA/MONOGRAM-!!!!!~'

J = `-10 / **C** = `-3

(10 + 3) = `-**13** = "A VERY PIVOTAL NUMBER"!!!!!~'

`-**13** = RECIPROCAL = `-**31**

`-31 + `-13 = `-**44** = "The `-YEAR of the "PROPHET'S" MOTHER'S `-BIRTH (`-19**44**)!!!!!~'

Julius Caesar was `-**ASSASSINATED** on (0**3**/1**5**/44) / **March 15**th of `-**44** B.C. (Before `-CHRIST)!!!!!~'

`-**35** = RECIPROCAL = `-**53** / `-1**5** + `-**3** = `-**18** = RECIPROCAL = `-**81**

(3 + 15 + 44) = `-**62** = RECIPROCAL = `-**26** / `-62 (-) `-26 = `-**36** = RECIPROCAL = `-**63**

Julius Caesar was `-**BORN (07/13/100)** / **July 13**th**, 100 B.C.**

Julius Caesar was `-**ASSASSINATED** at the `-**AGE** of `-**56**!!!!!~'

Abraham Lincoln was `-**ASSASSINATED** at the `-**AGE** of `-**56**!!!!~'

`-56 + `-56 = `-**112** / Date: (7 + 13 + 100) = `-**120**

`-**112** = (1 x 12) = `-**12** / `-120 = (12 + 0) = `-**12** / `-12 + `-12 = `-**24**

`-24 (-) `-1 = `-**23** = -a Prophetic Number!!!!!~'

`-120 + `-24 = `-**144** = (1 x 44) = `-**44** = "The "PROPHET'S" MOTHER & JULIUS CAESAR"!!!!!~'

John Wilkes Booth starred in **JULIUS CAESAR** of the **calendar year** of `-18**64**!!!!!~'

`-64 (-) `-18 = `-**46** = **RECIPROCAL** = `-**64**

`-**46** = `-**23** x `-**2** = `-**232** = Reciprocal-**S**equenced-**N**umerology-**RSN**!!!!!~'

`-64 + `-18 = `-**82** = **RECIPROCAL** = `-**28**

`-82 (-) `-28 = `-**54** = "EARTHQUAKES"!!!!!~'

`-**35** = **RECIPROCAL** = `-**53** = "WAR of the WORLDS"!!!!!~'

`-44 + `-35 = `-**79** = "AGE of `-DEATH of `-H. G. WELLS!!!!!~'

`-**79** = **RECIPROCAL** = `-**97** / `-44 + `-53 = `-**97** / `-97 (-) `-79 = `-**18**

`-18 + `-18 = `-**36** = **RECIPROCAL** = `-**63** / `-31 (-) `-13 = `-**18** = **RECIPROCAL** = `-**81**

`-81 (-) `-18 = `-**63** = "AGE of `-DEATH of the "PROPHET'S" MOTHER!!!!!~'

`-**36** = **RECIPROCAL** = `-**63**

`-63 (-) `-36 = `-**27** = "The ROMAN EMPIRE"!!!!!~'

`-44 x `-35 = `-**1540** = (15 + 40) = `-**55** = (`-**23** + `-**32**) = "The "PROPHET" & "JESUS" `-SAVES LIVES"!!!!!~'

`-44 x `-53 = `-**2332**

`-**23** = **RECIPROCAL** = `-**32** = "Two `-PROPHETIC `-NUMBERS"!!!!!~'

John Wilkes Booth = JWB = `-INSIGNIA/MONOGRAM-!!!!!~'

J = `-10 / **W** = `-23 / **B** = `-2

(10 + 23 + 2) = `-**35** = **RECIPROCAL** = `-**53** = "WAR of the WORLDS"!!!!!~'

John Wilkes Booth was `-**BORN** on **(05/10/1838) / May 10**th**, 1838**; and, `-**DIED** on **(04/26/1865) / April 26**th**, 1865**!!!!!~'

`-**38** = `-**1938** = The `-19**38** radio broadcast of the H. G. Wells' story "WAR of the WORLDS" by the Mr. George Orson Welles!!!!!~'

John Wilkes Booth `-DIED within `-**13** (`-**4** + `-**9**) DAYS lying in `-BETWEEN his Death/Day; and, `-BIRTHDAY; from TURNING, `-**27** years of age = **"The Roman Empire"!!!!!~'**

`-**94** = **RECIPROCAL** = `-**49**

`-94 (-) `-35 = `-**59** = **"AGE of `-DEATH of JESUS CHRIST'S MOTHER `-MARY"!!!!!~'**

`-49 (-) `-35 = `-**14** = **RECIPROCAL** = `-**41** = **"WAR of the WORLDS"!!!!!~'**

John Wilkes Booth `-DIED at the tender `-AGE of `-26** = `-13** x `-**2** = `-**132** = **(1 x 32) = `-32 = -a Prophetic Number!!!!!~'**

`-**26** = **RECIPROCAL** = `-**62** / `-62 (-) `-26 = `-**36** = **RECIPROCAL** = `-**63**

John Wilkes Booth `-BIRTHDAY `-NUMBER - # = (5 + 10 + 18 + 38) = `-**71**

John Wilkes Booth `-DEATH/DAY `-NUMBER - # = (4 + 26 + 18 + 65) = `-**113** = (1 x 13) = `-**13** = **"A VERY PIVOTAL NUMBER"!!!!!~'**

`-113 (-) `-71 = `-**42** = **RECIPROCAL** = `-**24**

`-**42** + `-**24** = `-**66** = **"AGE of `-DEATH of the "PROPHET'S" FATHER!!!!!~'**

John Wilkes Birth = (5 + 10 + 18 + 38)

John Wilkes Death = (4 + 26 + 18 + 65)

= (54) (36) (36) (27) = `-**153** = (1 x 53) = `-**53** = **"WAR of the WORLDS"!!!!!~'**

`-**65** + `-**38** = `-**103** = `-**103**...(...)...`-`` = `-**206** = `-**26** = **"AGE of `-DEATH of John Wilkes Booth!!!!!~'**

Abraham Lincoln/Julius Caesar = `-**56** / John Wilkes Booth = `-**26**

`-**56** x `-2 = `-**112** / `-112 + `-26 = `-**138**!!!!!~'

`-138 = (83 (-) 1) = `-**82** / `-56 + `-26 = `-**82**

`-82 + `-82 = `-**164** = `-**1864** = **John Wilkes Booth played in "Julius Caesar"!!!!!~'**

Dwayne W. Anderson = **DWA** = `-**INSIGNIA/MONOGRAM**-!!!!!~'

41

D = `-4 / **W** = `-23 / **A** = `-1 = `-**28** = **RECIPROCAL** = `-**82** = `-**ARMAGEDDON!!!!!**~'

(4 + 23 + 1) = `-**28** = **RECIPROCAL** = `-**82** = "AGE of `-DEATH of the "PROPHET'S" FATHER'S MOTHER/`-GRANDMOTHER"!!!!!~'

`-82 (-) `-28 = `-**54** = "EARTHQUAKES"!!!!!~'

(54 - 1) = `-**53** = "WAR of the WORLDS"!!!!!~'

(23 - 4 - 1) = `-**18** = **RECIPROCAL** = `-**81**

`-81 (-) `-18 = `-**63** = "AGE of `-DEATH of the "PROPHET'S" MOTHER!!!!!~'

D = `-4 / **A** = `-1

(1/4) = `-**14** = **RECIPROCAL** = `-**41** = "The `-YEAR the "PROPHET'S" FATHER was `-BORN (`-19**41**)" = "WAR of the WORLDS"!!!!!~'

`-41 (-) `-14 = `-**27** = "The ROMAN EMPIRE"!!!!!~'

From **John Wilkes Booth** `-BIRTH to **Julius Caesar's** `-DEATH there are `-**1,882** Years!!!!!~'

`-**1838** A.D./C.E. + `-**44** B.C./B.C.E. = `-**1882**

`-82 + `-18 = `-**100** = "YEAR of the Julius Caesar's `-BIRTH!!!!!~'

`-82 (-) `-18 = `-**64** = `-**1864** = "The `-**YEAR** that **John Wilkes Booth** played **Marc Anthony;** in the `-**PLAY,** 'SHAKESPEARES' "JULIUS CAESAR"!!!!!~'

'SHAKESPEARES' "JULIUS CAESAR" was first `-PERFORMED on (09/21/1599) / September 21st, 1599 A.D./C.E.!!!!!~'

`-**1864** (-) `-1599 = `-**265** = ((65 (-) 2)) = `-**63**

`-**1864** (-) `-1599 = `-**265** = (2 x 65) = `-**130**

`-**130** + `-**63** = `-**193** = (1 x 93) = `-**93** = **RECIPROCAL** = `-**39** = 3(9's) = `-**999**

`-**21** + `-15 = `-**36** = **RECIPROCAL** = `-**63**

`-(**999**) = <u>RECIPROCAL</u> = `-(**666**)!!!!!~'

`-999 + `-666 = `-**1665** / `-65 + `-16 = `-**81** / `-65 (-) `-16 = `-**49**

`-81 (-) `-49 = `-**32** = -a Prophetic Number!!!!!~'

`-81 + `-49 = `-**130** = (13 + 0) = `-**13** = "A VERY PIVOTAL NUMBER"!!!!!~'

`-09 + `-21 + `-15 = `-**45** = <u>RECIPROCAL</u> = `-**54** = "EARTHQUAKES"!!!!!~'

`-09 + `-21 + `-15 + `-99 = `-**144** = (1 x 44) = `-**44** = "The "PROPHET'S" MOTHER & JULIUS CAESAR"!!!!!~'

There are some `-**64** Days that lie in between the **Sept. 21ˢᵗ (1ˢᵗ Shakespeare Performance in `-1599)** and, the **opening night for John Wilkes Booth's Performance in 'Shakespeare's' Julius Caesar on November 25ᵗʰ** in `-**1864**!!!!!~'

Tom <u>C</u>ruise = <u>TC</u> = `-<u>INSIGNIA/MONOGRAM</u>-!!!!!~'

<u>T</u> = `-20 / <u>C</u> = `-3

(20 + 3) = `-**23** = -a Prophetic Number!!!!!~' / `-**23** = <u>RECIPROCAL</u> = `-**32**

Tom Cruise was `-<u>BORN</u> on **(07/03/1962)** / **July 3ʳᵈ** in `-**1962**!!!!!~'

(07/03) = (7/3) = (3/7) / `-**37** = <u>RECIPROCAL</u> = `-**73**

`-73 (-) `-37 = `-**36** = <u>RECIPROCAL</u> = `-**63**`-...(...)...'

(7 + 3 + 19) = `-**29** = <u>RECIPROCAL</u> = `-**92** / `-92 (-) `-29 = `-**63**`-...(...)...'

(7 + 3 + 19 + 62) = `-**91** = <u>RECIPROCAL</u> = `-**19**

`-91 (-) `-19 = `-**72** = <u>RECIPROCAL</u> = `-**27** = "The ROMAN EMPIRE"!!!!!~'

At the time of this `-WRITING **(10/31/2015)**, Tom Cruise is `-**53** years of `-AGE!!!!!~'

Tom Cruise is **5' 7"** in `-HEIGHT!!!!!~'

`-**57** = <u>RECIPROCAL</u> = `-**75**

43

`-75 + `-57 = `-**132** = (1 x 32) = `-**32** = -a Prophetic Number!!!!!~'

"WAR of the WORLDS" – RELEASE DATE – June 29ᵗʰ, `-2005 (USA)!!!!!~'

BUDGET: `-**$132** MILLION (USD)!!!!!~'

June 29ᵗʰ = (06/29) = (6 + 29) = `-**35** = **RECIPROCAL** = `-**53** = **"WAR of the WORLDS"!!!!!~'**

`-2005 = (0 + 0 + 25) = `-**25** = **RECIPROCAL** = `-**52**

`-52 (-) `-25 = `-**27** = **"The ROMAN EMPIRE"!!!!!~'**

NARRATOR: **"MORGAN FREEMAN"!!!!!~'**

DIRECTOR: **"STEVEN SPIELBERG"!!!!!~'**

ADAPTED from: "The WAR of the WORLDS"!!!!!~'

Steven Spielberg = SS = `-INSIGNIA/MONOGRAM-!!!!!~'

S = `-19 / **S** = `-19

(19 + 19) = `-**38** = `-**1938** = The `-19**38** radio broadcast of the H. G. Wells' story "WAR of the WORLDS" by the Mr. George Orson Welles!!!!!~'

Steven Spielberg was `-**BORN** on **(12/18/1946) / December 18ᵗʰ in `-1946!!!!!~'**

(12 + 18 + 19 + 46) = `-**95** = **RECIPROCAL** = `-**59**

`-95 (-) `-59 = `-**36** = **RECIPROCAL** = `-**63**`...(...)...'

`-**46** = `-**23** x `-**2** = `-**232** = **Reciprocal-Sequenced-Numerology-RSN!!!!!~'**

At the time of this `-WRITING **(10/31/2015)**, Steven Spielberg is `-**68** years of `-**AGE!!!!!~'**

Soon `-HE will be `-69 "Years of Age" = "The `-CYCLE of `-LIFE"!!!!!~'

Steven Spielberg as of this `-DATE has a `-NET `-WORTH of `-$**3.6** Billion (USD) (`-2015)!!!!!~'

`-36 = **RECIPROCAL** = `-63`-...(...)...-'

Steven Spielberg is **5' 8"** in `-HEIGHT!!!!!~'

`-58 = **RECIPROCAL** = `-85 / `-85 (-) `-58 = `-27 = "The ROMAN EMPIRE"!!!!!~'

Morgan Freeman = MF = `-INSIGNIA/MONOGRAM-!!!!!~'

M = `-13 / **F** = `-6

(13 x 6) = `-78 = "Current `-AGE of **Mr. Morgan Freeman** at the `-TIME of the "PROPHET'S" WRITINGS"!!!!!~'

(13 + 6) = `-19 = **RECIPROCAL** = `-91

`-91 (-) `-19 = `-72 = **RECIPROCAL** = `-27 = "The ROMAN EMPIRE"!!!!!~'

`-19 x `-2 = `-38 = `-1938 = The `-1938 radio broadcast of the H. G. Wells' story "WAR of the WORLDS" by the Mr. George Orson Welles!!!!!~'

(**13/6**) = (1 x 36) = `-36 = **RECIPROCAL** = `-63`-...(...)...-'

`-63 (-) `-36 = `-27 = "The ROMAN EMPIRE"!!!!!~'

Morgan Freeman was `-**BORN** on (**06/01/1937**) / **June 1st** `-**1937**!!!!!~'

(60 + 10 + 19 + 37) = `-**126**

(12 x 6) = `-72 = **RECIPROCAL** = `-27 = The ROMAN EMPIRE"!!!!!~'

(6 + 1 + 19) = `-**26** = **RECIPROCAL** = `-**62** / (6 + 1 + 19 + 37) = `-**63**`-...(...)...-'

Morgan Freeman is **6' 2"** in `-HEIGHT!!!!!~'

`-**62** = **RECIPROCAL** = `-**26** / `-62 (-) `-26 = `-**36** = **RECIPROCAL** = `-**63**`-...(...)...-'

(60 + 10 + 91 + 73) = `-**234** = "Prophetic-Linear-Progression"!!!!!~'

At the time of this `-WRITING (**10/31/2015**), Morgan Freeman is `-**78** years of `-AGE!!!!!~'

Soon `-HE will be `-79 "Years of Age" = "The `-AGE of `-DEATH of Mr. H. G. WELLS" from the "WAR of the WORLDS"!!!!!~'

The **2**nd President of the United States of America President John Adams lived `-**23** years longer than the very **1**st President of the United States of America – President George Washington!~'

`-**23** = <u>RECIPROCAL</u> = `-**32**

President George Washington was `-<u>BORN</u> in `-17**32**!!!!!~'

(`-**3**) of the very `-First-' (`-**5**) U. S. Presidents had `-DIED on <u>July 4</u>th!!!!!~'

`-**35** = <u>RECIPROCAL</u> = `-**53** = "WAR of the WORLDS"!!!!!~'

President John Adams was `-<u>BORN</u> in `-17**35**!!!!!~'

President John Adams; and, **President Thomas Jefferson** `-<u>DIED</u> on <u>July 4</u>th in `-<u>**1826**</u>!!!!!~' July 4th = (`-**74**)!!!!!~'

(7 + 4 + 18) = `-**29** = <u>RECIPROCAL</u> = `-**92**

`-**92** (-) `-**29** = `-**63**`-...(...)...` = "The `-AGE of the "PROPHET'S" MOTHER for `-WHEN SHE HAD `-DIED!!!!!~'

(18 + 26) = `-**44** = "The `-YEAR that the "PROPHET'S" MOTHER was `-BORN (`-19**44**)!!!!!~'

(7 + 4 + 18 + 26) = `-**55** = `-**23** + `-**32** = "The "PROPHET" & "JESUS CHRIST" SAVE `-LIVES!!!!!~'

President John Adams; and, President Thomas Jefferson `-BOTH `-<u>DIED</u> on the `-**50**th `-Anniversary of the `-BIRTH of the United States of America!!!!!~'

`-**50** = <u>RECIPROCAL</u> = `-**05**

The `-5th President of the United States of America President James Monroe `-<u>DIED</u> `-**5** years later in the calendar year of `-<u>**1831**</u>!!!!!~'

`-<u>**1831**</u> = (31 - 18) = `-**13** = "A VERY PIVOTAL NUMBER"!!!!!~'

President James Monroe `-**DIED** on the `-**55**th `-Anniversary of the `-BIRTH of the United States of America!!!!!~'

President Thomas Jefferson `-DIED at the `-AGE of `-**83**!!!!!~'

`-**83** = **RECIPROCAL** = `-**38**

As of this `-DATE (10/31/2015), of the `-**38** U. S. Presidents that have `-**DIED**, `-**23** eventually became the `-**OLDEST** of their `-**TIME**!!!!!~'

There have been `-5 U. S. Presidents that have either `-DIED exactly at the `-AGES of `-66, `-67, or, `-68!!!!!~' These Presidents are by `-NUMBER, Presidents: **#1, #9, #17, #23; and, #28**!!!!!~'

The `-**NUMBERS** in `-**BETWEEN** these `-**NUMBERS** are the `-**NUMBERS**: `-**8**, `-**8**, `-**6**; and, `-**5**!!!!!~'

(88 (-) 65) = `-**23** = **-a Prophetic Number!!!!!~'**

(8 + 8 + 6 + 5) = `-**27** = **"The ROMAN EMPIRE"**!!!!!~'

#1 = President George Washington (`-**67**) = `-DEATH `-AGE!!!!!~'

#9 = President William Henry Harrison (`-**68**) = `-DEATH `-AGE!!!!!~'

#17 = President Andrew Johnson (`-**66**) = `-DEATH `-AGE!!!!!~'

#23 = President Benjamin Harrison (**67**) = `-DEATH `-AGE!!!!!~'

#28 = President Woodrow Wilson (`-**67**) = `-DEATH `-AGE!!!!!~'

When `-**YOU** `-**ADD** `-**UP** *all* of the `-**NUMBERS** `-**YOU** *arrive* `-**AT**:

(67 + 68 + 66 + 67 + 67) = `-**335**

(33 + 5) = `-**38** = `-**1938** = The `-1938 radio broadcast of the H. G. Wells' story "WAR of the WORLDS" by the Mr. George Orson Welles!!!!!~'

`-**35** = **RECIPROCAL** = `-**53** = **"WAR of the WORLDS"**!!!!!~'

When `-**YOU** take the `-**MEAN**; or, the `-**AVERAGE**; `-**YOU** get the `-**NUMBER** `-**67** = **"The `-YEAR at which `-TIME the "PROPHET'S" BROTHER was `-BORN (`-19**67**)**!!!!!~'

47

(President George Washington-**67** + President William Henry Harrison-**68**) = `-**135** = (1 x 35) = `-**35** = **RECIPROCAL** = `-**53** = "**WAR of the WORLDS**"!!!!!~'

When `-YOU `-ADD up `-ALL of the `-NUMBERS from `-EACH; and, `-EVERY `-PRESIDENTS `-AGE of `-DEATH in `-BETWEEN the `-NUMBERS; `-YOU arrive `-AT the `-FOLLOWING `-RESULTS:

President #1 to President #8 = `-**635** = '-…(**63**)…-' / '-…(**53**)…-'

(#1/President George Washington `-DIED at the tender `-AGE of `-**67** = **RECIPROCAL** = `-**76**!!!!!~' President George Washington `-LIVED for some `-24,**767** `-DAYS `-**ENTIRELY!!!!!~'**)

(#8/President Martin Van Buren `-SURVIVED for some `-**231** DAYS after his `-BIRTHDAY!!!!!~' (`-**231** = (23 x 1) = `-**23** = -**a Prophetic Number!!!!!~'**)

President #1 to President #9 = `-**703** / `-**73** = **RECIPROCAL** = `-**37**

73 (-) 37 = `-**36** = **RECIPROCAL** = `-**63**'-…(…)…-'

President #9 to President #16 = `-**528** = `-**52.8** = ROUNDED = `-**53** = "**WAR of the WORLDS**"!!!!!~'

(#9/President William Henry Harrison had `-**311**/`-**312** days remaining in the `-YEAR after his untimely `-DEATH!!!!!~'

(`-**311**) = (31 x 1) = `-**31** = **RECIPROCAL** = `-**13** = "**A VERY PIVOTAL NUMBER**"!!!!!~'

(`-**312**) = (32 x 1) = `-**32** = -**a Prophetic Number!!!!!~'**

(311 + 312) = `-**623** = (6 x 23) = `-**138** = (1 x 38) = `-**38** = `-**1938** = The `-19**38** radio broadcast of the H. G. Wells' story "WAR of the WORLDS" by the Mr. George Orson Welles!!!!!~'

President #9 to President #17 = `-**594** = (59 x 4) = `-**236** = '-…(**23**)…-' / '-…(**36**)…-'

`-**23** (…) = **RECIPROCAL** = `-**32** (…) / `-**36** (…) = **RECIPROCAL** = `-**63** (…)

President #10 to President #16 = `-**406** = (0 + 46) = `-**46** = `-**23** x `-**2** = `-**232** = **Reciprocal-Sequenced-Numerology-RSN!!!!!~'**

(#16/President Abraham Lincoln `-DIED at the tender `-AGE of `-**56** = **RECIPROCAL** = `-**65** in `-19**65**)!!!!!~' President Abraham Lincoln `-SURVIVED for some `-**62** DAYS after his `-BIRTHDAY!!!!!~' (**62** + 1) = `-**63**`-...(...)...-'!!!!!~' President Abraham Lincoln `-LIVED for some `-20,**516** `-DAYS `-**ENTIRELY!!!!!~'**)

(#**16**/President Abraham Lincoln = **RECIPROCAL** = `-**61**)!!!!!~'

(61 + 16) = `-**77** = 2(7's) = `-**27** = **"The ROMAN EMPIRE"!!!!!~'**

President #10 to President #17 = `-**526**

(526 = `-**52.6** = ROUNDED = `-**53** = **"WAR of the WORLDS"!!!!!~'**

(#17/President Andrew Johnson `-DIED at the tender `-AGE of `-**66** = **RECIPROCAL** = `-**66** / `-66 + `-66 = `-**132**!!!!!~' `-**23** = **RECIPROCAL** = `-**32** / President Andrew Johnson `-SURVIVED for some `-**214** DAYS (24 - 1 = `-**23**) after his `-BIRTHDAY!!!!!~' President Andrew Johnson `-LIVED for some `-24,**320** `-DAYS `-**ENTIRELY!!!!!~'**)

(`-**320** = **"The "PROPHET'S" `-BIRTHDAY!!!!!~'**)

(#**18**/President Ulysses S. Grant `-DIED at the tender `-AGE of `-**63**!!!!!~')

(63 / 18) = `-**3.5** = `-**35** = **RECIPROCAL** = `-**53** = **"WAR of the WORLDS"!!!!!~'**

President #17 to President #22 = `-**376** = "Emphatic `-WITNESS to the `-NUMBER **76** = **RECIPROCAL** = `-**67**!!!!!~' **President #23 `-DIED** at the tender `-**AGE** of `-**67**!!!!!~'

President #17 to President #23 = `-**443** = "Emphatic `-WITNESS of `-Emphasis to the `-NUMBER `-**44** (44 x 3 = `-**132** = (1 x 32) = `-**32** = **-a Prophetic Number**)!!!!!~'

President #18 to President #22 = `-**310** = (31 + 0) = `-**31** = **RECIPROCAL** = `-**13** = **"A VERY PIVOTAL NUMBER"!!!!!~'**

President #18 to President #23 = `-**377** = (3 x 77) = `-**231** = (23 x 1) = `-**23** = **-a Prophetic Number!!!!!~'**

49

President #23 to President #27 = `-**328** = (28 + 3) = `-**31** = **RECIPROCAL** = `-**13** = **"A VERY PIVOTAL NUMBER"!!!!!~'**

(#23/President Benjamin Harrison `-DIED at the tender `-AGE of `-**67** = **RECIPROCAL** = `-**76**!!!!!~' President Benjamin Harrison `-LIVED for some `-24,**676** `-DAYS `-**ENTIRELY!!!!!~'**)

(#**23**/President Benjamin Harrison is the `-**RECIPROCAL** of #**1**/President George Washington as of: / President Benjamin Harrison (`-24,**676**); and, President George Washington (`-24,**767**)!!!!!~' The `-**23**rd `-**PRESIDENT!!!!!~'**

(**Minus #24/President Grover Cleveland** for the **2**nd `-**ENTRY as** `-**PRESIDENT** (`-71) = {(328 (-) 71)|} = `-**257** = (25 + 7) = `-**32** = -**a Prophetic Number!!!!!~'**)

(`-**257**) = (57 (-) 2) = `-**55** = `-**23** + `-**32…!!!!!~'**

President #23 to President #28 = `-**395** = (**35** x 9) = `-**315** = `-**31.5** = ROUNDED = `-**32** = -**a Prophetic Number!!!!!~'**

(**Minus #24/President Grover Cleveland** for the **2**nd `-**ENTRY as** `-**PRESIDENT** (`-71) = {(395 (-) 71)|} = `-**324** = (24 x 3) = `-**72** = **"The ROMAN EMPIRE"!!!!!~'**)

President #24 to President #27 = `-**261** = (26 + 1) = `-**27** = **"The ROMAN EMPIRE"!!!!!~'**

(2 + 61) = `-**63**`-…(…)…-`!!!!!~'

President #24 to President #28 = `-**328** = (28 + 3) = `-**31** = **RECIPROCAL** = `-**13** = **"A VERY PIVOTAL NUMBER"!!!!!~'**

When `-YOU `-TAKE the `-AGE of the `-PRESIDENT `-ABOVE; and, `-BELOW these `-SAME `-DESIGNATED `-NUMBERS of `-PRESIDENTS: #**9**, #**17**, #**23**; and, #**28**; and, `-ADD `-THEM `-TOGETHER; and, `-DIVIDE `-THEM by `-TWO for an `-AVERAGE; `-YOU in `-FACT get; `-the `-AGE `-NUMBER of the `-INITIAL `-PRESIDENT (`-**67**)!!!!!~'

`-**67** = **RECIPROCAL** = `-**76**

(`-**76** + `-**76**) = `-**152** = (1 + 52) = `-**53** = **"WAR of the WORLDS"!!!!!~'**

#**1** = President George Washington (`-**67**) = `-DEATH `-AGE!!!!!~'

#**8** = President Martin Van Buren (`-**79**) = `-DEATH `-AGE!!!!!~'

#**9** = President William Henry Harrison (`-**68**) = `-DEATH `-AGE!!!!!~'

#**10** = President John Tyler (`-**71**) = `-DEATH `-AGE!!!!!~'

#**16** = President Abraham Lincoln (`-**56**) = `-DEATH `-AGE!!!!!~'

#**17** = President Andrew Johnson (`-**66**) = `-DEATH `-AGE!!!!!~'

#**18** = President Ulysses S. Grant (`-**63**) = `-DEATH `-AGE!!!!!~'

#**22** = President Grover Cleveland (`-**71**) = `-DEATH `-AGE!!!!!~'

#**23** = President Benjamin Harrison (**67**) = `-DEATH `-AGE!!!!!~'

#**24** = President Grover Cleveland (`-**71**) = `-DEATH `-AGE!!!!!~'

#**27** = President William Howard Taft (`-**72**) = `-DEATH `-AGE!!!!!~'

#**28** = President Woodrow Wilson (`-**67**) = `-DEATH `-AGE!!!!!~'

#**29** = President Warren G. Harding (`-**57**) = `-DEATH `-AGE!!!!!~'

#**29** = President Warren G. Harding (`-**57**) = `-DEATH `-AGE `-DIED in `-19**23** within `-HIS `-**58**th `-YEAR of `-EXISTING!!!!!~' President Warren G. Harding `-**DIED** within `-HIS `-**57**th `-YEAR with `-**273** `-DAYS after `-HIS `-BIRTHDAY!!!!!~'

(365 (-) 273) = `-**92** = **RECIPROCAL** = `-**29**

`-**92** = "DAYS remaining; `-UNTIL, `-HIS `-NEXT `-**58**th `-BIRTHDAY!!!!!~'

(29 x 2) = `-**58** = "Double `-HIS PRESIDENCY # `-NUMBER; and, `-YOU `-ARRIVE at his `-TIME of the `-YEAR of `-HIS `-DEATH!!!!!~'

`-**58** = (5 + 8) = `-**13** = "A VERY PIVOTAL NUMBER"!!!!!~'

`-**57** = **RECIPROCAL** = `-**75**

(75 + 57) = `-**132** = (1 x 32) = `-**32** = -a Prophetic Number!!!!!~'

(58 (-) 23) = `-**35** = **RECIPROCAL** = `-**53** = "WAR of the WORLDS"!!!!!~'

President Warren G. Harding `-SURVIVED for some `-**273** DAYS after his 57th `-BIRTHDAY!!!!!~'

`-**273** = `-Emphatic `-WITNESS for an `-EMPHASIS on the `-NUMBER `-**27** = "The ROMAN EMPIRE"!!!!!~'

`-**273** = (73 + 2) = `-**75** = **RECIPROCAL** = `-**57**

#**30** = President Calvin Coolidge (`-**60**) = `-DEATH `-AGE `-DIED in `-19**33** right after `-HIS `-**60**th `-YEAR of `-EXISTING had `-TURNED into a `-NEW `-YEAR!!!!!~'

(30 x 2) = `-**60** = "Double `-HIS PRESIDENCY # `-NUMBER; and, `-YOU `-ARRIVE at his `-TIME of the `-YEAR of `-HIS `-DEATH!!!!!~'

`-**1872** = (72 + 18) = `-**90** = (30/60/90) = `-**123** = Prophetic-**L**inear-**P**rogressions-**PLP's**!!!!!~'

NOTICE the `-**PATTERNS** = The `-NEXT `-PRESIDENT #31/President Herbert Hoover lived to the `-AGE of `-**90** `-plus `-**71** `-DAYS!!!!!~' AND; the #30th/President Calvin Coolidge's `-DEATH/DAY # `-NUMBER `-EQUALED (=) the YEAR of `-DEATH of the `-PREVIOUS `-PRESIDENT / #29 = Mr. President Warren G. Harding whose `-DEATH `-YEAR was the `-NUMBER `-**58**!!!!!~'

#31/President Herbert Hoover was `-BORN on August 10th in `-1874; and, `-DIED on October 20th of `-1964!!!!!~'

(8 + 10 + 18 + 74) = `-**110** / (10 + 20 + 19 + 64) = `-**113**

(113 + 110) = `-**223** = "`-EMPHATIC `-WITNESS to the `-NUMBER `-**23** = -a Prophetic Number!!!!!~'

(8 + 10 + 18) = `-**36** = **RECIPROCAL** = `-**63** = "AGE of `-DEATH of #32/ President Franklin Delano Roosevelt!!!!!~'

President #**32**/Franklin Delano Roosevelt `-LIVED to the `-AGE of `-**63** `-**YEARS**; and, plus `-**72** `-**DAYS!!!!!~**' President #**32**/Franklin Delano Roosevelt `-**LIVED** for some `-**23**,0**82** `-DAYS `-ENTIRELY!!!!!~'

`-**32** = **RECIPROCAL** = `-**23** / `-**82** = **RECIPROCAL** = `-**28**

(82 - 28) = `-**54** = (`-27 x `-2) = **"EMPHATIC `-WITNESS to The ROMAN EMPIRE"!!!!!~**'

#33/President Harry S. Truman `-LIVED to the `-AGE of `-88 `-YEARS; and, plus some `-232 `-DAYS!!!!!~' President #**33**/Harry S. Truman `-**LIVED** for some `-**32**,373 `-**DAYS `-ENTIRELY!!!!!~**'

`-**323** = **Reciprocal-Sequencing-Numerology-RSN!!!!!~**'

The `-PATTERNS in `-DEATH in `-DAYS are `-RECIPROCALS = `-**32** = **RECIPROCAL** = `-**23** = **RECIPROCAL** = `-**32**

#31/President Herbert Hoover `-LIVED for some `-**32,943**...(...)...-'

#32/President Franklin Delano Roosevelt `-LIVED for some `-**23,082**...(...)...-'

#33/President Harry S. Truman `-LIVED for some `-**32,373**...(...)...-'

(943 - 373) = `-**570** = (57 + 0) = `-**57** = **RECIPROCAL** = `-**75**

(75 + 57) = `-**132** = (1 x 32) = `-**32** = -a Prophetic Number!!!!!~'

(570 + 082) = `-**652** = (65 + 2) = `-**67**...(...)...-'

(943 + 373) = `-**1316** = (1 x 1 x 36) = `-**36** = **RECIPROCAL** = `-**63** = "AGE of `-DEATH of #32/President Franklin Delano Roosevelt!!!!!~'

`-**373** = (37) ... / (73) ... / `-**73** = **RECIPROCAL** = `-**37**

(73 - 37) = `-**36** = **RECIPROCAL** = `-**63** = "AGE of `-DEATH of #32/ President Franklin Delano Roosevelt!!!!!~'

`-1316 (-) `-082 = `-**1234** = **P**rophetic-**L**inear-**P**rogression-**PLP**!!!!!~'

`-PRESIDENTS #31, #32; and, #33 = `-**96**

(31 + 32 + 33) = `-**96** = **RECIPROCAL** = `-**69** = "The `-CYCLES of `-LIFE"!!!!!~'

#35/President John F. Kennedy `-LIVED to the `-AGE of `-46 `-YEARS; and, plus some `-177 `-DAYS!!!!!~' President #**35**/John F. Kennedy `-**LIVED** for some `-**16,978** `-DAYS `-ENTIRELY!!!!!~' `-**16** x `-**2** `-PRESIDENTS = `-EQUALS `-**32**!!!!!~' (62 + 1) = `-**63**…(…)…-"

`-**46** = `-**23** x `-**2** = `-**232** = **R**eciprocal-**S**equencing-**N**umerology-**RSN**!!!!!~'

`-**16,978** = (78 (-) 9 (-) 16) = `-**53** = "WAR of the WORLDS"!!!!!~'

`-**35**th President = **RECIPROCAL** = `-**53** = "WAR of the WORLDS"!!!!!~'

(`-**978**) = (78 (-) 9) = `-**69** = "The `-CYCLE of `-LIFE"!!!!!~'

(`-**232**) = (2 x 32) = `-**64** = "AGE of `-DEATH of the #36/President Lyndon B. Johnson"!!!!!~'

#35 President John F. Kennedy (`-**46**) = **RECIPROCAL** = #36 President Lyndon B. Johnson (`-**64**)!!!!!~'

#**36**/President Lyndon B. Johnson `-LIVED to the `-AGE of `-64 `-YEARS; and, plus some `-148 `-DAYS!!!!!~' President #**36**/Lyndon B. Johnson `-**LIVED** for some `-**23,524** `-DAYS `-ENTIRELY!!!!!~' `-**36**th PRESIDENT = **RECIPROCAL** = `-**63** = "YEAR the `-PREVIOUS `-PRESIDENT was `-KILLED; or, had `-DIED!!!!!~'

`-148 = (1 x 48) = `-**48** = **RECIPROCAL** = `-**84**

(84 + 48) = `-**132** = (1 x 32) = `-**32** = -a Prophetic Number!!!!!~'

(84 - 48) = `-**36** = **RECIPROCAL** = `-**63** = "Year of `-DEATH of #35/ President John F. Kennedy!!!!!~"

(`-524) = `-**52.4** = ROUNDED UP = `-**53** = "WAR of the WORLDS"!!!!!~'

(`-524) = (52 + 4) = `-**56** = "The `-AGE of `-DEATH of #**16**/**President Abraham Lincoln** who `-TIED President Lyndon B. Johnson as the tallest `-PRESIDENTS `-EVER in the WHITEHOUSE at the `-HEIGHT of **6' 4"**!!!!!~'

#38/President Gerald Ford; and, #40/President Ronald Reagan `-BOTH `-DIED at the `-AGE of `-**93** with `-**45** days `-**SEPARATING their** `-**LENGTH of** `-**DAYS!!!!!~'**

`-93 + `-45 = `-**138** = (38 x 1) = `-**38** = `-**1938** = The `-19**38** radio broadcast of the H. G. Wells' story "WAR of the WORLDS" by the Mr. George Orson Welles!!!!!~'

`-93 (-) `-45 = `-**48** = **RECIPROCAL** = `-**84**

(84 + 48) = `-**132** = (1 x 32) = `-**32** = -a Prophetic Number!!!!!~'

#40/President Ronald Reagan `-DIED on (06/05/2004)!!!!!~'

(6 + 5 + 20 + 4) = `-**35** = **RECIPROCAL** = `-**53** = "**WAR of the WORLDS**"!!!!!~'

#40/President Ronald Reagan was `-BORN on (02/06/1911)!!!!!~'

(2 + 6 + 19 + 11) = `-**38** = `-**1938** = The `-19**38** radio broadcast of the H. G. Wells' story "WAR of the WORLDS" by the Mr. George Orson Welles!!!!!~'

#40/President Ronald Reagan `-DEATH/DAY # `-NUMBER (`-**35**) + `-PLUS `-HIS `-BIRTHDAY # `-NUMBER (`-**38**) = `-**73**!!!!!~'

#38/President Gerald Ford `-DEATH/DAY # `-NUMBER (`-**64**) + `-PLUS `-HIS `-BIRTHDAY # `-NUMBER (`-**53**) = `-**117**!!!!!~'

#38/President Gerald Ford (`-117) (-) `-MINUS #40/**President Ronald Reagan** (`-73) = `-**44** = "The `-YEAR that the "PROPHET'S" MOTHER was `-BORN (`-19**44**)!!!!!~'

#38/President Gerald Ford `-DIED on (12/26/2006)!!!!!~'

(12 + 26 + 20 + 6) = `-**64** = **RECIPROCAL** = `-**46** = `-**23** x `-**2** = `-**232** = Reciprocal-**S**equencing-**N**umerology-**RSN**!!!!!~'

#38/President Gerald Ford has the `-AGE of `-DEATH of **#35/President John F. Kennedy**; and, **#36/President Lyndon B. Johnson** `-<u>BOTH</u> within `-<u>HIS</u> `-DEATH/DAY # `-NUMBER!!!!!~'

#<u>38</u>/President Gerald Ford = `-<u>38</u><sup>th</sup> `-PRESIDENT of the UNITED STATES of AMERICA = `-<u>38</u> = `-<u>1938</u> = The `-19<u>38</u> radio broadcast of the H. G. Wells' story "WAR of the WORLDS" by the Mr. George Orson Welles!!!!!~'

#38/President Gerald Ford was `-BORN on (07/14/1913)!!!!!~'

(7 + 14 + 19 + 13) = `-<u>53</u> = "WAR of the WORLDS"!!!!!~'

#38/President Gerald Ford `-<u>DIED</u> on the very `-<u>DAY</u> (#`-<u>26</u><sup>th</sup>) **of the very same `-YEAR that** `-<u>HE</u> `-<u>DIED</u> on (`-<u>200</u><u>6</u>)!!!!!~' There is `-ALSO a `-<u>RECIPROCAL</u> `-AGAIN on the `-BIRTH `-DAY; and, `-BIRTH `-MONTH of the #40/President Ronald Reagan's `-DAY of `-BIRTH as (0<u>2</u>/0<u>6</u> of `-<u>1911</u>) with the #38/President Gerald Ford's **2(6's)!!!!!~'**

`-<u>1911</u> = (91 + 1 + 1) = `-<u>93</u> = `-AGE of `-DEATH of `-BOTH `-PRESIDENTS!!!!!~'

(19 + 11 + 6 + 2) = `-<u>38</u> = **#<u>38</u>**/President Gerald Ford's PRESIDENCY = `-<u>1938</u> = The `-19<u>38</u> radio broadcast of the H. G. Wells' story "WAR of the WORLDS" by the Mr. George Orson Welles!!!!!~' Both `-PRESIDENTS that `-DIED at the very same `-AGE of (`-<u>93</u>) are `-RECIPROCALS on the `-NUMBERS `-<u>35</u> = **<u>RECIPROCAL</u>** = `-<u>53</u> = "WAR of the WORLDS" with `-<u>EACH</u> of `-THEIR `-BIRTHS; and, `-DEATHS as `-PRESIDENTS for their `-BIRTHDAY # `-NUMBERS; and, their `-DEATH/DAY # `-NUMBERS!!!!!~'

Presidents #38, #39; and, #40 = "THREE `-3 SEPARATE `-PRESIDENTS!!!!!~

`-<u>45</u> days `-SEPARATING their `-LENGTH of `-DAYS **#38/President Gerald Ford/#40 President Ronald Reagan = (45 x 3) = `-<u>135</u> = (1 x 35) = `-<u>35</u> = <u>RECIPROCAL</u> = `-<u>53</u> = "WAR of the WORLDS"!!!!!~'**

(45 x 2) = `-<u>90</u> + 3 `-PRESIDENTS = `-<u>93</u> = `-AGE of `-DEATH of `-BOTH `-PRESIDENTS!!!!!~'

(45 / 2) = `-<u>22.5</u> = ROUNDED UP = `-<u>23</u> = -a **Prophetic Number!!!!!~'**

`-**45** = **RECIPROCAL** = `-**54** / (54 / 2) = `-**27** = "The **ROMAN EMPIRE**"!!!!!~'

#38/President Gerald Ford `-LENGTH of `-DAYS = `-EQUALS `-**34,133**!!!!!~'

#40/President Ronald Reagan `-LENGTH of `-DAYS = `-EQUALS `-**34,088**!!!!!~'

(34 + 34) = `-**68** = **RECIPROCAL** = `-**86**

(86 + 68) = `-**154** = (1 x 54) = `-**54**…(…)…~"

(133 - 88) = `-**45**…(…)…~"

`-**93** = **RECIPROCAL** = `-**39** / (93 - 39) = `-**54**…(…)…~"

(133 + 88) = `-**221** = "The `-CYCLE of `-PRESIDENTS in `-SUCCESSION that `-SHARE the `-SAME `-AGE!!!!!~'

(22 + 1) = `-**23** = -a **Prophetic Number**!!!!!~'

`-TWO `-SUCCESSIONS as `-PRESIDENT = The `-NUMBER (#2) `-SEPARATES these `-TWO in `-AGES of `-DEATH - #38/President Gerald Ford; and, #40/President Ronald Reagan `-BEING `-BOTH at the `-AGE of `-**93**!!!!!~'

`-TWO `-SUCCESSIONS as `-PRESIDENT = The `-NUMBER (#2) `-SEPARATES these `-TWO in `-AGES of `-LIVING at the `-TIME of this `-WRITING **(10/31/2015)** - #39/President Jimmy Carter; and, #41/President George H. W. Bush at the `-AGES ` of `-LIVING for `-BOTH of `-THEM `-CURRENTLY `-BEING at the `-AGE of `-**91**!!!!!~' DIFFERENCE in `-DAYS of `-LIVING is `-**111**…(…)…!!!!!~'

`-**91** = **RECIPROCAL** = `-**19**

(91 – 19) = `-**72** = **RECIPROCAL** = `-**27** = "The **ROMAN EMPIRE**"!!!!!~'

`-ONE `-SUCCESSION as `-PRESIDENT = The `-NUMBER (#1) `-SEPARATES these `-TWO in `-AGES of `-LIVING at the `-TIME of this `-WRITING **(10/31/2015)** - #42/President Bill Clinton; and, #43/President George W. Bush at the `-AGES ` of `-LIVING for `-BOTH of `-THEM `-CURRENTLY `-BEING at the `-AGE of `-**69**!!!!!~' DIFFERENCE in `-DAYS of `-LIVING is `-**44**…(…)…!!!!!~'

At this `-TIME there are `-73 `-DAYS beyond the `-BIRTHDAY for #42/ President Bill Clinton; and, `-117 DAYS beyond the `-BIRTHDAY FOR #43/ President George W. Bush!!!!!~'

= (+/-) =

`-73 = (73 - 1) = `-72

= **RECIPROCAL** =

`-117 = (1 x 17) = `-17 = **RECIPROCAL** = `-71 = (71 + 1) = `-72

(73 + 71) / 2 = `-72 = **RECIPROCAL** = `-27 = "The ROMAN EMPIRE"!!!!!~'

(73 + 71) = `-144 = (1 x 44) = `-44...(...)...-"

At this `-TIME of (10/31/2015); #44/President Barack H. Obama is `-54 `-YEARS of `-AGE with `-88 DAYS beyond `-HIS `-BIRTHDAY!!!!!~'

`-54 = (`-27 x `-2) = "EMPHATIC `-WITNESS to The ROMAN EMPIRE"!!!!!~'

(88 / 2) = `-44...(...)...-"

President Calvin Coolidge was `-BORN on **July 4th in `-1872!!!!!~'**

(7 + 4 + 18 + 72) = `-101 / (72 (-) 18 (-) 4 (-) 7) = `-43 = (`-SEE `-Below)...(...)...-"

(07/04) = `-74 = RECIPROCAL = `-47 / (74 - 47) = `-27 = "The ROMAN EMPIRE"!!!!!~'

`-1872 = (72 - 18) = `-54 = (27 x 2) = **(Below)...(...)... = `-EMPHATIC `-WITNESS to The ROMAN EMPIRE!!!!!~'**

`-27 = **RECIPROCAL** = `-72

President Calvin Coolidge `-DIED on January 5th of `-1933!!!!!~'

`-**BORN** on the `-4th; and, `-**DIED** on the `-5th = `-45 = **RECIPROCAL** = `-54...(...)...-"

(1 + 5 + 19 + 33) = `-58 = (5 + 8) = `-13 = "A VERY PIVOTAL NUMBER"!!!!!~'

(58 - 5) = `-53 = "WAR of the WORLDS"!!!!!~'

(101 - 58) = `-**43** = (`-SEE `-Above)...(...)...-"

#8 (`-79) + #10 (`-71) + #16 (`-56) + #18 (`-63) = `-**269** = (26 + 9) = `-**35** = **RECIPROCAL** = `-**53** = **"WAR of the WORLDS"**!!!!!~'

(79 + 71 + 56 + 63) = `-**269** = (69 (-) 2) = `-**67**...(...)...-'"

(269 / 4) = `-**67.25** = **ROUNDED** = `-**67**...(...)...-'"

#8 (`-79) + #10 (`-71) + #16 (`-56) + #18 (`-63) + #22 (`-71) + #24 (`-71) + #27 (`-72) + #29 (`-57) =

(79 + 71 + 56 + 63 + 71 + 71 + 72 + 57) = `-**540** = (54 + 0) = `-**54** = **"EARTHQUAKES"**!!!!!~'

`-**54** = `-**27** x 2 = **"The ROMAN EMPIRE"**!!!!!~'

(540 / 8) = `-**67.5** = **ROUNDED DOWN** = `-**67**...(...)...-'"

(Minus #24/President **Grover Cleveland** for the 2nd `-**ENTRY as** `-**PRESIDENT** (`-71) = (540 (-) 71) = `-**469** = (46 + 9) = `-**55** = `-**23** + `-**32**...(...)...-"

(469 / 7) = `-**67** = **"AGE** of the `-**PRESIDENTS** that have `-**DIED in** `-**SUCCESSION** as of (10.31.2015)!!!!!~'

`-**1867** `-YEARS is the `-NUMBER of `-AGES for the `-TOTAL `-NUMBER of `-YEARS adding `-UP to the President #**27** = President William Howard Taft (`-**72**) = `-DEATH `-AGE!!!!!~' `-HE `-DIED on the `-RECIPROCAL `-AGE of his `-PRESIDENCY!!!!!~'

`-**27** = **RECIPROCAL** = `-**72** / `-**1867** = (67 + 18) = `-**85** = **RECIPROCAL** = `-**58**

(85 - 58) = `-**27** = **"The ROMAN EMPIRE"**!!!!!~'

`-**1934** `-YEARS is the `-NUMBER of `-AGES for the `-TOTAL `-NUMBER of `-YEARS adding `-UP to the President #**28** = President Woodrow Wilson (`-**67**) = `-DEATH `-AGE!!!!!~'

`-**1934** = (34 + 19) = `-**53** = "WAR of the WORLDS"!!!!!~'

`-**3234** = (323)… (234)…

`-**323** = Reciprocal-**S**equencing-**N**umerology-**RSN**!!!!!~'

`-**234** = **P**rophetic-**L**inear-**P**rogression-**PLP**!!!!!~'

`-**2747** `-YEARS is the `-NUMBER of `-AGES for the `-TOTAL `-NUMBER of `-YEARS adding `-UP for `-ALL `-PRESIDENTS as `-DOCUMENTED as of (10/31/2015) that have `-DIED!!!!!~'

`-**2747** = (47 + 27) = `-**74** = **RECIPROCAL** = `-**47**

(74 - 47) = `-**27** = "The ROMAN EMPIRE"!!!!!~'

`-**2676** `-YEARS is the `-NUMBER of `-AGES for the `-TOTAL `-NUMBER of `-YEARS adding `-UP for `-ALL `-PRESIDENTS as `-DOCUMENTED as of (10/31/2015) that have `-DIED!!!!!~' (**Minus #24/President Grover Cleveland** for the 2nd `-**ENTRY as** `-**PRESIDENT** (`-71))!!!!!~'

`-**2676** = `-**EMPHATIC** `-**WITNESS** for `-**676** = Reciprocal-**S**equencing-**N**umerology-**RSN**!!!!!~'

`-**2747** / `-**39** PRESIDENTIAL TERMS that are `-USED in the `-CALCULATIONS for those `-PRESIDENTS that have `-DIED = `-**70.435**

`-**43** = **RECIPROCAL** = `-**34**

(43 + 34) = `-**77** = 2(7's) = `-**27** = "The ROMAN EMPIRE"!!!!!~'

`-**70** = "The `-YEAR that the `-PROPHET" was `-BORN!!!!!~'

`-**70** = (`-**35** x `-**2**) = `-EMPHATIC `-WITNESS as to the `-NUMBER `-**35** = **RECIPROCAL** = `-**53** = "WAR of the WORLDS"!!!!!~'

`-2676 / `-38 PRESIDENTS that have `-ACTUALLY `-DIED as of (10/31/2015) = `-70.421052

`-70.421052 = (42 + 10 + 52) - (70) = `-34 = **RECIPROCAL** = `-43

`-70 = **RECIPROCAL** = `-07 / (70 - 07) = `-63...(...)...-"!!!!!~'

`-38 = `-1938 = The `-1938 radio broadcast of the H. G. Wells' story "WAR of the WORLDS" by the Mr. George Orson Welles!!!!!~'

(10/31/2015) = (10 + 31 + 20 + 15) = `-76 = **RECIPROCAL** = `-67... (...)...-"!!!!!~'

(76 + 67) = `-143

(143 / 2) = `-71.5 = ROUNDED = `-72 = "The ROMAN EMPIRE"!!!!!~'

`-CURRENTLY `-4 `-FOUR U. S. Presidents `-SITTING in `-OFFICE have been killed in `-OFFICE (all with a `-GUN; or, by `-GUNSHOT) with #16/ President Abraham Lincoln, #20/President James A. Garfield, #25/President William McKinley; and, #35/President John F. Kennedy!!!!!~'

{(16 (-) 20) / (20 (-) 25) / (25 (-) 35)} = (4/5/10) = (4 + 5 + 10) = `-19 = **RECIPROCAL** = `-91

(91 - 19) = `-72 = **RECIPROCAL** = `-27 = "The ROMAN EMPIRE"!!!!!~'

(16 + 20 + 25 + 35) = `-96 = **RECIPROCAL** = `-69 = "The `-CYCLE of `-LIFE"!!!!!~'

(61 + 02 + 52 + 53) = `-168 = (1 x 68) = `-68 = **RECIPROCAL** = `-86

(86 + 68) = `-154 = (1 x 54) = `-54 = `-27 x `-2 = "`-EMPHATIC `-WITNESS to The "HOLY" ROMAN EMPIRE"!!!!!~'

(168 – 96) = `-72 = **RECIPROCAL** = 27 = "The ROMAN EMPIRE"!!!!!~'

#16/Abraham Lincoln (`-56 `-YEARS; and, `-62 `-DAYS; with `-20,516 `-DAYS `-TOTAL) was `-ASSASSINATED on April 15th of `-1865!!!!!~' President Abraham Lincoln was `-SHOT on April 14th of `-1865!!!!!~' #16/ President Abraham Lincoln was `-BORN on February 12th in `-1809!!!!!~'

(04/14) = `-**414** = **R**eciprocal-**S**equencing-**N**umerology-**RSN**!!!!!~'

`-**414** = (44 x 1) = `-**44**...(...)...-''~'

`-**ASSASSINATION SHOT/DAY #** `-**NUMBER** = (04/14/18/65) = (4 + 14 + 18 + 65) = `-**101**

(**04/14**) = (0 + 44 x 1) = `-**44**...(...)...-''~'

DEATH/DAY # `-**NUMBER** = (04/15/18/65) = (4 + 15 + 18 + 65) = `-**102**

BIRTHDAY # `-**NUMBER** = (02/12/18/09) = `-**41** = "WAR of the WORLDS"!!!!!~'

(16 x 2) = `-**32** = -a Prophetic Number!!!!!~'

(02/12/18) = (2 + 12 + 18) = `-**32** = -a Prophetic Number!!!!!~'

(02/12/18/09) = (2 + 12 + 18 - 9) = `-**23** = -a Prophetic Number!!!!!~'

(101 - 41) = `-**60** = (6 + 0) = `-**6** = `-2 x `-3 = `-**23** = -a Prophetic Number!!!!!~'

(101 - 41) = `-**60** = (6 + 0) = `-**6** = `-3 x `-2 = `-**32** = -a Prophetic Number!!!!!~'

(6/6) = `-**66** = "AGE of `-DEATH of the "PROPHET'S" FATHER!!!!!~'

(102 + 41) = `-**143** = (1 + 43) = `-**44** = "The `-YEAR that the "PROPHET'S" MOTHER was `-BORN (`-19**44**)!!!!!~'

(1944 (-) `-1865 = `-**79** = "AGE of `-DEATH of Mr. H. G. Wells of "WAR of the WORLDS"!!!!!~'

(02/12) = `-**212** = **R**eciprocal-**S**equencing-**N**umerology-**RSN**!!!!!~'

#16/President Abraham Lincoln was `-**BORN** on a `-**212**; and, was `-**SHOT** on a `-**414**!!!!!~

(414 + 212) = `-**626** = (62)... (26)... / `-**62** = **RECIPROCAL** = `-**26**

(62 - 26) = `-**36** = **RECIPROCAL** = `-**63** = "The `-ASSASSINATION of #35/President John F. Kennedy!!!!!~'

`-**YEARLY** `-**SUBTRACTION** = (`-**365** - **62**) = `-**303** = `-**30** = **RECIPROCAL** = `-**03**

(30 - 03) = `-**27** = "The ROMAN EMPIRE"!!!!!~'

`-**YEARLY** `-**SUBTRACTION** = (`-**366** - **62**) = `-**304** = (30 + 4) = `-**34** = **RECIPROCAL** = `-**43**

(43 + 34) = `-**77** = 2(7's) = `-**27** = "The ROMAN EMPIRE"!!!!!~'

`-DAYS in `-LIVING beyond `-BIRTHDAY = `-**62** = **RECIPROCAL** = `-**26**

(62 - 26) = `-**36** = **RECIPROCAL** = `-**63** = "The `-ASSASSINATION of #35/President John F. Kennedy!!!!!~'

#16/President Abraham Lincoln = (`-**56** `-YEARS; and, `-**62** `-DAYS; with `-20,**516** `-**DAYS** `-**TOTAL**)

`-**56** YEARS in `-LIVING (**=**) (`-**516** `-DAYS in `-LIVING)!!!!!~'

`-**516** = (56 x 1) = `-**56** = "AGE at `-TIME of #16/President Abraham Lincoln's `-DEATH!!!!!~'

#**20**/President James A. Garfield (`-**49** `-YEARS; and, `-**304** `-DAYS; with `-**18,202** `-**DAYS** `-**TOTAL**) was `-ASSASSINATED `-**16** `-**YEARS** `-**LATER** after the `-ASSASSINATION of #**16**/President Abraham Lincoln!!!!!~' #20/ President James A. Garfield was `-ASSASSINATED on **September 19th** `-**1881**!!!!!~' #20/President James A. Garfield was `-BORN on November 19th in `-1831!!!!!~' `-**16** + `-**16** = `-**32** = -a **Prophetic Number!!!!!~'** #20/President James A. Garfield was `-BORN in `-18**31** = `-**31** = **RECIPROCAL** = `-**13** = **"A VERY PIVOTAL NUMBER"!!!!!~'** (31 + 13) = `-**44**…(…)…-'~'

(20 + 16) = `-**36** = **RECIPROCAL** = `-**63**…(…)…-'~'

(16 + 16) = `-**32** = -a **Prophetic Number!!!!!~'**

(09/19/18) = (9 + 19 + 18) = `-**46** = `-**23** x `-**2** = `-**232** = **Reciprocal-Sequencing-Numerology-RSN!!!!!~'**

DEATH/DAY # `-NUMBER** = (09/19/18/81) = (9 + 19 + 18 + 81) = `-127** = (1 x 27) = `-**27** = "The ROMAN EMPIRE"!!!!!~'

(09/19) = `-**919** = **Reciprocal-Sequencing-Numerology-RSN!!!!!~'**

`-**91** = **RECIPROCAL** = `-**19**

(91 - 19) = `-**72** = <u>**RECIPROCAL**</u> = `-**27** = "The ROMAN EMPIRE"!!!!!~'

(18/81) = `-**18** = <u>**RECIPROCAL**</u> = `-**81** / (81 - 18) = `-**63**...(...)...-'~'

#20/President James A. Garfield was `-<u>**BORN**</u> on the `-**19**th; and, `-<u>**DIED**</u> on the `-**19**th!!!!!~

(19 + 19) = `-**38** = `-**1938** = The `-19**38** radio broadcast of the H. G. Wells' story "WAR of the WORLDS" by the Mr. George Orson Welles!!!!!~'

BIRTHDAY # `-NUMBER = (11/19/18/31) = `-79 = "AGE of `-DEATH of Mr. H. G. Wells of "WAR of the WORLDS"!!!!!~'

`-YEARLY `-SUBTRACTION = (`-**365** - **304**) = `-**61** = <u>RECIPROCAL</u> = `-**16**

(61 - 16) = `-**45** = <u>**RECIPROCAL**</u> = `-**54** = `-**27** x `-**2** = `-**27** = "`-EMPHATIC `-WITNESS to The "HOLY" ROMAN EMPIRE"!!!!!~'

`-YEARLY `-SUBTRACTION = (`-**366** - **304**) = `-**62** = <u>RECIPROCAL</u> = `-**26**

(62 - 26) = `-**36** = <u>**RECIPROCAL**</u> = `-**63** = "The `-ASSASSINATION of #35/President John F. Kennedy!!!!!~'

`-**304** = (30 + 4) = `-**34** = <u>**RECIPROCAL**</u> = `-**43**

(43 + 34) = `-**77** = 2(7's) = `-**27** = "The ROMAN EMPIRE"!!!!!~'

#**25**/President William McKinley (`-**58** `-YEARS; and, `-**228** `-DAYS; with `-**21,412** `-DAYS `-TOTAL) was `-ASSASSINATED nearly `-**20** `-YEARS `-LATER after the `-ASSASSINATION of #**20**/President James A. Garfield!!!!!~' #25/President William McKinley had `-DIED on September 14<sup>th</sup> `-1901!!!!!~' #25/President William McKinley was `-BORN on January 29<sup>th</sup> in `-1843!!!!!~' There are some `-**69** `-DAYS that `-SEPARATE the `-ASSASSINATION of #**25**/President William McKinley; and, the `-ASSASSINATION of #**35**/President John F. Kennedy!!!!!~' There is a `-SPAN of `-TIME of some `-**62** YEARS!!!!!~'

`-**58** = (5 + 8) = `-**13** = "A VERY PIVOTAL NUMBER"!!!!!~

President #25/President #20 = (25 - 20) = (`-5`) / (`-20 `-YEAR `-SPAN `-BETWEEN `-ASSASSINATIONS) = (20) = (4 x 5) = `-45` = **RECIPROCAL** = **54** = **"EARTHQUAKES"!!!!!~'**

(52 - 25) = `-27` = **"The ROMAN EMPIRE"!!!!~'**

(09/14) = (9 + 14) = `-23` = **-a Prophetic Number!!!!!~'**

**DEATH/DAY # `-NUMBER** = **(09/14/19/01)** = `-43` = **RECIPROCAL** = `-34`

#25/President William McKinley's `-DEATH/DAY # `-NUMBER (`-43`) = `-EQUALS the `-CALENDAR `-YEAR that #25/**President William McKinley** was `-**BORN!!!!!~'**

(43 + 34) = `-77` = `-2(7's)` = `-27` = **"The ROMAN EMPIRE"!!!!!~'**

**BIRTHDAY # `-NUMBER** = **(01/29/18/43)** = `-91` = **RECIPROCAL** = `-19`

(91 - 19) = `-72` = **RECIPROCAL** = `-27` = **"The ROMAN EMPIRE"!!!!!~'**

(91 - 43) = `-48` = **RECIPROCAL** = `-84`

(84 + 48) = `-132` = (1 x 32) = `-32` = **-a Prophetic Number!!!!!~'**

`-62` = **RECIPROCAL** = `-26`

(62 - 26) = `-36` = **RECIPROCAL** = `-63` = **"The `-ASSASSINATION of #35/President John F. Kennedy!!!!!~'**

`-69` = **"The `-CYCLE of `-LIFE"!!!!!~'**

`-**YEARLY `-SUBTRACTION** = (`-365 - 228`) = `-137` = (37 - 1) = `-36` = **RECIPROCAL** = `-63` = **"The `-ASSASSINATION of #35/President John F. Kennedy!!!!!~'**

`-**YEARLY `-SUBTRACTION** = (`-366 - 228`) = `-138` = (1 x 38) = `-38` = `-**1938** = The `-1938 radio broadcast of the H. G. Wells' story "WAR of the WORLDS" by the Mr. George Orson Welles!!!!!~'

`-**228** = (22 x 8) = `-**176** = (1 x 76) = `-**76** = **RECIPROCAL** = `-**67** = "The `-YEAR that the "PROPHET'S" BROTHER was `-BORN; and, the `-**SUCCESSIVE**/`-**CONSECUTIVE** `-**DEATH** `-**AGE** of the U. S. `-PRESIDENTS from (#1 to #28)!!!!!~'

(43 + 34) = `-**77** = 2(7's) = `-**27** = "The ROMAN EMPIRE"!!!!!~'

`-**21,412** = (21 x 2) = `-**42** = #25/**President William McKinley's** `-**DAYS in** `-**LIVING** are `-**TWICE** the `-**AMOUNT** of `-**HIS** `-**YEARS** in `-**LIVING!!!!!~'**

#**35**/President John F. Kennedy (`-**46** `-YEARS; and, `-**177** `-DAYS; with `-**16**,978 `-**DAYS** `-**TOTAL**) was `-ASSASSINATED nearly `-**63** `-**YEARS** `-**LATER** after the `-ASSASSINATION of #**25**/President William McKinley!!!!!~' #35/President John F. Kennedy had `-DIED on November 22nd `-19**63**!!!!!~' #35/President John F. Kennedy was `-BORN on May 29th in `-1917!!!!!~'

`-**1917** = (19 + 17) = `-**36** = **RECIPROCAL** = `-**63** = "The `-ASSASSINATION of #35/President John F. Kennedy!!!!!~'**

`-**1963** = (63 - 19) = `-**44**...(...)...-'-' / (05/29) = `-**34** = **RECIPROCAL** = `-**43**

(43 + 34) = `-**77** = 2(7's) = `-**27** = "The ROMAN EMPIRE"!!!!!~'

`-**77** = "AGE of `-DEATH of `-BROTHER Edward "Ted" Kennedy!!!!!~'

(05/29/19) = (5 + 29 + 19) = `-**53** = "WAR of the WORLDS" = **RECIPROCAL** = "35th President of the UNITED STATES of AMERICA"!!!!!~'

President #35/President #25 = **RECIPROCAL** = President#53/President #52 = (53 - 52) = `-**01** = **RECIPROCAL** = `-**10** = (35 - 25)!!!!!~'

(05/29/19/17) = (5 + 29 + 19 + 17) = `-**70** = "The `-**AVERAGE** `-**AGE** of a UNITED STATES `-**PRESIDENT**"!!!!!~'

`-**YEARLY** `-**SUBTRACTION** = (`-**365** - **177**) = `-**188** = (18 + 8) = `-**26** = `-**13** x `-**2** = (1 x 32) = `-**32** = -a Prophetic Number!!!!!~'

`-**YEARLY** `-**SUBTRACTION** = (`-**365** - **177**) = `-**188** = (18 x 8) = `-**144** = (1 x 44) = `-**44** = "The `-YEAR that the "PROPHET'S" MOTHER was `-BORN (`-19**44**)!!!!!~'

`-YEARLY `-SUBTRACTION = (`-**366** - **177**) = `-**189** = (18 + 9) = `-**27** = "The ROMAN EMPIRE"!!!!!~'

`-YEARLY `-SUBTRACTION = (`-**366** - **177**) = `-**189** = (18 x 9) = `-**162** = (1 + 62) = `-**63** = "The `-YEAR #35/President John F. Kennedy was `-KILLED (`-19**63**)!!!!!~'

`-**177** = (77 - 1) = `-**76** = **RECIPROCAL** = `-**67** = "The `-YEAR that the "PROPHET'S" BROTHER was `-BORN; and, the `-**SUCCESSIVE**/`-**CONSECUTIVE** `-**DEATH** `-**AGE** of the U. S. `-PRESIDENTS from (#1 to #28)!!!!!~'

`-CURRENTLY `-**4** `-**FOUR** U. S. Presidents `-SITTING in `-OFFICE have died in `-OFFICE (by `-NATURAL `-CAUSES) with #**9**/President William Henry Harrison, #**12**/President Zachary Taylor, #**29**/President Warren G. Harding; and, #**32**/President Franklin Delano Roosevelt!!!!!~'

{(9 (-) 12) / (12 (-) 29) / (29 (-) 32)} = (3/17/3) = (3 + 17 + 3) = `-**23** = -a **Prophetic Number!!!!!~'**

(9 + 12 + 29 + 32) = `-**82** = **RECIPROCAL** = `-**28**

(82 - 28) = `-**54** = `-**27** x `-**2** = "`-**EMPHATIC** `-**WITNESS as to the** `-**NUMBER** `-**27** = "The ROMAN EMPIRE"!!!!!~'

(90 + 21 + 92) = `-**203** = `-**23** = **RECIPROCAL** = `-**32** = -a **Prophetic Number!!!!!~'**

#9/President William Henry Harrison (`-**68** `-YEARS; and, `-**54** `-DAYS) only `-SERVED `-**31** `-DAYS in `-OFFICE; and, had `-DIED on April 4th of `-1841!!!!!~' #9/President William Henry Harrison was `-BORN on February 9th in `-1773!!!!!~'

`-**31** = **RECIPROCAL** = `-**13** = "A VERY PIVOTAL NUMBER"!!!!!~

April 4th = (4/4) = `-**44**...(...)...-'~'

`-**1841** = (41 - 18) = `-**23** = -a **Prophetic Number!!!!!~'**

DEATH/DAY # `-**NUMBER** = (04/04/18/41) = `-**67** = "The `-YEAR that the "PROPHET'S" BROTHER was `-BORN; and, the

`-**SUCCESSIVE**/`-**CONSECUTIVE** `-DEATH `-AGE of the U. S. `-PRESIDENTS from (#1 to #28)!!!!!~'

BIRTHDAY # `-NUMBER** = (02/09/17/73) = `-101**

(101 – 67) = `-**34** = **RECIPROCAL** = `-**43**

(43 + 34) = `-**77** = `-**2(7's)** = `-**27** = "The ROMAN EMPIRE"!!!!!~'

(101 + 67) = `-**168** = (1 x 68) = `-**68** = "**AGE of `-DEATH of President William Henry Harrison/#9!!!!!~'**

`-**68** = **RECIPROCAL** = `-**86**

(86 + 68) = `-**154** = (1 x 54) = `-**54** = "**The `-DAYS `-LIVING `-PAST `-HIS/`-THE `-BIRTHDAY of President William Henry Harrison/#9!!!!!~'**

`-**YEARLY `-SUBTRACTION** = (`-**365** - **54**) = `-**311** = (31 x 1) = `-**31** = **RECIPROCAL** = `-**13** = "**A VERY PIVOTAL NUMBER**"!!!!!~'

`-**YEARLY `-SUBTRACTION** = (`-**366** - **54**) = `-**312** = (32 x 1) = `-**32** = -**a Prophetic Number!!!!!~'**

#12/President Zachary Taylor (`-**65** `-YEARS; and, `-**227** `-DAYS / `-**23**,**967** `-TOTAL `-DAYS) `-SERVED in `-OFFICE; and, had `-DIED on July 9th of `-1850!!!!!~' #12/President Zachary Taylor was `-BORN on November 24th in `-1784!!!!!~'

(65 x 2) = `-**130** = (13 + 0) = `-**13** = "**A VERY PIVOTAL NUMBER**"!!!!!~

`-**23,967** = (67 - 23) = (44) = `-**44**...(...)...-'~'

`-**23,967** = (67 - 23 + 9) = `-**53** = "**WAR of the WORLDS**"!!!!!~'

`-**1850** = (50 - 18) = `-**32** = -**a Prophetic Number!!!!!~'**

DEATH/DAY # `-NUMBER** = (07/09/18/50) = `-84** = **RECIPROCAL** = `-**48**

(84 - 48) = `-**36** = **RECIPROCAL** = `-**63** = "**AGE of `-DEATH of #32/ President Franklin Delano Roosevelt!!!!!~'**

(84 + 48) = `-**132** = (1 x 32) = `-**32** = -**a Prophetic Number!!!!!~'**

#12/President Zachary Taylor `-DEATH/DAY # `-NUMBER (`-**84**) = `-EQUALS the very `-YEAR that `-HE/#12/President Zachary Taylor was `-**BORN**!!!!!~'

BIRTHDAY # `-NUMBER = (11/24/17/84) = `-**136** = (1 x 36) = `-**36** = **RECIPROCAL** = `-**63** = "AGE of `-DEATH of #32/President Franklin Delano Roosevelt!!!!!~'

(136 - 84) = `-**52** = **RECIPROCAL** = `-**25**

(52 - 25) = `-**27** = "The ROMAN EMPIRE"!!!!!~'

(11 + 24) = `-**35** = **RECIPROCAL** = `-**53** = "WAR of the WORLDS"!!!!!~'

(84 - 17) = `-**67** = "The `-YEAR that the "PROPHET'S" BROTHER was `-BORN; and, the `-**SUCCESSIVE**/`-**CONSECUTIVE** `-DEATH `-AGE of the U. S. `-PRESIDENTS from (#1 to #28)!!!!!~'

`-(11/24/17/84) = (84 (-) 17 (-) 24 (-) 11) = `-**32** = -a Prophetic Number!!!!!~'

`-**YEARLY** `-**SUBTRACTION** = (`-**365** - **227**) = `-**138** = (1 x 38) = `-**38** = `-**1938** = The `-19**38** radio broadcast of the H. G. Wells' story "WAR of the WORLDS" by the Mr. George Orson Welles!!!!!~'

`-**YEARLY** `-**SUBTRACTION** = (`-**366** - **227**) = `-**139** = (2 x 39 + 1) = `-**79** = "AGE of `-DEATH of Mr. H. G. Wells of "WAR of the WORLDS"!!!!!~'

`-**277** = (77 + 2) = `-**79** = "AGE of `-DEATH of Mr. H. G. Wells of "WAR of the WORLDS"!!!!!~'

#29/President Warren G. Harding (`-**57** `-YEARS; and, `-**273** `-DAYS) `-SERVED in `-OFFICE; and, had `-DIED on August 2nd of `-1923!!!!!~' #29/ President Warren G. Harding was `-BORN on November 2nd in `-1865!!!!!~'

`-**57** = **RECIPROCAL** = `-**75**

(75 + 57) = `-**132** = (1 x 32) = `-**32** = -a Prophetic Number!!!!!~'

#29/President Warren G. Harding was `-**BORN** on the `-**2ⁿᵈ**; and, `-**DIED** on the `-**2ⁿᵈ**!!!!!~ Much `-**LIKE** #20/President James A. Garfield was `-**BORN** on the `-**19ᵗʰ**; and, `-**DIED** on the `-**19ᵗʰ**!!!!!~

#29ᵗʰ **President** = (2 x 19) = `-**38**

69

`-($2^{nd}$/$19^{th}$) = `-(2 x 19) = `-**38** = `-**1938** = The `-19**38** radio broadcast of the H. G. Wells' story "WAR of the WORLDS" by the Mr. George Orson Welles!!!!!~'

(August) **2**nd `-**1923** = (23 + 19 + 2) = (4/4) = `-**44**...(...)...-".'

`-**1923** = (1 x 9 + 23) = `-**32** = -a Prophetic Number!!!!!~'

DEATH/DAY # `-NUMBER = (08/02/19/23) = `-**52** = RECIPROCAL = `-**25**

(52 - 25) = `-**27** = "The ROMAN EMPIRE"!!!!!~'

BIRTHDAY # `-NUMBER = (11/02/18/65) = `-**96** = RECIPROCAL = `-**69** = "The `-CYCLE of `-LIFE"!!!!!~'

(96 - 69) = `-**27** = "The ROMAN EMPIRE"!!!!!~'

(96 - 52) = `-**44** = "The `-YEAR that the "PROPHET'S" MOTHER was `-BORN (`-19**44**)!!!!!~'

(96 + 52) = `-**148** = (1 x 48) = `-**48** = RECIPROCAL = `-**84**

(84 - 48) = `-**36** = RECIPROCAL = `-**63** = "The `-AGE of `-DEATH of the "PROPHET'S" MOTHER & the "AGE of `-DEATH of #32/President Franklin Delano Roosevelt!!!!!~'

(84 + 48) = `-**132** = (1 x 32) = `-**32** = -a Prophetic Number!!!!!~'

`-YEARLY `-SUBTRACTION = (`-**365** - **273**) = `-**92** = RECIPROCAL = `-**29**

(92 - 29) = `-**63** = "The `-AGE of `-DEATH of the "PROPHET'S" MOTHER & the "AGE of `-DEATH of #32/President Franklin Delano Roosevelt!!!!!~'

`-YEARLY `-SUBTRACTION = (`-**366** – **273**) = `-**93** = RECIPROCAL = `-**39**

(93 - 39) = `-**54** = `-**27** x `-**2** = "`-EMPHATIC `-WITNESS to the `-NUMBER `-**27** = "The ROMAN EMPIRE"!!!!!~'

`-273 = "`-EMPHASIS to an `-EMPHATIC `-WITNESS on the `-NUMBER of `-27 for "The "HOLY" ROMAN EMPIRE"!!!!!~'

#32/President Franklin Delano Roosevelt (`-63 `-YEARS; and, `-72 `-DAYS / `-23,082 `-TOTAL `-DAYS) `-SERVED in `-OFFICE; and, had `-DIED on April 12th of `-1945!!!!!~' #32/President Franklin Delano Roosevelt was `-BORN on January 30th in `-1882!!!!!~'

January 30th = (130) = `-130 = (13 + 0) = `-13 = "A VERY PIVOTAL NUMBER"!!!!!~

(72 + 72) = `-144 = (1 x 44) = `-44...(...)...-"'

`-1945 = (45 + 19) = `-64 = RECIPROCAL = `-46 = `-23 x `-2 = `-232 = Reciprocal-Sequencing-Numerology-RSN!!!!!~'

`-1882 = (82 - 18) = `-64 = RECIPROCAL = `-46 = `-23 x `-2 = `-232 = Reciprocal-Sequencing-Numerology-RSN!!!!!~'

#32/President Franklin Delano Roosevelt was `-BORN; and, `-DIED in the `-YEAR of (`-64)!!!!!~'

(64 / 2) = `-32nd PRESIDENT of the UNITED STATES of AMERICA!!!!!~'

(64 x 2) = `-128 = (12 x 8) = `-96 = RECIPROCAL = `-69 = "The `-CYCLE of `-LIFE"!!!!!~'

DEATH/DAY # `-NUMBER = (04/12/19/45) = `-80 = RECIPROCAL = `-08

(80 - 08) = `-72 = RECIPROCAL = `-27 = "The ROMAN EMPIRE"!!!!!~'

BIRTHDAY # `-NUMBER = (01/30/18/82) = `-131 = (1 + 31) = `-32 = -a Prophetic Number!!!!!~'

Month/Day (1/30) = (30 + 1) = `-31 of `-BIRTH = `-EQUALS (131) = (1 x 31) = `-31 of the Birthday # `-Number!!!!!~'

(131 - 80) = `-51 = RECIPROCAL = `-15

(51 - 15) = `-36 = RECIPROCAL = `-63 = "The `-AGE of `-DEATH of the "PROPHET'S" MOTHER & the "AGE of `-DEATH of #32/President Franklin Delano Roosevelt!!!!!~'

71

(51 + 15) = `-**66** = "AGE of `-DEATH of the "PROPHET'S" FATHER!!!!!~'

`-**23,082** = (82 - 23) = `-**59** = "The `-AGE of `-DEATH of JESUS CHRIST'S MOTHER `-MARY"!!!!!~'

(95 - 59) = `-**36** = **RECIPROCAL** = `-**63** = "The `-AGE of `-DEATH of the "PROPHET'S" MOTHER & the "AGE of `-DEATH of #32/President Franklin Delano Roosevelt!!!!!~'

`-YEARLY `-SUBTRACTION = (`-**365** - **72**) = `-**293** = (93 / 2) = `-**46.5** = ROUNDED DOWN = `-**46** = `-**23** x `-**2** = `-**232** = Reciprocal-**S**equencing-**N**umerology-**RSN**!!!!!~'

`-YEARLY `-SUBTRACTION = (`-**366** - **72**) = `-**294** = (94 x 2) = `-**188** = (18 + 8) = `-**26** = `-**13** x `-**2** = (1 x 32) = `-**32** = -a Prophetic Number!!!!!~'

`-YEARLY `-SUBTRACTION = (`-**366** - **72**) = `-**294** = (94 / 2) = `-**47** = RECIPROCAL = `-**74**

(74 - 47) = `-**27** = **RECIPROCAL** = `-**72** = `-DAYS `-LIVING `-PAST `-HIS `-BIRTHDAY that of #32/President Franklin Delano Roosevelt!!!!!~'!!!!!~'

`-**72** = "The "HOLY" ROMAN EMPIRE"!!!!!~'

`-**79** = "AGE of `-DEATH of Mr. H. G. Wells of "WAR of the WORLDS"!!!!!~'

(**79** + **53**) = `-**132** = (1 x 32) = `-**32** = `-**32**nd President of the United States Franklin Delano Roosevelt = -a Prophetic Number!!!!!~'

`-CURRENTLY `-4 `-FOUR U. S. Presidents `-ASSASSINATED / `-CURRENTLY `-4 `-FOUR U. S. Presidents `-DYING in `-OFFICE of `-NATURAL `-CAUSES!!!!!~'

(4/4) = `-**44**...(...)...-"~'

`-The `-PRESIDENTS `-PRESENTED in their `-ENTIRETY!!!!!~'

President John F. Kennedy's `-BIRTH equals **5/29/1917!!!!!~**' President Franklin Delano Roosevelt's `-BIRTH equals **1/30/1882!!!!!~**' `-1917 (-) `-1882 = `-**35** YEARS!!!!!~' President John F. Kennedy's `-YEAR of `-DEATH equals **11/22/1963!!!!!~**' President Franklin Delano Roosevelt's `-YEAR of `-DEATH equals **4/12/1945!!!!!~**' `-1963 (-) `-1945 = `-**18!!!!!~**' `-35 + `-18 = `-**53** / `-**35** = **RECIPROCAL** = `-**53** = "WAR of the `-WORLDS"!!!!!~'

(82 (-) 29) = `-**53** = "WAR of the WORLDS"!!!!!~'

#35/President John F. Kennedy `-BIRTH/`-DEATH = (1917 + 1963) = `-**3880**

`-**38** = `-**1938** = The `-19**38** radio broadcast of the H. G. Wells' story "WAR of the WORLDS" by the Mr. George Orson Welles!!!!!~'

`-**88** = (44 x 2) = `-**442** = (42 + 4) = `-**46** = "AGE of `-DEATH of #35/ President John F. Kennedy"!!!!!~'

(38 + 38) = `-**76** = **RECIPROCAL** = `-**67** = "See `-BELOW"!!!!!~'

(88 + 88) = `-**176** = (1 x 76) = `-**76** = **RECIPROCAL** = `-**67** = "The `-YEAR that the "PROPHET'S" BROTHER was `-BORN; and, the `-**SUCCESSIVE**/`-**CONSECUTIVE** `-**DEATH** `-**AGE** of the U. S. `-PRESIDENTS from (#1 to #28)!!!!!~'

`-**88** = (**35** + **53**) = "WAR of the WORLDS"!!!!!~'

#36/President Lyndon B. Johnson `-BIRTH/`-DEATH = (1908 + 1973) = `-**3881**

`-**38** = `-**1938** = The `-19**38** radio broadcast of the H. G. Wells' story "WAR of the WORLDS" by the Mr. George Orson Welles!!!!!~'

`-**88** = (44 x 2) = `-**442** = (42 + 4) = `-**46** = **RECIPROCAL** = `-**64** = "AGE of `-DEATH of #36/President Lyndon B. Johnson"!!!!!~'

(38 + 38) = `-**76** = **RECIPROCAL** = `-**67** = "See `-BELOW"!!!!!~'

(88 + 88) = `-**176** = (1 x 76) = `-**76** = **RECIPROCAL** = `-**67** = "The `-YEAR that the "PROPHET'S" BROTHER was `-BORN; and, the `-**SUCCESSIVE**/`-**CONSECUTIVE** `-**DEATH** `-**AGE** of the U. S. `-PRESIDENTS from (#1 to #28)!!!!!~'

`-**88** = (**35** + **53**) = "WAR of the WORLDS"!!!!!~'

(80 + 81) = `-**161** = (16 x 1) = `-**16** = "**#16/President Abraham Lincoln**"!!!!!~'

(161 x 2) = `-**322** = "`-EMPHATIC `-WITNESS to the `-NUMBER `-**32**"!!!!!~'

`-**322** + 1 = `-**323** = **Reciprocal-Sequencing-Numerology-RSN**!!!!!~'

`-**23** = **RECIPROCAL** = `-**32** / `-32 / `-2 = `-**16** = "**HONEST** `-**ABE**"!!!!!~'

#16/President Abraham Lincoln `-BIRTH/`-DEATH = (1809 + 1865) = `-**3674**

`-**3674** = (74 (-) 36) = `-**38** = "**The `-LIFE; and, `-DEATHS of `-BOTH `-PRESIDENTS #/35 John F. Kennedy (Reciprocal); and, #36/Lyndon B. Johnson (Direct)**!!!!!~'

`-**YEARS of `-BIRTH; and, `-DEATH** = (1917 + 1882 + 1945 + 1963) = `-**7707**" = `-**1** `-YEAR `-AWAY from #**36**/President Lyndon B. Johnson!!!!!~'"

(19 + 17 + 18 + 82 + 19 + 45 + 19 + 63) = `-**282**

`-**82** = **RECIPROCAL** = `-**28**

(82 (-) 28) = `-**54** = `-**27** x `-**2** = "**The ROMAN EMPIRE**"!!!!!~'

`-**7707** = (77 (-) 07) = `-**70** = "**The `-YEAR the "PROPHET" was `-BORN**"!!!!!~'

`-**7707** = (77 + 07) = `-**84** = **RECIPROCAL** = `-**48**

(84 (-) 48) = `-**36** = **RECIPROCAL** = `-**63** = "**AGE of `-DEATH of the "PROPHET'S" MOTHER; and, The `-YEAR the #35/President John F. Kennedy was `-ASSASSINATED**"!!!!!~'

(84 + 48) = `-**132** = (1 x 32) = `-**32** = **-a Prophetic Number**!!!!!~'

President Lyndon B. Johnson's `-BIRTH equals **8/27/1908**!!!!!~' President Franklin Delano Roosevelt's `-BIRTH in `-DIFFERENCE equals `-**26**YEARS!!!!!~ `-1908 (-) `-1882 = `-**26**!!!!!~ President Lyndon B. Johnson's `-YEAR of `-DEATH equals **1/22/1973**!!!!!~' President Franklin Delano Roosevelt's `-DEATH in `-DIFFERENCE equals `-**27** YEARS!!!!!~' `-1972 (-) `-1945 = `-**27**!!!!!~' `-26 + `-27 = `-**53** = "**WAR of the `-WORLDS**"!!!!!~'

#36/President Lyndon B. Johnson was `-BORN on a $27^{th}$ = **RECIPROCAL** = `-**72** = **RECIPROCAL** = `-**27** = "The ROMAN EMPIRE"!!!!!~'

Just `-LIKE Mr. BRUCE LEE!!!!!~' (27th/72nd)!!!!!~'

`-**1972** = (72 (-) 19) = `-**53** = "The WAR of the WORLDS"!!!!!~'

`-**1973** = (73 (-) 19) = `-**54** = `-**27** x `-**2** = "`-EMPHATIC `-WITNESS to the `-NUMBER `-**27** = The ROMAN EMPIRE"!!!!!~'

BIRTHDAY # `-NUMBER = **(8/27/19/08)** = (8 + 27 + 19 + 8) = `-**62**
DEATHDAY # `-NUMBER = **(1/22/19/73)** = (1 + 22 + 19 + 73) = `-**115**
(115 (-) 62) = `-**53** = "WAR of the WORLDS"!!!!!~'

`-**YEARS of `-BIRTH; and, `-DEATH** = (1908 + 1882 + 1945 + 1973) = `-**7708** = "`-**1** `-YEAR `-AWAY from **#35/President John F. Kennedy**!!!!!~'"

(19 + 08 + 18 + 82 + 19 + 45 + 19 + 73) = `-**283** = (28 x 3) = `-**84** = "See `-**ABOVE**"!!!!!~'

`-**283** = (83 x 2) = `-**166** = (1 x 66) = `-**66** = "AGE of `-DEATH of the "PROPHET'S" FATHER"!!!!!~'

President Abraham Lincoln's `-BIRTH equals **2/12/1809**!!!!!~' President Franklin Delano Roosevelt's `-BIRTH in `-DIFFERENCE equals `-**73** YEARS!!!!!~' `-1882 (-) `-**1809** = `-**73**!!!!!~ President Abraham Lincoln's `-YEAR of `-DEATH equals **4/15/1865**!!!!!~' President Franklin Delano Roosevelt's `-DEATH in `-DIFFERENCE equals `-**20** YEARS; and, `-**3** DAYS = (20 + 3) = `-**23**!!!!!~' `-65 (-) `-45 = `-**20**!!!!!~' `-73 (-) `-20 = `-**53** ="WAR of the `-WORLDS"!!!!!~'

`-**73** = **RECIPROCAL** = `-**37**

(73 (-) 37) = `-**36** = **RECIPROCAL** = `-**63** = "The "YEAR" that the `-**36**$^{th}$ President took the `-PRESIDENCY"!!!!!~'

The **36**th President Lyndon B. Johnson `-**DIED** in `-**1973**!!!!!~'

(45 (-) 9) = `-**36** = **RECIPROCAL** = `-**63** = "The `-YEAR #35/President John F. Kennedy was `-**KILLED**"!!!!!~'

`-**Day of `-BIRTH; and, `-DAY of `-DEATH** = (12 + 15) = `-**27** = "#36/ President Lyndon B. Johnson; and, the # `-NUMBER `-**27**!!!!!~'

`-YEARS of `-BIRTH; and, `-DEATH = (1809 + 1882 + 1945 + 1865) = `-**7501** = (75 + 1) = `-**76** = **RECIPROCAL** = `-**67** = "The `-YEAR that the "PROPHET'S" BROTHER was `-BORN; and, the `-**SUCCESSIVE**/`-**CONSECUTIVE** `-**DEATH** `-**AGE** of the U. S. `-PRESIDENTS from (#1 to #28)!!!!!~'

`-7501 = (501 (-) 7) = `-**494** = "`-**NUMBERS of** `-**DEATH**" = Reciprocal-**S**equencing-**N**umerology-**RSN**!!!!!~'

(18 + 09 + 18 + 82 + 19 + 45 + 18 + 65) = `-**274** = (2 x 74) = `-**148** = (1 x 48) = `-**48** = **RECIPROCAL** = `-**84** = "See `-**ABOVE**"!!!!!~'

`-YEARS of `-BIRTH; and, `-DEATH = #35/President John F. Kennedy; and, #36/President Lyndon B. Johnson = (7707 + 7708) = `-**15415**

`-**15415** = (1 x 545 x 1) = `-**545** = "See `-**ABOVE**" = Reciprocal-**S**equencing-**N**umerology-**RSN**!!!!!~'

`-**15415** = (1 x 54 + 15) = `-**69** = "The `-CYCLE of `-LIFE"!!!!!~'

`-54 = `-**27** x `-**2** = "`-**EMPHATIC** `-**WITNESS** to The ROMAN EMPIRE"!!!!!~'

`-**51** = **RECIPROCAL** = `-**15**

(51 (-) 15) = `-**36** = **RECIPROCAL** = `-**63** = "#35/President John F. Kennedy; and, #36/President Lyndon B. Johnson!!!!!~'

`-**15415** = (1 + 5 + 4 + 1 + 5) = `-**16** = "The #16th/President Abraham Lincoln `-**REPRESENTED**; and, `-**TABULATED** `-by the `-**EQUATIONS**"!!!!!~'

`-YEARS of `-BIRTH; and, `-DEATH = #35/President John F. Kennedy, #36/President Lyndon B. Johnson; and, #16/President Abraham Lincoln = (15415 + 7501) = `-**22916**

`-**22916** = `-**22.916** = ROUNDED = `-**23** = -a Prophetic Number!!!!!~'

`-**916** = (96 x 1) = `-**96** = **RECIPROCAL** = `-**69** = "The `-CYCLE of `-LIFE"!!!!!~'

`-YEARS of `-BIRTH; and, `-DEATH = #35/President John F. Kennedy, #36/President Lyndon B. Johnson; and, #16/President Abraham Lincoln = (15415 (-) 7501) = `-**7914**

`-7914 = `-79.14 = ROUNDED = `-79 = "AGE of `-DEATH of Mr. H. G. Wells of "WAR of the WORLDS"!!!!!~'

`-14 = RECIPROCAL = `-41 = "WAR of the WORLDS" with #32/ PRESIDENT FRANKLIN DELANO ROOSEVELT!!!!!~'

(#16 x 2) = `-32 = -a Prophetic Number!!!!!~'

(79 (-) 14) = `-65 = "YEAR that #16/President Abraham Lincoln was `-ASSASSINATED"!!!!!~'

#16, #35; and, #36 `-PRESIDENTS = (16 + 35 + 36) = `-87 = RECIPROCAL = `-78 ...(...)...-'-'

(87 + 78) = `-165 = (1 x 65) = `-65 = "The `-YEAR that the #16/President Abraham Lincoln was `-ASSASSINATED"!!!!!~'

`-16 = RECIPROCAL = `-61 / `-35 = RECIPROCAL = `-53 /

`-36 = RECIPROCAL = `-63

(61 + 53 + 63) = `-177 = (1 x 77) = `-77 = 2(7's) = `-27 = "The ROMAN EMPIRE"!!!!!~'

(16 + 53 + 63) = `-132 = (1 x 32) = `-32 = -a Prophetic Number!!!!!~'

BIRTHDAY # `-NUMBER = (2 + 12 + 18 + 9) = `-41 = "WAR of the WORLDS" = "The `-YEAR that the "PROPHET'S" FATHER was `-BORN (`-1941)!!!!!~'

DEATHDAY # `-NUMBER = (4 + 15 + 18 + 65) = `-102

(102 + 41) = `-143 = (1 + 43) = `-44 = "The `-YEAR that the "PROPHET'S" MOTHER was `-BORN (`-1944)!!!!!~'

(102 (-) 41) = `-61 = RECIPROCAL = `-16 = "The #16th/PRESIDENT of the UNITED STATES of AMERICA as President Abraham Lincoln"!!!!!~'

First `-LADY LAURA BUSH was `-BORN on `-11/04/1946...(...)...-'-'

Birthday # `-NUMBER = (11 + 4 + 19 + 46) = `-80

77

(11 + 4 + 19) = `-34 = **RECIPROCAL** = `-**43**

`-**1946** = (46 (-)19) = `-**27** = "The ROMAN EMPIRE"

`-**27** = **2(7's)** = `-**77** = "**YEAR** that `-**SHE** `-**MARRIED** President #**43** = President George W. Bush (**in** `-**1977**)!!!!!~'

She is **5' 5"** = `-**55** = "**SAVES LIVES**"!!!!!~'

Laura Bush is now `-**69** `-YEARS of `-AGE = `-**69** = "The CYCLE of `-LIFE"!!!!!~'

`-**69** = **RECIPROCAL** = `-**96**

(96 (-) 69) = `-**27** = "The ROMAN EMPIRE"!!!!!~'

`-19**77** = (77 + 19) = `-**96**

`-BOTH/ `-HUSBAND; and, `-WIFE were `-BORN in `-19**46** = `-**46** = `-**23** x `-**2** = `-**232** = **Reciprocal-Sequencing-Numerology-RSN**!!!!!~'

`-**1946** = (46 (-) 19) = `-**27** = "The ROMAN EMPIRE"!!!!!~'

`-**1946** = (46 + 19) = `-**65** = **RECIPROCAL** = `-**56**

(65 + 56) = `-**121** = "The `-DAYS `-EXISTING `-BETWEEN `-BIRTHS of `-PRESIDENT George W. Bush; and, His `-**BIRTHDAY** `-WIFE; First `-LADY LAURA BUSH!!!!!~'

(11 x 4) = `-**44** = "The `-DAYS `-EXISTING `-BETWEEN the `-PRESIDENT George W. Bush `-BIRTH; and, the `-PRESIDENT Bill Clinton `-BIRTH!!!!!~'

(121 (-) 44) = `-**77** = `-**1977** = "The `-YEAR that the FIRST `-LADY was `-MARRIED to `-HER `-HUSBAND President George W. Bush!!!!!~'

(121 + 44) = `-**165** = (16 x 5) = `-**80** = "The Laura Bush `-BIRTHDAY # `-NUMBER!!!!!~'

President George W. Bush was `-BORN on **07/06/1946** = `-BIRTHDAY # `-NUMBER = `-**78**

(7 + 6 + 19) = `-**32** = -a Prophetic Number!!!!!~'

`-23 = **RECIPROCAL** = `-32

Husband & Wife `-BIRTHDAY # `-NUMBERS = (80 + 78) = `-**158** = (1 x 58) = `-**58** = (5 + 8) = `-**13** = **"A VERY PIVOTAL NUMBER"!!!!!~'**

`-**158** = (15 + 8) = `-**23** = -a **Prophetic Number!!!!!~'**

Did `-YOU `-NOTICE; that there are `-**23** days that lie in between the `-BIRTHDAYS of President George H. W. Bush; and, President George W. Bush!!!!!~' During this `-TIME of `-**23** days, they are `-**23** years apart in `-LIVING!!!!!~'

There are `-**67** days that lie in between the births of President Bill Clinton; and, President George H. W. Bush!!!!!~' `-**67** = "The `-YEAR of the `-**SUCCESSIVE**/`-**CONSECUTIVE** `-DEATHS of `-AGE of the U. S. `-PRESIDENTS from (President#1 to President #28)!!!!!~'

`-**111** (Jimmy Carter/George H. W. Bush) (-) `-**44** (Bill Clinton/George W. Bush) = `-**67**!!!!!~'

`-**67** = (6 + 7) = `-**13** = **"A VERY PIVOTAL NUMBER"!!!!!~'**

`-**67** = **RECIPROCAL** = `-**76** = The #43/President George W. Bush `-**BIRTHDAY!!!!!~'**

(67 (-) 44 = `-**23** = -a **Prophetic Number!!!!!~'**

President Jimmy Carter being married to his wife Rosa**lynn** Carter for some `-**69** years standing as equals to the lives of both President George W. Bush; and, President Bill Clinton!!!!!~'

(111 + 44) = `-**155** = (1 x 55) = `-**55** = **"The `-HEIGHT of FIRST `-LADY LAURA BUSH!!!!!~'**

HOW'S `-THIS for a `-BIRTHDAY `-GIFT?????~'

"The Real Prophet Of Doom (Kismet) – Introduction – Pendulum Flow" was `-PUBLISHED on `-DECEMBER 18th of `-2014!!!!!~ **The `-LAST `-UPDATE** was made **on SEPTEMBER 11th of `-2015 (9/11)!!!!!~'** The Movie - **"STAR WARS"** - will be `-**RELEASED** on `-DECEMBER 18th of `-2015!!!!!~'

(12 + 18 + 20 + 14) = `-**64** = "`-AGE of `-DEATH for #36/President Lyndon B. Johnson"!!!!!~'

(9 + 11 + 20 + 15) = `-**55** = "SAVES LIVES"!!!!!~'

(12 + 18 + 20 + 15) = `-**65** = "`-YEAR #16/President Abraham Lincoln was `-**KILLED**"!!!!!~'

(64 + 55 + 65) = `-**184** = (1 x 84) = `-**84** = **RECIPROCAL** = `-**48**

(84 (-) 48) = `-**36** = **RECIPROCAL** = `-**63** = "#36/President `-TOOK ON the `-OFFICE of `-PRESIDENCY in `-**1963**"!!!!!~'

(84 + 48) = `-**132** = (1 x 32) = `-**32** = -a Prophetic Number!!!!!~'

`-**32** = `-**16** x `-**2** = "`-EMPHATIC `-WITNESS to the # `-NUMBER #16/President of the UNITED STATES of AMERICA / Abraham Lincoln"!!!!!~'

(64 + 55 + 65) = `-**184** = (184/3) = `-**61.33** = ROUNDED = `-**61** = **RECIPROCAL** = `-**16** = "#16/President Abraham Lincoln"!!!!!~'

The **"-The-"** on the `-TOP of the `-FACE of the "PROPHET'S" `-BOOK `-LOOKS `-LIKE the `-**SWORD of the `-JEDI**; of - "STAR WARS" -!!!!!~'

"STAR WARS" - was `-FIRST `-RELEASED on MAY 25th in `-19**77**!!!!!~'

(5 + 25 + 19 + 77) = `-**126**

(126) = (1 x 26) = `-**26** = **RECIPROCAL** = `-**62**

(62 (-) 26) = `-**36** = **RECIPROCAL** = `-**63** = "#36/President `-TOOK ON the `-OFFICE of `-PRESIDENCY in `-19**63**"!!!!!~'

NOW; "The FORCE AWAKENS", is about to be; `-RELEASED!!!!!~'

Lyndon B Johnson = LBJ = `-INSIGNIA/MONOGRAM-!!!!!~'
L = `-12 / **B** = `-2 / **J** = `-10
(12 + **2** + 10) = `-**24** = **RECIPROCAL** = `-**42**

(42 + 24) = `-**66** *(-2)* = `-**64** = `-The `-**AGE** of `-**DEATH**!!!!!~'

…(…)…

John F. Kennedy = JFK = `-INSIGNIA/MONOGRAM-!!!!!~'

J = `-10 / F = `-6 / K = `-11

(10 + 6 + 11) = `-27 = "The ROMAN EMPIRE"!!!!!~'

`-27 = RECIPROCAL = `-72

(72 (-) 27) = `-45 (+1) = `-46 = `-The `-AGE of `-DEATH!!!!!~'

...(...)...

Abraham Lincoln = AL = `-INSIGNIA/MONOGRAM-!!!!!~'

A = `-1 / L = `-12 / = `-(12) = (1,2 = Above)...(...)...-'-'

(1 + 12) = `-13 = "A VERY PIVOTAL NUMBER"!!!!!~'

`-13 = RECIPROCAL = `-31

(31 + 13 + 12) = `-56 = `-The `-AGE of `-DEATH!!!!!~'

...(...)...

Martin Luther King, Jr. = MLK = `-INSIGNIA/MONOGRAM-!!!!!~'

M = `-13 / L = `-12 / K = `-11

11, 12, 13 = Prophetic-Linear-Progression!!!!!~'

`-11 (+) `-12 (+) `-13 = `-36 = RECIPROCAL = `-63

M = `-13 / L = `-12 / K = `-11 / J = `-10

(13 + 12 + 11 + 10) = `-46 = "AGE that JOHN F. KENNEDY was `-ASSASSINATED"!!!!!~'

10,11, 12,13 = Prophetic-Linear-Progression!!!!!~'

`-46 = RECIPROCAL = `-64 = "AGE of `-DEATH of #36/President Lyndon B. Johnson"!!!!!~'

`-64 (-) `-46 = `-18 = RECIPROCAL = `-81

`-81 (-) `-18 = `-**63** = "**AGE of `-DEATH of the "PROPHET'S"
MOTHER & `-YEAR that the `-PRESIDENT JOHN F. KENNEDY was
`-ASSASSINATED!!!!!~'**

(81 (-) 46 = `-**35** = **RECIPROCAL** = `-**53** = "**WAR of the WORLDS**"!!!!!~'

...(...)...

Some might `-THINK that because of the `-**FIXED** `-**NUMBER**
`-**ARRANGEMENTS** of `-**LIFE**; of `-WHAT `-I would call
a `-**NUMEROLOGY**, that `-WE are `-ALL a `-BUNCH of
`-**AUTOMATONS**!!!!!~' This is not `-TRUE!!!!!~' If `-IT were `-TRUE; `-WE
would have no `-PERSONALITY in our `-RELATIONSHIP `-To; and,
`-With `-GOD!!!!!~' He would `-SEE; and, `-HAVE no `-VALUE in `-HIS
`-CREATION at `-ALL!!!!!~' `-GOD allows `-US to be `-FREE `-MORAL
`-AGENTS with `-OUR `-DIVINE `-POWER of `-REASON that `-WE
can `-LIVE as a `-SACRIFICE `-LIVING; and, `-GOD just `-GUIDES `-US
to a `-COMPLETION of `-PURPOSE; and, `-DIRECTS `-US towards an
`-ACHIEVEMENT of `-HIS `-ARRANGEMENT!!!!!~'

#1/President George Washington was `-**BORN** in `-17**32**!!!!!~' (`-**44**) `-YEARS
later from his `-**BIRTH** was "**INDEPENDENCE DAY**" in `-17**76**!!!!!!~'
`-**32** = **RECIPROCAL** = `-**23** / `-**76** = **RECIPROCAL** = `-**67**!!!!!~' From
"**INDEPENDENCE DAY**" (`-**23**) `-YEARS `-LATER, #1/President George
Washington `-**DIED** at the tender `-**AGE of the `-RECIPROCAL (`-#) of**
`-**INDEPENDENCE DAY** (`-**67**!)!!!!!~'

`-**R**eciprocal-**S**equencing-**N**umerology-RSN!!!!!~'

#2/President John Adams `-LIVED `-**23** `-YEARS `-LONGER than the #1/
President George Washington!!!!!~' The `-NEXT #**2**/#**3** (`-**23**) PRESIDENTS
#**2**/John Adams; and, #**3**/Thomas Jefferson `-**DIED on the `-EXACT**
`-**SAME** `-**DAY** of (**July 4th** `-**TWICE** = (`-**44**) = `-TWO for `-ONE `-DAY)
= "**INDEPENDENCE DAY**"!!!!!~' #**2**/President John Adams `-**DIED** at
the `-AGE of `-**90**; while, #**3**/President Thomas Jefferson `-**DIED** at the
`-AGE of `-**83**!!!!!~' (90 + 83) = `-**173** = (1 x 73) = `-**73** = `-AGE of `-DEATH
of the `-**3**rd President to `-**DIE** on `-**JULY 4th** in `-**5 TERMS**: #**5**/President

James Monroe**!!!!!~'** #5/President James Monroe `-DIED at the `-AGE of `-**73** `-YEARS; and, `-**67** `-DAYS `-**TOTAL**; in `-LIVING!!!!!~' (`-67/`-76)

`-**76** = **RECIPROCAL** = `-**67** = "The`-**SUCCESSIVE/**`-**CONSECUTIVE** `-**DEATH** `-**AGE** of the U. S. `-PRESIDENTS from (President #1 (**WHO** died at the tender `-**AGE** of `-**67**) to President #28 (**WHO** died at the tender `-**AGE** of `-**67**) a `-**123** `-**YEARS** `-**APART!!!!!~'**

`-**23** = **RECIPROCAL** = `-**32**

`-**123** `-YEARS after the `-DEATH of #1/President George Washington; #28/President Woodrow Wilson `-**DIED** at the `-AGE of `-**67**!!!!!~

`-**76** `-YEARS after the `-DEATH of #1/President George Washington; #17/President Andrew Johnson `-**DIED** in his `-**67**th `-YEAR of `-EXISTING at the `-AGE of `-**66**!!!!!~' #17/President Andrew Johnson's `-WIFE; FIRST `-LADY "Eliza McCardle Johnson" `-DIED at the tender `-AGE of `-**65** in `-HER `-**66**th `-YEAR of `-LIVING in `-18**76**!!!!!~'

From #1/President George Washington's; and, #17/President Andrew Johnson's `-**DEATH** `-**DAYS** to `-**DEATH** `-**DAYS**; there are/they are `-**23**0 days `-**APART!!!!!~'** (`-**23**0 = (23 + 0) = `-**23** = -a **Prophetic Number!!!!!~'** `-**67** = **RECIPROCAL** = `-**76** / There are `-**76** years in between their `-**DEATHS!!!!!~'**

With President **Andrew** Johnson; and, President Abraham Lincoln (`-**BIRTH** to `-**BIRTH**) = `-**46 DAYS** = `-**23** x `-**2** = `-**232** = **Reciprocal-Sequenced-Numerology!!!!!~'** With President **Andrew** Jackson; and, President Abraham Lincoln (`-**BIRTH to** `-**BIRTH**) = `-**32 DAYS** = -a **Prophetic Number!!!!!~'** President **Andrew** Jackson was `-BORN in `-1**767**!!!!!~ `-**76** = **RECIPROCAL** = `-**67** / `-**32** years later; President George Washington, was `-**DEAD!!!!!~'**

(**Minus #24/President Grover Cleveland** for the 2nd `-**ENTRY** as `-**PRESIDENT** (`-71) = (540 (-) 71) = `-**469** = (46 + 9) = `-**55** = `-**23** + `-**32**...(...)...-"

(469 / 7) = `-**67** = "**AGE** of the `-**PRESIDENTS** that have `-**DIED** in `-**SUCCESSION** as of (10.31.2015)!!!!!~'

`-**1867** `-YEARS is the `-NUMBER of `-AGES for the `-TOTAL `-NUMBER of `-YEARS adding `-UP to the President #**27** = President William Howard Taft (`-**72**) = `-**DEATH `-AGE!!!!!~'** `-**HE `-DIED on the `-RECIPROCAL `-AGE of his `-PRESIDENCY #27!!!!!~'**

President Jimmy Carter was `-BORN on **10/01/1924** = `-BIRTHDAY `# = `-**54**

President George H. W. Bush was `-BORN on **06/12/1924** = `-BIRTHDAY `# = `-**61**

(61 + 54) = `-**115** = (`-**23** x `-**5**) = `-**2/35** = "`-EMPHATIC `-WITNESS to the # `-NUMBER `-**35** = **RECIPROCAL** = `-**53** = "WAR of the WORLDS"!!!!!~'

According to `-**HISTORY**; and, Reciprocal-Sequencing-Numerology; `-**93 for** `-**BOTH (Ronald Reagan & Gerald Ford); and, `-RECIPROCALLY; `-39** = (Martin Luther King, Jr. & Mr. Malcolm X)!!!!!~'

#40/President Ronald Reagan `-DIED on (06/05/2004)!!!!!~'

(6 + 5 + 20 + 4) = `-**35** = **RECIPROCAL** = `-**53** = "WAR of the WORLDS"!!!!!~'

#40/President Ronald Reagan was `-BORN on (02/06/1911)!!!!!~'

(2 + 6 + 19 + 11) = `-**38** = `-**1938** = The `-19**38** radio broadcast of the H. G. Wells' story "WAR of the WORLDS" by the Mr. George Orson Welles!!!!!~'

#40/President Ronald Reagan `-DEATH/DAY # `-NUMBER (`-35) +** `-PLUS `-HIS `-BIRTHDAY # `-NUMBER (`-38) = `-73!!!!!~'**

#38/President Gerald Ford `-DEATH/DAY # `-NUMBER (`-64) + `-PLUS `-**HIS `-BIRTHDAY # `-NUMBER (`-53) = `-117!!!!!~'**

#38/President Gerald Ford (`-117) (-) `-MINUS #40/President Ronald Reagan (`-73) = `-44 = "The `-YEAR that the "PROPHET'S" MOTHER was `-BORN (`-1944)!!!!!~'

#38/President Gerald Ford `-DIED on (12/26/2006)!!!!!~'

(12 + 26 + 20 + 6) = `-**64** = **RECIPROCAL** = `-**46** = `-**23** x `-**2** = `-**232** = **Reciprocal-Sequencing-Numerology-RSN!!!!!~'**

#38/President Gerald Ford has the `-AGE of `-DEATH of **#35/President John F. Kennedy**; and, **#36/President Lyndon B. Johnson** `-BOTH within `-HIS `-DEATH/DAY # `-NUMBER!!!!!~'

#38/President Gerald Ford was `-BORN on (07/14/1913)!!!!!~'

(7 + 14 + 19 + 13) = `-**53** = **"WAR of the WORLDS"!!!!!~'**

Martin Luther King, Jr. `-BIRTHDAY # `-NUMBER for January 15th, 1929 (01/15/19/29) = (1 + 15 + 19 + 29) = `-**64**

Martin Luther King, Jr. `-DEATH/DAY # `-NUMBER for April 4th, 1968 (04/04/19/68) = (4 + 4 + 19 + 68) = `-**95**

Mr. Malcolm X = `-BIRTHDAY # `-NUMBER for May 19th, 1925 (05/19/19/25) = (5 + 19 + 19 + 25) = `-**68**

Mr. Malcolm X `-DEATH/DAY # `-NUMBER for February 21st, 1965 (02/21/19/65) = (2 + 21 + 19 + 65) = `-**107**

The `-BIRTHDAY # `-NUMBERS of Martin Luther King, Jr.; and, Mr. Malcolm X give the `-YEAR `-COMPLETED; and, the `-YEAR of; /`-ASSASSINATIONS/, of `-EACH `-OTHER!!!!!~'

(64 + 68) = `-**132** = (1 x 32) = `-**32** = -a **Prophetic Number!!!!!~'**

Mr. Martin Luther King, Jr.

(95 + 64) = `-**159**

(95 (-) 64 = `-**31**

(159 + 31) = `-**190**

Mr. Malcolm X

(107 + 68) =`-**175**

(107 (-) 68) = `-**39**

(175 + 39) = `-**214**

(214 (+) 190 = `-**404** = (44 + 0) = `-**44**...(...)...-'-'!!!!!~'

#38/President Gerald Ford

`-BIRTHDAY # `-NUMBER = `-**53**

`-DEATH/DAY # `-NUMBER = **64**

(64 + 53) = `-**117**

#40/President Ronald Reagan

`-BIRTHDAY # `-NUMBER = `-**38**

`-DEATH/DAY # `-NUMBER = `-**35**

(38 + 35) = `-**73** / (117 (-) 73 = `-**44**...(...)...-'-'!!!!!~'

(MLK/MX (44) + GF/RR (44)) = `-88 = (`-35 + `-53) = "WAR of the WORLDS"!!!!!~'

President Bill Clinton was `-BORN on **08/19/1946** = `-BIRTHDAY `# = `-**92**

8 + 19 + 19 = `-**46** = `-23 x `-2 = `-**232** = **R**eciprocal-**S**equenced-**N**umerology**!!!!!~'**

46 + 46 = `-**92** = BIRTHDAY #!!!!!~'

`-**92** = (`-**23** x `-**4**) = `-**234** = "**P**rophetic-**L**inear-**P**rogression-**PLP**"!!!!!~'

`-**67** = **RECIPROCAL** = `-**76**

President George W. Bush was `-BORN on **07/06/1946** = `-BIRTHDAY `# = `-**78**

`-**46** = `-23 x `-2 = `-**232** = **R**eciprocal-**S**equenced-**N**umerology**!!!!!~'**

(92 + 78) = `-**170** = (1 x 70) = `-**70** = "The `-AVERAGE `-AGE of the `-HISTORY of the United States `-PRESIDENTS"!!!!!~'

`-**323** = **R**eciprocal-**S**equenced-**N**umerology!!!!!~'

(3 x 23) = `-**69** = "They `-**BOTH** are `-**AT** the `-**AGE** of `-**69**!!!!!~'

There are `-**44** days that `-SEPARATE their `-BIRTHS!!!!!~'

`-**44** = `-4 x `-11 = *Multiple of* `-11 = "Yin/Yang" = "The Cycle of `-LIFE"!!!!!~'

Same `-BIRTH `-YEAR; and, the Same `-AGE!!!!!~'

Did `-YOU `-NOTICE; that there are `-**23** days that lie in between the `-BIRTHDAYS of President George H. W. Bush; and, President George W. Bush!!!!!~' During this `-TIME of `-**23** days, they are `-**23** years apart in `-LIVING!!!!!~'

There are `-**67** days that lie in between the births of President Bill Clinton; and, President George H. W. Bush!!!!!~' `-**67** = "The `-YEAR of the `-**SUCCESSIVE**/`-**CONSECUTIVE** `-**DEATHS** of `-AGE of the U. S. `-PRESIDENTS from (President#1 to President #28)!!!!!~'

`-**111** (Jimmy Carter/George H. W. Bush) (**-**) `-**44** (Bill Clinton/George W. Bush) = `-**67**!!!!!~'

`-**67** = **RECIPROCAL** = `-**76** = The #43/President George W. Bush `-**BIRTHDAY**!!!!!~'

(67 (-) 44 = `-**23** = -a **Prophetic Number**!!!!!~'

President Jimmy Carter being married to his wife Rosa**lynn** Carter for some `-**69** years standing as equals to the lives of both President George W. Bush; and, President Bill Clinton!!!!!~'

`-**2747** `-YEARS is the `-NUMBER of `-AGES for the `-TOTAL `-NUMBER of `-YEARS adding `-UP for `-ALL `-PRESIDENTS as `-DOCUMENTED as of (10/31/2015) that have `-DIED!!!!!~'

`-**2747** = (47 + 27) = `-**74** = **RECIPROCAL** = `-**47**

(74 - 47) = `-27 = "The ROMAN EMPIRE"!!!!!~'

`-2676 `-YEARS is the `-NUMBER of `-AGES for the `-TOTAL `-NUMBER of `-YEARS adding `-UP for `-ALL `-PRESIDENTS as `-DOCUMENTED as of (10/31/2015) that have `-DIED!!!!!~' (**Minus #24/President Grover Cleveland** for the 2nd `-ENTRY as `-PRESIDENT (`-71))!!!!!~'

`-**2676** = `-**EMPHATIC `-WITNESS** for `-**676** = **R**eciprocal-**S**equencing-**N**umerology-**RSN**!!!!!~'

`-**2747** / `-**39** PRESIDENTIAL TERMS that are `-USED in the `-CALCULATIONS for those `-PRESIDENTS that have `-DIED = `-**70.435**

`-**43** = **RECIPROCAL** = `-**34** = **RECIPROCAL** = #**43**/President George W. Bush!!!!!~'

(43 + 34) = `-**77** = 2(7's) = `-**27** = "The ROMAN EMPIRE"!!!!!~'

`-**70** = "The `-YEAR that the `-PROPHET" was `-BORN!!!!!~'

`-**70** = (`-**35** x `-**2**) = `-EMPHATIC `-WITNESS as to the `-NUMBER `-**35** = **RECIPROCAL** = `-**53** = "WAR of the WORLDS"!!!!!~'

`-**2676** / `-**38** PRESIDENTS that have `-ACTUALLY `-DIED as of **(10/31/2015)** = `-**70**.4210**52**

`-**38** = `-**1938** = The `-19**38** radio broadcast of the **H. G. Wells'** story **"WAR of the WORLDS"** by the **Mr. George Orson Welles**!!!!!~'

`-**70.421052** = (42 + 10 + 52) - (70) = `-**34** = **RECIPROCAL** = `-**43**

`-**70** = **RECIPROCAL** = `-**07**

(70 + 7) = `-**77** = 2(7's) = `-**27** = "The ROMAN EMPIRE"!!!!!~'

`-**1453** = "The ROMAN EMPIRE `-ENDED"!!!!!~'

(53 (-) 14 = `-**39** = "The `-AGE of `-DEATH of Mr. Martin Luther King, Jr.; and, Mr. Malcolm X"!!!!!~'

`-2015 (-) `-1776 (`-INDEPENDENCE `-DAY) = `-2(39) = (23 + 9) = `-32 = -a Prophetic Number!!!!!~'

`-1776 = (76 + 17) = `-93 = RECIPROCAL = `-39 = "The `-AGE of `-DEATH of Mr. Martin Luther King, Jr.; and, Mr. Malcolm X"; and, "#38/President Gerald Ford; and, #40/President Ronald Reagan"!!!!!~'

(38 + 40) / `-2 = `-39 = #39/President Jimmy Carter that is `-CURRENTLY `-91 `-YEARS; and, `-35 `-DAYS in `-LIVING!!!!!~'

`-2015 = (20 + 15) = `-35 = RECIPROCAL = `- 53 = "WAR of the WORLDS"!!!!!~'

#41/President George H. W. Bush = `-CURRENTLY `-91 `-YEARS; and, `-146 `-DAYS in `-LIVING!!!!!~'

`-146 = (1 x 46) = `-46 = `-23 x `-2 = Reciprocal-Sequencing-Numerology-RSN!!!!!~'

#42/President Bill Clinton = `-CURRENTLY `-69 `-YEARS; and, `-78 `-DAYS in `-LIVING!!!!!~'

`-78 = `-39 x `-2 = "The `-EMPHATIC `-WITNESS to The `-AGE of `-DEATH of Mr. Martin Luther King, Jr.; and, Mr. Malcolm X"; and, "#38/President Gerald Ford (`-93); and, #40/President Ronald Reagan (`-93)"!!!!!~'

#43/President George W. Bush = `-CURRENTLY `-69 `-YEARS; and, `-122 `-DAYS in `-LIVING!!!!!~'

`-122 = (1 + 22) = `-23 = -a Prophetic Number!!!!!~'

#44/President Barack H. Obama = `-CURRENTLY `-54 `-YEARS; and, `-93 `-DAYS in `-LIVING!!!!!~'

`-93 = (93 (-) 54) = `-39 = "The `-AGE of `-DEATH of Mr. Martin Luther King, Jr.; and, Mr. Malcolm X"; and, "#38/President Gerald Ford (`-93); and, #40/President Ronald Reagan (`-93)"!!!!!~'

(122 (-) 93) = `-29 / (78 (-) 93) = `-15 / (29 + 15) = `-44…(…)…-'~'

(146 (-) 93) = `-53 = "WAR of the `-WORLDS"!!!!!~'

The `-ENDING of the `-ROMAN `-EMPIRE = `-1453 = (53 + 14) = `-67 = "The `-AVERAGE `-AGE of the United States Presidents 1 to 28 in "SUCCESSION" above; and, below `-ALL `-PRESIDENTS that `-DIED at `-AGES `-66, `-67; and, `-68; and, The `-AGE of `-DEATH of the #1/ President George Washington"!!!!!~'

The `-**44**th President of the United States of America #**44**/President Barack H. Obama has **(60 (-) 54) = `-6 / (67 (-) 60) = `-7 / (`-6-to-7) `-YEARS**; until, **`-HE'S (`-67) `-YEARS `-OLD!!!!!~'**

ALEXANDER HAMILTON was `-BORN on **January 11**th **in `-1755 (01/11/1755);** and, `-HIS `-**BIRTHDAY # `-NUMBER** is: (1 + 11 + 17 + 55) = `-**84** = **RECIPROCAL** = `-**48**

(84 (-) 48) = `-**36** = **"RECIPROCAL of AARON BURR'S # `-NUMBER (`-63)!!!!!~'**

(84 + 48) = `-**132** = (1 x 32) = `-**32** = -a Prophetic Number!!!!!~'

`-**23** = **RECIPROCAL** = `-**32**

`-**BIRTHDAY; and, `-DEATH/DAY** = (Jan. 11th / July 12th) = (11 + 12) = `-**23** = -a Prophetic Number!!!!!~'

ALEXANDER HAMILTON had `-DIED on **July 12**th **in `-1804 (07/12/1804);** and, `-HIS `-**DEATH/DAY # `-NUMBER** is: (7 + 12 + 18 + 4) = `-**41** = **RECIPROCAL** = `-**14**

`-**BIRTH/YEAR** = `-**1755** = (55 + 17) = `-**72**

`-**DEATH/YEAR** = `-**1804** = (18 x 4) = `-**72**

(41 (-) 14) = `-**27** = **RECIPROCAL** = `-**72** / `-**1755** = (55 + 17) = `-**72**

(72 + 72) = `-**144** = (1 x 44) = `-**44** = "**AGE** of #1/President George Washington at the `-**TIME** of the `-**1**st `-INDEPENDENCE `-DAY; and, the `-**AGE** of ALEXANDER HAMILTON at the `-**TIME** of #1/President George Washington's `-**DEATH**!!!!!~'

(84 + 14) = `-**98** = `-**49** x `-2

`-**98** = `-ONE (`-1) `-YEAR before #1/President George Washington had `-**DIED** (`-17**99**)!!!!!~'

`-**48** = `-ONE (`-1) `-YEAR before the `-AGE that ALEXANDER HAMILTON had `-**DIED** (`-**49**)!!!!!~'

(41 + 14) = `-**55** = "The `-YEAR ALEXANDER HAMILTON was `-**BORN** (`-**1755**)!!!!!~'

`-**55** = `-**32** + `-**23**

(84 + 41) = `-**125** = (25 + 1) = `-**26** = `-**13** x `-**2** = (**132**) = (1 x 32) = `-**32** = -a Prophetic Number!!!!!~'

ALEXANDER HAMILTON was `-**BORN** `-**23** `-**YEARS** after the `-BIRTH of #1/President George Washington; and, was `-**44** `-YEARS of `-AGE at the `-TIME of #1/President George Washington's `-**DEATH**!!!!!~'

#1/President George Washington = `-**67** `-DEATH `-AGE!!!!!~' (`-BORN in `-**1732**)!!!!!~'

`-**67** = (6 + 7) = `-**13** = "A VERY PIVOTAL NUMBER"!!!!!~

`-**1732** = (17 + 32) = `-**49** = "AGE of `-DEATH of SIR / ALEXANDER HAMILTON!!!!!~'

ALEXANDER HAMILTON = `-**49** `-DEATH `-AGE!!!!!~' (`-BORN in `-**1755**)!!!!!~'

`-**49** = (4 + 9) = `-**13** = "A VERY PIVOTAL NUMBER"!!!!!~

(13 + 13) = `-**26** = `-**13** x `-**2** = (**132**) = (1 x 32) = `-**32** = -a Prophetic Number!!!!!~'

`-**AGE** of `-**DEATHS** = (67 (-) 49) = `-**18** = (1 x 8) = `-**8** = "ALEXANDER HAMILTON `-DIED `-**8** `-DAYS `-PAST `-INDEPENDENCE `-DAY (`-**44**)!!!!!~' #1/President George Washington was `-**44** `-YEARS of `-AGE on the `-INITIAL `-INDEPENDENCE `-DAY!!!!!~'

VICE-PRESIDENT AARON BURR was `-**BORN** on February 6th in `-1756; and, `-HIS `-**BIRTHDAY #** `-**NUMBER** is: (2 + 6 + 17 + 56) = `-**81** = **RECIPROCAL** = `-**18**

91

February 6th = (26) = `-**26** = `-**13** x `-**2** = (**132**) = (1 x 32) = `-**32** = -a **Prophetic Number!!!!!~'**

(81 (-) 18 = `-**63** = "**RECIPROCAL of ALEXANDER HAMILTON'S #** `-**NUMBER** (`-**36**)!!!!!~'**

VICE-PRESIDENT AARON BURR had `-**DIED** on September 14$^{th}$ in `-1836; and, `-HIS `-**DEATH/DAY #** `-**NUMBER** is: (9 + 14 + 18 + 36) = `-**77** = **RECIPROCAL** = `-**77**

(77 + 77) = `-**154** = (54 + 1) = `-**55** = "The `-**YEAR** that ALEXANDER HAMILTON was `-**BORN** in (`-17**55**)!!!!!~'**

(9 + 1**4**) = `-**23** = -a **Prophetic Number!!!!!~'**

(1**4** + 18) = `-**32** = -a **Prophetic Number!!!!!~'**

`-**55** = `-**23** + `-**32**

(**9** + 1**4**) = (1 x 94) = `-**94** = **RECIPROCAL** = `-**49** = "AGE of `-DEATH of SIR / ALEXANDER HAMILTON"!!!!!~'**

`-**1836** = (1 x (8 + 36)) = `-**44** = `-**AGE** of ALEXANDER HAMILTON at the `-**TIME** of #1/President George Washington's `-**DEATH**!!!!!~'**

VICE-PRESIDENT AARON BURR `-DIED at the `-AGE of `-**80** = **RECIPROCAL** = `-**08**

(80 (-) 08) = `-**72** = "The # `-**NUMBERS of SIR / ALEXANDER HAMILTON"!!!!!~'**

`-**72** = **RECIPROCAL** = `-**27** = "The ROMAN EMPIRE"!!!!!~'**

(72 (-) 27) = `-**45** = **RECIPROCAL** = `-**54**

(54 + 45) = `-**99** = "The `-**YEAR** that #1/President George Washington had `-**DIED** (`-17**99**)!!!!!~'**

`-**AGE** of `-**DEATHS** = (80 (-) 67) = `-**13** = "A VERY PIVOTAL NUMBER"!!!!!~'**

`-**AGE** of `-**DEATHS** = (80 (-) 49) = `-**31** = **RECIPROCAL** = `-**13** = "A VERY PIVOTAL NUMBER"!!!!!~'**

(31 + 13) = `-**44** = "#1/President George Washington's `-AGE at `-INITIAL `-INDEPENDENCE `-DAY; and, `-AGE of ALEXANDER HAMILTON as the `-TIME of #1/President George Washington's `-DEATH"!!!!!~'

(`-1/`-3) = `-**13** = "A VERY PIVOTAL NUMBER"!!!!!~'

`-**1**/President George Washington / `-**3**/President Thomas Jefferson/Vice-President Aaron Burr!!!!!~'

VICE-PRESIDENT AARON BURR was `-**BORN** in `-**1756**!!!!!~'

`-**1756** = (17 + 56) = `-**73** = "AGE of `-DEATH of #5/President James Monroe plus `-**67** days `-**EQUALS** `-**AGE** of `-**DEATH** of #1/President George Washington"!!!!!~'

#5/ President James Monroe was `-BORN on **April 28th in `-1758 (04/28/1758)**; and, `-HIS `-**BIRTHDAY # `-NUMBER** is: (4 + 28 + 17 + 58) = `-**107**

(4 + 28) = `-**32** = -a Prophetic Number!!!!!~'

(4 + 28 + 17) = `-**49** = "`-AGE of `-DEATH of SIR / ALEXANDER HAMILTON"!!!!!~'

(4 + 28 + 17) = `-**49** / (49 (-) 18) = `-**31** = "**YEAR of `-DEATH**"!!!!!~'

#5/ President James Monroe had `-DIED on **July 4th in `-1831 (07/04/1831)**; and, `-HIS `-**DEATH/DAY # `-NUMBER** is: (7 + 4 + 18 + 31) = `-**60**

(7 + 4 + 18) = `-**29** / (29 x 2) = `-**58** = "**YEAR** of `-**BIRTH**"!!!!!~'

`-**BIRTHDAY # `-NUMBER/`-DEATH/DAY # `-NUMBER** (107 + 60) = `-**167** = (1 x 67) = `-**67** = "**AGE** of `-**DEATH** of #1/President George Washington"!!!!!~'

`-**1831** = (31 + 18) = `-**49** = "`-AGE of `-DEATH of SIR / ALEXANDER HAMILTON"!!!!!~'

`-**DEATH-MONTH/`-BIRTH-MONTH = (07/04)** = "`-INDEPENDENCE `-DAY" = "DAY of `-DEATH"!!!!!~'

`-**74** = **RECIPROCAL** = `-**47** / (107 (-) 60) = `-**47**

(47 + 47) = `-**94** = **RECIPROCAL** = `-**49** = "`-**AGE** of `-**DEATH** of SIR / **ALEXANDER HAMILTON**"!!!!!~'

#1/President George Washington (1732/1799) = (1732 + 1799) = `-**3531**

`-**3531** = (35 + 31) = `-**66** / (66 / 2) = `-**33**

`-**AGE** of `-**DEATH** = `-**67** = **RECIPROCAL** = `-**76** = (67 + 76) = `-**143**

`-**143** = (43 + 1) = `-**44**…(…)…-'~'

#2/President John Adams (1735/1826) = (1735 + 1826) = `-**3561**

`-**3561** = (53 + 61) = `-**114** = (11 x 4) = `-**44**

`-**AGE** of `-**DEATH** = `-**90** = **RECIPROCAL** = `-**09** = (90 + 09) = `-**99**

(143 (-) 99) = `-**44**…(…)…-'~'

#3/President Thomas Jefferson (1743/1826) = (1743 + 1826) = `-**3569**

(69 (-) 35) = `-**34** = **RECIPROCAL** = `-**43**

`-**AGE** of `-**DEATH** = `-**83** = **RECIPROCAL** = `-**38** = (83 + 39) = `-**121**

(144 (-) 121) = `-**23** = **RECIPROCAL** = `-**32**

#4/President James Madison (1751/1836) = (1751 + 1836) = `-**3587**

(78 (-) 35) = `-**43**

`-**AGE** of `-**DEATH** = `-**85** = **RECIPROCAL** = `-**58** = (85 + 58) = `-**143**

`-**143** = (43 + 1) = `-**44**…(…)…-'~'

#5/President James Monroe (1758/1831) = (1758 + 1831) = `-**3589**

(98 (-) 35) = `-**63**…(…)…-'~'

`-**AGE** of `-**DEATH** = `-**73** = **RECIPROCAL** = `-**37** = (73 + 37) = `-**110**

(144 (-) 110) = `-**34** = **RECIPROCAL** = `-**43**

Vice-President Aaron Burr (1756/1836) = (1756 + 1836) = `-35**92**

`-**92** = **RECIPROCAL** = `-**29** / (92 (-) 29) = `-**63**...(...)...-`-`

`-**AGE** of `-**DEATH** = `-**80** = **RECIPROCAL** = `-**08** = (80 + 08) = `-**88**

(88 / 2) = `-**44**...(...)...-`-`

(88 x 2) = `-**176** = (1 x 76) = `-**76** = **RECIPROCAL** = `-**67**...(...)...-`-`

(144 + 88) = `-**232** = **Reciprocal-Sequencing-Numerology-RSN!!!!!~`**

`-**59** = **"ALEXANDER HAMILTON"!!!!!~`**

(59 x 4) = `-**236** = **"`-EMPHATIC `-WITNESS to the `-NUMBER `-36"!!!!!~`**

ALEXANDER HAMILTON (1755/1804) = (1755 + 1804) = `-**3559**

`-**59** = **RECIPROCAL** = `-**95** / (95 (-) 59) = `-**36** = **RECIPROCAL** = `-**63**...(...)...-`-`

`-**AGE** of `-**DEATH** = `-**49** = **RECIPROCAL** = `-**94** = (49 + 94) = `-**143**

`-**143** = (43 + 1) = `-**44**...(...)...-`-`

`-**59** = **"VICE-PRESIDENT AARON BURR"!!!!!~`**

(59 x 4) = `-**236** = **"`-EMPHATIC `-WITNESS to the `-NUMBER `-36"!!!!!~`**

#**3**/ President Thomas Jefferson was `-BORN on **April 13**th in `-**1743** (**04**/**13**/**1743**); and, `-HIS `-**BIRTHDAY # `-NUMBER** is: (**4** + **13** + 17 + **43**) = `-**77**

(4 + 13 + 17) = `-**34** = **RECIPROCAL** = `-**43** / (43 + 34) = `-**77**

#**3**/ President Thomas Jefferson had `-DIED on **July 4**th in `-**1826** (**07**/**04**/**1826**); and, `-HIS `-**DEATH/DAY # `-NUMBER** is: (7 + 4 + 18 + 26) = `-**55**

(77 + 55) = `-**132** = (1 x 32) = `-**32** = **-a Prophetic Number!!!!!~`**

#**4**/ President James Madison was `-BORN on **March 16**th in `-**1751** (**03**/**16**/**1751**); and, `-HIS `-**BIRTHDAY # `-NUMBER** is: (3 + 16 + 17 + 51) = `-**87**

(3 + 16 + 17) = `-**36** = "**YEAR of `-DEATH**"!!!!!~'

`-**51** = **RECIPROCAL** = `-**15** / (3 + 16 + 17 + 15) = `-**51** = "**YEAR of `-BIRTH**"!!!!!~'

#**4**/ President James Madison had `-DIED on **June 28**th **in `-1836 (06/28/1836)**; and, `-HIS `-**DEATH/DAY # `-NUMBER** is: (6 + 28 + 18 + 36) = `-**88**

(6 + 28) = `-**34** = **RECIPROCAL** = `-**43**

(6 + 28 + 18) = `-**52** = "**ONE** (`-**1**) `-**YEAR** `-**AWAY** from `-**YEAR of `-BIRTH**"!!!!!~'

(88 + 87) = `-**175** = (1 + 75) = `-**76** = **RECIPROCAL** = `-**67**...(...)...-'-' = "**AGE of `-DEATH of #1/President George Washington**"!!!!!~'

Take #1/President George Washington's `-**DEATH** `-**AGE** (`-**67**-Reciprocal-**76**); and, #4/President James Madison's `-**DEATH** `-**AGE** (`-**85**-Reciprocal-**58**); and, `-**ADD them `-TOGETHER**"!!!!!~'

(76 + 58) = `-**134** = (1 x 34) = `-**34** = **RECIPROCAL** = `-**43**...(...)...-'-'

(67 + 85) = `-**152** = (52 + 1) = `-**53** = "**WAR of the WORLDS**...(...)...-'-'"!!!!!~'

"There are #'s `-NUMBERS to the `-SCRIPTURES"!!!!!~'-'"

ROMANS 14:**5,13,15** (-) "(**5**) One man esteemeth one day above another: another esteemeth every day alike. Let each man be fully assured in his own mind. (**13**) Let us not therefore judge one another any more: but judge ye this rather, that no man put a stumbling block in his brother's way, or an occasion of falling. (**15**) For if because of meat thy brother is grieved, thou walkest no longer in love. Destroy not with thy meat him for whom Christ died." **-(ENGLISH REVISED EDITION - 1885)-**

(14 + **5** + 1**3**) = `-**32** = -a PROPHETIC NUMBER!!!!!~'

(**5** + 1**3** + 1**5**) = `-**33** = "**Yin/Yang**" = "**Multiple of `-ELEVEN**" = "**The `-CYCLE of `-LIFE**"!!!!!~'

ROMANS 14:19,20 (-) "(19) So then let us follow after things which make for peace, and things whereby we may edify one another. (20) Overthrow not for meat's sake the work of God. All things indeed are clean; howbeit it is evil for that man who eateth with offence." -(ENGLISH REVISED EDITION - 1885)-

(14 + 19 + 20) = `-**53** = "WAR of the WORLDS"!!!!!~'

ROMANS 2:14,15 (-) "(14) for when Gentiles which have no law do by nature the things of the law, these, having no law, are a law unto themselves; (15) in that they shew the work of the law written in their hearts, their conscience bearing witness therewith, and their thoughts one with another accusing or else excusing them;" -(ENGLISH REVISED EDITION - 1885)-

(2 + 14 + 15) = `-**31** = **RECIPROCAL** = `-**13** = "A PIVOTAL NUMBER"!!!!!~'

----

1 TIMOTHY 4:8 (-) "(8) for bodily exercise is profitable for a little; but godliness is profitable for all things, having promise of the life which now is, and of that which is to come." -(ENGLISH REVISED EDITION - 1885)-

(1 + 4 + 8) = `-**13** = "A PIVOTAL NUMBER"!!!!!~'

PROVERBS 13:20 (-) "(20) Walk with wise men, and thou shalt be wise: but the companion of fools shall smart for it." -(ENGLISH REVISED EDITION - 1885)-

`-**32** = -a PROPHETIC NUMBER!!!!!~'

(13 + 20) = `-**33** = "Yin/Yang" = "Multiple of `-ELEVEN" = "The `-CYCLE of `-LIFE"!!!!!~'

----

1 CORINTHIANS 9:16 (-) "(16) For if I preach the gospel, I have nothing to glory of; for necessity is laid upon me; for woe is unto me, if I preach not the gospel." -(ENGLISH REVISED EDITION - 1885)-

(1 + 9 + 16) = `-**26** = `-**13** x `-**2** = `-**132** = (1 x 32) = `-**32** = -a Prophetic Number!!!!!~'

ROMANS 14:13,19 (-) "(13) Let us not therefore judge one another any more: but judge ye this rather, that no man put a stumblingblock in his brother's way, or an occasion of falling. (19) So then let us follow after things which make for peace, and things whereby we may edify one another." -(ENGLISH REVISED EDITION - 1885)-

(14 + 13 + 19) = `-46 = `-23 x `-2 = `-232 = Reciprocal-Sequenced-Numerology-RSN!!!!!~'

ACTS: 16:2 (-) "(2) The same was well reported of by the brethren that were at Lystra and Iconium." -(ENGLISH REVISED EDITION - 1885)-

(16 x 2) = `-32 = -a Prophetic Number!!!!!~'

Acts 16:2 / `-32km / Lystra/Iconium / Timothy, Paul; Silas; and, Barnabas!!!!!~'

REVELATION 16:16 (-) "(16) And they gathered them together into the place which is called in Hebrew Har-Magedon." -(ENGLISH REVISED EDITION - 1885)-

Revelation 16:16 /`-ARMAGEDDON!!!!!~'

(16 + 16) = `-32 = -a Prophetic Number!!!!!~'

MARK 13:32,33 (-) "(32) But of that day or that hour knoweth no one, not even the angels in heaven, neither the Son, but the Father. (33) Take ye heed, watch and pray: for ye know not when the time is." -(ENGLISH REVISED EDITION - 1885)-

(13,32,33)...(...)...'-'~'

(13 + 32 + 33) = `-78 = (39 / 2) = "`-EMPHATIC `-WITNESS to the `-NUMBER `-39 = 3(9's) = `-999 = RECIPROCAL = `-666!!!!!~'

JEREMIAH 5:31 (-) "(31) the prophets prophesy falsely, and the priests bear rule by their means; and my people love to have it so: and what will ye do in the end thereof?" -(ENGLISH REVISED EDITION - 1885)-

(31 (-) 5) = `-**26** = `-**13** x `-**2** = `-**132** = (1 x 32) = `-**32** = -a **Prophetic Number!!!!!~'**

(31 + 5) = `-**36** = **RECIPROCAL** = `-63 = "AGE of `-DEATH of the "PROPHET'S" MOTHER"!!!!!~'**

MATTHEW 7:21-**23** (-) "(21) Not every one that saith unto me, Lord, Lord, shall enter into the kingdom of heaven; but he that doeth the will of my Father which is in heaven. (22) Many will say to me in that day, Lord, Lord, did we not prophesy by thy name, and by thy name cast out devils, and by thy name do many mighty works? (23) And then will I profess unto them, I never knew you: depart from me, ye that work iniquity. -**(ENGLISH REVISED EDITION - 1885)-**

MATTHEW **7**: / (**21 + 22 + 23**) = `-**66** = "AGE of `-DEATH of the "PROPHET'S" FATHER"!!!!!~'**

(66 (-) 7) = `-**59** = "AGE of `-DEATH of `-JESUS `-CHRIST'S MOTHER `-**MARY**"!!!!!~'**

AGE of `-**MOTHERS** = (63 + 59) = `-**122** = (22 + 1) = `-**23** = -a **Prophetic Number!!!!!~'**

MATTHEW 7:6 (-) "(6) Give not that which is holy unto the dogs, neither cast your pearls before the swine, lest haply they trample them under their feet, and turn and rend you." -**(ENGLISH REVISED EDITION - 1885)-**

JAMES **4**:**14** (-) "(14) whereas ye know not what shall be on the morrow. What is your life? For ye are a vapour, that appeareth for a little time, and then vanisheth away." -**(ENGLISH REVISED EDITION - 1885)-**

(4/14) = (44 x 1) = `-**44** = "The `-YEAR of the "PROPHET'S" MOTHER'S `-BIRTH (`-19**44**)"!!!!!~'**

ISAIAH 46:10 (-) "(10) declaring the end from the beginning, and from ancient times things that are not yet done; saying, My counsel shall stand, and I will do all my pleasure:" -**(ENGLISH REVISED EDITION - 1885)-**

(46 x 1 + 0) = `-**46** = `-**23** x `-**2** = `-**232** =
Reciprocal-Sequenced-Numerology-RSN!!!!!~'

REVELATION 7:9,14 (-) "(9) After these things I saw, and behold, a great multitude, which no man could number, out of every nation and of all tribes and peoples and tongues, standing before the throne and before the Lamb, arrayed in white robes, and palms in their hands; (14) And I say unto him, My lord, thou knowest. And he said to me, These are they which come out of the great tribulation, and they washed their robes, and made them white in the blood of the Lamb." -(ENGLISH REVISED EDITION - 1885)-

(9 + 14) = `-**23** = -a PROPHETIC NUMBER!!!!!~'

`-**723** = (72 (-) 3) = `-**69** = "Yin/Yang" = "The `-CYCLE of `-LIFE"!!!!!~'

ROMANS **6:7** (-) "(7) for he that hath died is justified from sin." -(ENGLISH REVISED EDITION - 1885)-

(6 + 7) = `-**13** = "A PIVOTAL NUMBER"!!!!!~'

MATTHEW 24:7 (-) "(7) For nation shall rise against nation, and kingdom against kingdom: and there shall be famines and earthquakes in divers places." -(ENGLISH REVISED EDITION - 1885)-

(247) = (24 + 7) = `-**31** = **RECIPROCAL** = `-**13** = "A PIVOTAL NUMBER"!!!!!~'

(247) = (47 + 2) = `-**49** = **RECIPROCAL** = `-**94** = "The `-DEATH `-NUMBERS"!!!!!~'

(247) = (2 x 47) = `-**94** = **RECIPROCAL** = `-**49**

(9 + 4) = `-**13** = "A PIVOTAL NUMBER"!!!!!~'

LUKE 21:11 (-) "(11) and there shall be great earthquakes, and in divers places famines and pestilences; and there shall be terrors and great signs from heaven." -(ENGLISH REVISED EDITION - 1885)-

(21 + 11) = `-**32** = -a Prophetic Number!!!!!~'

"The Last Days" are `-MARKED by `-WARS, `-FOOD `-SHORTAGES, `-EARTHQUAKES; and, `-PESTILENCES"!!!!!~'

----

2 TIMOTHY **3**:1-**5** (-) "(1) But realize this, that in the last days difficult times will come. (2) For men will be lovers of self, lovers of money, boastful, arrogant, revilers, disobedient to parents, ungrateful, unholy, (3) unloving, irreconcilable, malicious gossips, without self-control, brutal, haters of good, (4) treacherous, reckless, conceited, lovers of pleasure rather than lovers of God, (5) holding to a form of godliness, although they have denied its power; Avoid such men as these." -**(ENGLISH REVISED EDITION - 1885)**-

(2 + 3 + 1 + 2 + 3 + 4 + 5) = `-**20** = "The `-<u>DAY</u> the "**PROPHET**" was `-**BORN** (`-**03/20**)"!!!!!~'

(20 + 3) = `-**23** = -a **Prophetic Number!!!!!~'**

`-**35** = **RECIPROCAL** = `-**53** = "**WAR of the WORLDS**"!!!!!~'

"In The Last Days" – "Many `-LOVE many `-OTHER `-THINGS than `-LOVE `-GOD"!!!!!~'

MATTHEW 24:14 (-) "(14) And this gospel of the kingdom shall be preached in the whole world for a testimony unto all the nations; and then shall the end come." -**(ENGLISH REVISED EDITION - 1885)**-

(24 + 14) = `-**38** = **RECIPROCAL** = `-**83**

(83 (-) 38) = `-**45** = "**CURRENT `-AGE of the "PROPHET"-**"!!!!!~'

(24 x 14) = `-**336**

`-**33** = "Yin/Yang" = "Multiple of `-ELEVEN" = "The `-CYCLE of `-LIFE"!!!!!~'

`-**36** = **RECIPROCAL** = `-**63** = "AGE of `-DEATH of the "PROPHET'S" MOTHER"!!!!!~'

(33 + 36) = `-**69** = "Yin/Yang" = "The `-CYCLE of `-LIFE"!!!!!~'

"This `-GOOD `-NEWS of the `-KINGDOM will be `-PREACHED in `-ALL the `-EARTH during "These Last Days"-"

"There are #'s `-NUMBERS to the `-SCRIPTURES"!!!!!~'~'"

(FIRST LADY)...(...)...-"~'

MARTHA WASHINGTON was `-BORN on June 13th in `-1731 (06/13/1731); and, the `-BIRTHDAY # `-NUMBER is: (6 + 13 + 17 + 31) = `-**67** = **RECIPROCAL** = `-**76**

(67 + 76) = `-**143** = (1 x 43) = `-**43** = **RECIPROCAL** = `-**34**

(**6** + 1**3** + 17) = `-**36** = **RECIPROCAL** = `-**63**

MARTHA WASHINGTON'S `-BIRTHDAY # `-NUMBER = `-**67** = "The `-AGE of `-DEATH of `-HER `-HUSBAND #1/President George Washington, The `-YEAR that the "PROPHET'S" BROTHER was `-BORN; and, the `-**SUCCESSIVE**/`-**CONSECUTIVE** `-DEATH `-AGE of the U. S. `-PRESIDENTS from (#1 to #28)!!!!!~'

MARTHA WASHINGTON `-**DIED** at the tender `-**AGE** of `-**70** = **"The `-YEAR that the "PROPHET" was `-BORN in** (`-19**70**); and, the **`-AVERAGE `-DEATH `-AGE of `-ALL `-38 `-PRESIDENTS** that have **`-DIED as of the `-DATE - (11/08/2015)"!!!!!~'**

MARTHA WASHINGTON had `-DIED on May 22nd in `-1802 (05/22/1802); and, the `-DEATH/DAY # `-NUMBER is: (5 + 22 + 18 + 02) = `-**47** = **RECIPROCAL** = `-**74**

(74 (-) 47) = `-**27** = **"The ROMAN EMPIRE"!!!!!~'**

(143 + 27) = `-**170** = (1 x 70) = `-**70** = **"AGE of `-DEATH of FIRST LADY MARTHA WASHINGTON"!!!!!~'**

(5 + 22 + 18 - 2) = `-**43** = **RECIPROCAL** = `-**34**

BIRTHYEAR / DEATHYEAR = (1731/1802) = (1731 + 1802) = `-**3533**

`-**3533** = (3533 / 2) = `-**1766.5** = **ROUNDED** = `-**1767** = (1 x 767) = `-**767** = **R**eciprocal-**S**equencing-**N**umerology-**RSN**!!!!!~'

(FIRST LADY)…(…)…-'-'

ABIGAIL ADAMS was `-BORN on November 22nd in `-1744 (11/22/1744); and, the `-BIRTHDAY # `-NUMBER is: (11 + 22 + 17 + 44) = `-**94** = **RECIPROCAL** = `-**49**

(94 + 49) = `-**143** = (1 x 43) = `-**43** = **RECIPROCAL** = `-**34**

(11+ 22 + 17) = `-**36** = **RECIPROCAL** = `-**63**

`-17**44** = (44 (-) 17) = `-**27** = "The ROMAN EMPIRE"!!!!!-'

`-17**44** = "DEATH/DAY # `-NUMBER in the `-MIDDLE of the `-BIRTHDAY # `-NUMBER"!!!!!-'

`-17**44** = `-**44**…(…)…-'-'

ABIGAIL ADAMS `-BIRTHDAY # `-NUMBER = `-**94** = **RECIPROCAL** = `-**49** = "The `-AGE of `-DEATH of ALEXANDER HAMILTON!!!!!-'

ABIGAIL ADAMS `-**DIED** at the tender `-**AGE** of `-**73** = "The `-AGE of `-DEATH of #5/President James Monroe!!!!!-'

ABIGAIL ADAMS had `-DIED on October 28th in `-1818 (10/28/1818); and, the `-DEATH/DAY # `-NUMBER is: (10 + 28 + 18 + 18) = `-**74** = **RECIPROCAL** = `-**47**

ABIGAIL ADAMS `-DEATH/DAY # `-NUMBER = (`-**74**) is the `-**RECIPROCAL** of MARTHA WASHINGTON'S `-DEATH/DAY # `-NUMBER = (`-**47**)!!!!!-'

(74 + 47) = `-**121** = (12 + 1) = `-**13** = "A VERY PIVOTAL NUMBER"!!!!!-'

(74 (-) 47) = `-**27** = "The ROMAN EMPIRE"!!!!!-'

(143 + 27) = `-**170** = (1 x 70) = `-**70** = "AGE of `-DEATH of FIRST LADY MARTHA WASHINGTON"!!!!!-'

(10 + 28 + 18) = `-**56** = "AGE of `-DEATH of #16/President Abraham Lincoln"!!!!!-'

There are some `-**26** `-**DAYS** from **ABIGAIL ADAMS `-DEATH/DAY** to her `-**74**th `-**BIRTHDAY**!!!!!-'

`-26 = `-13 x `-2 = `-132 = (1 x 32) = `-32 = -a Prophetic Number!!!!!~'

BIRTHYEAR / DEATHYEAR = (1744/1818) = (1744 + 1818) = `-3562

`-3562 = (3562 / 2) = `-1781 = (81 (+) 17) = `-98 = (98 / 2) = `-49 = "AGE of `-DEATH of ALEXANDER HAMILTON; and, ABIGAIL ADAMS was `-BORN in the `-YEAR of `-44 in (`-1744)"!!!!!~'

`-3562 = (3562 / 2) = `-1781 = (81 (-) 17) = `-64 = "AGE of `-DEATH of #36/President Lyndon B. Johnson"!!!!!~'

(FIRST LADY)...(...)...-"-'

MARTHA JEFFERSON was `-BORN on October 30th in `-1748 (10/30/1748); and, the `-BIRTHDAY # `-NUMBER is: (10 + 30 + 17 + 48) = `-105

`-1748 = (48 + 17) = `-65 = "The `-YEAR #16/President Abraham Lincoln was `-ASSASSINATED"!!!!!~'

MARTHA JEFFERSON `-DIED at the tender `-AGE of `-33 = "MARTHA JEFFERSON `-DIED some `-23 `-DAYS before `-HER `-34th `-BIRTHDAY!!!!!~'

`-23 = RECIPROCAL = `-32

MARTHA JEFFERSON had `-DIED on September 6th in `-1782 (09/06/1782); and, the `-DEATH/DAY # `-NUMBER is: (9 + 6 + 17 + 82) = `-114

(9 + 6) = `-96 = `-32 x `-3 = `-323 = Reciprocal-Sequencing-Numerology-RSN!!!!!~'

(9 + 6 + 17) = `-32 = -a Prophetic Number!!!!!~'

`-1782 = (82 (-) 17) = `-65 = "The `-YEAR #16/President Abraham Lincoln was `-ASSASSINATED"!!!!!~'

(65 + 65) = `-130 = (13 + 0) = `-13 = "A VERY PIVOTAL NUMBER"!!!!!~'

`-1782 = (82 + 17) = `-99 = "The `-YEAR that #1/President George Washington had `-DIED (`-1799)"!!!!!~'

BIRTHYEAR / DEATHYEAR = (1748/1782) = (1748 + 1782) = `-**3530**

`-**3530** = (3530 / 2) = `-**1765** = (765 x 1) = `-**765** =
Prophetic-Linear-Progression-PLP!!!!!~'

`-**3530** = (353 + 0) = `-**353** = **Reciprocal-Sequencing-Numerology-RSN** =
"WAR of the WORLDS"!!!!!~'

(FIRST LADY)...(...)...-'~'

MARTHA JEFFERSON RANDOLPH -(Daughter)- of #3/President Thomas Jefferson was `-BORN on September 27th in `-1772 (09/27/1772); and, the `-BIRTHDAY # `-NUMBER is: (9 + 27 + 17 + 72) = `-**125**

(9 + 27) = `-**36** = **"YEAR of `-DEATH (`-1836)"!!!!!~'**

(9 + 27 + 17) = `-**53** = **"WAR of the WORLDS"!!!!!~'**

MARTHA JEFFERSON RANDOLPH -(Daughter)- of #3/President Thomas Jefferson `-**DIED** at the tender `-**AGE** of `-**64** / `-**13** `-**DAYS** / `-**TOTAL** of `-**23,388** `-**DAYS of** `-**LIFE** = **"The `-AGE of `-DEATH of #36/President Lyndon B. Johnson"!!!!!~'**

MARTHA JEFFERSON RANDOLPH -(Daughter)- of #3/President Thomas Jefferson had `-DIED on October 10th in `-1836 (10/10/1836); and, the `-DEATH/DAY # `-NUMBER is: (10 + 10 + 18 + 36) = `-**74** = **RECIPROCAL** = `-**47**

(74 (-) 47) = `-**27** = **"The ROMAN EMPIRE"!!!!!~'**

(125 + 27) = `-**152** = (52 + 1) = `-**53** = **"WAR of the WORLDS"!!!!!~'**

MARTHA JEFFERSON RANDOLPH -(Daughter)- of #3/President Thomas Jefferson `-DEATH/DAY # `-NUMBER is = `-EQUAL to FIRST LADY ABIGAIL ADAMS `-DEATH/DAY # `-NUMBER = (`-**74**); and, a `-**RECIPROCAL** of MARTHA WASHINGTON'S `-DEATH/DAY # `-NUMBER = (`-**47**)!!!!!~'

BIRTHYEAR / DEATHYEAR = (1772/1836) = (1772 + 1836) = `-**3608**

`-**3608** = (36 + 8) = `-**44**...(...)....-'~'

`-**3608** = (3608 / 2) = `-1804 = (1 + 8 + 0 + 4) = `-**13** = "A VERY PIVOTAL NUMBER"!!!!!~'

(44 (-) 13) = `-**31** = **RECIPROCAL** = `-**13**

MARY JEFFERSON EPPES -(Daughter)- of #3/President Thomas Jefferson was `-BORN on August 1ˢᵗ in `-1778 (08/01/1778); and, the `-BIRTHDAY # `-NUMBER is: (8 + 1 + 17 + 78) = `-**104**

(8 + 1 + 17) = `-**26** = `-**13** x `-**2** = `-**132** = (1 x 32) = `-**32** = -a **Prophetic Number**!!!!!~'

MARY JEFFERSON EPPES -(Daughter)- of #3/President Thomas Jefferson `-**DIED** at the tender `-**AGE** of `-**25**!!!!!~'

`-**25** = **RECIPROCAL** = `-**52**!!!!!~' / (52 (-) 25) = `-**27** = "The ROMAN EMPIRE"!!!!!~'

(52 + 25) = `-**77** = "Yin/Yang" = "Multiple of `-ELEVEN" = "The `-CYCLE of `-LIFE"!!!!!~'

MARY JEFFERSON EPPES -(Daughter)- of #3/President Thomas Jefferson had `-DIED on April 17ᵗʰ in `-1804 (04/17/1804); and, the `-DEATH/DAY # `-NUMBER is: (4 + 17 + 18 + 4) = `-**43** = **RECIPROCAL** = `-**34**

(43 + 34) = `-**77** = **2(7's)** = `-**27** = "The ROMAN EMPIRE"!!!!!~'

(104 + 27) = `-**131** = (31 + 1) = `-**32** = -a **Prophetic Number**!!!!!~'

BIRTHDAY # `-NUMBER / DEATH/DAY # `-NUMBER = (104/43) = (104 + 43) = `-**147** = (1 x 47) = `-**47** = **RECIPROCAL** = `-**74**

MARY JEFFERSON EPPES has a `-**VARIATION** on the `-DEATH # `-NUMBERS of MARY JEFFERSON EPPES -(Daughter)- of #3/President Thomas Jefferson `-DEATH/DAY # `-NUMBER is = `-EQUAL to FIRST LADY ABIGAIL ADAMS `-DEATH/DAY # `-NUMBER = (`-**74**); and, a `-**RECIPROCAL** of MARTHA WASHINGTON'S `-DEATH/DAY # `-NUMBER = (`-**47**)!!!!!~'

(104 (-) 43) = `-**61** / `-**1778** = (78 (-) 17) = `-**61**

(61 + 61) = `-**122** = (22 + 1) = `-**23** = -a Prophetic Number!!!!!~’

BIRTHYEAR / DEATHYEAR = (1778/1804) = (1778 + 1804) = `-**3582**

`-**3582** = (82 (-) 35) = `-**47** = **RECIPROCAL** = `-**74**

`-**3582** = (3582 / 2) = `-**1791** = (91 (-) 17) = `-**74** = **RECIPROCAL** = `-**47**

(FIRST LADY)…(…)…-'-'

DOLLEY MADISON was `-**BORN** on May 20th in `-1768 (05/20/1768); and, the `-BIRTHDAY # `-NUMBER is: (5 + 20 + 17 + 68) = `-**110**

`-**1768** = (68 + 17) = `-**85** = (8 + 5) = `-**13** = **“A VERY PIVOTAL NUMBER”!!!!!~’**

DOLLEY MADISON `-**DIED** at the `-**AGE** of `-**81** `-**YEARS**; and, `-**53** `-**DAYS**!!!!!~’

(81 + 53) = `-**134** = (34 x 1) = `-**34** = **RECIPROCAL** = `-**43**

DOLLEY MADISON had `-DIED on July 12th in `-1849 (07/12/1849); and, the `-DEATH/DAY # `-NUMBER is: (7 + 12 + 18 + 49) = `-**86** = **RECIPROCAL** = `-**68**

(110 + 86) = `-**196** = (96 x 1) = `-**96** = `-**32** x `-**3** = `-**323** = **Reciprocal-Sequencing-Numerology-RSN**!!!!!~’

(86 + 68) = `-**154** = (1 + 54) = `-**55** = **“SAVES LIVES”**!!!!!~’

(86 + 68) = `-**154** = (1 + 54) = `-**55** = **“The `-YEAR ALEXANDER HAMILTON was `-BORN in (`-17**55**)”**!!!!!~’

`-18**49** = `-**49** = **“The `-YEAR of `-DEATH for FIRST LADY DOLLEY MADISON; and, the `-AGE of `-DEATH of SIR / ALEXANDER HAMILTON”**!!!!!~’

`-**1849** = (49 (-) 18) = `-**31** = **RECIPROCAL** = `-**13** = **“A VERY PIVOTAL NUMBER”**!!!!!~’

BIRTHYEAR / DEATHYEAR = (1768/1849) = (1768 + 1849) = `-**3617**

`-**3617** = (36 + 17) = `-**53** = "WAR of the WORLDS"!!!!!~'

`-**3617** = (3617 / 2) = `-1808.5 = ROUNDED = `-**1809** = (1 x 89 + 0) = `-**89** = "The `-AGE of `-DEATH of the "PROPHET'S" GRANDMOTHER (MOTHER'S MOTHER)"!!!!!~'

(89 (-) 53) = `-**36** = **RECIPROCAL** = `-**63** = "The `-AGE of `-DEATH of the "PROPHET'S" MOTHER"!!!!!~'

(FIRST LADY)...(...)...-"~'

ELIZABETH MONROE was `-BORN on June 30th in `-1768 (06/30/1768); and, the `-BIRTHDAY # `-NUMBER is: (6 + 30 + 17 + 68) = `-**121**

(6 + 30) = `-**36** = **RECIPROCAL** = `-**63** = "The `-AGE of `-DEATH of the "PROPHET'S" MOTHER"!!!!!~'

(6 + 30 + 17) = `-**53** = "WAR of the WORLDS"!!!!!~'

`-**1768** = (68 + 17) = `-**85** = (8 + 5) = `-**13** = "A VERY PIVOTAL NUMBER"!!!!!~'

(85 (-) 53) = `-**32** = -a Prophetic Number!!!!!~'

ELIZABETH MONROE `-**DIED** at the `-**AGE** of `-**62** `-**YEARS**; and, `-**85** `-**DAYS**!!!!!~'

(62 + 85) = `-**147** = (47 x 1) = `-**47** = **RECIPROCAL** = `-**74**

(85 (-) 62) = `-**23** = -a Prophetic Number!!!!!~'

`-**1768** = (68 + 17) = `-**85** = "`-DAYS in `-LIVING after the FIRST LADY'S - ELIZABETH MONROE'S - `-LAST `-BIRTHDAY"!!!!!~'

ELIZABETH MONROE had `-DIED on September **23**th in `-1830 (09/**23**/1830); and, the `-DEATH/DAY # `-NUMBER is: (9 + 23 + 18 + 30) = `-**80** = **RECIPROCAL** = `-**08**

(9 + 23) = `-**32** = -a Prophetic Number!!!!!~'

(121 (-) 80) = `-**41** = "WAR of the WORLDS (WWII) - (`-19**41**)"!!!!!~'

`-**14** = <u>RECIPROCAL</u> = `-**41**

(41 + 14) = `-**55** = "The `-YEAR ALEXANDER HAMILTON was `-BORN in (`-17<u>55</u>)"!!!!!-'

(80 + 8) = `-**88** = (88 / 2) = `-**44**…(…)…-'-' / (80 (-) 08) = `-**72**

(121 (-) 72) = `-**49** = "The `-YEAR of `-DEATH for FIRST LADY DOLLEY MADISON; and, the `-AGE of `-DEATH of SIR / ALEXANDER HAMILTON"!!!!!-'

BIRTHYEAR / DEATHYEAR = (1768/1830) = (1768 + 1830) = `-**<u>3598</u>**

`-**<u>3598</u>** = (98 (-) 35) = `-**63** = "The `-AGE of `-DEATH of the "PROPHET'S" MOTHER"!!!!!-'

`-**<u>3598</u>** = (3598 / 2) = `-**1799** = "The `-<u>YEAR</u> that the #1/President George Washington `-<u>PASSED</u> `-<u>AWAY</u> in `-DEATH!!!!!-'-'

(99 (-) 17) = `-**82** = "The `-AGE of `-DEATH of the "PROPHET'S" GRANDMOTHER (FATHER'S MOTHER)"!!!!!-'

`-the `-<u>WEATHER</u>…(…)…-'-'

`-Matthew **16:2,3** – "**(2)** But he answered and said unto them, When it is evening, ye say, It will be fair weather: for the heaven is red. **(3)** And in the morning, It will be foul weather today: for the heaven is red and lowring. Ye know how to discern the face of the heaven; but ye cannot discern the signs of the times." -(**ENGLISH REVISED EDITION - 1885**)-

(16 + 16) = `-**32** = -a Prophetic Number!!!!!-' / `-**32** = <u>RECIPROCAL</u> = `-**23**

`-**35** = <u>RECIPROCAL</u> = `-**53** = "WAR of the WORLDS"!!!!!-'

<u>STRATOSPHERE</u>: the part of the `-EARTH'S `-ATMOSPHERE which extends from the top of the `-**TROPOSHERE** to about `-**30** `-MILES (`-**50** `-Kilometers) above the surface; and, in which the `-**TEMPERATURE** increases gradually to about `-**32°** `-DEGREES `-FAHRENHEIT (`-**0°** `-DEGREES CELSIUS); and, the clouds rarely form… (**Webster's Dictionary**)…(…)…-'-'

The `-**DIFFERENCE** `-BETWEEN `-**FAHRENHEIT**; and, `-**CELSIUS** is (`-**1.8**)!!!!!~' The `-**DIFFERENCE** `-BETWEEN `-**FAHRENHEIT; and, `-KELVIN** is (`-**0.556**)!!!!!~' {(1.8 / 0.556 = `-**3.23** = **R**eciprocal-**S**equencing-**N**umerology-**RSN**) (`-3.23(**74**)}!!!!!~'

Water/Freezing/`-**273.15**/Kelvin (**/**) Water/Boiling/`-**373.15**/Kelvin (**/**) (373.15 + 273.15 = `-**646.3**) = `-**AGE** of `-**DEATH** of #35/President John F. Kennedy (`-**46**); and, #**36**/President Lyndon B. Johnson (`-**64**) with a `-**BOILING** `-**POINT**; and, `-**COLD** `-**WAR** interchange in `-**1963**!!!!!~' {(1963 = (63 (-) 19) = `-**44**) = An `-**EMPHATIC** `-**WITNESS** for the `-**BOILING**; and, `-**FREEZING** `-**POINTS** of `-**FAHRENHEIT** = (`-32 Degrees + `-212 Degrees = `-**(2)44**)|}!!!!!~'

FAHRENHEIT: relating to; or, conforming to a `-**THERMOMETRIC** `-**SCALE** on which under `-**STANDARD** `-**ATMOSPHERIC** `-**PRESSURE** the `-**BOILING** `-**POINT** of `-**WATER** is at `-**212°** `-**DEGREES** (**R**eciprocal-**S**equenced-**N**umerology-**RSN**) above the zero of the scale, the `-**FREEZING** `-**POINT** is at `-**32°** `-**DEGREES** above `-**ZERO**... (**Webster's Dictionary**)...(...)...-"-' {(212 (-) 32 = `-**180**) = (%) **CELSIUS**}!!!!!~'

`-**212** = **R**eciprocal-**S**equenced-**N**umerology-**RSN** = (21 + 2) = `-**23** = -a **Prophetic Number!!!!!~'**

`-**23** = **RECIPROCAL** = `-**32** / `-**32** = -a **Prophetic Number!!!!!~'**

`-**1** `-**METER** = `-**39.37** inches

`-**39.37** inches / `-**12** inches = `-**3.**280833 feet

`-**1013.25** / `-**760** = `-**1.33**3223 **pascals** (**pa.**)

Blaise Pascal (*Lived `-From* (16**23**) (-) (16**62**) *Died `-From*) was a French mathematician, physicist, and a religious philosopher that had completed an original treatise on conic sections by the time he was `-**16** years of age. He undertook the study of geometry, hydrodynamics, and hydrostatic and atmospheric pressure... (**Webster's Dictionary**)...(...)...-"-'

Matthew **16:2,3** = (`-**1623**) = `-**FROM** the `-**SCRIPTURES** `-**ABOVE** = (62) = (13) = (23)...(...)...-"-'

(62 (-) 23) = `-**39** = "AGE of `-**DEATH** of Mr. Blaise Pascal"!!!!!~'

(16 + 16) = `-32 = -a Prophetic Number!!!!!~'

Blaise Pascal was `-BORN on June 19th in `-1623 (06/19/1623); and, with a `-BIRTHDAY # `-NUMBER of = (6 + 19 + 16 + 23) = `-64

Blaise Pascal had `-DIED on August 19th in `-1662 (08/19/1662); and, with a `-DEATH/DAY # `-NUMBER of = (8 + 19 + 16 + 62) = `-105

(105 + 64) = `-169 = (1 x 69) = `-69 = `-3 x `-23 = `-323 = Reciprocal-Sequenced-Numerology-RSN = "The `-CYCLE of `-LIFE"!!!!!~'

Blaise Pascal `-DIED at the tender `-AGE of `-39 = 3(9's) = `-999 = RECIPROCAL = `-666-!!!!!~'

`-1623 = (23 + 16) = `-39 = "AGE of `-DEATH of Blaise Pascal"!!!!!~'

`-1662 = (62 + 16) = `-78 = (78 / 2) = `-39 = "AGE of `-DEATH of Blaise Pascal"!!!!!~'

`-1662 = (62 (-) 16) = `-46 = `-23 x `-2 = `-232 = Reciprocal-Sequenced-Numerology-RSN!!!!!~'

`-1.333 = `-33 = "Yin/Yang" = "Multiple of `-ELEVEN" = "The `-CYCLE of `-LIFE"!!!!!~'

`-80833 = (8 + 0 + 8 + 3 + 3) = `-22

`-808 = Reciprocal-Sequenced-Numerology-RSN!!!!!~'

(62 + 23) = `-85 = (8 + 5) = `-13 = "A VERY PIVOTAL NUMBER"!!!!!~'

(11 + 11) = `-22 = "Yin/Yang" = "Multiple of `-ELEVEN" = "The `-CYCLE of `-LIFE"!!!!!~'

`-2015 = (20 + 15) = `-35 = RECIPROCAL = `-53 = "The WAR of the WORLDS"!!!!!~'

`-69 = "The `-CYCLE of `-LIFE"!!!!!~'

Evangelista Torricelli, in `-1643, an Italian Physicist `-INVENTED the `-BAROMETER; which is, a `-SIMPLE `-DEVICE that `-MEASURES `-AIR `-PRESSURE!!!!!~'

Evangelista Torricelli was `-<u>BORN</u> on October 15<sup>th</sup> in `-1608 (10/15/1608); and, with a `-**BIRTHDAY #** `-**NUMBER** of = (10 + 15 + 16 + 08) = `-**<u>49</u>**

Evangelista Torricelli had `-<u>DIED</u> on October 25<sup>th</sup> in `-1647 (10/25/1647); and, with a `-**DEATH/DAY #** `-**NUMBER** of = (10 + 25 + 16 + 47) = `-**<u>98</u>**

Blaise Pascal was `-BORN in (`-<u>1623</u>) = (62 (-) 13) = `-**<u>49</u>** = BIRTHDAY # `-NUMBER of Evangelista Torricelli!!!!!~'

(49 x 2) = `-**<u>98</u>** = Evangelista Torricelli's DEATH/DAY # `-NUMBER (`-**<u>98</u>**) is `-TWICE the `-AMOUNT of `-HIS BIRTHDAY # `-NUMBER (`-**<u>49</u>**)!!!!!~'

Evangelista Torricelli `-<u>DIED</u> at the `-EXACT `-SAME `-AGE as Blaise Pascal = `-**<u>39</u>** `-<u>YEARS</u> of `-<u>AGE</u> = "The `-<u>AGE</u> of `-<u>DEATH</u>"!!!!!~'

Blaise Pascal `-DIED on the `-EXACT same `-DAY (the `-19th); as `-HE was `-BORN on (the `-19th)!!!!!~'

(19 + 19) = `-**<u>38</u>**

Evangelista Torricelli `-DIED within the `-EXACT same `-MONTH (`-25th-October-'-10-'); as `-HE was `-BORN within (`-15<sup>th</sup>-October-'-10-');!!!!!~' There were `-<u>10</u> `-<u>DAYS</u> that `-<u>SEPARATED</u> `-HIS `-<u>BIRTH</u>; and, `-HIS `-<u>DEATH</u> / `-<u>DAYS</u>!!!!!~'

(25 + 15) = `-**<u>40</u>**

`-<u>AVERAGE</u> = (38 + 40) = `-**<u>78</u>** / (`-2) = `-**<u>39</u>** = "AGE of `-DEATH for `-BOTH `-MEN (Blaise Pascal; and, Evangelista Torricelli)!!!!!~'

`-<u>HYGROMETER</u> – For `-<u>MEASURING</u> the `-<u>HUMIDITY</u> in the `-<u>ATMOSPHERE</u> – First Known Use was in `-1<u>6</u>70!!!!!~'

(1<u>6</u>70 + 164<u>3</u>) = `-**<u>3313</u>** = (33 + 13) = `-**<u>46</u>** = `-**<u>23</u>** x `-**<u>2</u>** = `-**<u>232</u>** = <u>R</u>eciprocal-<u>S</u>equenced-<u>N</u>umerology-<u>RSN</u>!!!!!~'

`-<u>P</u>ASCAL = `-**<u>16</u>** = ECCLESIASTES 1:6 (-) "(6) The wind goeth toward the south, and turneth about unto the north; it turneth about continually in its course, and the wind returneth again to its circuits." -(ENGLISH REVISED EDITION - 1885)-

<u>AMERICAN/ENGLISH</u> `-<u>ALPHABET</u> '-to-' `-<u>NUMBERS</u> #'s:!!!!!~'

THE REAL PROPHET OF DOOM (KISMET) - INTRODUCTION - PENDULUM FLOW – II –

BLAISE PASCAL / EVANGELISTA TORRICELLI

BP = `-2, `-16 / **ET** = `-5, `-20

(2 + 16 + 5 + 20) = `-43 / (520 (-) 216) = `-304 = (34 + 0) = `-34

`-34 = **RECIPROCAL** = `-43 = "PRESIDENTIAL # `-NUMBER"!!!!!~'

(520 + 216) = `-736 = (73 (-) 6) = `-67 = "The `-YEAR that the "PROPHET'S" BROTHER was `-BORN, the `-AVERAGE `-AGE of the United States Presidents 1 to 28 in "SUCCESSION" above; and, below `-ALL `-PRESIDENTS that `-DIED at `-AGES `-66, `-67; and, `-68; and, The `-AGE of `-DEATH of the #1/President of the United States of America #1/President George Washington"!!!!!~'

(73 (-) 34) = `-39 = "AGE of `-DEATH for `-BOTH `-MEN (Blaise Pascal; and, Evangelista Torricelli)!!!!!~'

(73 (-) 29) = `-44 = "#1/President <u>George</u> Washington was `-44 `-YEARS of `-AGE in (`-1776) on the very `-FIRST `-INDEPENDENCE `-DAY of which `-HE `-DIED on the `-EXACT same `-DAY `-RECIPROCAL # `-NUMBER of which `-HE was at the `-AGE of (`-67)-'"!!!!!~'

`-736 = (36 (-) 7) = `-29

<u>Job</u> 36:29 – "(29) Yea, can any understand the spreadings of the clouds, the thunderings of his pavilion?" -(ENGLISH REVISED EDITION - 1885)-

(36 + 29) = `-65 = "The `-YEAR that #16/President Abraham Lincoln was `-ASSASSINATED in -(`-1865)-'"!!!!!~'

BLAISE PASCAL, EVANGELISTA TORRICELLI, MARTIN LUTHER KING, JR.; AND, MR. MALCOLM X; `-ALL `-DIED, at the tender `-AGE of (`-39)!!!!!~'

(39 x 4) = `-156 = (56 x 1) = `-56 = "AGE of `-DEATH of #16/President Abraham Lincoln"!!!!!~'

The `-SURFACE `-PRESSURE at `-SEA `-LEVEL varies minimally, as of this `-DATE (`-11/11/2015); the `-LOWEST `-VALUE `-MEASURED has been `-MEASURED at `-870.0 `-HECTOPASCALS (`-25.69 inHg);

and, the `-HIGHEST `-VALUE `-RECORDED has been `-<u>MEASURED</u> at `-<u>1,085.7</u> `-HECTOPASCALS (`-<u>32.06</u> inHg)!!!!!~'

(<u>25.69</u>inHg + <u>32.06</u>inHg) = `-<u>57.75</u> = <u>R</u>eciprocal-<u>S</u>equencing-<u>N</u>umerology-<u>RSN</u>!!!!!~'

`-BAROMETRIC `-PRESSURE; which, is sometimes `-CALLED; `-ATMOSPHERIC `-PRESSURE, has a/the `-WEIGHT at `-SEA `-LEVEL; of, `-14.7 (<u>PSI</u> - <u>P</u>ounds-<u>P</u>er-<u>S</u>quare-<u>I</u>nch)!!!!!~'

By `-DEFINITION; the `-STANDARD `-ATMOSPHERE, is a `-UNIT of `-PRESSURE that is `-10<u>1</u>3.25 `-HECTOPASCALS!!!!!~' (Equivalent to `-<u>760</u> mmHg, `-29.92 inHg; or, `-<u>14.696</u> (PSI)!!!!!~'

`-<u>1013</u> = (10 + 13) = `-<u>23</u> = -a Prophetic Number!!!!!~'

`-<u>87</u> = <u>RECIPROCAL</u> = `-<u>78</u>

(87 + 78) = `-<u>165</u> = (1 x 65) = `-<u>65</u> = "The `-YEAR #<u>16</u>/President Abraham Lincoln was `-<u>ASSASSINATED</u>"!!!!!~'

(100° `-DEGREES CELSIUS (-) 65) = `-<u>35</u> = "The # `-NUMBER of the #35ᵗʰ President #/<u>35</u> President John F. Kennedy being `-<u>ASSASSINATED</u>"!!!!!~'

`-<u>85</u> = <u>RECIPROCAL</u> = `-<u>58</u>

(85 (-) 58) = `-<u>27</u> = "The ROMAN EMPIRE"!!!!!~'

`-<u>85</u> = (5 + 8) = `-<u>13</u> = "A VERY PIVOTAL NUMBER"!!!!!~'

`-TODAY'S `-DATE = `-(11/11/2015) = (11 + 11 + 20 + 15) = `-<u>57</u>

`-<u>57</u> = <u>RECIPROCAL</u> = `-<u>75</u>

(57 + 75) = `-<u>132</u> = (32 x 1) = `-<u>32</u> = -a Prophetic Number!!!!!~'

`-<u>25</u> = <u>RECIPROCAL</u> = `-<u>52</u> / (52 (-) 25) = `-<u>27</u> = "The ROMAN EMPIRE"!!!!!~'

`-<u>760</u> mmHg = `-<u>76</u> = <u>RECIPROCAL</u> = `-<u>67</u> = "The `-YEAR that the "PROPHET'S" BROTHER was `-BORN, the `-AVERAGE `-AGE of the United States Presidents 1 to 28 in "SUCCESSION" above; and, below `-ALL `-PRESIDENTS that `-DIED at `-AGES `-66, `-67; and, `-68;

and, The `-AGE of `-DEATH of the #1/President of the United States of America #1/President George Washington"!!!!!~'

MmHg = "One `-MILLIMETER of `-MERCURY is approximately `-1 `-TORR; or, `-1/760 of `-STANDARD `-ATMOSPHERIC `-PRESSURE"!!!!!~'

`-29.92 inHg = Reciprocal-Sequenced-Numerology-RSN!!!!!~'

`-29 = RECIPROCAL = `-92

(92 (-) 29) = `-63 = "The `-AGE of `-DEATH of the "PROPHET'S" MOTHER"!!!!!~'

(92 + 29) = `-121 = (21 + 1) = `-22 = "Yin/Yang" = "Multiple of `-ELEVEN" = "The `-CYCLE of `-LIFE"!!!!!~'

`-14.696 (PSI) = `-696 = `-69 = RECIPROCAL = `-96

`-69 = `-3 x `-23 = `-323 = Reciprocal-Sequenced-Numerology-RSN!!!!!~'

`-96 = `-32 x `-3 = `-323 = Reciprocal-Sequenced-Numerology-RSN!!!!!~'

(69 + 96) = `-165 = (1 x 65) = `-65 = "The `-YEAR #16/President Abraham Lincoln was `-ASSASSINATED"!!!!!~'

(165 + 14) = `-179 = (1 x 79) = `-79 = "The `-AGE of `-DEATH of Mr. H. G. WELLS of; and, for; - the "WAR of the WORLDS"-"!!!!!~'

`-14.7 (PSI) = (1 x 47) = `-47 = RECIPROCAL = `-74

(74 (-) 47) = `-27 = "The ROMAN EMPIRE"!!!!!~'

(7 + 4) = `-11 = "Yin/Yang" = "Multiple of `-ELEVEN" = "The `-CYCLE of `-LIFE"!!!!!~'

(74 + 47) = `-121 = (21 + 1) = `-22 = "Yin/Yang" = "Multiple of `-ELEVEN" = "The `-CYCLE of `-LIFE"!!!!!~'

The `-HEIGHT of the `-TROPOSHERE varies with `-LATITUDE (`-POLES-LOWER; and, `-EQUATOR-HIGHER); and, with the `-SEASONS of the `-YEAR: `-SUMMER (`-HIGHER) and `-WINTER (`-LOWER); and, can be as `-HIGH as `-20km (`-12 miles; or, `-65,000 feet)

115

near the `-**EQUATOR in** `-**SUMMER**; and, as low as `-**7** km (`-**4** miles; or, `-**23**,000 feet) over the `-**POLES in** `-**WINTER**!!!!!~'

A `-**MILE** is a `-**UNIT** of `-**MEASUREMENT** that is `-**EQUAL** to `-**5,280** feet (ft.); or, `-**1,609** meters (m.)-'"!!!!!~'

`-**5,280** = `-**52.80** = ROUNDED = `-**53** = "WAR of the WORLDS"!!!!!~'

`-**1,609** = (69 x 1 + 0) = `-**69** = `-**3** x `-**23** = `-**323** = Reciprocal-**S**equenced-**N**umerology-**RSN** = "The `-**CYCLE of** `-**LIFE**"!!!!!~'

(5,280/1,609) = `-**3.28** = ROUNDED DOWN = `-**3.2** = `-**32** = -a Prophetic Number!!!!!~'

A `-**METER** is a `-**UNIT** of `-**MEASUREMENT** that is `-**EQUAL** to `-**39.37** inches (in./"); or, `-**3.28** feet (ft./')-'"!!!!!~'

`-**3.28** feet (x) `-**12** inches = `-**39.36** inches = 33(69) = (69 (-) 33) = `-**36** = 3(6's) = `-**666**!!!!!~'

Blaise Pascal `-**DIED** at the tender `-**AGE** of `-**39** = 3(9's) = `-**999** = RECIPROCAL = `-**666**-!!!!!~'

`-**69** = `-**3** x `-**23** = `-**323** = Reciprocal-**S**equenced-**N**umerology-**RSN**!!!!!~'

`-**96** = `-**32** x `-**3** = `-**323** = Reciprocal-**S**equenced-**N**umerology-**RSN**!!!!!~'

`-**HUMAN** `-**BLOOD** `-**PRESSURE** `-**READINGS**:...(...)...-'"~'

`-**120**mmHg = `-**2.3326984**psi ("**P**ounds-**P**er-**S**quare-**I**nch")...(...)...-'-'!!!!!~'

`-**80**mmHg = `-**1.5469473684**psi ("**P**ounds-**P**er-**S**quare-**I**nch")...(...)...-'-'!!!!!~'

`-**54** = "EARTHQUAKES"!!!!!~'

`-**84** = RECIPROCAL = `-**48**

(84 + 48) = `-**132** = (1 x 32) = `-**32** = -a Prophetic Number!!!!!~'

(2.3 + 1.54) = `-**3.84**

(3 x 84) = `-**252** = Reciprocal-**S**equenced-**N**umerology-**RSN**!!!!!~'

(2.332 + 1.546) = `-**3.878** / `-**87** = RECIPROCAL = `-**78**

(87 + 78) = `-165 = (1 x 65) = `-65 = "The `-YEAR that #16/President Abraham Lincoln was `-ASSASSINATED in -(`-1865)-""!!!!!~'

`-1865 = (65 (-) 18) = `-47 = RECIPROCAL = `-74

(74 (-) 47) = `-27 = "The ROMAN EMPIRE"!!!!!~'

`-1865 = (65 (+) 18) = `-83 = RECIPROCAL = `-38

(83 (-) 38) = `-45 = RECIPROCAL = `-54 = "THE `-EARTHQUAKES"!!!!!~'

`-the `-WEATHER...(...)...-'-"

`-the `-SCRIPTURES...(...)...-'-'

JAMES 1:13 - "GOD does not `-TEST `-PEOPLE with `-EVIL!!!!!~'

"Let no man say when he is tempted, I am tempted of God: for God cannot be tempted with evil, and he himself tempteth no man:" -(ENGLISH REVISED EDITION - 1885)-

PROVERBS 14:23 - There is `-BENEFIT in `-EVERY `-KIND of `-HARD `-WORK!!!!!~'

"In all labour there is profit: but the talk of the lips tendeth only to penury." -(ENGLISH REVISED EDITION - 1885)-

JAMES 3:2 - WE `-ALL make `-MISTAKES many `-TIMES!!!!!~'

"For in many things we all stumble. If any stumbleth not in word, the same is a perfect man, able to bridle the whole body also." -(ENGLISH REVISED EDITION - 1885)-

PROVERBS 13:4 - "The `-DILIGENT `-ONE will be `-FULLY `-SATISFIED!!!!!~'

"The soul of the sluggard desireth, and hath nothing: but the soul of the diligent shall be made fat. -(ENGLISH REVISED EDITION - 1885)-

`-the `-SCRIPTURES...(...)...-'-'

`-The `-<u>FAMILY</u>…(…)…-"-'

There are some `-<u>126</u> `-DAYS that `-LIE in from the `-BIRTH of the "PROPHET'S" MOTHER to the `-BIRTH of the "PROPHET" (`-BIRTH-to-`-BIRTH)!!!!!~'

`-<u>126</u> = (1 x 26) = `-<u>26</u> = `-<u>13</u> x `-<u>2</u> = `-<u>132</u> = (1 x 32) = `-<u>32</u> = -a Prophetic Number!!!!!~'

When the "PROPHET" was `-<u>BORN</u>, the "PROPHET'S" MOTHER was `-<u>26</u> `-YEARS of `-AGE!!!!!~'

`-<u>32</u> = <u>RECIPROCAL</u> = `-<u>23</u>

When the "PROPHET'S" BROTHER was `-<u>BORN</u>, the "PROPHET'S" MOTHER was just `-<u>23</u> `-YEARS of `-AGE!!!!!~'

(23 + 26) = `-<u>49</u> = (9 + 4) = `-<u>13</u> = "A VERY PIVOTAL NUMBER"!!!!!~'

`-<u>94</u> = <u>RECIPROCAL</u> = `-<u>49</u>

(94 (-) 49) = `-<u>45</u> = "CURRENT `-<u>AGE</u> of the "PROPHET"!!!!!~'

There are some `-<u>50</u> `-DAYS that `-LIE-in-Between- the `-BIRTH of the "PROPHET'S" MOTHER; and, the `-BIRTH of the "PROPHET'S" BROTHER (`-BIRTH-to-`-BIRTH)!!!!!~'

(126 + 50) = `-<u>176</u> = (1 x 76) = `-<u>76</u> = <u>RECIPROCAL</u> = `-<u>67</u> = "The `-YEAR that the "PROPHET'S" BROTHER was `-BORN, the `-AVERAGE `-AGE of the United States Presidents 1 to 28 in "SUCCESSION" above; and, below `-ALL `-PRESIDENTS that `-DIED at `-AGES `-66, `-67; and, `-68; and, The `-AGE of `-DEATH of the #1/President of the United States of America #1/President George Washington"!!!!!~'

There are some `-<u>76</u> `-DAYS that `-LIE in from the `-BIRTH of the "PROPHET'S" MOTHER to the `-BIRTH of the "PROPHET'S" MOTHER'S `-FATHER; and, the "PROPHET'S" FATHER (`-BIRTH-to-`-BIRTH)!!!!!~'

"PROPHET'S" `-BIRTH (-) (<u>03/20/1970</u>)

CURRENT `-<u>AGE</u> of the "PROPHET" is `-<u>45</u> `-YEARS of `-AGE!!!!!~'

"PROPHET'S" BROTHER'S `-BIRTH (-) (<u>09/25/1967</u>)

CURRENT `-**AGE** of the "PROPHET'S" BROTHER is `-**48** `-**YEARS of** `-**AGE!!!!!~'**

"PROPHET'S" MOTHER'S `-BIRTH (-) (<u>11/15/1944</u>)

The "PROPHETS" MOTHER `-**DIED** at the tender `-**AGE** of `-**63!!!!!~'**

(11 + 15) = `-**26** = "The "PROPHET'S" MOTHER'S `-AGE for `-WHEN the "PROPHET" was `-BORN"!!!!!~'

(11 + 15 + 44) = `-**70** = "The `-YEAR the "PROPHET" was `-BORN"!!!!!~'

(11 + 15 + 19) = `-**45** = "CURRENT `-AGE of the "PROPHET"!!!!!~'

"PROPHET'S" FATHER'S `-BIRTH (-) (<u>09/01/1941</u>)

The "PROPHETS" FATHER `-**DIED** at the tender `-**AGE** of `-**66!!!!!~'**

"PROPHET'S" MOTHER'S `-FATHER'S `-BIRTH (-) (<u>09/01/1906</u>)

The "PROPHETS" GRANDFATHER `-**DIED** at the `-**AGE** of `-**86!!!!!~'**

(70 + 67 + 44 + 41 + 06) = `-**228** = `-**22.8** = **ROUNDED** = `-**23** = -a **Prophetic Number!!!!!~'**

`-**23** = **RECIPROCAL** = `-**32**

"PROPHET'S" `-BIRTHDAY = (0<u>3</u>/<u>2</u>0) = `-**32** = -a Prophetic Number!!!!!~'

"PROPHET'S" MOTHER'S `-MOTHER'S `-BIRTH (-) (<u>12/10/1914</u>)

The "PROPHET'S GRANDMOTHER `-**DIED** at the `-**AGE** of `-**89!!!!!~'**

(12 + 10 + 19) = `-**41** = **RECIPROCAL** = `-**14**

(12 + 10) = `-**22** / (19 + 14) = `-**33**

(`-22/`-33) = (22 + 33) = `-**55** = `-23 + `-32 / `-**23** = **RECIPROCAL** = `-**32**

(89 / 2) = `-**44.5** = **ROUNDED DOWN** = `-**44** = "The `-YEAR that the "PROPHET'S"
MOTHER was `-BORN / `-HER `-DAUGHTER / "!!!!!~'

"PROPHET'S" FATHER'S `-MOTHER'S `-BIRTH (-) (09/19/1924) /`-Died (09/30/2006)

(93 (-) 26) = `-67 = "The `-YEAR that the "PROPHET'S" BROTHER was `-BORN (`-HER `-GRANDSON), the `-AVERAGE `-AGE of the United States Presidents 1 to 28 in "SUCCESSION" above; and, below `-ALL `-PRESIDENTS that `-DIED at `-AGES `-66, `-67; and, `-68; and, The `-AGE of `-DEATH of the #1/President of the United States of America #1/President George Washington"!!!!!~'

The "PROPHET'S" GRANDMOTHER `-DIED at the `-AGE of `-82!!!!!~'

(9 + 19) = `-28 = RECIPROCAL = `-82 = "AGE of `-DEATH"!!!!!~'

(9 + 19 + 19) = `-47 = "AGE of `-DEATH of (`-MICHAEL); the `-SON, that `-DIED on `-HER `-BIRTHDAY"!!!!!~'

`-HER `-BIRTHDAY # `-NUMBER = (9 + 19 + 19 + 24) = `-71

`-71 = RECIPROCAL = `-17

(71 + 17) = `-88 = "AGE of `-DEATH of `-HER `-HUSBAND (-) `-BELOW!!!!!~'

`-919 = `-Reciprocal-Sequenced-Numerology-RSN!!!!!~'

DEATH/DAY # `-NUMBER = (9 + 30 + 20 + 6) = `-65

(9 + 30) = `-39 = "AGE of `-DEATH of Blaise Pascal"!!!!!~'

(9 + 30 + 20) = `-59 = "AGE of `-DEATH of JESUS CHRIST'S MOTHER `-MARY"!!!!!~'

`-65 = RECIPROCAL = `-56 = "AGE; and, `-YEAR of `-DEATH of #16/President Abraham Lincoln"!!!!!~'

(71 + 65) = `-136 = (1 x 36) = `-36 = RECIPROCAL = `-63 = "AGE of `-DEATH of the "PROPHET'S" MOTHER"!!!!!~'

"PROPHET'S" FATHER'S `-FATHER'S `-BIRTH (-) (12/30/1916)

The "PROPHETS" GRANDFATHER `-DIED at the `-AGE of `-88!!!!!~'

(24 + 16 + 14) = `-**54** = **RECIPROCAL** = `-**45** = "CURRENT `-AGE of the "PROPHET"!!!!!~'

(228 + 54) = `-**282** = **R**eciprocal-**S**equenced-**N**umerology-**RSN**!!!!!~'

`-**28** = **RECIPROCAL** = `-**82**

(82 (-) 28) = `-**54** = **RECIPROCAL** = `-**45** = "CURRENT `-AGE of the "PROPHET"!!!!!~'

(45 + 48 + 63 + 66 + 86 + 89 + 82 + 88) = `-**567** = (56 + 7) = `-**63** = "AGE of `-DEATH of the "PROPHET'S" MOTHER"!!!!!~'

`-567 = (56 (-) 7) = `-**49** = "The `-SUM of the `-AGES of the "PROPHET'S" MOTHER at the `-TIME of `-HER giving `-BIRTH to the "PROPHET"; and, of the "PROPHET'S" `-BROTHER"!!!!!~'

`-**567** = (567 / 8) = `-**70.875** = ROUNDED DOWN = `-**70** = "YEAR of the "PROPHET" being `-BORN" (`-19**70**)!!!!!~'

`-**875** = (87 (-) 5) = `-**82** = "AGE of `-DEATH of the "PROPHET'S" GRANDMOTHER (FATHER'S MOTHER)"!!!!!~'

`-**875** = (**87.5**) = ROUNDED UP = `-**88** = "AGE of `-DEATH of the "PROPHET'S" GRANDFATHER (FATHER'S FATHER)"!!!!!~'

(63 + 66 + 86 + 89 + 82 + 88) = `-**474** = **R**eciprocal-**S**equenced-**N**umerology-**RSN** =
(47 (-) 4) = `-**43** = "PRESIDENTIAL # `-NUMBER"!!!!!~'

`-**47** = **RECIPROCAL** = `-**74**

(74 (-) 47) = `-**27** = "The ROMAN EMPIRE"!!!!!~'

`-**474** = (474 / 6) = `-**79** = "AGE of `-DEATH of Mr. H. G. Wells from the "WAR of the WORLDS"!!!!!~'

`-FATHER; and, `-GRANDFATHER `-BORN on the very `-SAME `-DAY = `-EXACTLY - (09/01) = (1941 (-) 1906) = `-**35** = **RECIPROCAL** = `-**53** = "WAR of the `-WORLDS"!!!!!~'

`-The `-<u>FAMILY</u>…(…)…-`-`

`-The `-<u>BIBLE</u> `-<u>AGAIN</u>…(…)…-`-`

`-<u>NOAH</u> was `-<u>BORN</u> `-<u>126</u> `-<u>YEARS</u> after the `-<u>DEATH</u> of `-<u>ADAM</u>!!!!!~

`-<u>NOAH was</u> `-<u>BORN in</u> `-<u>2970</u>B.C./B.C.E.; `-<u>SIX</u> `-<u>HUNDRED</u> (`-600) `-<u>YEARS before the</u> `-<u>FLOOD</u>!!!!!~`

<u>GENESIS</u> 7:11 (-) "In the six hundredth year of Noah's life, in the second month, on the seventeenth day of the month, on the same day were all the fountains of the great deep broken up, and the windows of heaven were opened. -(ENGLISH REVISED EDITION - 1885)-

`-<u>7:11</u> = (7 x 11) = `-<u>77</u> = "Yin/Yang" = "Multiple of `-<u>ELEVEN</u>" = "The `-CYCLE of `-LIFE"!!!!!~`

`-<u>92</u> = <u>RECIPROCAL</u> = `-<u>29</u> / `-<u>2970</u>…(…)…-`-`

(92 (-) 29) = `-<u>63</u> = "<u>AGE</u> of `-<u>DEATH</u> of the "<u>PROPHET'S</u> MOTHER</u>"!!!!!~`

`-<u>70</u> = "YEAR of `-BIRTH of the "PROPHET"- (`-19<u>70</u>)"!!!!!~

`-<u>AGE</u> of `-<u>DEATH</u> of the "PROPHET'S" FATHER; and, MOTHER (63 + 66) = `-<u>129</u> = (1 x 29) = `-<u>29</u> = <u>RECIPROCAL</u> = `-<u>92</u>

`-<u>NOAH</u> was `-<u>600</u> `-<u>YEARS</u> of `-<u>AGE</u> at the `-<u>TIME</u> of the `-<u>FLOOD</u>!!!!!~`

<u>GENESIS</u> 7:6 (-) "And Noah was six hundred years old when the flood of waters was upon the earth." -(ENGLISH REVISED EDITION - 1885)-

<u>GENESIS</u> 6:3 (-) "And the LORD said, My spirit shall not strive with man for ever, for that he also is flesh: yet shall his days be an hundred and twenty years." -(ENGLISH REVISED EDITION - 1885)-

`-<u>120</u> = (1 x 20) = `-<u>20</u> = "<u>DAY of</u> `-<u>BIRTH</u> of the "<u>PROPHET</u>"-"!!!!!~`

`-<u>NOAH'S</u> `-<u>CHILDREN</u> were `-<u>BORN</u> around `-<u>2470</u>B.C./B.C.E.!!!!!~`

`-**2470** = (70 (-) 24) = `-**46** = `-**23** x `-**2** = `-**232** =
Reciprocal-**S**equenced-**N**umerology-**RSN**!!!!!~'

`-**2470** = (70 (-) 24) = `-**94**

`-**93**, `-**94**, `-**95** = "**P**rophetic-**L**inear-**P**rogression-**PLP**"!!!!!~'

GENESIS 5:32 (-) "And Noah was five hundred years old: and Noah begat Shem, Ham, and Japheth. -(**ENGLISH REVISED EDITION - 1885**)-

`-**NOAH** `-**DIED** `-**35**0 `-**YEARS** after the `-**FLOOD of** `-**NOAH'S** `-**DAY** that had occurred in `-**2370**B.C./B.C.E at the `-**AGE** of `-**95**0 `-**YEARS-OF-AGE-**"!!!!!~' NOAH had `-**LIVED** `-**20** `-YEARS `-LONGER than `-ADAM who had `-LIVED to the `-AGE of `-**93**0 `-**YEARS-OF-AGE-**"!!!!!~'

`-**35** = **RECIPROCAL** = `-**53** = "**WAR of the WORLDS**"!!!!!~'

GENESIS 5:(**3-5**) (-) "(3) And Adam lived an hundred and thirty years, and begat a son in his own likeness, after his image; and called his name Seth: (4) and the days of Adam after he begat Seth were eight hundred years: and he begat sons and daughters. (5) And all the days that Adam lived were nine hundred and thirty years: and he died." -(**ENGLISH REVISED EDITION - 1885**)-

GENESIS 9:28,29 (-) "(28) And Noah lived after the flood three hundred and fifty years. (29) And all the days of Noah were nine hundred and fifty years: and he died." -(**ENGLISH REVISED EDITION - 1885**)-

(9 + 28 + 29) = `-**66** = "**AGE of** `-**DEATH of the "PROPHET'S" FATHER**"!!!!!~'

(9 + 28 + 29) = `-**66** = "Yin/Yang" = "Multiple of `-**ELEVEN**" = "The `-CYCLE of `-LIFE"!!!!!~'

NOAH `-**DIED in** `-**2020**B.C./B.C.E. = 2* `-**20** = "`-**EMPHATIC** `-**WITNESS as to the DAY of the** `-**BIRTH of the "PROPHET"**-"!!!!!~'

`-**2020** = (22 + 0 + 0) = `-**22** = "Yin/Yang" = "Multiple of `-**ELEVEN**" = "The `-CYCLE of `-LIFE"!!!!!~'

NOAH'S `-**GRANDFATHER** `-**METHUSELAH** `-lived to the `-AGE of `-**969**; that's, `-**31** `-YEARS short of a `-**1,000** `-YEARS-OF-AGE-"!!!!!~'

123

`-31 = <u>RECIPROCAL</u> = `-13 = "A VERY PIVOTAL NUMBER"!!!!!~'

<u>GENESIS</u> 5:21-27 (-) "(21) And Enoch lived sixty and five years, and begat Methuselah: (22) and Enoch walked with God after he begat Methuselah three hundred years, and begat sons and daughters: (23) and all the days of Enoch were three hundred sixty and five years: (24) and Enoch walked with God: and he was not; for God took him. (25) And Methuselah lived an hundred eighty and seven years, and begat Lamech: (26) and Methuselah lived after he begat Lamech seven hundred eighty and two years, and begat sons and daughters: (27) And all the days of Methuselah were nine hundred sixty and nine years: and he died." -(ENGLISH REVISED EDITION - 1885)-

(5 + 21) = `-<u>26</u> = "EQUALS plus `-100 the `-DISTANCE in `-YEARS from the `-TIME of `-ADAMS `-DEATH; and, `-NOAH'S `-BIRTH!!!!!~'

(5 + 21 + 27) = `-<u>53</u> = "WAR of the WORLDS"!!!!!~'

`-<u>969</u> = `-<u>96</u> = <u>RECIPROCAL</u> = `-<u>69</u>

`-<u>96</u> = `-<u>32</u> x `-<u>3</u> = `-<u>323</u> = <u>Reciprocal-Sequenced-Numerology-RSN</u>!!!!!~'

`-<u>69</u> = `-<u>3</u> x `-<u>23</u> = `-<u>323</u> = <u>Reciprocal-Sequenced-Numerology-RSN</u>!!!!!~'

`-<u>23</u> = <u>RECIPROCAL</u> = `-<u>32</u>

<u>1 PETER 3:20</u> (-) "which aforetime were disobedient, when the longsuffering of God waited in the days of Noah, while the ark was a preparing, wherein few, that is, eight souls, were saved through water:" -(ENGLISH REVISED EDITION - 1885)-

<u>GENESIS</u> 5:23 (-) "(<u>23</u>) and all the days of Enoch were three hundred sixty and five years:"

`-ENOCH `-lived the `-AMOUNT of `-DAYS that there are in the `-AMOUNT of `-YEARS within a `-YEAR - (`-365 `-YEARS-OF-AGE-'")!!!!!~'

(969 – 930) = `-<u>39</u> `-YEARS-in-AGE-'" = "DIFFERENCE between `-METHUSELAH; and, `-ADAM"!!!!!~'

Blaise Pascal `-<u>DIED</u> at the tender `-<u>AGE</u> of `-<u>39</u> = <u>3(9's)</u> = `-<u>999</u> = <u>RECIPROCAL</u> = `-<u>666</u>-!!!!!~'

`-<u>1623</u> = (23 + 16) = `-<u>39</u> = "AGE of `-DEATH of Blaise Pascal"!!!!!~'

`-**1662** = (62 + 16) = `-**78** = (78 / 2) = `-**39** = "AGE of `-DEATH of Blaise Pascal"!!!!!~'

(62 + 23 + 16) = `-101 = "An `-<u>EDUCATION</u> on the # `-<u>NUMBERS</u>"!!!!!~'

(16 + 16) = `-**32** = -a Prophetic Number!!!!!~'

`-**1513** B.C./B.C.E. `-When <u>GOD'S LAW</u> was `-<u>IMPLEMENTED</u> FOR `-<u>ISRAEL</u>!!!!!~'

`-**33** A.D./C.E. `-When "<u>THE LAW OF THE CHRIST</u>" was `-<u>IMPLEMENTED</u> to the `-<u>CHRISTIANS</u>!!!!!~'

`-**1513** = (53 x 1 x 1) = `-**53** = "WAR of the WORLDS"!!!!!~'

`-**11** = "Yin/Yang" = "Multiple of `-ELEVEN" = "The `-CYCLE of `-LIFE"!!!!!~'

`-**33** = "Yin/Yang" = "Multiple of `-ELEVEN" = "The `-CYCLE of `-LIFE"!!!!!~'

`-<u>NOTICE</u> `-<u>ALL</u> of the `-<u>SCRIPTURAL</u> # `-<u>NUMBERS</u> in `-<u>REFERENCE</u>:-"

(11/15/2015) - In the `-STATE of `-CALIFORNIA in the UNITED STATES of AMERICA; there on `-AVERAGE are `-1 (`-ONE) `-TORNADOS in the `-MONTH of `-NOVEMBER; and, `-11 (`-ELEVEN) `-TORNADOS that `-AVERAGE for the `-ENTIRE `-YEAR!!!!!~'

"-1-to-11-" = <u>RECIPROCAL</u> = "-11-to-1-"

`-**111** = (11 x 1) = `-**11** = "Yin/Yang" = "Multiple of `-ELEVEN" = "The `-CYCLE of `-LIFE"!!!!!~'

`-READ; `-The `-<u>BIBLE</u> `-<u>AGAIN</u>…(…)…-"~'

The `-TERRORIST `-ATTACKS in `-PARIS; and, `-RUSSIA!!!!!~"

`-LET'S `-MAKE the `-WORLD a `-BETTER `-PLACE!!!!!~' `-START `-TALKING about the `-"PROPHET" - Dwayne W. Anderson!!!!!~' I'm not `-AFRAID of the `-TERRORISTS!!!!!~' Did `-YOU `-EXAMINE; `-PARIS,

`-yet!!!!!~' I've `-HEARD that `-**132** have been `-KILLED!!!!!~' They say now that `-**129** have been `-KILLED!!!!!~'**Analyze the # `-NUMBERS!!!!!~'**

(129) = (1 x 29) = `-**29** = **RECIPROCAL** = `-**92**

The `-FIRST `-BOMB went `-OFF at `-**9:2**0PM by a `-**29 Year-OLD `-TERRORIST!!!!!~'**

`-**292** = **Reciprocal-Sequenced-Numerology-RSN!!!!!~'**

`-**ANALYZE** the `-**DATA;** `-**Again!!!!!~'**

`-**352** `-INJURED!!!!!~' `-**99** `-SURVIVORS are in `-CRITICAL `-CONDITION!!!!!~'

`-**35** = **RECIPROCAL** = `-**53** = **"WAR of the WORLDS"!!!!!~'**

`-**23** YEAR-OLD `-**killed** FROM `-**AMERICA!!!!!~'**

`-**23** = **RECIPROCAL** = `-**32** / `-**23** `-**YEARS** `-**AGO** was `-**1992!!!!!~'**

`-A `-RUSSIAN `-PLANE goes down `-OVER `-EGYPT with the number `-A**32** on `-IT; going down after `-FLYING for some `-**23** `-MINUTES!!!!!~' There were `-**224** on board that were `-KILLED!!!!!~' The `-PLANE at the `-TIME was at `-**6:17**AM / `-AT (**31**,000FT)!!!!!~' It was an `-AERBUS **321**!!!!~' `-**321** = **RECIPROCAL** = `-**123**!!!!!~' (`-**123** - **"Prophetic-Linear-Progression-PLP"**)!!!!!~' MetroJET `-FLIGHT `-**92**68 (**92** (-) 68) = `-**24**!!!!!~' `-2**24** `-**DIED** on `-**BOARD!!!!!~'**

(6 + 17) = `-**23** = -a Prophetic Number!!!!!~'

`-**LIFE'S** `-**PURPOSE** with `-**EXPLANATIONS!!!!!~'**

`-EXAMINE the `-LIFE; and, `-DEATHS; of `-PRESIDENTS of the United States of America; and, the `-FIRST `-LADY'S!!!!!~'

`-GOD didn't `-DO `-IT; but, `-IT has been `-ORCHESTRATED by `-HIS `-HOLY `-SPIRIT drawing `-IT out; without `-US, even `-KNOWING about `-IT!!!!!~'

Some might `-THINK that because of the `-**FIXED** `-**NUMBER** `-**ARRANGEMENTS** of `-**LIFE**; of `-WHAT `-I would call a `-**NUMEROLOGY**, that `-WE are `-ALL a `-BUNCH of

'-**AUTOMATONS**!!!!!~' This is not '-TRUE!!!!!~' If '-IT were '-TRUE; '-WE would have no '-PERSONALITY in our '-RELATIONSHIP '-To; and, '-With '-GOD!!!!!~' He would '-SEE; and, '-HAVE no '-VALUE in '-HIS '-CREATION at '-ALL!!!!!~' '-GOD allows '-US to be '-FREE '-MORAL '-AGENTS with '-OUR '-DIVINE '-POWER of '-REASON that '-WE can '-LIVE as a '-SACRIFICE '-LIVING; and, '-GOD just '-GUIDES '-US to a '-COMPLETION of '-PURPOSE; and, '-DIRECTS '-US towards an '-ACHIEVEMENT of '-HIS '-ARRANGEMENT!!!!!~'

'-**ANALYZE the # '-NUMBERS, '-AGAIN!!!!!~'**

#43/President George W. Bush!!!!!~'

'-*PRESIDENTS; and, the # '-NUMBER* '-**53**!!!!!~' #**43**/President George W. Bush won the '-ELECTION just after being '-AGE '-**53**!!!!!~' #43/President George W. Bush won the '-ELECTION by '-**53**% of the '-VOTE; and, #43/President George W. Bush attended '-FLIGHT '-SCHOOL for just '-**53** '-WEEKS at '-MOODY '-AIR '-FORCE '-BASE in '-GEORGIA!!!!!~' #43/President George W. Bush ranked '-**22** out of '-**53** '-STUDENTS in '-HIS '-FLIGHT '-SCHOOL '-CLASS with a '-GRADE of '-**88** on '-HIS total '-AIRMANSHIP!!!!!~'

'-**23** = **RECIPROCAL** = '-**32**

(53 (-) 22) = '-**31** = **RECIPROCAL** = '-**13** = **"A VERY PIVOTAL NUMBER"!!!!!~'**

(31 + 13) = '-**44** = **"43ʳᵈ '-PRESIDENT"!!!!!~'**

(44 x 2) = '-**88** / (88 + 44) = '-**132** = (1 x 32) = '-**32** = **-a Prophetic Number!!!!!~'**

#43/President George W. Bush's '-BIRTHDAY # '-NUMBER is '-**78**!!!!!~'

July 6ᵗʰ, 1946 / (7 + 6 + 19) = '-**32** = **-a Prophetic Number!!!!!~'**

(7 + 6 + 19 + 46) = '-**78**

#**41**/President George H. W. Bush's '-BIRTHDAY # '-NUMBER is '-**61**!!!!!~'

(#43 + #41) = '-**84** = **RECIPROCAL** = '-**48**

(84 + 48) = `-**132** = (1 x 32) = `-**32** = -a Prophetic Number!!!!!~'

(78 + 61) = `-**139** = (1 x 39) = `-**39** = <u>RECIPROCAL</u> = `-**93** = "AGE of `-DEATH of #38/President Gerald Ford; and, #40/President Ronald Reagan"!!!!!~'

`-<u>**Do**</u> `-<u>**YOU**</u> `-<u>**WANT**</u> `-<u>**MORE**</u>?????~'

<u>#43/President George W. Bush!!!!!~'</u>

`-<u>**A**</u> `-<u>**PENDULUM**</u> `-<u>**SHIFT**</u>!!!!!~' / `-(<u>UFC</u> <u>193</u>)-'"

<u>Ronda</u> <u>Rousey</u> vs. <u>Holly</u> <u>Holm</u> (<u>33,2,3</u>)-(Boxing `-RECORD) – <u>UFC 193</u> = (1 x 93) = `-**93** = <u>RECIPROCAL</u> = `-**39**

<u>Holly</u> <u>Holm</u>-(33,2,3) = (33 (-) 2 (-) 3) = `-**28** = "The `-AGE of Ronda Rousey"!!!!!~'

`-**23** = <u>RECIPROCAL</u> = -**32**

Ronda Rousey's `-FIGHTS before this `-FIGHT have balanced an `-AVERAGE of just `-**32** `-SECONDS!!!!!~'

<u>UFC</u> `-**193** = (139) = (39 (-) 1) = `-**38** = `-**3(8's)** = `-**888** = (8 x 8 x 8) = `-**512**

`-**512** / `-**32** = `-**16** = (`-2 x `-8) = `-**2(8's)** = `-2(H's) = `-**HH** = "<u>Holly</u> <u>Holm</u> would be the `-DEFEATER"!!!!!~'

<u>AMERICAN/ENGLISH</u> `-<u>**ALPHABET**</u> '-to-' `-<u>**NUMBERS**</u> #'s:!!!!!~'

<u>HH</u> = `-**8**, `-**8** / <u>RR</u> = `-**18**, `-**18**

`-**18** = <u>RECIPROCAL</u> = `-**81**

`-**818** = (8 + 1 + 8) = `-**17** x (`-2) = `-**34** = "The `-<u>**AGE**</u> of the Winner Holly Holm"!!!!!~'

`-**818** = (81 (-) 18) = `-**63** = "AGE of `-DEATH of the "PROPHET'S" MOTHER – A `-FIGHTER"!!!!!~'

(88/2) = `-**44** = "The `-YEAR that the "PROPHET'S" MOTHER was `-BORN (`-19**44**)"!!!!!~'

(Ronda Rousey-**18** x Holly Holm-**8**) = (18 x 8) = `-**144** = (1 x 44) = `-**44**...(...)...-"-'

(8 + 8) = `-**16** x (`-2) = `-**32** = -a Prophetic Number!!!!!~'

(8 x 8) = `-**64** = "AGE of `-DEATH of #36/President Lyndon B. Johnson who `-TOOK the `-OFFICE of the `-PRESIDENCY in (`-19**63**)"!!!!!~'

(18 + 18) = `-**36** = **RECIPROCAL** = `-**63**

(18 x 18) = `-**324** = `-**(32)4** = (32 x 4) = `-**128** = (1 x 28) = `-**28** = "AGE of Ronda Rousey at the `-TIME of the `-DEFEAT"!!!!!~'

`-**(32)4** = (32 (-) 4) = `-**28** = "AGE of Ronda Rousey at the `-TIME of the `-DEFEAT"!!!!!~'

Ronda Rousey is `-**CURRENTLY** (`-28) `-YEARS of `-AGE!!!!!~'

Ronda Rousey was `-**BORN** on February 1ˢᵗ in `-1987 (02/01/1987); and, `-HER `-BIRTHDAY # `-NUMBER is = (2 + 1 + 19 + 87) = `-**109**

`-**109** = (9 (-) 1 (+) 0) = `-**8** = "The `-**MONOGRAM/INSIGNIA** of HOLLY HOLM that would `-**DEFEAT** RONDA ROUSEY"!!!!!~'

Ronda Rousey's `-WEIGHT is `-**135 lbs**. = (1 x 35) = `-**35** = **RECIPROCAL** = `-**53** = "WAR of the WORLDS"!!!!!~'

Ronda Rousey's `-HEIGHT is **5' 7**" = `-**57** = **RECIPROCAL** = `-**75**

(57 + 75) = `-**132** = (1 x 32) = `-**32** = -a Prophetic Number!!!!!~'

Holly Holm is `-**CURRENTLY** (`-34) `-YEARS of `-AGE!!!!!~'

Holly Holm was `-**BORN** on October 17ᵗʰ in `-19**81** (10/17/1981); and, `-HER `-BIRTHDAY # `-NUMBER is = (10 + 17 + 19 + 81) = `-**127**

`-**127** = (1 + 27) = `-**28** = "AGE of Ronda Rousey at the `-TIME of the `-PENDULUM `-FLOW `-**DEFEAT**"!!!!!~'

Holly Holm's `-WEIGHT is `-**134 lbs**. = (1 x 34) = `-**34** = "AGE of Holly Holm at the `-TIME of the `-PENDULUM `-"**VICTORY**"-"!!!!!~'

Holly Holm's `-HEIGHT is **5' 8**" = `-**58** = **RECIPROCAL** = `-**85**

(58 + 85) = `-**143** = (1 x 43) = `-**43** = <u>RECIPROCAL</u> = `-**34** = "AGE of Holly Holm at the `-TIME of this `-PENDULUM `-"<u>VICTORY</u>"-"!!!!!~'

`-BIRTHDAY # `-NUMBER HOLLY HOLM (`-**127**) (-)MINUS(-) `-BIRTHDAY # `-NUMBER RONDA ROUSEY (`-109) = `-**18**

HOLLY HOLM was `-<u>**BORN**</u> in `-19**81** = `-**81** = <u>RECIPROCAL</u> = `-**18**

`-BIRTHDAY # `-NUMBER HOLLY HOLM (`-**127**) (+)PLUS(+) `-BIRTHDAY # `-NUMBER RONDA ROUSEY (`-109) = `-**236**

`-**236** = `-(23)6 = (23 x 6) = `-**138** = (1 + 38) = `-**39** = <u>RECIPROCAL</u> = `-**93** = "UFC `-1**93** of the HOLLY HOLM'S `-VICTORY"!!!!!~'

`-**236** = `-(23)6 = (23 (-) 6) = `-**17** x (`-2) = `-**34** = "AGE for the `-VICTORY of HOLLY HOLM'S"!!!!!~'

`-**236** = (36 (-) 2) = `-**34** = "AGE for the `-VICTORY of HOLLY HOLM'S over RONDA ROUSEY"!!!!!~'

<u>UFC</u> `-**193** (`-FIGHT `-NIGHT) was on (**11/15/2015**) = "The "PROPHET'S" MOTHER'S `-BIRTHDAY"!!!!!~'

"The "PROPHET'S" MOTHER; if, `-SHE were `-ALIVE; would have been `-**71** `-YEARS of `-AGE = (7 + 1) = `-**8** = "The `-<u>MONOGRAM/ INSIGNIA</u> of <u>H</u>OLLY <u>H</u>OLM"!!!!!~'

(Ronda Rousey-**18** + Holly Holm-**8**) = (18 + 8) = `-**26** = "The `-<u>AGE</u> of the "PROPHET'S" MOTHER for when the "PROPHET" was `-<u>BORN</u>"!!!!!~'

The `-FIGHT (UFC-193) took place `-**126** `-DAYS from the "PROPHET'S" BIRTHDAY on (03/**20**) for when the "PROPHET" will be `-**46** `-YEARS of `-AGE = `-**46** = `-**23** x `-**2** = `-**232** = <u>R</u>eciprocal-<u>S</u>equencing-<u>N</u>umerology-<u>RSN</u>!!!!!~'

`-**126** = (`-12)6 = (12 x 6) = `-**72** = <u>RECIPROCAL</u> = `-**27**

(72 (-) 27) = `-**45** = The "PROPHET" is `-<u>CURRENTLY</u> `-**45** `-YEARS of `-AGE!!!!!~'

DIFFERENCE in `-AGES = (45 (-) 34) = `-**11** = "Yin/Yang" = "Multiple of `-ELEVEN" = "The `-CYCLE of `-LIFE"!!!!!~'

DIFFERENCE in `-AGES = (45 (-) 28) = `-17 x (`-2) = `-34 = "AGE for the `-VICTORY of HOLLY HOLM'S over RONDA ROUSEY"!!!!!~'

DIFFERENCES `-ADDED = (17 + 11) = `-28 = "AGE of RONDA ROUSEY"!!!!!~'

`-AGES `-ADDED = (45 + 34) = `-79 = "AGE of `-DEATH of Mr. H. G. Wells for the "WAR of the WORLDS"-"!!!!!~'

(7 + 9) = `-16 = (`8 x `-2) = `-2(8's) = `-2(H's) = `-HH = "HOLLY HOLM the `-VICTOR"!!!!!~'

UFC `-193 = (`-19)3 = (19 x 3) = `-57 = RECIPROCAL = `-75

(75 + 57) = `-132 = (1 x 32) = `-32 = -a Prophetic Number!!!!!~'

(75 (-) 57) = `-18 = `-RR = "RONDA ROUSEY"!!!!!~'

TODAY'S `-DATE = (11/23/2015) = !!!!!~'

(11 + 23) = `-34 = "The `-AGE of HOLLY HOLM"!!!!!~'

(11 + 23 + 20) = `-54 = RECIPROCAL = `-45 = "The `-AGE of the "PROPHET"-"!!!!!~'

(11 + 23 + 20 + 15) = `-69 = `-3 x `-23 = `-323 = Reciprocal-Sequencing-Numerology-RSN!!!!!~'

TODAY'S `-DATE = (11/23/2015) (-)MINUS(-) THE `-DATE of the FIGHT `-NIGHT (UFC-193) = (11/15/2015) = `-8 = "The `-MONOGRAM/INSIGNIA of the `-VICTOR `-HOLLY `-HOLM"!!!!!~'

(11 + 15 + 20 + 15) = `-61 = RECIPROCAL = `-16

(11 + 15) = `-26 = (2 + 6) = `-8 = "The `-MONOGRAM/INSIGNIA of the `-CHAMPION `-HOLLY `-HOLM"!!!!!~'

(11 + 15 + 20) = `-46 = `-23 x `-2 = `-232 = Reciprocal-Sequencing-Numerology-RSN!!!!!~'

(61 (-) 16) = `-45 = "The `-AGE of the "PROPHET"-"!!!!!~'

(69 + 61) = `-130 = (13 + 0) = `-13 = "A VERY PIVOTAL NUMBER"!!!!!~'

`-13, `-23; &, `-32 = "A `-PARADIGM `-SHIFT within `-PENDULUM `-FLOW"!!!!!~'

(13 + 23 + 32) = `-68 = RECIPROCAL = `-86

(86 (-) 68) = `-18 = `-RR = "RONDA ROUSEY"!!!!!~'

`-A `-PENDULUM `-FLOW `-SHIFT!!!!!~' / `-(UFC 193)-'"

(FIRST LADY)…(…)…-'~'

The "PROPHET'S" MOTHER `-DIED at the tender `-AGE of `-63 `-YEARS; and, `-153 `-DAYS in `-LIVING!!!!!~ A `-TOTAL of `-23,163 `-DAYS in `-LIVING!!!!!~' The `-BOILING `-POINT, there were `-212 `-DAYS left remaining in the `-YEAR before the "PROPHET'S" MOTHER'S `-NEXT `-BIRTHDAY!!!!!~' `-LEAP `-YEAR; there were `-213 `-DAYS left remaining in the `-YEAR before the "PROPHET'S" MOTHER'S `-NEXT `-BIRTHDAY!!!!!~'

`-153 = (1 x 53) = `-53 = "WAR of the WORLDS"!!!!!~'

`-215 = (51 + 2) = `-53 = "WAR of the WORLDS"!!!!!~'

`-23,163/`-23,226 = (226 (-) 163) = `-63 = "AGE of `-DEATH of `-BOTH!!!!!~'

FIRST LADY; MARY TODD LINCOLN, `-DIED at the tender `-AGE of `-63 `-YEARS; and, `-215 `-DAYS in `-LIVING!!!!!~ A `-TOTAL of `-23,226 `-DAYS in `-LIVING!!!!!~' There were `-150 `-DAYS left remaining in the `-YEAR before the FIRST LADY'S `-NEXT `-BIRTHDAY!!!!!~' From `-HER `-DEATH `-YEAR of `-1882; plus, `-150 `-YEARS = `-EQUALS = `-2032!!!!!~' At this `-TIME, the "PROPHET" will be `-62 `-YEARS of `-AGE!!!!!~'

(FIRST LADY)…(…)…-'~'

MARY TODD LINCOLN was `-BORN on December 13th in `-1818 (12/13/1818); and, the `-BIRTHDAY # `-NUMBER is: (12 + 13 + 18 + 18) = `-61 = RECIPROCAL = `-16

(12 + 13 + 18) = `-43 = RECIPROCAL = `-34

(43 + 34) = `-_77_ / (61 + 16) = `-_77_

(77 + 77) = `-_154_ = (1 x 54) = `-_54_ = "__EARTHQUAKES__"!!!!!~'

(61 (-) 16) = `-_45_ = __RECIPROCAL__ = `-_54_

MARY TODD LINCOLN `-__DIED__ at the tender `-__AGE__ of `-_63_ = "The `-AGE of the "PROPHET'S" MOTHER'S `-DEATH at `-AGE `-_63_; `-just as well!!!!!~' Including the `-_32_nd President of the United States of America Franklin Delano Roosevelt that had also `-__DIED__ at the tender `-AGE of `-_63_; just (`-_63_) `-YEARS after the `-DEATH of the FIRST LADY MARY TODD LINCOLN; and then, from the `-PRESIDENT; `-_63_ `-YEARS to the "PROPHET'S" MOTHER'S `-DEATH!!!!!~' (63, 63, 63, 63, 63) = (`-63 x `-5) = `-_315_ = (35 x 1) = `-_35_ = __RECIPROCAL__ = `-_53_ = "WAR of the WORLDS"-"!!!!!~'

MARY TODD LINCOLN had `-DIED on July 16th in `-1882 (07/16/1882); and, the `-DEATH/DAY # `-NUMBER is: (7 + 16 + 18 + 82) = `-_123_ = __P__rophetic-__L__inear-__P__rogression-__PLP__!!!!!~'

(7 + 16) = `-_23_ = -a Prophetic Number!!!!!~'

(123 (-) 61) = `-_62_ = "AGE of the "PROPHET" in (`-_2032_)"!!!!!~'

BIRTHYEAR / DEATHYEAR = (1818/1882) = (1818 + 1882) = `-_3700_

`-_3700_ = (37 + 0 + 0) = `-_37_ = `-_3(7's)_ = (777) = (7 x 7 x 7) = `-_343_ = Reciprocal-__S__equencing-__N__umerology-__RSN__ = "The `-__PRESIDENTIAL #'s__ `-__NUMBERS__"!!!!!~'

(FIRST LADY)...(...)...-"~'

FIRST LADY; ELIZA MCCARDLE JOHNSON, `-__DIED__ at the **tender** `-__AGE__ of `-_65_ `-__YEARS__; and, `-_103_ `-__DAYS in__ `-__LIVING__!!!!!~' A `-TOTAL of `-_23,844_ `-DAYS in `-LIVING!!!!!~' There were `-_262_ `-DAYS left remaining in the `-YEAR before the FIRST LADY'S `-NEXT `-BIRTHDAY!!!!!~'

FIRST LADY; ELIZA MCCARDLE JOHNSON, `-HER `-AGE of `-DEATH = `-EQUALS the `-YEAR of `-DEATH for #16/President Abraham Lincoln (`-18_65_)"!!!!!~'

133

'-**103** = (13 + 0) = '-**13** = "A VERY PIVOTAL NUMBER"!!!!!~'

ELIZA MCCARDLE JOHNSON was '-BORN on October 4th in '-1810 (10/04/1810); and, the '-BIRTHDAY # '-NUMBER is: (10 + 4 + 18 + 10) = '-**42** = **RECIPROCAL** = '-**24**

(42 + 24) = '-**66** = "AGE of '-DEATH of '-HER '-HUSBAND #17/President Andrew Johnson"!!!!!~'

(42 (-) 24) = '-**18** / (10 + 4 + **18**) = '-**32** = -a Prophetic Number!!!!!~'

(66 + 18) = '-**84** = "PART of '-HER '-DAYS in '-LIVING"!!!!!~'

'-**84** = **RECIPROCAL** = '-**48**

(84 + 48) = '-**132** = (1 x 32) = '-**32** = -a Prophetic Number!!!!!~'

ELIZA MCCARDLE JOHNSON had '-DIED on January 15th in '-1876 (01/15/1876); and, the '-DEATH/DAY # '-NUMBER is: (1 + 15 + 18 + 76) = '-**110**

(1 + 15 + 18) = '-**34** = **RECIPROCAL** = '-**43** = "The '-**PRESIDENTIAL #'s** '-**NUMBERS**"!!!!!~'

'-**110** = (11 + 0) = '-**11** = "Yin/Yang" = "Multiple of '-ELEVEN" = "The '-CYCLE of '-LIFE"!!!!!~'

(110 + 42) = '-**152** = (52 + 1) = '-**53** = "WAR of the WORLDS"!!!!!~'

(110 (-) 42) = '-**68** = **RECIPROCAL** = '-**86** / (86 (-) 68) = '-**18**

(152 (-) 18) = '-**134** = (1 x 34) = '-**34** = **RECIPROCAL** = '-**43** = "The '-**PRESIDENTIAL #'s** '-**NUMBERS**"!!!!!~'

BIRTHYEAR / DEATHYEAR = (1810/1876) = (1810 + 1876) = '-**3686**

'-**3686** = (86 + 36) = '-**122** = (1 + 22) = '-**23** = -a Prophetic Number!!!!!~'

(FIRST LADY)...(...)...-'~'

FIRST LADY; JULIA BOGGS GRANT, '-**DIED** at the '-AGE of '-**76** '-**YEARS**; and, '-**322** '-**DAYS** in '-LIVING!!!!!~ A '-TOTAL of '-**28,080**

'-DAYS in '-LIVING!!!!!~' There were '-**43** '-DAYS left remaining in the '-YEAR before the FIRST LADY'S '-NEXT '-BIRTHDAY!!!!!~'

FIRST LADY; JULIA BOGGS GRANT, '-HER '-AGE of '-DEATH = '-EQUALS the '-YEAR of '-DEATH for FIRST LADY ELIZA MCCARDLE JOHNSON ('-18<u>76</u>)"!!!!!~'

'-**322** = (32 + 2) = '-**34** = **RECIPROCAL** = '-**43** = "The '-**PRESIDENTIAL #'s '-NUMBERS**"!!!!!~'

JULIA BOGGS GRANT was '-BORN on January 26th in '-1826 (01/26/1826); and, the '-BIRTHDAY # '-NUMBER is: (1 + 26 + 18 + 26) = '-**71** = **RECIPROCAL** = '-**17**

(1 + 26 + 18) = '-**45** = **RECIPROCAL** = '-**54** = "**EARTHQUAKES**"!!!!!~'

(71 + 17) = '-**88** / (71 (-) 17) = '-**54** = "**EARTHQUAKES**"!!!!!~'

(88 (-) 54) = '-**34** = **RECIPROCAL** = '-**43** = "The '-**PRESIDENTIAL #'s '-NUMBERS**"!!!!!~'

JULIA BOGGS GRANT had '-DIED on December 14th in '-1902 (12/14/1902); and, the '-DEATH/DAY # '-NUMBER is: (12 + 14 + 19 + 02) = '-**47** = **RECIPROCAL** = '-**74**

(12 + 14 + 19) = '-**45** = **RECIPROCAL** = '-**54** = "**EARTHQUAKES**"!!!!!~'

(74 (-) 47) = '-**27** = "The ROMAN EMPIRE"!!!!!~' / (74 + 47) = '-**121**

'-**121** = (12 (-) 1) = '-**11** = "Yin/Yang" = "Multiple of '-ELEVEN" = "The '-CYCLE of '-LIFE"!!!!!~'

(71 + 47) = '-**118** / (71 (-) 47) = '-**24** = **RECIPROCAL** = '-**42** / (42 (-) 24) = '-**18**

'-**18**/'-**118** = (118 + 18) = '-**136** = (36 x 1) = '-**36** = **RECIPROCAL** = '-**63** = "AGE of '-DEATH of '-HER '-HUSBAND #18/President Ulysses S. Grant"!!!!!~'

FIRST LADY JULIA BOGGS GRANT was '-MARRIED to '-HER '-HUSBAND #18/President Ulysses S. Grant for '-<u>37</u> '-YEARS = '-<u>3(7's)</u> = '-<u>777</u> = (7 x 7 x 7) = '-<u>343</u> = "<u>R</u>eciprocal-<u>S</u>equenced-<u>N</u>umerology-RSN" = "The '-PRESIDENTIAL #'s '-NUMBERS"!!!!!~' /|\ Just like FIRST

135

LADY LUCY WEBB HAYES; and, `-HER `-HUSBAND #19/President Rutherford B. Hayes!!!!!~'

BIRTHYEAR / DEATHYEAR = (1826/1902) = (1826 + 1902) = `-**3728**

`-**3728** = (37 + 28) = `-**65** = "The `-YEAR that #16/President Abraham Lincoln was `-ASSASSINATED (`-18**65**)"!!!!!~'

`-**1865** = (65 (-) 18) = `-**47** = "The `-DEATH/DAY # `-NUMBER of FIRST LADY JULIA BOGGS GRANT"!!!!!~'

(FIRST LADY)…(…)…-"-'

FIRST LADY; LUCY WEBB HAYES, `-DIED** at the tender `-AGE** of `-**57** `-**YEARS**; and, `-**301** `-**DAYS** in `-**LIVING**!!!!!~ A `-TOTAL of `-**21,121** `-DAYS in `-LIVING!!!!!~' There were `-**64** `-DAYS left remaining in the `-YEAR before the FIRST LADY'S `-NEXT `-BIRTHDAY!!!!!~'

`-**301** = (31 + 0) = `-**31** = **RECIPROCAL** = `-**13** = "A VERY PIVOTAL NUMBER"!!!!!~'

FIRST LADY; LUCY WEBB HAYES, `-DIED `-13 `-YEARS `-YOUNGER than `-HER `-HUSBAND #19/President Rutherford B. Hayes!!!!!~'

FIRST LADY; LUCY WEBB HAYES, `-HER `-AGE of `-DEATH = `-EQUALS the `-YEAR of `-DEATH for FIRST LADY GRACE ANNA COOLIDGE (`-1957**)"!!!!!~'**

LUCY WEBB HAYES was `-BORN on August 28th in `-1831 (0**8**/**28**/18**31**); and, the `-BIRTHDAY # `-NUMBER is: (8 + 28 + 18 + 31) = `-**85** = **RECIPROCAL** = `-**58**

(85 + 58) = `-**143** = (1 x 43) = `-**43** = **RECIPROCAL** = `-**34** = "The `-**PRESIDENTIAL #'s `-NUMBERS**"!!!!!~'

(85 (-) 58) = `-**27** = "The ROMAN EMPIRE"!!!!!~'

LUCY WEBB HAYES had `-DIED on June 25th in `-1889 (06/25/1889); and, the `-DEATH/DAY # `-NUMBER is: (6 + 25 + 18 + 89) = `-**138**

`-**138** = (38 x 1) = `-**38** = **3(8's)** = `-**888** = (8 x 8 x 8) = `-**512** = (5 (1 + 2)) = `-**53** = "WAR of the WORLDS"!!!!!~'

(138 (-) 85) = `-**53** = "WAR of the WORLDS"!!!!!~'

(138 + 85) = `-**223** = `-**23** x `-**2** = `-**232** = Reciprocal-**S**equenced-**N**umerology-**RSN**!!!!!~'

FIRST LADY LUCY WEBB HAYES was `-MARRIED to `-HER `-HUSBAND #19/President Rutherford B. Hayes for `-**37** `-YEARS = `-**3(7's)** = `-**777** = (7 x 7 x 7) = `-**343** = "Reciprocal-**S**equenced-**N**umerology-RSN" = "**The** `-**PRESIDENTIAL #'s** `-**NUMBERS**"!!!!!~' /|\ Just like FIRST LADY JULIA BOGGS GRANT; and, `-HER `-HUSBAND #18/ President Ulysses S. Grant!!!!!~'

BIRTHYEAR / DEATHYEAR = (1831/1889) = (1831 + 1889) = `-**3720**

`-**3720** = (37 + 20) = `-**57** = "The `-AGE of `-DEATH of FIRST LADY LUCY WEBB HAYES"!!!!!~'

`-**3720** = (70 (-) 32) = `-**38** = **3(8's)** = `-**888** = (8 x 8 x 8) = `-**512** = (5 (1 + 2)) = `-**53** = "WAR of the WORLDS"!!!!!~'

(FIRST LADY)...(...)...-'~'

FIRST LADY; LUCRETIA GARFIELD, `-**DIED** at the `-AGE of `-**85** `-**YEARS**; and, `-**329** `-DAYS in `-LIVING!!!!!~ A `-TOTAL of `-**31,374** `-DAYS in `-LIVING!!!!!~' There were `-**36** `-DAYS left remaining in the `-YEAR before the FIRST LADY'S `-NEXT `-BIRTHDAY!!!!!~'

FIRST LADY; LUCRETIA GARFIELD, `-LIVED `-**36** `-YEARS `-LONGER than `-HER `-HUSBAND #20/President James A. Garfield!!!!!~'

FIRST LADY; LUCRETIA GARFIELD, `-HER `-AGE of `-DEATH = `-EQUALS the `-YEAR of `-DEATH for #18/President Ulysses S. Grant (`-18**85**)"!!!!!~'

LUCRETIA GARFIELD was `-BORN on April 19th in `-1832 (04/19/1832); and, the `-BIRTHDAY # `-NUMBER is: (4 + 19 + 18 + 32) = `-**73** = **RECIPROCAL** = `-**37**

(4 + 19) = `-**23** = -a Prophetic Number!!!!!~' / `-**23** = **RECIPROCAL** = `-**32**

`-**1832** = (82 (-) 13) = `-**69** = "Yin/Yang" = "The `-CYCLE of `-LIFE"!!!!!~'

(73 (-) 37) = `-**36** = "The `-YEARS `-LIVING `-LONGER than `-HER `-HUSBAND – FIRST LADY LUCRETIA GARFIED; and, `-HER `-HUSBAND #20/PRESIDENT JAMES A. GARFIELD"!!!!!~'

(73 + 37) = `-**110** = (11 + 0) = `-**11** = "Yin/Yang" = "Multiple of `-ELEVEN" = "The `-CYCLE of `-LIFE"!!!!!~'

LUCRETIA GARFIELD had `-DIED on March 14th in `-1918 (0**3**/1**4**/1918); and, the `-DEATH/DAY # `-NUMBER is: (0**3** + 1**4** + 19 + 18) = `-**54** = **RECIPROCAL** = `-**45**

(0**3** + 1**4** + 19) = `-**36** = "The `-YEARS `-LIVING `-LONGER than `-HER `-HUSBAND – FIRST LADY LUCRETIA GARFIED; and, `-HER `-HUSBAND #20/PRESIDENT JAMES A. GARFIELD"!!!!!~'

(0**3** + 1**4** + 19 + 18) = `-**54** = "**EARTHQUAKES**"!!!!!~'

(73 + 54) = `-**127** = (27 x 1) = `-**27** = "#27/President William Howard Taft that `-DIED on the `-RECIPROCAL `-AGE of `-**72** of `-HIS `-PRESIDENCY #2**7**-"!!!!!~'

(73 + 54) = `-**127** = (27 (-) 1) = `-**26** = "#26/President Theodore Roosevelt who was `-MARRIED to `-HIS `-WIFE FIRST LADY EDITH KERMIT ROOSEVELT for a `-RECIPROCAL `-TIME of some `-**32** `-YEARS when `-COMPARED to FIRST LADY LUCRETIA GARFIELD"!!!!!~'

`-**32** = **RECIPROCAL** = `-**23**

FIRST LADY LUCRETIA GARFIELD was `-MARRIED to `-HER `-HUSBAND #20/President James A. Garfield for `-**Twenty-Three** `-**YEARS** = `-**23** = -a Prophetic Number!!!!!~'

BIRTHYEAR / DEATHYEAR = (1832/1918) = (1832 + 1918) = `-**3750**

`-**3750** = (70 (-) 35) = `-**35** = <u>RECIPROCAL</u> = `-**53** = "WAR of the WORLDS"!!!!!~'

(FIRST LADY)...(...)...-`~'

FIRST LADY; EDITH KERMIT ROOSEVELT, `-<u>DIED</u> at the `-AGE of `-87 `-YEARS; and, `-**55** `-**DAYS in** `-**LIVING**!!!!!~ A `-TOTAL of `-**31,831** `-DAYS in `-LIVING!!!!!~' There were `-**310** `-DAYS left remaining in the `-YEAR before the FIRST LADY'S `-NEXT `-BIRTHDAY!!!!!~'

`-**301** = (31 + 0) = `-**31** = <u>RECIPROCAL</u> = `-**13** = "A VERY PIVOTAL NUMBER"!!!!!~'

EDITH KERMIT ROOSEVELT was `-BORN on August 6<sup>th</sup> in `-1861 (08/06/1861); and, the `-BIRTHDAY # `-NUMBER is: (8 + 6 + 18 + 61) = `-**93** = <u>RECIPROCAL</u> = `-**39**

(8 + 6 + 18) = `-**32** = -a Prophetic Number!!!!!~'

(93 + 39) = `-**132** = (1 x 32) = `-**32** = -a Prophetic Number!!!!!~'

(93 (-) 39) = `-**54** = "<u>EARTHQUAKES</u>"!!!!!~'

EDITH KERMIT ROOSEVELT had `-DIED on September 30<sup>th</sup> in `-1948 (09/30/1948); and, the `-DEATH/DAY # `-NUMBER is: (09 + 30 + 19 + 48) = `-**106**

(9 + 30) = `-**39** = <u>RECIPROCAL</u> = `-**93** = "FIRST LADY EDITH KERMIT ROOSEVELT'S `-BIRTHDAY # `-NUMBER"!!!!!~'

(106 (-) 93) = `-**13** = "A VERY PIVOTAL NUMBER"!!!!!~'

`-**13** x `-**2** = "#26 `-HER `-HUSBAND #26/President Theodore Roosevelt"!!!!!~'

FIRST LADY EDITH KERMIT ROOSEVELT was `-MARRIED to `-HER `-HUSBAND #26/President Theodore Roosevelt for `-<u>Thirty-Two</u> `-YEARS** = `-32** = -a Prophetic Number!!!!!~'

BIRTHYEAR / DEATHYEAR = (1861/1948) = (1861 + 1948) = `-**3809**

139

`-**3809** = (38 (-) 09) = `-**29** = "FIRST LADY EDITH KERMIT ROOSEVELT `-LIVED `-**29** `-YEARS `-LONGER than `-HER `-HUSBAND #26/President Theodore Roosevelt"!!!!!~'

(FIRST LADY)…(…)…-"~'

FIRST LADY; HELEN LOUISE TAFT, `-**DIED** at the `-AGE of `-**81** `-**YEARS**; and, `-**354** `-DAYS in `-LIVING!!!!!~ A `-TOTAL of `-**29,938** `-DAYS in `-LIVING!!!!!~' There were `-**11** `-DAYS left remaining in the `-YEAR before the FIRST LADY'S `-NEXT `-BIRTHDAY!!!!!~'

`-**11** = "Yin/Yang" = "Multiple of `-ELEVEN" = "The `-CYCLE of `-LIFE"!!!!!~'

FIRST LADY; HELEN LOUISE TAFT, `-DIED `-**13** `-YEARS after the `-DEATH of `-HER `-HUSBAND #27/President William Howard Taft!!!!!~'

HELEN LOUISE TAFT was `-BORN on June 2nd in `-1861 (06/02/1861); and, the `-BIRTHDAY # `-NUMBER is: (6 + 2 + 18 + 61) = `-**87** = **RECIPROCAL** = `-**78**

(87 + 78) = `-**165** = (1 x 65) = `-**65** = **RECIPROCAL** = `-**56** = "The `-AGE; and, `-YEAR of `-DEATH of #16/President Abraham Lincoln `-LIKENED to `-HER `-HUSBAND'S `-RECIPROCALS in `-TIME of `-DEATH"!!!!!~' #29/President Warren G. Harding was `-BORN `-165 `-DAYS away in `-REVERSE from the `-ASSASSINATION of #16/President Abraham Lincoln with `-HIS `-DEATH being `-TWICE `-HIS `-PRESIDENCIAL # `-NUMBER in (`-19**23**)!!!!!~' #16/President Abraham Lincoln was `-MARRIED to `-HIS `-WIFE FIRST LADY MARY TODD LINCOLN for some `-23 `-YEARS; until, `-HIS `-ASSASSINATION"!!!!!~'

HELEN LOUISE TAFT had `-DIED on May 22nd in `-19**43** (05/22/19**43**); and, the `-DEATH/DAY # `-NUMBER is: (5 + 22 + 19 + **43**) = `-**89** = **RECIPROCAL** = `-**98**

(5 + 22) = `-**27** = "`-HER `-HUSBAND #27/President William Howard Taft"!!!!!~'

(5 + 22 + 19) = `-**46** = `-**23** x `-**2** = `-**232** = Reciprocal-**S**equencing-**N**umerology-**RSN**!!!!!~'

(89 + 98) = `-**187** = (1 x 87) = `-**87** = "AGE of `-DEATH of FIRST LADY EDITH KERMIT ROOSEVELT"!!!!!~'

(89 + 87) = `-**176** = (1 x 76) = `-**76** = **RECIPROCAL** = `-**67** = "The `-YEAR that the "PROPHET'S" BROTHER was `-BORN, the `-AVERAGE `-AGE of the United States Presidents 1 to 28 in "SUCCESSION" above; and, below `-ALL `-PRESIDENTS that `-DIED at `-AGES `-66, `-67; and, `-68; and, The `-AGE of `-DEATH of the #1/President of the United States of America #1/President George Washington"!!!!!~'

FIRST LADY HELEN LOUISE TAFT was `-MARRIED to `-HER `-HUSBAND #27/President William Howard Taft for `-**44** `-**YEARS**"!!!!!~' #1/President George Washington was `-**44** `-YEARS of `-AGE in the `-CALENDAR `-YEAR of (`-17**76**)!!!!~'

BIRTHYEAR / DEATHYEAR = (1861/1943) = (1861 + 1943) = `-**3804**

`-**3804** = (38 (-) 04) = `-**34** = **RECIPROCAL** = `-**43** = "The `-PRESIDENTIAL **#'s** `-**NUMBERS**"!!!!!~'

(FIRST LADY)...(...)...-"-'

FIRST LADY; FLORENCE HARDING, `-**DIED** at the tender `-**AGE** of `-**64** `-**YEARS**; and, `-**98** `-**DAYS** in `-**LIVING**!!!!!~ A `-TOTAL of `-**23,473** `-DAYS in `-LIVING!!!!!~' There were `-**267** `-DAYS left remaining in the `-YEAR before the FIRST LADY'S `-NEXT `-BIRTHDAY!!!!!~'

`-**267** = `-2(67) = (2 x 67) = `-**134** = (1 x 34) = `-**34** = **RECIPROCAL** = `-**43** = "The `-**PRESIDENTIAL #'s** `-**NUMBERS**"!!!!!~'

FLORENCE HARDING was `-BORN on August 15th in `-1860 (08/15/1860); and, the `-BIRTHDAY # `-NUMBER is: (8 + 15 + 18 + 60) = `-**101**

(8 + 15) = `-**23** = -a Prophetic Number!!!!!~'

`-**101** = (11 + 0) = `-**11** = "Yin/Yang" = "Multiple of `-ELEVEN" = "The `-CYCLE of `-LIFE"!!!!!~'

FLORENCE HARDING had `-DIED on November 21ˢᵗ in `-1924 (11/21/1924); and, the `-DEATH/DAY # `-NUMBER is: (11 + 21 + 19 + 24) = `-**75** = **RECIPROCAL** = `-**57**

(11 + 21) = `-**32** = -a Prophetic Number!!!!!~'

(75 + 57) = `-**132** = (1 x 32) = `-**32** = -a Prophetic Number!!!!!~'

(101 (-) 75) = `-**26** = `-**13** x `-**2** = `-**132** = (1 x 32) = `-**32** = -a Prophetic Number!!!!!~'

(101 + 75) = `-**176** = (1 x 76) = `-**76** = **RECIPROCAL** = `-**67** = "The `-YEAR that the "PROPHET'S" BROTHER was `-BORN, the `-AVERAGE `-AGE of the United States Presidents 1 to 28 in "SUCCESSION" above; and, below `-ALL `-PRESIDENTS that `-DIED at `-AGES `-66, `-67; and, `-68; and, The `-AGE of `-DEATH of the #1/President of the United States of America #1/President George Washington"!!!!!~'

BIRTHYEAR / DEATHYEAR = (1860/1924) = (1860 + 1924) = `-**3784**

`-**3784** = (78 (-) 34) = `-**44** = "The `-YEAR that the "PROPHET'S" MOTHER was `-BORN in (`-19**44**)"!!!!!~'

`-**3784** = (78 (-) 43) = `-**35** = **RECIPROCAL** = `-**53** = "WAR of the WORLDS"!!!!!~'

(FIRST LADY)...(...)...-"~'

FIRST LADY; GRACE ANNA COOLIDGE, `-**DIED** at the `-AGE of `-**78** `-**YEARS**; and, `-**186** `-DAYS in `-LIVING!!!!!~ A `-TOTAL of `-**28,675** `-DAYS in `-LIVING!!!!!~' There were `-**179** `-DAYS left remaining in the `-YEAR before the FIRST LADY'S `-NEXT `-BIRTHDAY!!!!!~'

`-**179** = (79 (-) 1) = `-**78** = "AGE of `-DEATH of FIRST LADY GRACE ANNA COOLIDGE"!!!!!~'

`-**179** = (79 x 1) = `-**79** = "The `-YEAR FIRST LADY GRACE ANNA COOLIDGE was `-BORN (`-18**79**)"!!!!!~'

FIRST LADY; LOU HENRY HOOVER, was the `-**RECIPROCAL** `-**BETWEEN FIRST LADYS GRACE ANNA COOLIDGE; and,**

ELEANOR ROOSEVELT; as `-THESE `-TWO FIRST LADYS; Respectively, `-BOTH `-DIED; at the `-AGE of `-78!!!!!~'

GRACE ANNA COOLIDGE was `-BORN on January 3rd in `-1879 (01/03/1879); and, the `-BIRTHDAY # `-NUMBER is: (1 + 3 + 18 + 79) = `-101

`-101 = (11 + 0) = `-11 = "Yin/Yang" = "Multiple of `-ELEVEN" = "The `-CYCLE of `-LIFE"!!!!!~'

GRACE ANNA COOLIDGE had `-DIED on July 8th in `-1957 (07/08/1957); and, the `-DEATH/DAY # `-NUMBER is: (7 + 8 + 19 + 57) = `-91 = RECIPROCAL = `-19

(7 + 8 + 19) = `-34 = RECIPROCAL = `-43 = "The `-PRESIDENTIAL #'s `-NUMBERS"!!!!!~'

(91 (-) 19) = `-72 = "AGE of `-DEATH of #27/President William Howard Taft"!!!!!~'

(91 + 19) = `-110 = (11 + 0) = `-11 = "Yin/Yang" = "Multiple of `-ELEVEN" = "The `-CYCLE of `-LIFE"!!!!!~'

(101 + 91) = `-192 = (19 x 2) = `-38 = `-3(8's) = `-888 = (8 x 8 x 8) = `-512 = (5 (1 + 2)) = `-53 = "WAR of the WORLDS"!!!!!~'

(101 (-) 91) = `-10 = "EARTHLY COMPLETENESS"!!!!!~'

GRACE ANNA COOLIDGE was `-44 `-YEARS of `-AGE at the `-TIME of `-BECOMING FIRST LADY!!!!!~'

BIRTHYEAR / DEATHYEAR = (1879/1957) = (1879 + 1957) = `-3836

`-3836 = (38 (-) 36) = `-74 = RECIPROCAL = `-47 = "The `-DEATH/DAY; and, `-BIRTHDAY #'s of the FIRST LADYS"!!!!!~'

`-3836 = (86 (-) 33) = `-53 = "WAR of the WORLDS"!!!!!~'

`-3836 = (83 (-) 36) = `-47 = RECIPROCAL = `-74 = "The `-DEATH/DAY; and, `-BIRTHDAY #'s of the FIRST LADYS"!!!!!~'

(FIRST LADY)…(…)…'-'

FIRST LADY; LOU HENRY HOOVER, `-<u>DIED</u>** at the tender `-AGE** of `-**69** `-<u>**YEARS**</u>; and, `-**284** `-**DAYS in** `-**LIVING!!!!!**~ A `-TOTAL of `-**<u>25,485</u>** `-**DAYS in** `-**LIVING!!!!!**~' There were `-**<u>81</u>** `-**DAYS** left remaining in the `-YEAR before the FIRST LADY'S `-**NEXT** `-**BIRTHDAY!!!!!**~'

`-**<u>69</u>** = "Yin/Yang" = "The `-**CYCLE** of `-**LIFE**"!!!!!~'

FIRST LADY; LOU HENRY HOOVER, was the `-<u>RECIPROCAL</u> `-BETWEEN FIRST LADYS GRACE ANNA COOLIDGE; and, ELEANOR ROOSEVELT; as `-THESE `-TWO FIRST LADYS; Respectively, `-BOTH `-DIED; at the `-AGE of `-<u>78</u>!!!!!~'

LOU HENRY HOOVER was `-BORN on March 29[th] in `-1874 (03/29/1874); and, the `-BIRTHDAY # `-NUMBER is: (3 + 29 + 18 + 74) = `-**<u>124</u>**

(3 + 29) = `-**<u>32</u>** = -a **Prophetic Number!!!!!**~' / `-**<u>32</u>** = **<u>RECIPROCAL</u>** = `-**<u>23</u>**

`-**<u>124</u>** = (24 (-) 1) = `-**<u>23</u>** = -a **Prophetic Number!!!!!**~'

LOU HENRY HOOVER had `-DIED on January 7[th] in `-1944 (01/07/1944); and, the `-DEATH/DAY # `-NUMBER is: (1 + 7 + 19 + 44) = `-**<u>71</u>** = **<u>RECIPROCAL</u>** = `-**<u>17</u>**

(71 + 17) = `-**<u>88</u>** = `-**<u>HH</u>** = MONOGRAM/INSIGNIA for `-HER `-HUSBAND #31/President <u>H</u>erbert <u>H</u>oover"!!!!!~'

(71 + 17) = `-**<u>88</u>** / (`-2) = `-**<u>44</u>** = "The `-YEAR that the "PROPHET'S" MOTHER was `-BORN in (`-19<u>44</u>)"!!!!!~'

FIRST LADY LOU HENRY HOOVER had `-<u>**DIED**</u> `-**312** `-**DAYS before** the `-**BIRTH of the "PROPHET'S" MOTHER**"!!!!!~'

`-**<u>312</u>** = (32 x 1) = `-**<u>32</u>** = -a **Prophetic Number!!!!!**~'

At the `-TIME of this `-WRITING; if, the "PROPHET'S" MOTHER were `-ALIVE; the "PROPHET'S" MOTHER would, just have had; `-HER `-<u>71</u>[st] `-BIRTHDAY on (<u>11/15/2015</u>)!!!!!~'

(71 (-) 17) = `-**<u>54</u>** = **<u>RECIPROCAL</u>** = `-**<u>45</u>** = "The `-AMOUNT of `-YEARS that the FIRST LADY LOU HENRY HOOVER was `-MARRIED to `-HER `-HUSBAND #31/President <u>H</u>erbert <u>H</u>oover"!!!!!~'

(71 (-) 17) = `-**54** = "The `-AGE of FIRST LADY LOU HENRY HOOVER at the `-TIME of `-HER `-BECOMING A FIRST LADY!!!!!~'

(124 (-) 71) = `-**53** = "WAR of the WORLDS"!!!!!~'

BIRTHYEAR / DEATHYEAR = (1874/1944) = (1874 + 1944) = `-**3818**

`-**3818** = (38 (-) 18) = `-**20** = "The `-DAY of `-BIRTH for the "PROPHET" (`-03/20)-"!!!!!~'

`-**3818** = (38 (-) 18) = `-**56** = "AGE of `-DEATH of the #16/President Abraham Lincoln"!!!!!~'

`-**3818** = (81 (-) 38) = `-**43** = RECIPROCAL = `-**34** = "The `-PRESIDENTIAL #'s `-NUMBERS"!!!!!~'

`-**3818** = (81 + 83) = `-**164** = (64 + 1) = `-**65** = "YEAR of `-DEATH of the #16/President Abraham Lincoln (`-18**65**)"!!!!!~'

(FIRST LADY)…(…)…-'~'

FIRST LADY; ELEANOR ROOSEVELT, `-DIED at the `-AGE of `-**78** `-**YEARS**; and, `-**27** `-DAYS in `-LIVING!!!!!~ A `-TOTAL of `-**28,515** `-DAYS in `-LIVING!!!!!~' There were `-**338** `-DAYS left remaining in the `-YEAR before the FIRST LADY'S `-NEXT `-BIRTHDAY!!!!!~'

FIRST LADY; LOU HENRY HOOVER, was the `-RECIPROCAL `-BETWEEN FIRST LADYS GRACE ANNA COOLIDGE; and, ELEANOR ROOSEVELT; as `-THESE `-TWO FIRST LADYS; Respectively, `-BOTH `-DIED; at the `-AGE of `-**78**!!!!!~'

ELEANOR ROOSEVELT was `-BORN on October 11th in `-1884 (10/11/1884); and, the `-BIRTHDAY # `-NUMBER is: (10 + 11 + 18 + 84) = `-**123**

(10 + 11 + 18) = `-**39** = RECIPROCAL = `-**93**

(93 + 39) = `-**132** = (1 x 32) = `-**32** = -a Prophetic Number!!!!!~'

`-**32** = RECIPROCAL = `-**23** / `-**123** = (23 x 1) = `-**23** = -a Prophetic Number!!!!!~'

145

ELEANOR ROOSEVELT had `-DIED on November 7ᵗʰ in `-1962 (11/07/1962); and, the `-DEATH/DAY # `-NUMBER is: (11 + 7 + 19 + 62) = `-**99** = **RECIPROCAL** = `-**66**

(99/66) = (96) = `-**96** = **RECIPROCAL** = `-**69** = "Yin/Yang" = "The `-CYCLE of `-LIFE"!!!!!~'

FIRST LADY ELEANOR ROOSEVELT had `-**DIED** at the `-**AGE** of `-**78**; the `-**RECIPROCAL** `-**AGE** of FIRST LADY EDITH KERMIT ROOSEVELT who was standing at the `-AGE of `-**87** at the `-**TIME of** `-**HER** `-**DEATH!!!!!~'**

`-**87** = **RECIPROCAL** = `-**78**

(78 + 87) = `-**165** = (65 x 1) = `-**65** = "YEAR of `-DEATH of the #16/ President Abraham Lincoln (`-18**65**)"!!!!!~'

(123 + 99) = `-**222** = (2 x 22) = `-**44** = "The `-YEAR that the "PROPHET'S" MOTHER was `-BORN in (`-19**44**)!!!!!~'

BIRTHYEAR / DEATHYEAR = (1884/1962) = (1884 + 1962) = `-**3846**

`-**3846** = (68 (-) 34) = `-**34** = **RECIPROCAL** = `-**43** = "The `-**PRESIDENTIAL** #'s `-**NUMBERS**"!!!!!~'

(FIRST LADY)…(…)…-''~'

FIRST LADY; ELIZABETH VIRGINIA "BESS" TRUMAN, `-DIED** at the `-AGE** of `-**97** `-**YEARS**; and, `-**247** `-**DAYS in** `-**LIVING!!!!!~** A `-**TOTAL of** `-**35,675** `-DAYS in `-LIVING!!!!!~' There were `-**118** `-DAYS left remaining in the `-YEAR before the FIRST LADY'S `-NEXT `-BIRTHDAY!!!!!~'

FIRST LADY; ELIZABETH VIRGINIA "BESS" TRUMAN'S HUSBAND #33/President Harry S. Truman, `-DIED** at the `-AGE of `-**88** `-YEARS; and, `-**232** `-DAYS in `-LIVING!!!!!~' A `-TOTAL of `-**32,373** `-DAYS in `-LIVING!!!!!~' There were `-133** `-DAYS left remaining in the `-YEAR before the PRESIDENT'S `-NEXT `-BIRTHDAY!!!!!~'

ELIZABETH VIRGINIA "BESS" TRUMAN was `-BORN on February 13th in `-1885 (02/13/1885); and, the `-BIRTHDAY # `-NUMBER is: (2 + 13 + 18 + 85) = `-**118**

FIRST LADY ELIZABETH VIRGINIA "BESS" TRUMAN'S `-BIRTHDAY # `-NUMBER (`-**118**) = `-EQUALS the `-AMOUNT of `-DAYS `-LEFT in the `-YEAR after `-HER `-DEATH before the FIRST LADY'S `-NEXT `-BIRTHDAY!!!!!~'

ELIZABETH VIRGINIA "BESS" TRUMAN had `-DIED on October 18th in `-1982 (10/18/1982); and, the `-DEATH/DAY # `-NUMBER is: (10 + 18 + 19 + 82) = `-**129**

(129 (-) 118) = `-**11** = "Yin/Yang" = "Multiple of `-ELEVEN" = "The `-CYCLE of `-LIFE"!!!!!~'

(129 + 118) = `-**247** = `-2(47) = (2 x 47) = `-**94** = "AGE of `-DEATH of FIRST LADY LADY BIRD JOHNSON"!!!!!~'

(129 + 118) = `-**247** = "EMPHATIC `-WITNESS to the `-DEATH/DAY; and, `-BIRTHDAY #'s of the FIRST LADYS"!!!!!~'

(29 + 18) = `-**47** = **RECIPROCAL** = `-**74** = "The `-DEATH/DAY; and, `-BIRTHDAY #'s of the FIRST LADYS"!!!!!~'

BIRTHYEAR / DEATHYEAR = (1885/1982) = (1885 + 1982) = `-**3867**

`-**3867** = (67 (-) 38) = `-**29** = "The `-DEATH/DAY # `-NUMBER of FIRST LADY ELIZABETH VIRGINIA "BESS" TRUMAN"!!!!!~'

`-**3867** = (86 (-) 37) = `-**49** = **RECIPROCAL** = `-**94** = "AGE of `-DEATH of the FIRST LADY LADY BIRD JOHNSON"!!!!!~'"!!!!!~'

`-**3867** = (86 + 37) = `-**123** = "**P**rophetic-**L**inear-**P**rogression-**PLP**"!!!!!~'

(FIRST LADY)...(...)...`-'

FIRST LADY; MAMIE GENEVA DOUD EISENHOWER, `-**DIED** at the `-**AGE** of `-**82** `-**YEARS**; and, `-**352** `-**DAYS in `-LIVING**!!!!!~ A `-TOTAL of `-**30,301** `-DAYS in `-LIVING!!!!!~' There were `-**13** `-DAYS left remaining in the `-YEAR before the FIRST LADY'S `-NEXT `-BIRTHDAY!!!!!~'

The FIRST LADY MAMIE GENEVA DOUD EISENHOWER was `-BORN in the `-SAME `-MONTH; and, `-DIED in the `-SAME `-MONTH of `-NOVEMBER!!!!!~'

MAMIE GENEVA DOUD EISENHOWER was `-BORN on November 14th in `-1896 (11/14/1896); and, the `-BIRTHDAY # `-NUMBER is: (11 + 14 + 18 + 96) = `-**139**

(11 + 14 + 18) = `-**43** = **RECIPROCAL** = `-**34** = "**The** `-**PRESIDENTIAL #'s** `-**NUMBERS**"!!!!!~'

`-139 = (1 x 39) = `-**39** = **RECIPROCAL** = `-**93** = (93 + 39) = `-**132** = (1 x 32) = `-**32** = **-a Prophetic Number!!!!!~'**

`-**32** = **RECIPROCAL** = `-**23** / (96 (-) **43** = `-**53** = "**WAR of the WORLDS**"!!!!!~'

MAMIE GENEVA DOUD EISENHOWER was `-MARRIED to `-HER `-HUSBAND #**34**/President Dwight D. Eisenhower for `-**53** `-**YEARS** = **"WAR of the WORLDS"!!!!!~'**

MAMIE GENEVA DOUD EISENHOWER had `-DIED on November 1st in `-1979 (11/01/1979); and, the `-DEATH/DAY # `-NUMBER is: (11 + 1 + 19 + 79) = `-**110**

(11 + 1 + 19) = `-**31** = **RECIPROCAL** = `-**13** = "A VERY PIVOTAL NUMBER"!!!!!~'

`-**110** = (11 + 0) = `-**11** = "Yin/Yang" = "Multiple of `-ELEVEN" = "The `-CYCLE of `-LIFE"!!!!!~'

(139 (-) 110) = `-29 = "The `-DEATH/DAY # `-NUMBER of FIRST LADY ELIZABETH VIRGINIA "BESS" TRUMAN"!!!!!~'

MAMIE GENEVA DOUD EISENHOWER had `-**DIED** in the `-**YEAR** of `-**79**; **the `-RECIPROCAL `-NUMBER to the `-AGE** of FIRST LADY ELIZABETH VIRGINIA "BESS" TRUMAN who was standing at the `-AGE of `-**97** at the `-**TIME of `-HER `-DEATH!!!!!~' FIRST LADY GRACE ANNA COOLIDGE was `-ALSO `-BORN in the # `-NUMBER of `-79 -/- in (`-18**79**)"!!!!!~'**

`-**79** = **RECIPROCAL** = `-**97**

(79 + 97) = `-**176** = (1 x 76) = `-**76** = **RECIPROCAL** = `-**67** = "The `-YEAR that the "PROPHET'S" BROTHER was `-BORN, the `-AVERAGE `-AGE of the United States Presidents 1 to 28 in "SUCCESSION" above; and, below `-ALL `-PRESIDENTS that `-DIED at `-AGES `-66, `-67; and, `-68; and, The `-AGE of `-DEATH of the #1/President of the United States of America #1/President George Washington"!!!!!~'

BIRTHYEAR / DEATHYEAR = (1896/1979) = (1896 + 1979) = `-**3875**

`-**3875** = (75 (-) 38) = `-**37** = `-**3(7's)** = (777) = (7 x 7 x 7) = `-**343** = **R**eciprocal-**S**equencing-**N**umerology-**RSN** = "The `-**PRESIDENTIAL #'s** `-**NUMBERS**"!!!!!~'

(FIRST LADY)…(…)…-"-'

FIRST LADY; JACQUELINE KENNEDY, `-**DIED** at the `-AGE of `-**64** `-**YEARS**; and, `-**295** `-**DAYS in** `-**LIVING**!!!!!~ A `-TOTAL of `-**23,671** `-DAYS in `-LIVING!!!!!~' There were `-**70** `-DAYS left remaining in the `-YEAR before the FIRST LADY'S `-NEXT `-BIRTHDAY!!!!!~'

FIRST LADY; JACQUELINE KENNEDY'S `-DAYS remaining in the `-YEAR before the FIRST LADY'S `-NEXT `-BIRTHDAY (`-**70**) = `-EQUALS `-HER `-HUSBAND'S #35/President John F. Kennedy's `-BIRTHDAY # `-NUMBER of (`-**70**)!!!!!~'

PRESIDENT JOHN F. KENNEDY was `-BORN on MAY 29th in `-1917 (05/29/1917)!!!!!~'

(05 + 29) = `-**34** = "AGE of FIRST LADY JACQUELINE KENNEDY for when `-HER `-HUSBAND PRESIDENT #35/President John F. Kennedy was `-ASSASSINATED"!!!!!~'

(05 + 29 + 19) = `-**53** = "WAR of the WORLDS"!!!!!~'

(05 + 29 + 19 + 17) = `-**70** = "The `-YEAR of the `-BIRTH of the "PROPHET" (`-19**70**)"!!!!!~'

JACQUELINE KENNEDY was `-BORN on July 28th in `-1929 (07/28/1929); and, the `-BIRTHDAY # `-NUMBER is: (7 + 28 + 19 + 29) = `-**83** = **RECIPROCAL** = `-**38**

(7 + 28) = `-**35** = **RECIPROCAL** = `-**53** = **"WAR of the WORLDS"!!!!!~'**

(7 + 28 + 19) = `-**54** = **"EARTHQUAKES"!!!!!~'** / `-**54** = **RECIPROCAL** = `-**45**

(83 (-) 38) = `-**45** = **"CURRENT `-AGE of the "PROPHET"-"!!!!!~'**

`-**83** = **RECIPROCAL** = `-**38** = **3(8's)** = `-**888** = (8 x 8 x 8) = `-**512** = (5 (1 + 2)) = `-**53** = **"WAR of the WORLDS"!!!!!~'**

`-**1929** = (929 x 1) = `-**929** = **Reciprocal-Sequenced-Numerology-RSN** = (92 (-) 9) = `-**83** = **"FIRST LADY JACQUELINE KENNEDY'S `-BIRTHDAY # `-NUMBER!!!!!~'**

JACQUELINE KENNEDY was `-MARRIED to `-HER `-HUSBAND #**35**/President John F. Kennedy from `-19**53** to `-19**63**"!!!!!~' The `-**35**th `-PRESIDENT of the United States of America was `-MARRIED in `-19**53** = **"WAR of the WORLDS"!!!!!~'**

FIRST LADY JACQUELINE KENNEDY was `-MARRIED to `-HER `-HUSBAND #35/President John F. Kennedy for `-**10** YEARS!!!!~' The FIRST LADY `-DIED `-**10** `-DAYS before the `-NEXT `-BIRTHDAY of `-HER `-HUSBAND PRESIDENT JOHN F. KENNEDY!!!!!~' The PRESIDENTIAL `-COUPLE have the `-RECIPROCAL on their MONTHS of `-BIRTH; and, `-DEATH; being `-BOTH, in the `-MONTH of `-MAY!!!!!~' The `-BIRTHDAY of PRESIDENT JOHN F. KENNEDY (The `-**29**th) is the `-BIRTHYEAR (The `-**29**th) of the FIRST LADY JACQUELINE KENNEDY!!!!!~' PRESIDENT KENNEDY `-DIED at the tender `-AGE of `-**46**; while, the FIRST LADY JACQUELINE KENNEDY `-DIED on the `-RECIPROCAL `-AGE of `-**64** being SIXTY-FOUR `-YEARS of `-AGE at `-TIME of `-DEATH!!!!!~' FIRST LADY JACQUELINE KENNEDY `-DIED at the `-EXACT `-AGE of (`-**64**) as did #36/President Lyndon B. Johnson (`-**64**)!!!!!~' FIRST LADY JACQUELINE KENNEDY `-DIED in the `-YEAR (`-19**94**) of the very same `-AGE of `-DEATH of FIRST LADY LADY BIRD JOHNSON (`-**94**)!!!!!~'

FIRST LADY JACQUELINE KENNEDY was `-**34** `-YEARS of `-AGE for when `-**HER** `-**HUSBAND** #35/President John F. Kennedy **was** `-**ASSASSINATED**"!!!!!~'

JACQUELINE KENNEDY had `-DIED on May 19th in `-1994 (05/19/1994); and, the `-DEATH/DAY # `-NUMBER is: (5 + 19 + 19 + 94) = `-**137**

(5 + 19 + 19) = `-**43** = **RECIPROCAL** = `-**34** = "The `-**PRESIDENTIAL #'s `-NUMBERS**"!!!!!~'

(137 (-) 83) = `-**54** = "**EARTHQUAKES**"!!!!!~'

(137 + 83) = `-**220** = (22 + 0) = `-**22** = **"Yin/Yang"** = **"Multiple of `-ELEVEN"** = **"The `-CYCLE of `-LIFE"**!!!!!~'

BIRTHYEAR / DEATHYEAR = (1929/1994) = (1929 + 1994) = `-**3923**

`-**3923** = (93 (-) 23) = `-**70** = **"The `-DAYS `-REMAINING in the `-YEAR after the `-DEATH of FIRST LADY JACQUELINE KENNEDY until `-HER `-NEXT `-BIRTHDAY, the `-BIRTHYEAR of the "PROPHET"; and, the `-BIRTHDAY #'s `-NUMBERS of the "PROPHET'S" FATHER; and, of the #35/PRESIDENT JOHN F. KENNEDY"**!!!!!~'

(FIRST LADY)…(…)…-"~'

FIRST LADY; LADY BIRD JOHNSON, `-DIED at the `-AGE of `-94 `-YEARS; and, `-**201 `-DAYS in `-LIVING**!!!!!~ A `-TOTAL of `-**34,534** `-**DAYS in `-LIVING**!!!!!~' There were `-**164** `-DAYS left remaining in the `-YEAR before the FIRST LADY'S `-NEXT `-BIRTHDAY!!!!!~'

`-**164** = (1 x 64) = `-**64** = **"AGE of `-DEATH of `-HER `-HUSBAND #36/ President Lyndon B. Johnson"**!!!!!~'

`-**34,53**4 = `-**34** = **RECIPROCAL** = `-**43** = **"The `-PRESIDENTIAL #'s `-NUMBERS; and, The "WAR of the WORLDS"-"**!!!!!~'

LADY BIRD JOHNSON `-MARRIED `-HER `-HUSBAND PRESIDENT LYNDON B. JOHNSON in `-1934; and, `-LIVED for `-34 `-YEARS `-BEYOND the `-DEATH; of `-HER `-HUSBAND #36/President Lyndon B. Johnson**!!!!!~' FIRST LADY JACQUELINE LEE KENNEDY was `-34** `-YEARS of `-AGE for when `-HER `-HUSBAND #35/President John F. Kennedy was `-ASSASSINATED; and, when FIRST LADY LADY BIRD JOHNSON'S `-HUSBAND #36/President Lyndon B. Johnson took over the `-PRESIDENCY in (`-1963)!!!!!~'

151

LADY BIRD JOHNSON was `-BORN on December 22^{nd} in `-1912 (12/22/1912); and, the `-BIRTHDAY # `-NUMBER is: (12 + 22 + 19 + 12) = `-**65** = **RECIPROCAL** = `-**56**

(12 + 22) = `-**34** = **RECIPROCAL** = `-**43** = "The `-**PRESIDENTIAL #'s** `-**NUMBERS**"!!!!!~'

(12 + 22 + 19) = `-**53** = "**WAR of the WORLDS**"!!!!!~'

`-**65** = **RECIPROCAL** = `-**56** = "The `-AGE; and, `-YEAR of `-DEATH of #16/President Abraham Lincoln!!!!!~' Both PRESIDENT ABRAHAM LINCOLN; and, `-HER `-HUSBAND PRESIDENT LYNDON B. JOHNSON were the `-TALLEST `-PRESIDENTS `-EVER at the `-HEIGHT of **6' 4**"!!!!!~' HER `-HUSBAND PRESIDENT LYNDON B. JOHNSON was `-BORN in `-1**908**; while, PRESIDENT ABRAHAM LINCOLN was `-BORN on the `-**RECIPROCAL `-YEAR** of `-1**809**!!!!!~'

(908 + 809) = `-**1717** = (17 + 17) = `-**34** = "**FIRST LADY LADY BIRD JOHNSON; and, PRESIDENT LYNDON B. JOHNSON**"!!!!!~'

LADY BIRD JOHNSON had `-DIED on July 11^{th} in `-2007 (07/11/2007); and, the `-DEATH/DAY # `-NUMBER is: (7 + 11 + 20 + 07) = `-**45** = **RECIPROCAL** = `-**54**

(7 + 11 + 20) = `-**38** = **3(8's)** = `-**888** = (8 x 8 x 8) = `-**512** = (5 (1 + 2)) = `-**53** = "**WAR of the WORLDS**"!!!!!~'

LADY BIRD JOHNSON was `-MARRIED to `-HER `-HUSBAND `-PRESIDENT #36/President Lyndon B. Johnson for some `-**39** `-YEARS!!!!!~'

`-**39** = **RECIPROCAL** = `-**93** = (93 + 39) = `-**132** = (1 x 32) = `-**32** = -a **Prophetic Number!!!!!~'**

`-**39** = **3(9's)** = `-**999** = (9 x 9 x 9) = `-**729** = (72 (-) 9) = `-**63** = "**HER `-HUSBAND #36/President Lyndon B. Johnson became `-PRESIDENT in (`-1963) - A `-RECIPROCAL- (36/63) = `-99**"!!!!!~'

`-**39** = **3(9's)** = `-**999** = (9 x 9 x 9) = `-**729** = (72 + 9) = `- **81** = "**AGE of `-DEATH of FIRST LADY THELMA "PAT" NIXON**"!!!!!~'

(45 + 54) = `-**99** = **RECIPROCAL** = `-**66**

(99/66) = (96) = `-**96** = **RECIPROCAL** = `-**69** = "Yin/Yang" = "The `-CYCLE of `-LIFE"!!!!!~'

FIRST LADY LADY BIRD JOHNSON `-LIVED `-13 `-YEARS `-LONGER than FIRST LADY THELMA "PAT" NIXON!!!!!~'

(94 + 81) = `-**175** = (75 + 1) = `-**76** = **RECIPROCAL** = `-**67** = "The `-YEAR that the "PROPHET'S" BROTHER was `-BORN, the `-AVERAGE `-AGE of the United States Presidents 1 to 28 in "SUCCESSION" above; and, below `-ALL `-PRESIDENTS that `-DIED at `-AGES `-66, `-67; and, `-68; and, The `-AGE of `-DEATH of the #1/President of the United States of America #1/President George Washington"!!!!!~'

FIRST LADY LADY BIRD JOHNSON had `-**DIED** at the `-**AGE** of `-**94**; the `-**YEAR** of `-**DEATH** of FIRST LADY JACQUELINE LEE KENNEDY in (`-19**94**) who was standing at the tender `-AGE of `-**64** at the `-**TIME** of `-HER `-DEATH!!!!!~' The `-SAME `-EXACT `-AGE of `-DEATH as of `-HER `-HUSBAND `-PRESIDENT #36/President Lyndon B. Johnson (`-**64**)!!!!!~'

(65 + 45) = `-**110** = (11 + 0) = `-**11** = "Yin/Yang" = "Multiple of `-ELEVEN" = "The `-CYCLE of `-LIFE"!!!!!~'

BIRTHYEAR / DEATHYEAR = (1912/2007) = (1912 + 2007) = `-**3919**

`-**3919** = (93 (-) 19) = `-**74** = **RECIPROCAL** = `-**47** = "The `-DEATH/DAY; and, `-BIRTHDAY #'s of the FIRST LADYS"!!!!!~'

(FIRST LADY)…(…)…-"~'

FIRST LADY; THELMA "PAT" NIXON, `-DIED** at the `-AGE of `-**81** `-YEARS**; and, `-**98** `-DAYS in `-LIVING!!!!!~ A `-TOTAL of `-**29,683** `-DAYS in `-LIVING!!!!!~' There were `-**267** `-DAYS left remaining in the `-YEAR before the FIRST LADY'S `-NEXT `-BIRTHDAY!!!!!~'

`-**267** = `-2(67) = (2 x 67) = `-**134** = (1 x 34) = `-**34** = **RECIPROCAL** = `-**43** = "The `-**PRESIDENTIAL #'s** `-**NUMBERS**"!!!!!~'

`-**29,683** = (2,96,83) = (2 + 96 + 83) = `-**181** = (81 x 1) = `- **81** = "AGE of `-DEATH of FIRST LADY THELMA "PAT" NIXON"!!!!!~'

THELMA "PAT" NIXON was `-BORN on March 16th in `-1912 (03/16/1912); and, the `-BIRTHDAY # `-NUMBER is: (03 + 16 + 19 + 12) = `-**50** = **RECIPROCAL** = `-**05**

(3 + 16 + 19) = `-**38** = **3(8's)** = `-**888** = (8 x 8 x 8) = `-**512** = (5 (1 + 2)) = `-**53** = **"WAR of the WORLDS"!!!!!~**

(50 + 5) = `-**55** = **"The "PROPHET"; and, "JESUS CHRIST" SAVE "LIVES"-"!!!!!~'**

(50 (-) 5) = `-**45** = **"The `-CURRENT `-AGE of the "PROPHET"-"!!!!!~'**

THELMA "PAT" NIXON had `-DIED on June 22nd in `-1993 (06/22/1993); and, the `-DEATH/DAY # `-NUMBER is: (6 + 22 + 19 + 93) = `-**140**

(6 + 22 + 19) = `-**47** = **RECIPROCAL** = `-**74** = **"The `-DEATH/DAY; and, `-BIRTHDAY #'s of the FIRST LADYS"!!!!!~'**

(140 + 50) = `-**190** / (140 (-) 50) = `-**90**

(190 + 90) = `-**280** = (82 + 0) = `-**82** = **"FIRST LADY THELMA "PAT" NIXON `-DIED within `-82 `-YEARS of `-LIVING"!!!!!~'**

THELMA "PAT" NIXON was `-MARRIED to `-HER `-HUSBAND `-PRESIDENT #37/President Richard Nixon for some `-**53** `-YEARS = `-WHICH; `-EQUALS = **"WAR of the WORLDS"!!!!!~'**

(1**4**0/**5**0) = `-**45** = **RECIPROCAL** = `-**54** = (45 + 54) = `-**99** = **RECIPROCAL** = `-**66**

(99/66) = (96) = `-**96** = **RECIPROCAL** = `-**69** = **"Yin/Yang"** = **"The `-CYCLE of `-LIFE"!!!!!~'**

BIRTHYEAR / DEATHYEAR = (1912/1993) = (1912 + 1993) = `-**3905**

`-3905 = (39 (-) 05) = `-**34** = **RECIPROCAL** = `-**43** = **"The `-PRESIDENTIAL #'s `-NUMBERS"!!!!!~'**

`-**3905** = **(39 + 05)** = `-**44** = **"#1/President George Washington was `-44 `-YEARS of `-AGE in (`-1776) on the very `-FIRST `-INDEPENDENCE `-DAY"!!!!!~'**

`-<u>1776</u> = (76 + 17) = `-<u>93</u> = "AGE of `-DEATH of FIRST LADY ELIZABETH ANN "BETTY" FORD"!!!!!~'

FIRST LADY THELMA "PAT" NIXON `-DIED in the `-YEAR (`-19<u>93</u>) of the `-AGE of `-DEATH; of (`-<u>93</u>), that was `-RESERVED for FIRST LADY ELIZABETH ANN "BETTY" FORD"!!!!!~'

FIRST LADY THELMA "PAT" NIXON'S `-HUSBAND #37/President Richard Nixon `-DIED in the `-YEAR of (`-19<u>94</u>) just like FIRST LADY JACQUELINE LEE KENNEDY `-DIED (`-19<u>94</u>); that the `-DEATH `-AGE of (`-<u>94</u>) was `-RESERVED for FIRST LADY LADY BIRD JOHNSON!!!!!~'

(FIRST LADY)…(…)…-"~'

FIRST LADY; ELIZABETH ANN "BETTY" FORD, `-<u>DIED</u> at the `-AGE of `-<u>93</u> `-<u>YEARS</u>; and, `-<u>91</u> `-DAYS in `-LIVING!!!!!~ A `-TOTAL of `-<u>34,059</u> `-DAYS in `-LIVING!!!!!~' There were `-<u>274</u> `-DAYS left remaining in the `-YEAR before the FIRST LADY'S `-NEXT `-BIRTHDAY!!!!!~'

`-<u>274</u> = "EMPHATIC `-WITNESS to the `-DEATH/DAY; and, `-BIRTHDAY #'s of the FIRST LADYS"!!!!!~'

`-<u>34,059</u> = (34,0,59) = (34 + 0 + 59) = `-<u>93</u> = "AGE of `-DEATH of FIRST LADY ELIZABETH ANN "BETTY" FORD"!!!!!~'

ELIZABETH ANN "BETTY" FORD was `-BORN on April 8[th] in `-1918 (04/08/1918); and, the `-BIRTHDAY # `-NUMBER is: (04 + 08 + 19 + 18) = `-<u>49</u> = <u>RECIPROCAL</u> = `-<u>94</u>

(4 + 8 + 19) = `-<u>31</u> = <u>RECIPROCAL</u> = `-<u>13</u> = "A VERY PIVOTAL NUMBER"!!!!!~'

`-<u>49</u> = "AGE of `-DEATH of ALEXANDER HAMILTON"!!!!!~'

`-<u>49</u> = <u>RECIPROCAL</u> = `-<u>94</u> = "AGE of `-DEATH for `-FIRST LADY LADY BIRD JOHNSON"!!!!!~'

ELIZABETH ANN "BETTY" FORD had `-DIED on July 8th in `-2011 (07/08/2011); and, the `-DEATH/DAY # `-NUMBER is: (7 + 8 + 20 + 11) = `-**46** = **RECIPROCAL** = `-**64**

(7 + 8 + 20) = `-**35** = **RECIPROCAL** = `-**53** = "WAR of the WORLDS"!!!!!~'

`-**46** = **RECIPROCAL** = `-**64** = "AGE of `-DEATH for #36/President Lyndon B. Johnson; and, FIRST LADY JACQUELINE LEE KENNEDY (`-64)-'"!!!!!~'

(49 + 46) = `-**95** = "FIRST LADY LADY BIRD JOHNSON `-DIED with `-**95** `-YEARS of `-EXISTING"!!!!!~'

`-**46** = `-**23** x `-**2** = `-**232** = **R**eciprocal-**S**equencing-**N**umerology-**RSN**!!!!!~'

ELIZABETH ANN "BETTY" FORD was `-MARRIED to `-HER `-HUSBAND `-PRESIDENT #38/President Gerald Ford for some `-**58** `-YEARS = `-WHICH; `-EQUALS = **(5 + 8) = `-13** = "A VERY PIVOTAL NUMBER"!!!!!~'

(93 (-) 58) = `-**35** = **RECIPROCAL** = `-**53** = "WAR of the WORLDS"!!!!!~'

`-**58** = **RECIPROCAL** = `-**85**

(85 + 58) = `-**143** = (1 x 43) = `-**43** = **RECIPROCAL** = `-**34** = "The `-PRESIDENTIAL #'s `-NUMBERS"!!!!!~'

BIRTHYEAR / DEATHYEAR = (1918/2011) = (1918 + 2011) = `-**3929**

`-**3929** = (92 (-) 39) = `-**53** = "WAR of the WORLDS"!!!!!~'

FIRST LADY ELIZABETH ANN "BETTY" FORD (`-93), #38/President Gerald Ford (`-93); and, #40/President Ronald Reagan (`-93) `-ALL `-DIED at the `-EXCESSIVE `-AGE of (`-93)-!!!!!~'

(93 x 3) = `-279 = `-(27)9 = (27 x 9) = `-243** = "EMPHATIC `-WITNESS as to the # `-NUMBER = `-43** = **RECIPROCAL** = `-**34** = "The `-PRESIDENTIAL #'s `-NUMBERS"!!!!!~'

The `-**PRESIDENTIAL** `-**PARALLELS** /|\ in `-**TIME**-'"!!!!!~'

#34/President Dwight D. Eisenhower was `-MARRIED to `-HIS `-WIFE FIRST LADY MAMIE GENEVA DOUD EISENHOWER for `-**53** `-YEARS = "WAR of the WORLDS"!!!!!~'

#34/President Dwight D. Eisenhower's Vice-President Richard M. Nixon was `-MARRIED to `-HIS `-WIFE FIRST LADY THELMA "PAT" NIXON for `-**53** `-YEARS = "WAR of the WORLDS"!!!!!~'

#**34**/President Dwight D. Eisenhower /|\ #**37**/President Richard M. Nixon

----

#37/President Richard M. Nixon `-**DIED** at the `-SAME `-AGE (`-**81**) as `-HIS `-WIFE FIRST LADY THELMA "PAT" NIXON (`-**81**)!!!!!~'

PRESIDENT RICHARD M. NIXON, `-**DIED** at the `-AGE of `-**81** `-**YEARS**; and, `-**103** `-DAYS in `-LIVING!!!!!~ A `-TOTAL of `-**29,688** `-DAYS in `-LIVING!!!!!~' There were `-**262** `-DAYS left remaining in the `-YEAR before the PRESIDENT'S `-NEXT `-BIRTHDAY!!!!!~'

`-**29,688** = (2,96,88) = (2 + 96 + 88) = `-**186** = `-(18)6 = (18 x 6) = `-**108** = (18 + 0) = `-**18** = **RECIPROCAL** = `-**81** = "AGE of `-DEATH of #37/President Richard M. Nixon"!!!!!~'

FIRST LADY; THELMA "PAT" NIXON, `-**DIED** at the `-AGE of `-**81** `-**YEARS**; and, `-**98** `-DAYS in `-LIVING!!!!!~ A `-TOTAL of `-**29,683** `-DAYS in `-LIVING!!!!!~' There were `-**267** `-DAYS left remaining in the `-YEAR before the FIRST LADY'S `-NEXT `-BIRTHDAY!!!!!~'

`-**29,683** = (2,96,83) = (2 + 96 + 83) = `-**181** = (81 x 1) = `-**81** = "AGE of `-DEATH of FIRST LADY THELMA "PAT" NIXON"!!!!!~'

(267 (-) 262) = `-**5** `-DAYS in `-SEPARATION of `-BOTH of `-ALL of `-THEIR `-DAYS on this `-EARTH = "THE `-HAND OF `-GOD"!!!!!~'

(267 + 262) = `-**529** = `-**52.9** = ROUNDED = `-**53** = "WAR of the WORLDS"!!!!!~'

#38/President Gerald Ford `-**DIED** at the `-SAME `-AGE (`-**93**) as `-HIS `-WIFE FIRST LADY ELIZABETH ANN "BETTY" FORD (`-**93**)!!!!!~'

PRESIDENT GERALD FORD, `-**DIED** at the `-**AGE** of `-**93** `-**YEARS**; and, `-**165** `-**DAYS** in `-**LIVING**!!!!!~ A `-TOTAL of `-**34,133** `-DAYS in `-LIVING!!!!!~' There were `-**200** `-DAYS left remaining in the `-YEAR before the PRESIDENT'S `-NEXT `-BIRTHDAY!!!!!~'

`-**34,133** = (34,133) = `-**167** = (67 x 1) = `-**67** = "The `-YEAR that the "PROPHET'S" BROTHER was `-BORN, the `-AVERAGE `-AGE of the United States Presidents 1 to 28 in "SUCCESSION" above; and, below `-ALL `-PRESIDENTS that `-DIED at `-AGES `-66, `-67; and, `-68; and, The `-AGE of `-DEATH of the #1/President of the United States of America #1/President George Washington"!!!!!~'

FIRST LADY; FIRST LADY ELIZABETH ANN "BETTY" FORD, `-**DIED** at the `-**AGE** of `-**93** `-**YEARS**; and, `-**91** `-**DAYS in** `-**LIVING**!!!!!~ A `-TOTAL of `-**34,059** `-DAYS in `-LIVING!!!!!~' There were `-**274** `-DAYS left remaining in the `-YEAR before the FIRST LADY'S `-NEXT `-BIRTHDAY!!!!!~'

`-**34,059** = (34,0,59) = (34 + 0 + 59) = `-**93** = "AGE of `-DEATH of FIRST LADY ELIZABETH ANN "BETTY" FORD"!!!!!~'

(165 (-) 91) = `-**74** = **RECIPROCAL** = `-**47** = "The `-DEATH/DAY; and, `-BIRTHDAY #'s of the FIRST LADYS"!!!!!~'

(274 (-) 200) = `-**74** = **RECIPROCAL** = `-**47** = "The `-DEATH/DAY; and, `-BIRTHDAY #'s of the FIRST LADYS"!!!!!~'

(93 + 81) = `-**174** = (74 x 1) = `-**74** = **RECIPROCAL** = `-**47** = "The `-DEATH/ DAY; and, `-BIRTHDAY #'s of the FIRST LADYS"!!!!!~'

#8/President Martin Van Buren (`-**79**) /|\ FIRST LADY HANNAH VAN BUREN (`-**35**)-'

PRESIDENT MARTIN VAN BUREN, `-**DIED** at the `-**AGE** of `-**79** `-**YEARS**; and, `-**231** `-**DAYS** in `-**LIVING**!!!!!~ A `-TOTAL of `-**29,085** `-DAYS in `-LIVING!!!!!~' There were `-**134** `-DAYS left remaining in the `-YEAR before the PRESIDENT'S `-NEXT `-BIRTHDAY!!!!!~'

`-**29,085** = (29,0,85) = (85 (-) 29) = `-**56** = "AGE of `-DEATH of #16/ President Abraham Lincoln"!!!!!~'

(92 (-) 58) = `-**34** = **RECIPROCAL** = `-**43** = "The `-**PRESIDENTIAL #'s** `-**NUMBERS**"!!!!!~'

`-**134** = (34 x 1) = `-**34** = **RECIPROCAL** = `-**43** = "The `-**PRESIDENTIAL #'s** `-**NUMBERS**"!!!!!~'

`-**231** = (23 x 1) = `-**23** = -a Prophetic Number!!!!!~'

`-**79** = "AGE of `-**DEATH** for Mr. H. G. Wells of the "WAR of the WORLDS"-"!!!!!~'

FIRST LADY; HANNAH VAN BUREN, `-**DIED** at the `-**AGE** of `-**35** `-**YEARS**; and, `-**334** `-**DAYS** in `-**LIVING**!!!!!~ A `-TOTAL of `-**13,117** `-**DAYS** in `-**LIVING**!!!!!~' There were `-**274** `-**DAYS** left remaining in the `-**YEAR** before the FIRST LADY'S `-**NEXT** `-**BIRTHDAY**!!!!!~'

`-**13,117** = (13,1,17) = (13 + 1 + 17) = `-**31** = **RECIPROCAL** = `-**13** = "A VERY PIVOTAL NUMBER"!!!!!~'

`-**334** = "**EMPHATIC** `-**EMPHASIS** for the # `-**NUMBER** = `-**34** = **RECIPROCAL** = `-**43** = "The `-**PRESIDENTIAL #'s** `-**NUMBERS**"!!!!!~'

`-**274** = "**EMPHATIC** `-**WITNESS** for the `-**DEATH/DAY**; and, `-**BIRTHDAY #'s** of the FIRST LADYS"!!!!!~'

FIRST LADY HANNAH VAN BUREN'S `-**DEATH** `-**AGE** = `-**35** = **RECIPROCAL** = `-**53** = "WAR of the WORLDS"!!!!!~'

(79 (-) 35) = `-**44** = "**#1/President George Washington was `-44 `-YEARS** of `-**AGE** in (`-17**76**) on the very `-**FIRST** `-**INDEPENDENCE** `-**DAY** of which `-**HE** `-**DIED** on the `-**EXACT** same `-**DAY** `-**RECIPROCAL #** `-**NUMBER** of which `-**HE** was at the `-**AGE** of (`-**67**)-'"!!!!!~'

#8/President Martin Van Buren (`-**79**) /|\ FIRST LADY HANNAH VAN BUREN (`-**35**)-' `-**THEIR** `-**CORRELATION** `-**PARALLEL** is the `-**MOVIE** - "The WAR of the WORLDS"-' (**ARMAGEDDON**)… (…)…-'"!!!!!~'

#11/President James K. Polk (`-**53**) /|\ FIRST LADY SARAH POLK (`-**87**)-'

159

PRESIDENT JAMES K. POLK, `-**DIED** at the `-**AGE** of `-**53** `-**YEARS**; and, `-**225** `-**DAYS in** `-**LIVING**!!!!!~ A `-TOTAL of `-**19,583** `-DAYS in `-LIVING!!!!!~' There were `-**140** `-DAYS left remaining in the `-YEAR before the PRESIDENT'S `-NEXT `-BIRTHDAY!!!!!~'

`-**19,583** = (1,95,83) = (1 + 95 + 83) = `-**179** = (79 x 1) = `-**79** = "AGE of `-**DEATH for Mr. H. G. Wells of the "WAR of the WORLDS"-"!!!!!~'

`-**225** = `-**22.5** = ROUNDED = `-**23** = -a Prophetic Number!!!!!~'

(140 + 53) = `-**193** = (93 x 1) = `-**93** = **RECIPROCAL** = `-**39** = `-**3(9's)** = `-**999** = (9 x 9 x 9) = `-**729** = `-**7(29)** = (7 x 29) = `-**203** = (23 + 0) = `-**23** = **-a Prophetic Number!!!!!~'**

`-**53** = "WAR of the WORLDS"!!!!!~'

FIRST LADY; SARAH POLK, `-**DIED** at the `-**AGE** of `-**87** `-**YEARS**; and, `-**344** `-**DAYS in** `-**LIVING**!!!!!~ A `-TOTAL of `-**32,121** `-DAYS in `-LIVING!!!!!~' There were `-**21** `-DAYS left remaining in the `-YEAR before the FIRST LADY'S `-NEXT `-BIRTHDAY!!!!!~'

`-**32,121** = (32,1,21) = (32 + 21 x 1) = `-**53** = **"WAR of the WORLDS"**!!!!!~'

`-**344** = (44 x 3) = `-**132** = (32 x 1) = `-**32** = -a Prophetic Number!!!!!~'

(53 (-) 21) = `-**32** = -a Prophetic Number!!!!!~'

`-**344** = (34 x 4) = `-**136** = (36 x 1) = `-**36** = **RECIPROCAL** = `-**63** = "AGE of `-**DEATH of the "PROPHET'S" MOTHER"**!!!!!~'

(87 (-) 21) = `-**66** = "AGE of `-DEATH of the "PROPHET'S" FATHER"!!!!!~'

(87 (-) 53) = `-**34** = **RECIPROCAL** = `-**43** = "The `-**PRESIDENTIAL** **#'s** `-**NUMBERS**"!!!!!~'

WHEN `-YOU `-TAKE **FIRST LADY GRACE ANNA COOLIDGE** who `-**DIED** at the `-AGE of `-**78**; and, **FIRST LADY ELEANOR ROOSEVELT** who `-**DIED** at the `-AGE of `-**78**; and, take `-THEIR `-HUSBANDS **#32/President Franklin Delano Roosevelt**; and, **#30/President Calvin Coolidge**; and, `-ADD `-UP `-THEIR `-YEARS of `-DEATH (`-**63** (+) `-**60**) = `-**EQUALS** = `-**123** = "**P**rophetic-**L**inear-**P**rogression-**PLP**"!!!!!~'

`-78 = **RECIPROCAL** = `-87

FIRST LADY EDITH KERMIT ROOSEVELT; and, FIRST LADY SARAH POLK `-BOTH `-DIED at the `-AGE of (`-87); which, is the `-RECIPROCAL `-AGE of `-DEATH with FIRST LADY ELEANOR ROOSEVELT (`-78)!!!!!~' FIRST LADY EDITH KERMIT ROOSEVELT'S HUSBAND #26/President Theodore Roosevelt `-ALSO, `-DIED at the `-AGE of (`-60); and, If; `-YOU `-ADD `-HIS `-DEATH `-AGE to the `-MIX, `-YOU arrive at (`-63 (+) `-60 (+) `-60) = `-183 = (83 x 1) = `-83 = RECIPROCAL = `-38 = 3(8's) = `-888 = (8 x 8 x 8) = `-512 = (5 (1 + 2)) = `-53 = "WAR of the WORLDS"!!!!!~

#21/President Chester A. Arthur (`-57) /|\ FIRST LADY ELLEN LEWIS HERNDON ARTHUR (`-42)-'

PRESIDENT CHESTER A. ARTHUR, `-DIED at the `-AGE of `-57 `-YEARS; and, `-44 `-DAYS in `-LIVING!!!!!~ A `-TOTAL of `-20,863 `-DAYS in `-LIVING!!!!!~' There were `-321 `-DAYS left remaining in the `-YEAR before the PRESIDENT'S `-NEXT `-BIRTHDAY!!!!!~'

`-**20,863** = (28,0,63) = (63 (-) 28 (-) 0) = `-**35** = **RECIPROCAL** = `-**53** = "WAR of the WORLDS"!!!!!~'

`-**44** = "#1/President George Washington was `-44 `-YEARS of `-AGE in (`-1776) on the very `-FIRST `-INDEPENDENCE `-DAY of which `-HE `-DIED on the `-EXACT same `-DAY `-RECIPROCAL # `-NUMBER of which `-HE was at the `-AGE of (`-67)-'"!!!!!~'

`-**321** = "**P**rophetic-**L**inear-**P**rogression-**PLP**"!!!!!~'

(57 (-) 42) = `-**15** = **RECIPROCAL** = `-**51**

(51 (-) 15) = `-**36** = **RECIPROCAL** = `-**63** = "AGE of `-DEATH of the "PROPHET'S" MOTHER"!!!!!~'

(51 + 15) = `-**66** = "AGE of `-DEATH of the "PROPHET'S" FATHER"!!!!!~'

FIRST LADY; ELLEN LEWIS HERNDON ARTHUR, `-DIED at the `-AGE of `-42 `-YEARS; and, `-135 `-DAYS in `-LIVING!!!!!~ A `-TOTAL of

`-15,475 `-DAYS in `-LIVING!!!!!~' There were `-230 `-DAYS left remaining in the `-YEAR before the FIRST LADY'S `-NEXT `-BIRTHDAY!!!!!~'

`-15,475 = (15,4,75) = (15 + 4 + 75) = `-94 = "AGE of `-DEATH of FIRST LADY LADY BIRD JOHNSON"!!!!!~'

`-15,475 = (1,54,75) = (1 + 54 + 75) = `-130 = (13 + 0) = `-13 = "A VERY PIVOTAL NUMBER"!!!!!~'

`-15,475 = (15,4,75) = (75 (-) 15 (-) 4) = `-56 = "AGE of `-DEATH of #16/ President Abraham Lincoln"!!!!!~'

#36/President Lyndon B. Johnson; and, #16/President Abraham Lincoln `-SUBTRACT {(36 (-) 16)|} = `-20 = #21/President Chester A. Arthur was the `-VERY `-NEXT `-PRESIDENT!!!!!~'

`-135 = `-(13)5 = (13 x 5) = `-65 = "YEAR of `-DEATH of #16/President Abraham Lincoln"!!!!!~'

`-135 = (35 x 1) = `-35 = RECIPROCAL = `-53 = "WAR of the WORLDS"!!!!!~'

`-230 = (23 + 0) = `-23 = -a Prophetic Number!!!!!~'

(57 + 42) = `-99 / `-99 = RECIPROCAL = `-66

(99/66) = (96) = `-96 = RECIPROCAL = `-69 = "Yin/Yang" = "The `-CYCLE of `-LIFE"!!!!!~'

The `-PRESIDENTIAL `-PARALLELS /|\ in `-TIME-"!!!!!~'

"`-NOTE- the `-NUMBERS-"!!!!!~'

#1/President George Washington `-TOOK the `-OFFICE of `-PRESIDENCY at the `-AGE of `-57 `-YEARS / `-67 `-DAYS!!!!!~'

`-57 = RECIPROCAL = `-75

(75 + 57) = `-132 = (32 x 1) = `-32 = -a Prophetic Number!!!!!~'

#3/President Thomas Jefferson `-TOOK the `-OFFICE of `-PRESIDENCY at the `-AGE of `-**57** `-YEARS / `-**325** `-DAYS!!!!!~'

`-**57** = **RECIPROCAL** = `-**75**

(75 + 57) = `-**132** = (32 x 1) = `-**32** = -a Prophetic Number!!!!!~'

`-**325** = `-**32.5** = **ROUNDED DOWN** = `-**32** = -a Prophetic Number!!!!!~'

#4/President James Madison `-TOOK the `-OFFICE of `-PRESIDENCY at the `-AGE of `-57 `-YEARS / `-353 `-DAYS!!!!!~'

`-**57** = **RECIPROCAL** = `-**75**

(75 + 57) = `-**132** = (32 x 1) = `-**32** = -a Prophetic Number!!!!!~'

`-**353** = **Reciprocal-Sequencing-Numerology-RSN** = `-**35** = **RECIPROCAL** = `-**53** = **"WAR of the WORLDS"**!!!!!~'

#6/President John Quincy Adams `-TOOK the `-OFFICE of `-PRESIDENCY at the `-AGE of `-**57** `-YEARS / `-**236** `-DAYS!!!!!~'

`-**57** = **RECIPROCAL** = `-**75**

(75 + 57) = `-**132** = (32 x 1) = `-**32** = -a Prophetic Number!!!!!~'

`-**236** = `-**23.6** = **ROUNDED DOWN** = `-**23** = -a Prophetic Number!!!!!~'

#8/President Martin Van Buren `-TOOK the `-OFFICE of `-PRESIDENCY at the `-AGE of `-**54** `-YEARS / `-**89** `-DAYS!!!!!~'

(89 (-) 54) = `-35 = RECIPROCAL** = `-53** = **"WAR of the WORLDS"**!!!!!~'

#19/President Rutherford B. Hayes `-TOOK the `-OFFICE of `-PRESIDENCY at the `-AGE of `-**54** `-YEARS / `-**151** `-DAYS!!!!!~'

(151 (-) 54) = `-**97** = **RECIPROCAL** = `-**79** = **"AGE of `-DEATH for Mr. H. G. Wells of the "WAR of the WORLDS"-"**!!!!!~'

#25/President William McKinley `-TOOK the `-OFFICE of `-PRESIDENCY at the `-AGE of `-**54** `-YEARS / `-**34** `-DAYS!!!!!~'

(54 (-) 34) = `-20 = "The `-BIRTHDAY of the "PROPHET"-"!!!!!~'

`-**34** = **RECIPROCAL** = `-**43** = "The `-**PRESIDENTIAL** #'s `-**NUMBERS**"!!!!!~'

#31/President Herbert Hoover `-TOOK the `-OFFICE of `-PRESIDENCY at the `-AGE of `-**54** `-YEARS / `-**206** `-DAYS!!!!!~'

(206 (-) 54) = `-**152** = (52 + 1) = `-**53** = "WAR of the WORLDS"!!!!!~'

(206 + 54) = `-**260** = (26 + 0) = `-**26** = `-**13** x `-**2** = `-**132** = (1 x 32) = `-**32** = -a **Prophetic Number!!!!!~'**

#**43**/President **George W**. Bush `-TOOK the `-OFFICE of `-PRESIDENCY at the `-AGE of `-**54** `-YEARS / `-**198** `-DAYS!!!!!~'

(198 (-) 54) = `-**144** = (44 x 1) = `-**44** = "**#1/President George Washington was `-44 `-YEARS of `-AGE in (`-1776) on the very `-FIRST `-INDEPENDENCE `-DAY of which `-HE `-DIED on the `-EXACT same `-DAY `-RECIPROCAL # `-NUMBER of which `-HE was at the `-AGE of (`-67)-'**"!!!!!~'

(76 + 67) = `-**143** = (43 x 1) = `-**43** = "**#43/President George W. Bush**"!!!!!~'

#16/President Abraham Lincoln `-TOOK the `-OFFICE of `-PRESIDENCY at the `-AGE of `-**52** `-YEARS / `-**20** `-DAYS!!!!!~'

(52 (-) 20) = `-**32** = **-a Prophetic Number!!!!!~'**

#35/President John F. Kennedy `-TOOK the `-OFFICE of `-PRESIDENCY at the `-AGE of `-**43** `-YEARS / `-**236** `-DAYS!!!!!~'

`-**236** = (36 (-) 2) = `-**34** = **RECIPROCAL** = `-**43** = "**The `-PRESIDENTIAL #'s `-NUMBERS**"!!!!!~'

#36/President Lyndon B. Johnson `-TOOK the `-OFFICE of `-PRESIDENCY at the `-AGE of `-**55** `-YEARS / `-**87** `-DAYS!!!!!~'

(87 (-) 55) = `-**32** = **-a Prophetic Number!!!!!~'**

#35/President John F. Kennedy `-LOST `-HIS `-LIFE at the tender `-AGE of `-46; while, #36/President Lyndon B. Johnson `-LOST `-HIS `-LIFE at the tender `-AGE of `-64!!!!!~'

`-46 = <u>RECIPROCAL</u> = `-64

#42/President Bill Clinton `-TOOK the `-OFFICE of `-PRESIDENCY at the `-AGE of `-46 `-YEARS / `-154 `-DAYS!!!!!~'

(64 + 46) = `-110 = (11 + 0) = `-11 = "Yin/Yang" = "Multiple of `-ELEVEN" = "The `-CYCLE of `-LIFE"!!!!!~'

(154 (-) 64) = `-90 = "AGE of `-DEATH of #31/President <u>H</u>erbert <u>H</u>oover"!!!!!~'

#41/President George H. W. Bush `-TOOK the `-OFFICE of `-PRESIDENCY at the `-AGE of `-64 `-YEARS / `-222 `-DAYS!!!!!~'

(222 (-) 46) = `-176 = (76 x 1) = `-76 = <u>RECIPROCAL</u> = `-67 = "The `-YEAR that the "PROPHET'S" BROTHER was `-BORN, the `-AVERAGE `-AGE of the United States Presidents 1 to 28 in "SUCCESSION" above; and, below `-ALL `-PRESIDENTS that `-DIED at `-AGES `-66, `-67; and, `-68; and, The `-AGE of `-DEATH of the #1/President of the United States of America #1/President George Washington"!!!!!~'

#<u>31</u>/President <u>H</u>erbert <u>H</u>oover!!!!!~'

<u>AMERICAN/ENGLISH</u> `-<u>ALPHABET</u> `-to-` `-<u>NUMBERS</u> #'s:!!!!!~'

<u>HH</u> = `-<u>8</u>, `-<u>8</u> / <u>RR</u> = `-<u>18</u>, `-<u>18</u>

`-<u>18</u> = <u>RECIPROCAL</u> = `-<u>81</u>

`-<u>818</u> = (8 + 1 + 8) = `-<u>17</u> x (`-2) = `-<u>34</u> = "The `-<u>BEGINNING</u> of the #40/President <u>R</u>onald <u>R</u>eagan's `-<u>PRESIDENCY</u>"!!!!!~'

#40/President <u>R</u>onald <u>R</u>eagan`-TOOK the `-OFFICE of `-PRESIDENCY at the `-AGE of `-<u>69</u> `-YEARS / `-<u>349</u> `-DAYS!!!!!~'

`-<u>69</u> = "Yin/Yang" = "The `-CYCLE of `-LIFE"!!!!!~'

#**31**/President **H**erbert **H**oover's `-WIFE FIRST LADY LOU HENRY HOOVER `-**DIED** at the `-AGE of `-**69**; and, was the `-**RECIPROCAL** `-**BETWEEN** FIRST LADY GRACE ANNA COOLIDGE; and, FIRST LADY ELEANOR ROOSEVELT!!!!!~'

`-**349** = `-**34(9)** = (34 x 9) = `-**306** = (36 + 0) = `-**36** = **RECIPROCAL** = `-**63** = "The `-AGE of `-DEATH of the "PROPHET'S" MOTHER; the `-YEAR of `-**ASSASSINATION** for #**35**/President John F. Kennedy; and, the `-YEAR of #**36**/President Lyndon B. Johnson taking over the `-**PRESIDENCY**"!!!!!~'

`-**49** = **RECIPROCAL** = `-**94**

`-**49** = "The `-AGE of `-DEATH of SIR ALEXANDER HAMILTON"!!!!!~'

`-**94** = "The `-AGE of `-DEATH of FIRST LADY LADY BIRD JOHNSON"!!!!!~'

(49 + 94) = `-**143** = (1 x 43) = `-**43** = **RECIPROCAL** = `-**34** = "The `-**PRESIDENTIAL #'s `-NUMBERS**"!!!!!~'

#**44**/President Barack H. Obama `-TOOK the `-OFFICE of `-PRESIDENCY at the `-AGE of `-**47** `-YEARS / `-**169** `-DAYS!!!!!~'

`-**47** = "The `-DEATH/DAY; and, `-BIRTHDAY #'s of the FIRST LADYS"!!!!!~'

`-**169** = (69 x 1) = `-**69** = "Yin/Yang" = "The `-CYCLE of `-LIFE"!!!!!~'

(169 + 47) = `-**216** = (2 x 16) = `-**32** = -a Prophetic Number!!!!!~'

`-**23** = **RECIPROCAL** = `-**32**

(169 (-) 47) = `-**122** = (22 + 1) = `-**23** = -a Prophetic Number!!!!!~'

#**44**/ FIRST LADY MICHELLE OBAMA at the `-START of being `-FIRST `-LADY was at the `-AGE of -**45** `-YEARS / `-**3** `-DAYS!!!!!~'

`-**43** = **RECIPROCAL** = `-**34** = "The `-**PRESIDENTIAL #'s `-NUMBERS**"!!!!!~'

(45 x 3) = `-**135** = (35 x 1) = `-**35** = **RECIPROCAL** = `-**53** = "WAR of the WORLDS"!!!!!~'

`-45 = **RECIPROCAL** = `-54

#43/FIRST LADY LAURA BUSH at the `-START of being `-FIRST `-LADY was at the `-AGE of -54 `-YEARS / `-77 `-DAYS!!!!!~'

(77 (-) 54) = `-23 = -a Prophetic Number!!!!!~'

#42/FIRST LADY HILLARY CLINTON at the `-START of being `-FIRST `-LADY was at the `-AGE of -45 `-YEARS / `-86 `-DAYS!!!!!~'

(86 + 45) = `-131 = (31 + 1) = `-32 = -a Prophetic Number!!!!!~'

#41/FIRST LADY BARBARA BUSH at the `-START of being `-FIRST `-LADY was at the `-AGE of -63 `-YEARS / `-226 `-DAYS!!!!!~'

(226 (-) 63) = `-163 = (63 x 1) = `-63 = "The `-AGE of `-DEATH of the "PROPHET'S" MOTHER; the `-YEAR of `-ASSASSINATION for #35/President John F. Kennedy; and, the `-YEAR of #36/President Lyndon B. Johnson taking over the `-PRESIDENCY"!!!!!~'

#40/FIRST LADY NANCY REAGAN at the `-START of being `-FIRST `-LADY was at the `-AGE of -59 `-YEARS / `-198 `-DAYS!!!!!~'

(198 (-) 59) = `-139 = (39 x 1) = `-39 = `-3(9's) = `-999 = (9 x 9 x 9) = `-729 = `-7(29) = (7 x 29) = `-203 = (23 + 0) = `-23 = -a Prophetic Number!!!!!~'

#39/FIRST LADY **ELEANOR** ROSA**LYNN** CARTER at the `-START of being `-FIRST `-LADY was at the `-AGE of -49 `-YEARS / `-155 `-DAYS!!!!!~'

`-49 = **RECIPROCAL** = `-94

`-49 = "The `-AGE of `-DEATH of SIR ALEXANDER HAMILTON"!!!!!~'

`-94 = "The `-AGE of `-DEATH of FIRST LADY LADY BIRD JOHNSON"!!!!!~'

(49 + 94) = `-143 = (1 x 43) = `-43 = **RECIPROCAL** = `-34 = "The `-PRESIDENTIAL #'s `-NUMBERS"!!!!!~'

`-155 = (55 x 1) = `-55 = `-23 + `-32

#**38**/FIRST LADY ELIZABETH ANN "BETTY" FORD at the `-START of being `-FIRST `-LADY was at the `-AGE of -**56** `-YEARS / `-**123** `-DAYS!!!!!~'

`-**56** = "AGE of `-DEATH of #16/President Abraham Lincoln"!!!!!~'

`-**123** = "Prophetic-Linear-Progression-PLP"!!!!!~'

(123 (-) 56) = `-**67** = "The `-YEAR that the "PROPHET'S" BROTHER was `-BORN, the `-AVERAGE `-AGE of the United States Presidents 1 to 28 in "SUCCESSION" above; and, below `-ALL `-PRESIDENTS that `-DIED at `-AGES `-66, `-67; and, `-68; and, The `-AGE of `-DEATH of the #1/President of the United States of America #1/President George Washington"!!!!!~'

(123 + 56) = `-**179** = (79 x 1) = `-**79** = "AGE of `-DEATH for Mr. H. G. Wells of the "WAR of the WORLDS"-"!!!!!~'

#**37**/FIRST LADY THELMA "PAT" NIXON at the `-START of being `-FIRST `-LADY was at the `-AGE of -**56** `-YEARS / `-**310** `-DAYS!!!!!~'

`-**56** = "AGE of `-DEATH of #16/President Abraham Lincoln"!!!!!~'

`-**310** = (31 + 0) = `-**31** = **RECIPROCAL** = `-**13** = "A VERY PIVOTAL NUMBER"!!!!!~'

#**36**/FIRST LADY LADY BIRD JOHNSON at the `-START of being `-FIRST `-LADY was at the `-AGE of -**50** `-YEARS / `-**335** `-DAYS!!!!!~'

`-**335** = `-(33)5 = (33 x 5) = `-**165** = (65 x 1) = `-**65** = "YEAR of `-DEATH of #16/President Abraham Lincoln"!!!!!~'

(94 (-) 50) = `-**44** = "#1/President George Washington was `-**44** `-YEARS of `-AGE in (`-17**76**) on the very `-FIRST `-INDEPENDENCE `-DAY of which `-HE `-DIED on the `-EXACT same `-DAY `-RECIPROCAL # `-NUMBER of which `-HE was at the `-AGE of (`-**67**)-"!!!!!~'

#**35**/FIRST LADY JACQUELINE LEE KENNEDY at the `-START of being `-FIRST `-LADY was at the `-AGE of -**31** `-YEARS / `-**176** `-DAYS!!!!!~'

`-**31** = **RECIPROCAL** = `-**13** = "A VERY PIVOTAL NUMBER"!!!!!~'

`-**176** = (76 x 1) = `-**76** = **RECIPROCAL** = `-**67** = "The `-YEAR that the "PROPHET'S" BROTHER was `-BORN, the `-AVERAGE `-AGE of the

United States Presidents 1 to 28 in "SUCCESSION" above; and, below `-ALL `-PRESIDENTS that `-DIED at `-AGES `-66, `-67; and, `-68; and, The `-AGE of `-DEATH of the #1/President of the United States of America #1/President George Washington"!!!!!~'

#**34**/FIRST LADY MAMIE GENEVA DOUD EISENHOWER at the `-START of being `-FIRST `-LADY was at the `-AGE of -**56** `-YEARS / `-**67** `-DAYS!!!!!~'

`-**56** = "AGE of `-DEATH of #16/President Abraham Lincoln"!!!!!~'

`-**67** = "The `-YEAR that the "PROPHET'S" BROTHER was `-BORN, the `-AVERAGE `-AGE of the United States Presidents 1 to 28 in "SUCCESSION" above; and, below `-ALL `-PRESIDENTS that `-DIED at `-AGES `-66, `-67; and, `-68; and, The `-AGE of `-DEATH of the #1/President of the United States of America #1/President George Washington"!!!!!~'

(56 + 67) = `-**123** = "Prophetic-**L**inear-**P**rogression-**PLP**"!!!!!~'

#**33**/FIRST LADY ELIZABETH VIRGINIA "BESS" TRUMAN at the `-START of being `-FIRST `-LADY was at the `-AGE of -**60** `-YEARS / `-**58** `-DAYS!!!!!~'

`-**60** = (6 + 0) = `-**6** = `-2 x `-3 = `-(**23**) = `-**23** = -a Prophetic Number!!!!!~'

`-**60** = (6 + 0) = `-**6** = `-3 x `-2 = `-(**32**) = `-**32** = -a Prophetic Number!!!!!~'

`-**58** = (5 + 8) = `-**13** = "A VERY PIVOTAL NUMBER"!!!!!~'

#**33**/President Harry S. Truman `-TOOK the `-OFFICE of `-PRESIDENCY at the `-AGE of `-**60** `-YEARS / `-**339** `-DAYS!!!!!~'

`-**60** = (6 + 0) = `-**6** = `-2 x `-3 = `-(**23**) = `-**23** = -a Prophetic Number!!!!!~'

`-**60** = (6 + 0) = `-**6** = `-3 x `-2 = `-(**32**) = `-**32** = -a Prophetic Number!!!!!~'

`-**339** = `-(33)9) = (33 x 9) = `-**297** = `-(**29**)7 = (29 x 7) = `-**203** = (23 + 0) = `-**23** = -a Prophetic Number"!!!!!~'

#**32**/FIRST LADY ELEANOR ROOSEVELT at the `-START of being `-FIRST `-LADY was at the `-AGE of -**48** `-YEARS / `-**144** `-DAYS!!!!!~'

`-**48** = **RECIPROCAL** = `-**84**

(84 + 48) = `-**132** = (32 x 1) = `-**32** = -a Prophetic Number!!!!!~'

`-**144** = (44 x 1) = `-**44** = "#1/President George Washington was `-**44** `-YEARS of `-AGE in (`-17**76**) on the very `-FIRST `-INDEPENDENCE `-DAY of which `-HE `-DIED on the `-EXACT same `-DAY `-RECIPROCAL # `-NUMBER of which `-HE was at the `-AGE of (`-**67**)-'"!!!!!~'

#**32**/President Franklin Delano Roosevelt `-TOOK the `-OFFICE of `-PRESIDENCY at the `-AGE of `-**51** `-YEARS / `-**33** `-DAYS!!!!!~'

`-**33** = "Yin/Yang" = "Multiple of `-ELEVEN" = "The `-CYCLE of `-LIFE"!!!!!~'

(51) = (5 x 1) = `-**5**

(5/33) = `-**53** = "WAR of the WORLDS"!!!!!~'

(5 + 33) = `-**38** = **3(8's)** = `-**888** = (8 x 8 x 8) = `-**512** = (5 (1 + 2)) = `-**53** = "WAR of the WORLDS"!!!!!~

(51 + 33) = `-**84** = **RECIPROCAL** = `-**48**

(84 + 48) = `-**132** = (32 x 1) = `-**32** = -a Prophetic Number!!!!!~'

`-**13** = "A VERY PIVOTAL NUMBER"!!!!!~'

`-**51** = (51 (-) **1**) = `-**5**0 / `-**33** = (33 (-) **3**) = `-**3**0

(**5**0/**3**0) = (53 + 0 + 0) = `-**53** = "WAR of the WORLDS"!!!!!~'

`-**33** = (33 (-) **1**) = `-**32** = -a Prophetic Number!!!!!~'

`-**51** = **RECIPROCAL** = `-**15**

#**32**/FIRST LADY ELEANOR ROOSEVELT `-OUTLIVED `-HER `-HUSBAND #**32**/President Franklin Delano Roosevelt `-by `-**15** `-YEARS!!!!!~'

#31/FIRST LADY LOU HENRY HOOVER at the `-START of being `-FIRST `-LADY was at the `-AGE of -**54** `-YEARS / `-**340** `-DAYS!!!!!~'

(340 (-) 54) = `-**286** = `-**(28)6** = (28 x 6) = `-**168** = (68 + 1) = `-**69** = "AGE of `-DEATH of FIRST LADY LOU HENRY HOOVER"!!!!!~'

(340 + 54) = `-**394** = `-**3(94)** = "EMPHATIC `-EMPHASIS to the # `-NUMBER (`-**94**)"!!!!!~'

`-**49** = **RECIPROCAL** = `-**94**

`-**49** = "The `-AGE of `-DEATH of SIR ALEXANDER HAMILTON"!!!!!~'

`-**94** = "The `-AGE of `-DEATH of FIRST LADY LADY BIRD JOHNSON"!!!!!~'

`-**340** = (34 + 0) = `-**34** = **RECIPROCAL** = `-**43** = "The `-PRESIDENTIAL #'s `-NUMBERS"!!!!!~'

#**30**/FIRST LADY GRACE ANNA COOLIDGE; at the `-START of being `-FIRST `-LADY was at the `-AGE of -**44** `-YEARS / `-**211** `-DAYS!!!!!~'

`-**44** = "#1/President George Washington was `-**44** `-YEARS of `-AGE in (`-17**76**) on the very `-FIRST `-INDEPENDENCE `-DAY of which `-HE `-DIED on the `-EXACT same `-DAY `-RECIPROCAL # `-NUMBER of which `-HE was at the `-AGE of (`-**67**)-"!!!!!~'

(211 (-) 44) = `-**167** = (67 x 1) = `-**67** = "The `-YEAR that the "PROPHET'S" BROTHER was `-BORN, the `-AVERAGE `-AGE of the United States Presidents 1 to 28 in "SUCCESSION" above; and, below `-ALL `-PRESIDENTS that `-DIED at `-AGES `-66, `-67; and, `-68; and, The `-AGE of `-DEATH of the #1/President of the United States of America #1/President George Washington"!!!!!~'

#**29**/FIRST LADY FLORENCE HARDING at the `-START of being `-FIRST `-LADY was at the `-AGE of -**60** `-YEARS / `-**201** `-DAYS!!!!!~'

(201 + 60) = `-**261** = (61 + 2) = `-**63** = "The `-AGE of `-DEATH of the "PROPHET'S" MOTHER; the `-YEAR of `-ASSASSINATION for #35/

President John F. Kennedy; and, the `-YEAR of #36/President Lyndon B. Johnson taking over the `-PRESIDENCY"!!!!!~'

(201 (-) 60) = `-**141** = `-**14** = **RECIPROCAL** = `-**41**

(41 + 14) = `-**55** = `-**23** + `-**32**

#**29**/President Warren G. Harding `-TOOK the `-OFFICE of `-PRESIDENCY at the `-AGE of `-**55** `-YEARS / `-**122** `-DAYS!!!!!~'

`-**55** = `-**23** + `-**32**

(122 (-) 55) = `-**67** = "The `-YEAR that the "PROPHET'S" BROTHER was `-BORN, the `-AVERAGE `-AGE of the United States Presidents 1 to 28 in "SUCCESSION" above; and, below `-ALL `-PRESIDENTS that `-DIED at `-AGES `-**66**, `-**67**; and, `-**68**; and, The `-AGE of `-DEATH of the #1/President of the United States of America #1/President George Washington"!!!!!~'

(67 + 63) = `-**130** = (13 + 0) = `-**13** = "A VERY PIVOTAL NUMBER"!!!!!~'

#**28**/FIRST LADY EDITH WILSON at the `-START of being `-FIRST `-LADY was at the `-AGE of -**43** `-YEARS / `-**64** `-DAYS!!!!!~'

`-**43** = **RECIPROCAL** = `-**34** = "The `-**PRESIDENTIAL** #'s `-**NUMBERS**"!!!!!~'

`-**64** = "The `-AGE of `-DEATH of #36/President Lyndon B. Johnson; and, FIRST LADY JACQUELINE LEE KENNEDY"!!!!!~'

#**28**/President Woodrow Wilson `-TOOK the `-OFFICE of `-PRESIDENCY at the `-AGE of `-**56** `-YEARS / `-**66** `-DAYS!!!!!~'

(56 + 66) = `-**122** = (22 + 1) = `-**23** = -a Prophetic Number!!!!!~'

(56 (-) 43) = `-**13** = "A VERY PIVOTAL NUMBER"!!!!!~'

(66 + 64) = `-**130** = (13 + 0) = `-**13** = "A VERY PIVOTAL NUMBER"!!!!!~'

#**28**/FIRST LADY ELLEN AXSON WILSON at the `-START of being `-FIRST `-LADY was at the `-AGE of -**52** `-YEARS / `-**293** `-DAYS!!!!!~'

(293 (-) 52) = `-**241** = (24 x 1) = `-**24** = "The `-YEAR of `-DEATH of `-HER `-HUSBAND #28/President Woodrow Wilson (`-19**24**)"!!!!!~'

`-**293** = (93 / 2) = `-**46.5** = ROUNDED DOWN = `-**46** = `-**23** x `-**2** = `-**232** = **Reciprocal-Sequencing-Numerology-RSN**!!!!!~'

(293 + 52) = `-**345** = "**Prophetic-Linear-Progression-PLP**" = `-**34.5** = ROUNDED DOWN = `-**34** = **RECIPROCAL** = `-**43** = "The `-PRESIDENTIAL #'s `-NUMBERS"!!!!!~'

(293 + 52) = `-**345** = "**Prophetic-Linear-Progression-PLP**" = `-**3(45)** = (3 x 45) = `-**135** = (35 x 1) = `-**35** = **RECIPROCAL** = `-**53** = "WAR of the WORLDS"!!!!!~'

#**27**/FIRST LADY HELEN LOUISE TAFT at the `-START of being `-FIRST `-LADY was at the `-AGE of -**47** `-YEARS / `-**275** `-DAYS!!!!!~'

(275 + 47) = `-**322** = `-**(32)2** = "EMPHATIC `-WITNESS to the # `-NUMBER `-**32** = -a Prophetic Number"!!!!!~'

`-**23** = **RECIPROCAL** = `-**32**

(275 (-) 47) = `-**228** = `-**22.8** = ROUNDED = `-**23** = -a Prophetic Number!!!!!~'

#**26**/FIRST LADY EDITH KERMIT ROOSEVELT at the `-START of being `-FIRST `-LADY was at the `-AGE of -**40** `-YEARS / `-**39** `-DAYS!!!!!~'

`-**39** = `-**3(9's)** = `-**999** = (9 x 9 x 9) = `-**729** = `-**7(29)** = (7 x 29) = `-**203** = (23 + 0) = `-**23** = -a Prophetic Number!!!!!~'

(39 + 40) = `-**79** = "AGE of `-DEATH for Mr. H. G. Wells of the "WAR of the WORLDS"-"!!!!!~'

#**26**/President Theodore Roosevelt `-TOOK the `-OFFICE of `-PRESIDENCY at the `-AGE of `-**42** `-YEARS / `-**322** `-DAYS!!!!!~'

(322 (-) 42) = `-**280** = (28 + 0) = "#28/President Woodrow Wilson"!!!!!~'

(322 + 42) = `-**364** = "#**36**/President Lyndon B. Johnson `-DYING at the `-AGE of (`-**64**)"!!!!!~'

(28 + 36) = `-**64** = "AGE of `-DEATH of #**36**/President Lyndon B. Johnson; and, FIRST LADY JACQUELINE LEE KENNEDY"!!!!!~'

`-**322** = `-**(32)2** = "EMPHATIC `-WITNESS to the # `-NUMBER `-**32** = -a Prophetic Number"!!!!!~'

#**25**/FIRST LADY IDA MCKINLEY at the `-START of being `-FIRST `-LADY was at the `-AGE of -**49** `-YEARS / `-**269** `-DAYS!!!!!~'

`-**49** = **RECIPROCAL** = `-**94**

`-**49** = "The `-AGE of `-DEATH of SIR ALEXANDER HAMILTON"!!!!!~'

`-**94** = "The `-AGE of `-DEATH of FIRST LADY LADY BIRD JOHNSON"!!!!!~'

`-**269** = (26 + 9) = `-**35** = **RECIPROCAL** = `-**53** = "WAR of the WORLDS"!!!!!~'

`-**269** = `-**(26)9** = (26 x 9) = `-**234** = "Prophetic-**L**inear-**P**rogression-**PLP**" = `-EMPHATIC `-WITNESS to the # `-NUMBER `-**34** = **RECIPROCAL** = `-**43** = "The `-**PRESIDENTIAL** #'s `-**NUMBERS**"!!!!!~'

`-**269** = `-**2(69)** = (2 x 69) = `-**138** = (38 x 1) = `-**38** = **3(8's)** = `-**888** = (8 x 8 x 8) = `-**512** = (5 (1 + 2)) = `-**53** = "WAR of the WORLDS"!!!!!~

`-**269** = "EMPHATIC `-WITNESS to the # `-NUMBER `-**69** = "Yin/Yang" = "The `-CYCLE of `-LIFE"!!!!!~'

(269 (-) 49) = `-**220** = (22 + 0) = `-**22** = "Yin/Yang" = "Multiple of `-ELEVEN" = "The `-CYCLE of `-LIFE"!!!!!~'

(269 + 49) = `-**318** = `-**31.8** = ROUNDED = `-**32** = -a Prophetic Number!!!!!~'

#**22**/#**24**/FIRST LADY FRANCES CLEVELAND at the `-START of being `-FIRST `-LADY was at the `-AGE of -**28** `-YEARS / `-**226** `-DAYS!!!!!~'

174

`-28 = "#28/President Woodrow Wilson"!!!!!~'

`-226 = `-22.6 = ROUNDED = `-23 = -a Prophetic Number!!!!!~'

(226 (-) 28) = `-198 = (98 + 1) = `-99 = "The `-YEAR that #1/President George Washington `-DIED (`-1799)"!!!!!~'

#22/#24/President Grover Cleveland `-TOOK the `-OFFICE of `-PRESIDENCY at the `-AGE of `-55 `-YEARS / `-351 `-DAYS!!!!!~'

`-55 = `-23 + `-32

`-351 = (35 x 1) = `-35 = RECIPROCAL = `-53 = "WAR of the WORLDS"!!!!!~'

`-351 = (3 x 51) = `-153 = (53 x 1) = `-53 = "WAR of the WORLDS"!!!!!~'

(351 + 55) = `-406 = (46 + 0) = `-46 = `-23 x `-2 = `-232 = Reciprocal-Sequencing-Numerology-RSN!!!!!~'

#22/#24/FIRST LADY FRANCES CLEVELAND at the `-START of being `-FIRST `-LADY was at the `-AGE of -21 `-YEARS / `-316 `-DAYS!!!!!~'

`-316 = (36 x 1) = `-36 = `-3(6's) = `-666 = (6 x 6 x 6) = `-216 = (2 x 16) = `-32 = -a Prophetic Number!!!!!~'

`-21 = RECIPROCAL = `-12

(21 + 12) = `-33 = "Yin/Yang" = "Multiple of `-ELEVEN" = "The `-CYCLE of `-LIFE"!!!!!~'

`-316 = `-31.6 = ROUNDED = `-32 = -a Prophetic Number!!!!!~'

(316 + 21) = `-337 = `-3(37) = `-111 = (11 x 1) = `-11 = "Yin/Yang" = "Multiple of `-ELEVEN" = "The `-CYCLE of `-LIFE"!!!!!~'

(316 + 21) = `-337 = `-(33)7) = `-231 = (23 x 1) = `-23 = -a Prophetic Number!!!!!~'

#22/#24/President Grover Cleveland `-TOOK the `-OFFICE of `-PRESIDENCY at the `-AGE of `-47 `-YEARS / `-351 `-DAYS!!!!!~'

`-351 = (35 x 1) = `-35 = RECIPROCAL = `-53 = "WAR of the WORLDS"!!!!!~'

`-351 = (3 x 51) = `-153 = (53 x 1) = `-53 = "WAR of the WORLDS"!!!!!~'

(351 (-) 47) = `-**304** = (34 + 0) = `-**34** = **RECIPROCAL** = `-**43** = "The `-PRESIDENTIAL #'s `-NUMBERS"!!!!!~'

(351 + 47) = `-**398** = `-**3(98)** = (98 + 3) = `-**101** = "A `-LESSON in `-PRESIDENTIAL `-POLITICS"!!!!!~'

(351 + 47) = `-**398** = `-**(39)8** = (39 x 8) = `-**312** = (32 x 1) = `-**32** = -a Prophetic Number!!!!!~'

#**23**/FIRST LADY CAROLINE HARRISON at the `-START of being `-FIRST `-LADY was at the `-AGE of -**56** `-YEARS / `-**154** `-DAYS!!!!!~'
#**23**/FIRST LADY CAROLINE HARRISON was `-BORN in `-18**32**!!!!!~'

`-**23** = **RECIPROCAL** = `-**32**

`-**56** = "AGE of `-DEATH of #16/President Abraham Lincoln"!!!!!~'

(154 (-) 55) = `-**99** = "The `-YEAR that #1/President George Washington `-DIED (`-17**99**)"!!!!!~'

#**23**/President Benjamin Harrison `-TOOK the `-OFFICE of `-PRESIDENCY at the `-AGE of `-**55** `-YEARS / `-**196** `-DAYS!!!!!~'

`-**55** = `-**23** + `-**32** / (196 (-) 55) = `-**141** = `-**14** = **RECIPROCAL** = `-**41**

(41 + 14) = `-**55** = `-**23** + `-**32**

(196 + 55) = `-**251** = (51 + 2) = `-**53** = "WAR of the WORLDS"!!!!!~'

#**23**/FIRST LADY CAROLINE HARRISON `-MARRIED `-HER `-HUSBAND #**23**/President Benjamin Harrison in (`-18**53**) = `-**53** = "WAR of the WORLDS"!!!!!~'

`-**1853** = (53 (-) 18) = `-**35** = **RECIPROCAL** = `-**53** = "WAR of the WORLDS"!!!!!~'

#**23**/FIRST LADY CAROLINE HARRISON was `-MARRIED to `-HER `-HUSBAND #**23**/President Benjamin Harrison for some `-**39** `-YEARS!!!!!~'

`-**39** = **RECIPROCAL** = `-**93**

(93 + 39) = `-**132** = (32 x 1) = `-**32** = -a Prophetic Number!!!!!~'

`-**39** = `-**3(9's)** = `-**999** = (9 x 9 x 9) = `-**729** = `-7(29) = (7 x 29) = `-**203** = (23 + 0) = `-**23** = -a Prophetic Number!!!!!~'

#21/President Chester A. Arthur `-TOOK the `-OFFICE of `-PRESIDENCY at the `-AGE of `-**51** `-YEARS / `-**349** `-DAYS!!!!!~'

`-**51** = **RECIPROCAL** = `-**15**

(51 (-) 15) = `-**36** = **RECIPROCAL** = `-**63** = "AGE of `-DEATH of the "PROPHET'S" MOTHER"!!!!!~

(51 + 15) = `-**66** = "AGE of `-DEATH of the "PROPHET'S" FATHER"!!!!!~

`-**349** = `-**34(9)** = (34 x 9) = `-**306** = (36 + 0) = `-**36** = **RECIPROCAL** = `-**63** = "The `-AGE of `-DEATH of the "PROPHET'S" MOTHER; the `-YEAR of `-ASSASSINATION for #35/President John F. Kennedy; and, the `-YEAR of #36/President Lyndon B. Johnson taking over the `-PRESIDENCY"!!!!!~'

(President #**36** (-) President #**21**) = `-**15** = **RECIPROCAL** = `-**51**

(President #**36** + President #**21**) = `-**57** = **RECIPROCAL** = `-**75**

(75 + 57) = `-**132** = (32 x 1) = `-**32** = -a Prophetic Number!!!!!~'

#20/FIRST LADY LUCRETIA GARFIELD at the `-START of being `-FIRST `-LADY was at the `-AGE of -**48** `-YEARS / `-**319** `-DAYS!!!!!~'
#20/FIRST LADY LUCRETIA GARFIELD was `-BORN in `-18**32**!!!!!~'

`-**319** = `-**31.9** = ROUNDED = `-**32** = -a Prophetic Number!!!!!!~'

(319 + 48) = `-**367** = "**EMPHATIC** `-**EMPHASIS** to the # `-NUMBER `-**67** = "The `-YEAR that the "PROPHET'S" BROTHER was `-BORN, the `-AVERAGE `-AGE of the United States Presidents 1 to 28 in "SUCCESSION" above; and, below `-ALL `-PRESIDENTS that `-DIED at `-AGES `-66, `-67; and, `-68; and, The `-AGE of `-DEATH

of the #1/President of the United States of America #1/President George Washington"!!!!!~'

(319 (-) 48) = `-**271** = (71 (-) 2) = `-**69** = "Yin/Yang" = "The `-CYCLE of `-LIFE"!!!!!~'

#**20**/President James A. Garfield `-TOOK the `-OFFICE of `-PRESIDENCY at the `-AGE of `-**49** `-YEARS / `-**105** `-DAYS!!!!!~'

`-**49** = **RECIPROCAL** = `-**94**

`-**49** = "The `-AGE of `-DEATH of SIR ALEXANDER HAMILTON"!!!!!~'

`-**94** = "The `-AGE of `-DEATH of FIRST LADY LADY BIRD JOHNSON"!!!!!~'

(105 (-) 49) = `-**56** = "AGE of `-DEATH of #16/President Abraham Lincoln"!!!!!~'

(105 + 49) = `-**154** = (54 + 1) = `-**55** = `-**23** + `-**32**

#**20**/FIRST LADY LUCRETIA GARFIELD `-MARRIED `-HER `-HUSBAND #**20**/President James A. Garfield in (`-1**858**); and, the `-**MARRIAGE** `-**ENDED** upon `-**HER** `-**HUSBAND'S** `-**DEATH** `-**IN** (`-**1881**)!!!!!~'

`-**1858** = (858 x 1) = `-**858** = "Reciprocal-Sequencing-Numerology-RSN"!!!!!~'

`-**1881** = `-**18** = **RECIPROCAL** = `-**81**

#**20**/FIRST LADY LUCRETIA GARFIELD was `-MARRIED to `-HER `-HUSBAND #**20**/President James A. Garfield for some `-**23** `-YEARS!!!!!~'

#**16**/FIRST LADY MARY TODD LINCOLN was `-MARRIED to `-HER `-HUSBAND #**16**/President Abraham Lincoln for some `-**23** `-YEARS; `-**just as well!!!!!~'**

#**19**/FIRST LADY LUCY WEBB HAYES at the `-START of being `-FIRST `-LADY was at the `-AGE of -**45** `-YEARS / `-**188** `-DAYS!!!!!~'

`-**45** = "CURRENT `-AGE of the "PROPHET"!!!!!~'

`-**188** = (88 x 1) = `-**88** = "AGE of `-DEATH of the "PROPHET'S" GRANDFATHER (FATHER'S FATHER)!!!!!~'

AMERICAN/ENGLISH `-ALPHABET '-to-' `-NUMBERS #'s:!!!!!~'

FF = `-**6**, `-**6** = "The "PROPHET'S" FATHER `-DIED at the `-AGE of (`-**66**)"!!!!!~'

`-**188** = `-**(18)8** = (18 x 8) = `-**144** = (44 x 1) = `-**44** = "The `-YEAR that the "PROPHET'S" MOTHER was `-BORN (`-19**44**)!!!!!~'

(188 (-) 45) = `-**143** = (43 x 1) = `-**43** = **RECIPROCAL** = `-**34** = "The `-PRESIDENTIAL #'s `-NUMBERS"!!!!!~'

(188 + 45) = `-**233** = `-**(23)3** = "EMPHATIC `-EMPHASIS on the # `-NUMBER `-**23** = -a Prophetic Number!!!!!~'

(188 + 45) = `-**233** = `-**2(33)** = (33 x 2) = `-**66** = "AGE of `-DEATH of the "PROPHET'S" FATHER"!!!!!~'

(188 + 45) = `-**233** = `-**23(3)** = `-**69** = "Yin/Yang" = "The `-CYCLE of `-LIFE"!!!!!~'

#**18**/FIRST LADY JULIA BOGGS GRANT at the `-START of being `-FIRST `-LADY was at the `-AGE of -**43** `-YEARS / `-**37** `-DAYS!!!!!~' #**18**/ FIRST LADY JULIA BOGGS GRANT was `-BORN in `-18**26** /|\ `-**26** = `-**13** x `-**2** = `-**132** = (1 x 32) = `-**32** = -a Prophetic Number!!!!!~'

`-**43** = **RECIPROCAL** = `-**34** = "The `-PRESIDENTIAL #'s `-NUMBERS"!!!!!~'

`-**37** = `-**3(7's)** = (777) = (7 x 7 x 7) = `-**343** = **Reciprocal-Sequencing-Numerology-RSN** = "The `-PRESIDENTIAL #'s `-NUMBERS"!!!!!~'

#**18**/President Ulysses S. Grant `-TOOK the `-OFFICE of `-PRESIDENCY at the `-AGE of `-**46** `-YEARS / `-**311** `-DAYS!!!!!~'

`-**46** = `-**23** x `-**2** = `-**232** = **Reciprocal-Sequencing-Numerology-RSN**!!!!!~'

`-**311** = (31 + 1) = `-**32** = -a Prophetic Number!!!!!~'

(311 + 46) = `-**357** = `-**(35)7** = (35 x 7) = `-**245** = (45 (-) 2) = `-**43** = **RECIPROCAL** = `-**34** = "The `-**PRESIDENTIAL** #'s `-**NUMBERS**"!!!!!~'

(311 (-) 46) = `-**265** = (65 + 2) = `-**67** = "The `-YEAR that the "PROPHET'S" BROTHER was `-BORN, the `-AVERAGE `-AGE of the United States Presidents 1 to 28 in "SUCCESSION" above; and, below `-ALL `-PRESIDENTS that `-DIED at `-AGES `-66, `-67; and, `-68; and, The `-AGE of `-DEATH of the #1/President of the United States of America #1/President George Washington"!!!!!~'

#**18**/FIRST LADY JULIA BOGGS GRANT was `-MARRIED to `-HER `-HUSBAND #**18**/President Ulysses S. Grant for some `-**37** `-YEARS!!!!!~'

`-**37** = `-**3(7's)** = (777) = (7 x 7 x 7) = `-**343** = **R**eciprocal-**S**equencing-**N**umerology-**RSN** = "The `-**PRESIDENTIAL** #'s `-**NUMBERS**"!!!!!~'

#**17**/FIRST LADY ELIZA MCCARDLE JOHNSON at the `-START of being `-FIRST `-LADY was at the `-AGE of -**54** `-YEARS / `-**193** `-DAYS!!!!!~' #**18**/FIRST LADY JULIA BOGGS GRANT `-DIED in `-18**76**!!!!!~'

`-**54** = **RECIPROCAL** = `-**45** = "CURRENT `-AGE of the "PROPHET"!!!!!~'

`-**193** = (93 x 1) = `-**93** = **RECIPROCAL** = `-**39** = `-**3(9's)** = `-**999** = (9 x 9 x 9) = `-**729** = `-**7(29)** = (7 x 29) = `-**203** = (23 + 0) = `-**23** = -a Prophetic Number!!!!!~'

(193 (-) 54) = `-**139** = (39 x 1) = `-**39** = `-**3(9's)** = `-**999** = (9 x 9 x 9) = `-**729** = `-**7(29)** = (7 x 29) = `-**203** = (23 + 0) = `-**23** = -a Prophetic Number!!!!!~'

(193 + 54) = `-**247** = `-**(24)7** = (24 x 7) = `-**168** = (68 (-) 1) = `-**67** = "The `-YEAR that the "PROPHET'S" BROTHER was `-BORN, the `-AVERAGE `-AGE of the United States Presidents 1 to 28 in "SUCCESSION" above; and, below `-ALL `-PRESIDENTS that `-DIED at `-AGES `-66, `-67; and, `-68; and, The `-AGE of `-DEATH of the #1/President of the United States of America #1/President George Washington"!!!!!~'

#**17**/President Andrew Johnson `-TOOK the `-OFFICE of `-PRESIDENCY at the `-AGE of `-**56** `-YEARS / `-**107** `-DAYS!!!!!~'

`-**56** = "AGE of `-DEATH of #16/President Abraham Lincoln"!!!!!~'

180

(107 + 56) = `-**163** = (63 x 1) = `-**63** = "The `-AGE of `-DEATH of the "PROPHET'S" MOTHER; the `-YEAR of `-ASSASSINATION for #35/President John F. Kennedy; and, the `-YEAR of #36/President Lyndon B. Johnson taking over the `-PRESIDENCY"!!!!!~'

(107 (-) 56) = `-**51** = **RECIPROCAL** = `-**15**

(51 + 15) = `-**66** = "AGE of `-DEATH of the "PROPHET'S" FATHER"!!!!!~'

(51 (-) 15) = `-**36** = `-**3(6's)** = `-**666** = (6 x 6 x 6) = `-**216** = (2 x 16) = `-**32** = -a Prophetic Number!!!!!~'

#**17**/FIRST LADY ELIZA MCCARDLE JOHNSON was `-MARRIED to `-HER `-HUSBAND #**17**/President Andrew Johnson for some `-**48** `-YEARS!!!!!~'

`-**48** = **RECIPROCAL** = `-**84**

(84 + 48) = `-**132** = (32 x 1) = `-**32** = -a Prophetic Number!!!!!~'

#**16**/FIRST LADY MARY TODD LINCOLN at the `-START of being `-FIRST `-LADY was at the `-AGE of -**42** `-YEARS / `-**81** `-DAYS!!!!!~'

#**16**/FIRST LADY MARY TODD LINCOLN was `-BORN in `-**1818** = (18 + 18) = `-**36** = `-**3(6's)** = `-**666** = (6 x 6 x 6) = `-**216** = (2 x 16) = `-**32** = -a Prophetic Number!!!!!~'

(81 (-) 42) = `-**39** = `-**3(9's)** = `-**999** = (9 x 9 x 9) = `-**729** = `-7(29) = (7 x 29) = `-**203** = (23 + 0) = `-**23** = -a Prophetic Number!!!!!~'

(81 + 42) = `-**123** = "**Prophetic-Linear-Progression-PLP**"!!!!!~'

#**16**/President Abraham Lincoln `-TOOK the `-OFFICE of `-PRESIDENCY at the `-AGE of `-**52** `-YEARS / `-**20** `-DAYS!!!!!~'

(52 (-) 20) = `-**32** = -a Prophetic Number!!!!!~'

`-**23** = **RECIPROCAL** = `-**32**

(52 + 20) = `-**72** = **RECIPROCAL** = `-**27**

(72 (-) 27) = `-**45** = "CURRENT `-AGE of the "PROPHET at the `-TIME of this `-WRITING"-'"!!!!!~'

#**16**/FIRST LADY MARY TODD LINCOLN was `-MARRIED to `-HER `-HUSBAND #**16**/President Abraham Lincoln for some `-**23** `-YEARS!!!!!~'

(#**16** x **2**) = `-**32** = -a Prophetic Number!!!!!~'

#**15**/President James Buchanan `-TOOK the `-OFFICE of `-PRESIDENCY at the `-AGE of `-**65** `-YEARS / `-**315** `-DAYS!!!!!~'

`-**65** = "YEAR of `-DEATH of #16/President Abraham Lincoln"!!!!!~'

`-**315** = `-**31.5** = ROUNDED = `-**32** = -a Prophetic Number!!!!!~'

`-**315** = (35 x 1) = `-**35** = **RECIPROCAL** = `-**53** = "WAR of the WORLDS"!!!!!~'

(315 + 65) = `-**380** = (38 + 0) = `-**38** = 3(8's) = `-**888** = (8 x 8 x 8) = `-**512** = (5 (1 + 2)) = `-**53** = "WAR of the WORLDS"!!!!!~

#**14**/FIRST LADY JANE MEANS PIERCE at the `-START of being `-FIRST `-LADY was at the `-AGE of -**46** `-YEARS / `-**357** `-DAYS!!!!!~'

#**14**/FIRST LADY JANE MEANS PIERCE was `-MARRIED in `-18**34**, was FIRST LADY in `-18**53**; and, `-DIED in `-18**63**!!!!!~'

`-**46** = `-**23** x `-**2** = `-**232** = Reciprocal-**S**equencing-**N**umerology-**RSN**!!!!!~'

`-**357** = `-**(35)7** = (35 x 7) = `-**245** = (45 (-) 2) = `-**43** = **RECIPROCAL** = `-**34** = "The `-PRESIDENTIAL #'s `-NUMBERS"!!!!!~'

(357 (-) 46) = `-**311** = (31 + 1) = `-**32** = -a Prophetic Number!!!!!~'

(357 + 46) = `-**403** = (43 + 0) = `-**43** = **RECIPROCAL** = `-**34** = "The `-PRESIDENTIAL #'s `-NUMBERS"!!!!!~'

#**14**/President Franklin Pierce `-TOOK the `-OFFICE of `-PRESIDENCY at the `-AGE of `-**48** `-YEARS / `-**101** `-DAYS!!!!!~'

`-**101** = "A `-LESSON in `-PRESIDENTIAL `-POLITICS"!!!!!~'

(101 + 48) = `-**149** = (49 x 1) = `-**49** = **RECIPROCAL** = `-**94**

`-**49** = "The `-AGE of `-DEATH of SIR ALEXANDER HAMILTON"!!!!!~'

`-**94** = "The `-AGE of `-DEATH of FIRST LADY LADY BIRD JOHNSON"!!!!!~'

(101 (-) 48) = `-**53** = "WAR of the WORLDS"!!!!!~'

#**14**/FIRST LADY JANE MEANS PIERCE was `-MARRIED to `-HER `-HUSBAND #**14**/President Franklin Pierce for some `-**29** `-YEARS!!!!!~'

`-ONE (`-1) `-YEAR `-AWAY in `-MARRIAGE from `-THEIR `-PRESIDENCY # `-NUMBER being `-DOUBLED!!!!!~'

`-**29** = **RECIPROCAL** = `-**92**

(92 + 29) = `-**121** = **Reciprocal-Sequencing-Numerology-RSN**!!!!!~'

The `-AGE of `-DEATHS `-ADDED `-UP for #**14**/FIRST LADY JANE MEANS PIERCE (`-**57**); and, `-HER `-HUSBAND #**14**/President Franklin Pierce (`-**64**) = `-**EQUALS** = `-**121** = **Reciprocal-Sequencing-Numerology-RSN**!!!!!~'

(64 + 57) = `-**121** = **Reciprocal-Sequencing-Numerology-RSN**!!!!!~'

`-**121** = (12 + 1) = `-**13** = "A VERY PIVOTAL NUMBER"!!!!!~'

#**13**/FIRST LADY ABIGAIL FILLMORE at the `-START of being `-FIRST `-LADY was at the `-AGE of -**52** `-YEARS / `-**118** `-DAYS!!!!!~'

#**13**/FIRST LADY ABIGAIL FILLMORE `-**DIED** in `-18**53**!!!!!~'

`-**1853** = (53 (-) 18) = `-**35** = **RECIPROCAL** = `-**53** = "WAR of the WORLDS"!!!!!~'

(118 (-) 52) = `-**66** = "AGE of `-DEATH of the "PROPHET'S" FATHER"!!!!!~'

(118 + 52) = `-**170** = (70 x 1) = "The `-YEAR that the "PROPHET" was `-BORN (`-19**70**)"!!!!!~'

(183 (-) 52) = `-**131** = **R**eciprocal-**S**equencing-**N**umerology-**RSN** = (31 + 1) = `-**32** = -a Prophetic Number!!!!!~'

#**13**/President Millard Fillmore `-TOOK the `-OFFICE of `-PRESIDENCY at the `-AGE of `-**50** `-YEARS / `-**183** `-DAYS!!!!!~'

(118 + 50) = `-**168** = (68 (-) 1) = `-**67** = "The `-YEAR that the "PROPHET'S" BROTHER was `-BORN, the `-AVERAGE `-AGE of the United States Presidents 1 to 28 in "SUCCESSION" above; and, below `-ALL `-PRESIDENTS that `-DIED at `-AGES `-66, `-67; and, `-68; and, The `-AGE of `-DEATH of the #1/President of the United States of America #1/President George Washington"!!!!!~'

(183 (-) 50) = `-**133** = (33 (-) 1) = `-**32** = -a Prophetic Number!!!!!~'

(183 + 50) = `-**233** = `-**(23)3** = "EMPHATIC `-EMPHASIS on the # `-NUMBER `-**23** = -a Prophetic Number!!!!!~'

(183 + 50) = `-**233** = `-**2(33)** = (33 x 2) = `-**66** = "AGE of `-DEATH of the "PROPHET'S" FATHER"!!!!!~'

(183 + 50) = `-**233** = `-**23(3)** = `-**69** = "Yin/Yang" = "The `-CYCLE of `-LIFE"!!!!!~'

#**13**/FIRST LADY ABIGAIL FILLMORE was `-MARRIED to `-HER `-HUSBAND #**13**/President Millard Fillmore for some `-**27** `-YEARS!!!!!~'

`-ONE (`-1) `-YEAR `-AWAY in `-MARRIAGE from `-THEIR `-PRESIDENCY # `-NUMBER being `-DOUBLED!!!!!~'

The `-AGE of `-DEATHS `-ADDED `-UP for #**13**/FIRST LADY ABIGAIL FILLMORE (`-**55**); and, `-HER `-HUSBAND #**13**/President Millard Fillmore (`-**74**) = `-**EQUALS** = `-**129** = `-**12.9** = ROUNDED = `-**13** = "A VERY PIVOTAL NUMBER"!!!!!~'

(74 + 55) = `-**129** = (29 x 1) = `-**29** = "FIRST LADY JANE MEANS PIERCE; and, President Franklin Pierce"!!!!!~'

#**14**/FIRST LADY JANE MEANS PIERCE was `-MARRIED to `-HER `-HUSBAND #**14**/President Franklin Pierce for some `-**29** `-YEARS!!!!!~'

(1<u>3</u>/1<u>4</u>) = (<u>34</u> x 1 x 1) = `-<u>34</u> = **RECIPROCAL** = `-<u>43</u> = "**The `-PRESIDENTIAL #'s `-NUMBERS**"!!!!!~'

#<u>12</u>/FIRST LADY MARGARET TAYLOR at the `-START of being `-FIRST `-LADY was at the `-AGE of -<u>60</u> `-YEARS / `-<u>164</u> `-DAYS!!!!!~'

#<u>12</u>/FIRST LADY MARGARET TAYLOR `-**DIED** at the `-AGE of (`-<u>63</u>)-"!!!!!~'

(164 + 60) = `-<u>224</u> = `-<u>22.4</u> = **ROUNDED UP** = `-<u>23</u> = -a **Prophetic Number**!!!!!~'

(164 + 60) = `-<u>224</u> = `-<u>(22)4</u> = (22 x 4) = `-<u>88</u> = "**AGE of `-DEATH of the "PROPHET'S" GRANDFATHER (FATHER'S FATHER)**!!!!!~'

AMERICAN/ENGLISH `-ALPHABET '-to-' `-NUMBERS #'s:!!!!!~'

FF = `-<u>6</u>, `-<u>6</u> = "**The "PROPHET'S" FATHER `-DIED at the `-AGE of (`-66)**"!!!!!~'

#<u>12</u>/President Zachary Taylor `-TOOK the `-OFFICE of `-PRESIDENCY at the `-AGE of `-<u>64</u> `-YEARS / `-<u>100</u> `-DAYS!!!!!~'

(100 + 64) = `-<u>164</u> = "**DAYS of #12/FIRST LADY MARGARET TAYLOR taking on the `-ROLE of `-FIRST LADY**"!!!!!~'

(100 (-) 64) = `-<u>36</u> = `-<u>3(6's)</u> = `-<u>666</u> = (6 x 6 x 6) = `-<u>216</u> = (2 x 16) = `-<u>32</u> = -a **Prophetic Number**!!!!!~'

#<u>12</u>/FIRST LADY MARGARET TAYLOR was `-MARRIED to `-HER `-HUSBAND #<u>12</u>/President Zachary Taylor for some `-<u>40</u> `-YEARS!!!!!~'

The `-AGE of `-DEATHS `-ADDED `-UP for #<u>12</u>/FIRST LADY MARGARET TAYLOR (`-<u>63</u>); and, `-HER `-HUSBAND #<u>12</u>/President Zachary Taylor (`-<u>65</u>) = `-**EQUALS** = `-<u>128</u> = `-<u>12.8</u> = **ROUNDED** = `-<u>13</u> = "**A VERY PIVOTAL NUMBER**"!!!!!~'

(65 + 63) = `-<u>128</u> = (28 + 1) = `-<u>29</u> = "**FIRST LADY JANE MEANS PIERCE; and, President Franklin Pierce**"!!!!!~'

#**14**/FIRST LADY JANE MEANS PIERCE was `-MARRIED to `-HER `-HUSBAND #**14**/President Franklin Pierce for some `-**29** `-YEARS!!!!!~'

#**11**/FIRST LADY SARAH POLK at the `-START of being `-FIRST `-LADY was at the `-AGE of -**41** `-YEARS / `-**181** `-DAYS!!!!!~'

`-181 = (81 + 1) = `-**82** = "AGE of `-DEATH of the "PROPHET'S" GRANDMOTHER (FATHER'S MOTHER)!!!!!~'

`-**181** = **R**eciprocal-**S**equencing-**N**umerology-**RSN**!!!!!~'

(181 + 41) = `-**222** = `-**3(2's)** = `-**32** = -a Prophetic Number!!!!!~'

(181 + 122) = `-**303** = (33 + 0) = `-**33** = "Yin/Yang" = "Multiple of `-ELEVEN" = "The `-CYCLE of `-LIFE"!!!!!~'

#**12**/President James K. Polk `-TOOK the `-OFFICE of `-PRESIDENCY at the `-AGE of `-**49** `-YEARS / `-**122** `-DAYS!!!!!~'

`-**49** = **RECIPROCAL** = `-**94**

`-**49** = "The `-AGE of `-DEATH of SIR ALEXANDER HAMILTON"!!!!!~'

`-**94** = "The `-AGE of `-DEATH of FIRST LADY LADY BIRD JOHNSON"!!!!!~'

`-**122** = (22 + 1) = `-**23** = -a Prophetic Number!!!!!~'

(122 (-) 49) = `-**73** = **RECIPROCAL** = `-**37** = `-**3(7's)** = (777) = (7 x 7 x 7) = `-**343** = **R**eciprocal-**S**equencing-**N**umerology-**RSN** = "The `-PRESIDENTIAL #'s `-NUMBERS"!!!!!~'

(122 (-) 41) = `-**81** = "DAYS of #**11**/FIRST LADY SARAH POLK taking on the `-ROLE of `-FIRST LADY"!!!!!~'

(122 + 41) = `-**163** = (63 x 1) = `-**63** = "The `-AGE of `-DEATH of the "PROPHET'S" MOTHER; the `-YEAR of `-ASSASSINATION for #**35**/President John F. Kennedy; and, the `-YEAR of #**36**/President Lyndon B. Johnson taking over the `-PRESIDENCY"!!!!!~'

#**11**/FIRST LADY SARAH POLK was `-MARRIED to `-HER `-HUSBAND #**11**/President James K. Polk for some `-**25** `-YEARS!!!!!~'

The `-AGES of `-DEATH `-SUBTRACTED for #**11**/FIRST LADY SARAH POLK (`-**87**); and, `-HER `-HUSBAND #**11**/President James K. Polk (`-**53**)!!!!!~'

(87 (-) 53) = `-**34** = **RECIPROCAL** = `-**43** = "The `-**PRESIDENTIAL** #'s `-**NUMBERS**"!!!!!~'

#**10**/FIRST LADY JULIA GARDINER TYLER at the `-START of being `-FIRST `-LADY was at the `-AGE of -**24** `-YEARS / `-**53** `-DAYS!!!!!~'

`-**53** = "WAR of the WORLDS"!!!!!~'

(53 + 24) = `-**77** = "Yin/Yang" = "Multiple of `-ELEVEN" = "The `-CYCLE of `-LIFE"!!!!!~'

#**10**/President John Tyler `-TOOK the `-OFFICE of `-PRESIDENCY at the `-AGE of `-**51** `-YEARS / `-**6** `-DAYS!!!!!~'

`-**51** = **RECIPROCAL** = `-**15**

(51 + 15) = `-**66** = "AGE of `-DEATH of the "PROPHET'S" FATHER"!!!!!~'

(**51**/**6**) = (56 x 1) = `-**56** = "AGE of `-DEATH of #16/President Abraham Lincoln"!!!!!~'

(**51**/**6**) = (56 (-) 1) = `-**55** = `-**23** + `-**32**

#**10**/FIRST LADY LETITIA CHRISTIAN TYLER at the `-START of being `-FIRST `-LADY was at the `-AGE of `-**50** `-YEARS / `-**143** `-DAYS!!!!!~'

(143 (-) 50) = `-**93** = **RECIPROCAL** = `-**39** = `-**3(9's)** = `-**999** = (9 x 9 x 9) = `-**729** = `-7(29) = (7 x 29) = `-**203** = (23 + 0) = `-**23** = -a Prophetic Number!!!!!~'

(143 + 50) = `-**193** = (93 x 1) = `-**93** = **RECIPROCAL** = `-**39** = `-**3(9's)** = `-**999** = (9 x 9 x 9) = `-**729** = `-7(29) = (7 x 29) = `-**203** = (23 + 0) = `-**23** = -a Prophetic Number!!!!!~'

`-143 = (43 x 1) = `-**43** = **RECIPROCAL** = `-**34** = "**The** `-**PRESIDENTIAL #'s** `-**NUMBERS**"!!!!!~'

`-**143** = (43 + 1) = `-**44** = "**#1/President** George **Washington was** `-**44** `-**YEARS of** `-**AGE in** (`-17**76**) **on the very** `-**FIRST** `-**INDEPENDENCE** `-**DAY of which** `-**HE** `-**DIED on the** `-**EXACT same** `-**DAY** `-**RECIPROCAL #** `-**NUMBER of which** `-**HE was at the** `-**AGE of** (`-**67**)-`"!!!!!~'

#10/FIRST LADY JULIA GARDINER TYLER was `-MARRIED to **#10**/President John Tyler for (`-**18**) `-YEARS!!!!!~' **#10**/FIRST LADY LETITIA CHRISTIAN TYLER was `-MARRIED to **#10**/President John Tyler for (`-**29**) `-YEARS!!!!!~'

(29 (-) 18) = `-**11** = "**Yin/Yang**" = "**Multiple of** `-**ELEVEN**" = "**The** `-**CYCLE of** `-**LIFE**"!!!!!~'

#10/FIRST LADY JULIA GARDINER TYLER `-DIED at the `-AGE of (`-**69**) `-YEARS; `-**54** `-DAYS!!!!!~'

#10/FIRST LADY LETITIA CHRISTIAN TYLER `-DIED at the `-AGE of (`-**51**) `-YEARS; `-**3**0**2** `-DAYS!!!!!~'

#10/President John Tyler `-DIED at the `-AGE of (`-**71**) `-YEARS; `-**295** `-DAYS!!!!!~'

`-**295** = `-**(29)5** = (29 x 5) = `-**145** = (45 x 1) = `-**45** = **RECIPROCAL** = `-**54** = "**#10/FIRST LADY JULIA GARDINER TYLER**"!!!!!~'

(71 + 51) = `-**122** = (22 + 1) = `-**23** = -a Prophetic Number!!!!!~'

(122 (-) 69) = `-**53** = "**WAR of the WORLDS**"!!!!!~'

`-**69** = "**Yin/Yang**" = "**The** `-**CYCLE of** `-**LIFE**"!!!!!~'

#9/FIRST LADY ANNA HARRISON at the `-START of being `-FIRST `-LADY was at the `-AGE of -**65** `-YEARS / `-**222** `-DAYS!!!!!~'

`-**65** = "**YEAR of** `-**DEATH of #16/President Abraham Lincoln**"!!!!!~'

`-**222** = `-**3(2's)** = `-**32** = -a Prophetic Number!!!!!~'

(222 + 65) = `-**287** = `-**(28)7** = (28 + 7) = `-**35** = **RECIPROCAL** = `-**53** = "**WAR of the WORLDS**"!!!!!~'

(222 (-) 65) = `-**157** = (57 x 1) = `-**57** = **RECIPROCAL** = `-**75**

(75 + 57) = `-**132** = (32 x 1) = `-**32** = -a **Prophetic Number!!!!!~'**

#**9**/President William Henry Harrison `-TOOK the `-OFFICE of `-PRESIDENCY at the `-AGE of `-**68** `-YEARS / `-**23** `-DAYS!!!!!~'

`-**68** = **RECIPROCAL** = `-**86**

(86 + 68) = `-**154** = (54 + 1) = `-**55** = `-**23** + `-**32** / `-**23** = -a **Prophetic Number!!!!!~'**

(68 (-) 23) = `-**45** = **RECIPROCAL** = `-**54** = "**EARTHQUAKES**" = "(`-**68** `-YEARS; and, `-**54** `-DAYS in `-LIVING**"!!!!!~'**

#**9**/FIRST LADY ANNA HARRISON was `-MARRIED to `-HER `-HUSBAND #**9**/President William Henry Harrison for some `-**46** `-YEARS!!!!!~'

`-**46** = `-**23** x `-**2** = `-**232** = **Reciprocal-Sequencing-Numerology-RSN!!!!!~'**

The `-AGE of `-DEATHS `-ADDED `-UP for #**9**/FIRST LADY ANNA HARRISON (`-**88**); and, `-HER `-HUSBAND #**9**/President William Henry Harrison (`-**68**) = `-**EQUALS** = `-**156** = (56 x 1) = `-**56** = "**AGE of `-DEATH of #16/President Abraham Lincoln**"!!!!!~'

(88 + 68) = `-**156** = (56 (-) 1) = `-**55** = `-**23** + `-**32**

(88 + 68) = `-**156** = (56 + 1) = `-**57** = **RECIPROCAL** = `-**75**

(75 + 57) = `-**132** = (32 x 1) = `-**32** = -a **Prophetic Number!!!!!~'**

#**7**/FIRST LADY EMILY DONELSON at the `-START of being `-FIRST `-LADY was at the `-AGE of -**21** `-YEARS / `-**276** `-DAYS!!!!!~'

`-**276** = "**EMPHATIC `-WITNESS to the # `-NUMBER `-76 in being `-INDEPENDENCE `-DAY**"!!!!!~'

189

`-**276** = `-**2(76)** = (2 x 76) = `-**152** = (52 + 1) = `-**53** = "WAR of the WORLDS"!!!!!~'

`-**276** = `-**(27)6** = (27 x 6) = `-**162** = (62 + 1) = `-**63** = "The `-AGE of `-DEATH of the "PROPHET'S" MOTHER; the `-YEAR of `-ASSASSINATION for #**35**/President John F. Kennedy; and, the `-YEAR of #**36**/President Lyndon B. Johnson taking over the `-PRESIDENCY"!!!!!~'

(276 (-) 21) = `-**255** = `-**2(55)** = (55 x 2) = `-**110** = (11 + 0) = `-**11** = "Yin/Yang" = "Multiple of `-ELEVEN" = "The `-CYCLE of `-LIFE"!!!!!~'

(276 + 21) = `-**297** = `-**(29)7** = (29 x 7) = `-**203** = (23 + 0) = `-**23** = -a Prophetic Number"!!!!!~'

#**7**/President Andrew Jackson `-TOOK the `-OFFICE of `-PRESIDENCY at the `-AGE of `-**61** `-YEARS / `-**354** `-DAYS!!!!!~'

`-**61** = (6 x 1) = `-**6** = `-**2** x `-**3** = `-**23** = -a Prophetic Number!!!!!~'

`-**61** = (6 x 1) = `-**6** = `-**3** x `-**2** = `-**32** = -a Prophetic Number!!!!!~'

`-**354** = `-**3(54)** = (54 x 3) = `-**162** = (62 + 1) = `-**63** = "The `-AGE of `-DEATH of the "PROPHET'S" MOTHER; the `-YEAR of `-ASSASSINATION for #**35**/President John F. Kennedy; and, the `-YEAR of #**36**/President Lyndon B. Johnson taking over the `-PRESIDENCY"!!!!!~'

(354 (-) 61) = `-**293** = "EMPHATIC `-WITNESS to the # `-NUMBER (`-93) = RECIPROCAL = (`-39) = (93 + 39) = `-**132** = (32 x 1) = `-**32** = -a Prophetic Number"!!!!!~'

(354 + 61) = `-**415** = (45 x 1) = `-**45** = "CURRENT `-AGE of the "PROPHET"-"!!!!!~'

#**7**/President Andrew Jackson's `-WIFE; RACHEL JACKSON, was `-BORN in `-1**767** as `-HE was; and, `-SHE had `-DIED in `-1**828**!!!!!~'

`-1**767** = (767 x 1) = `-**767** = Reciprocal-Sequencing-Numerology-RSN!!!!!~'

`-1**828** = (828 x 1) = `-**828** = Reciprocal-Sequencing-Numerology-RSN!!!!!~'

#**7**/President Andrew Jackson's `-WIFE; RACHEL JACKSON, `-DIED at the `-AGE of (`-**61**)!!!!!~' The `-SAME `-AGE (`-**61**) that #**7**/President Andrew Jackson was for `-WHEN `-HE took `-OFFICE of the `-PRESIDENCY!!!!!~'

(61 + 61) = `-**122** = (22 + 1) = `-**23** = -**a Prophetic Number!!!!!**~'

SARAH JACKSON was `-**31** `-YEARS; and, `-**133** `-DAYS when #**7**/President Andrew Jackson became `-PRESIDENT!!!!!~'

`-**31** = **RECIPROCAL** = `-**13** = **"A VERY PIVOTAL NUMBER"!!!!!**~'

`-**133** = (33 (-) 1) = `-**32** = -**a Prophetic Number!!!!!**~'

`-**133** = `-**(13)3** = (13 x 3) = `-**39** = `-**3(9's)** = `-**999** = (9 x 9 x 9) = `-**729** = `-7(29) = (7 x 29) = `-**203** = (23 + 0) = `-**23** = -**a Prophetic Number!!!!!**~'

#**6**/FIRST LADY LOUISA ADAMS at the `-START of being `-FIRST `-LADY was at the `-AGE of `-**50** `-YEARS / `-**20** `-DAYS!!!!!~'

(50 + 20) = `-**70** = **"The `-YEAR of the "PROPHET'S" BIRTH (`-19**_**70**_**)"!!!!!**~'

#**6**/President John Quincy Adams `-TOOK the `-OFFICE of `-PRESIDENCY at the `-AGE of `-**57** `-YEARS / `-**236** `-DAYS!!!!!~'

`-**57** = **RECIPROCAL** = `-**75**

(75 + 57) = `-**132** = (32 x 1) = `-**32** = -**a Prophetic Number!!!!!**~'

`-**236** = `-**(23)6** = (23 x 6) = `-**138** = (38 x 1) = `-**38** = **3(8's)** = `-**888** = (8 x 8 x 8) = `-**512** = (5 (1 + 2)) = `-**53** = **"WAR of the WORLDS"!!!!!**~

(236 (-) 57) = `-**179** = (79 x 1) = `-**79** = **"AGE of `-DEATH for Mr. H. G. Wells of the "WAR of the WORLDS"-"!!!!!**~'

(236 + 57) = `-**293** = **"EMPHATIC `-WITNESS to the # `-NUMBER (`-93) = RECIPROCAL = (`-39) = (93 + 39) = `-132 = (32 x 1) = `-32 = -a Prophetic Number"!!!!!**~'

#**6**/FIRST LADY LOUISA ADAMS was `-MARRIED to `-HER `-HUSBAND #**6**/President John Quincy Adams for some `-**51** `-YEARS!!!!!~'

`-**51** = **RECIPROCAL** = `-**15**

(51 + 15) = `-**66** = **"AGE of `-DEATH of the "PROPHET'S" FATHER"!!!!!**~'

(51 (-) 15) = `-**36** = `-**3(6's)** = `-**666** = (6 x 6 x 6) = `-**216** = (2 x 16) = `-**32** = -a **Prophetic Number!!!!!~'**

(51 (-) 15) = `-**36** = **RECIPROCAL** = `-**63** = "AGE of `-DEATH of the "PROPHET'S" MOTHER"!!!!!~'**

The `-AGE of `-DEATHS `-ADDED `-UP for #**6**/FIRST LADY LOUISA ADAMS (`-**77**); and, `-HER `-HUSBAND #**6**/President John Quincy Adams (`-**80**) = `-**EQUALS** = `-**157** = (57 (-) 1) = `-**56** = "AGE of `-DEATH of #16/ President Abraham Lincoln"!!!!!~'**

#**6**/President John Quincy Adams was `-BORN in (`-1**767**) just as well; and, had `-DIED on the `-**23**ʳᵈ of the `-MONTH in `-1**848**!!!!!~'

`-**1767** = (767 x 1) = `-**767** = **R**eciprocal-**S**equencing-**N**umerology-**RSN**!!!!!~'

`-**1848** = (848 x 1) = `-**848** = **R**eciprocal-**S**equencing-**N**umerology-**RSN**!!!!!~'

#**5**/FIRST LADY ELIZABETH MONROE at the `-START of being `-FIRST `-LADY was at the `-AGE of `-**48** `-YEARS / `-**247** `-DAYS!!!!!~'

`-**48** = **RECIPROCAL** = `-**84**

(84 + 48) = `-**132** = (32 x 1) = `-**32** = -a **Prophetic Number!!!!!~'**

`-**247** = `-**(24)7** = (24 x 7) = `-**168** = (68 (-) 1) = `-**67** = "The `-YEAR that the "PROPHET'S" BROTHER was `-BORN, the `-AVERAGE `-AGE of the United States Presidents 1 to 28 in "SUCCESSION" above; and, below `-ALL `-PRESIDENTS that `-DIED at `-AGES `-66, `-67; and, `-68; and, The `-AGE of `-DEATH of the #1/President of the United States of America #1/President George Washington"!!!!!~'

(247 (-) 48) = `-**199** = (99 x 1) = `-**99** = "The `-YEAR that #1/President George Washington `-**DIED** (`-1**799**)"!!!!!~'

#**5**/President James Monroe `-TOOK the `-OFFICE of `-PRESIDENCY at the `-AGE of `-**58** `-YEARS / `-**310** `-DAYS!!!!!~'

`-**58** = (5 + 8) = `-**13** = "A VERY PIVOTAL NUMBER"!!!!!~'

`-**310** = (31 + 0) = `-**31** = **RECIPROCAL** = `-**13** = "A VERY PIVOTAL NUMBER"!!!!!~'

(310 (-) 58) = `-**252** = Reciprocal-**S**equenced-**N**umerology-**RSN**!!!!!~'

(310 + 58) = `-**368** = `-**(36)8** = (36 x 8) = `-**288** = (88 / 2) = `-**44** = "#1/ President **George** Washington was `-**44** `-YEARS of `-AGE in (`-1776) on the very `-FIRST `-INDEPENDENCE `-DAY of which `-HE `-DIED on the `-EXACT same `-DAY `-RECIPROCAL # `-NUMBER of which `-HE was at the `-AGE of (`-67)-'"!!!!!~'

#**5**/FIRST LADY ELIZABETH MONROE was `-MARRIED to `-HER `-HUSBAND #**5**/President James Monroe for some `-**44** `-YEARS!!!!!~'

`-**44** = "**#1/President George** Washington was `-**44** `-YEARS of `-AGE in (`-1776) on the very `-FIRST `-INDEPENDENCE `-DAY of which `-HE `-DIED on the `-EXACT same `-DAY `-RECIPROCAL # `-NUMBER of which `-HE was at the `-AGE of (`-67)-'"!!!!!~'

The `-AGE of `-DEATHS `-ADDED `-UP for #**5**/FIRST LADY ELIZABETH MONROE (`-62); and, `-HER `-HUSBAND #**5**/President James Monroe (`-73) = `-**EQUALS** = `-**135** = (35 x 1) = `-**35** = **RECIPROCAL** = `-**53** = "WAR of the WORLDS"!!!!!~'

#**5**/FIRST LADY ELIZABETH MONROE was `-BORN on (`-06/30) and, had `-DIED on the `-**23**rd of the `-MONTH within **September** (`-09) in `-18**3**0!!!!!~'

`-**69** = "Yin/Yang" = "The `-CYCLE of `-LIFE"!!!!!~'

#**4**/FIRST LADY DOLLEY MADISON at the `-START of being `-FIRST `-LADY was at the `-AGE of `-**40** `-YEARS / `-**288** `-DAYS!!!!!~'

(288 + 40) = `-**328** = `-**3(28)** = (3 x 28) = `-**84** = **RECIPROCAL** = `-**48**

(84 + 48) = `-**132** = (32 x 1) = `-**32** = -a Prophetic Number!!!!!~'

(288 (-) 40) = `-**248** = (48 (-) 2) = `-**46** = `-**23** x `-**2** = `-**232** = **R**eciprocal-**S**equencing-**N**umerology-**RSN**!!!!!~'

#**4**/President James Madison `-TOOK the `-OFFICE of `-PRESIDENCY at the `-AGE of `-**57** `-YEARS / `-**353** `-DAYS!!!!!~'

`-**57** = **RECIPROCAL** = `-**75**

(75 + 57) = `-**132** = (32 x 1) = `-**32** = -a **Prophetic Number!!!!!~'**

`-**353** = **Reciprocal-Sequencing-Numerology-RSN** = `-**35** = **RECIPROCAL** = `-**53** = **"WAR of the WORLDS"!!!!!~'**

(353 (-) 57) = `-**296** = `-**(29)6** = (29 x 6) = `-**174** = (74 x 1) = `-**74** = **RECIPROCAL** = `-**47** = **"The `-DEATH/DAY; and, `-BIRTHDAY #'s of the FIRST LADYS"!!!!!~'**

(353 + 57) = `-**410** = (41 + 0) = `-**41** = **"WAR of the WORLDS"; and, the `-YEAR that the "PROPHET'S" FATHER was `-BORN (`-19_41_)!!!!!~'**

#**4**/FIRST LADY DOLLEY MADISON was `-MARRIED to `-HER `-HUSBAND #**4**/President James Madison for some `-**42** `-YEARS!!!!!~'

`-**42** = (**6** x **7**) = `-**(67)** = `-**67** = **"The `-YEAR that the "PROPHET'S" BROTHER was `-BORN, the `-AVERAGE `-AGE of the United States Presidents 1 to 28 in "SUCCESSION" above; and, below `-ALL `-PRESIDENTS that `-DIED at `-AGES `-66, `-67; and, `-68; and, The `-AGE of `-DEATH of the #1/President of the United States of America #1/President George Washington"!!!!!~'**

The `-AGE of `-DEATHS `-ADDED `-UP for #**4**/FIRST LADY DOLLEY MADISON (`-**81**) `-YEARS / `-**53** `-DAYS; and, `-HER `-HUSBAND #**4**/ President James Madison (`-**85**) `-YEARS / `-**104** `-DAYS = `-**EQUALS** = `-**166** = (66 + 1) = `-**67** = **"The `-YEAR that the "PROPHET'S" BROTHER was `-BORN, the `-AVERAGE `-AGE of the United States Presidents 1 to 28 in "SUCCESSION" above; and, below `-ALL `-PRESIDENTS that `-DIED at `-AGES `-66, `-67; and, `-68; and, The `-AGE of `-DEATH of the #1/President of the United States of America #1/President George Washington"!!!!!~'**

(104 + 53) = `-**157** = (57 x 1) = `-**57** = "AGE at which `-TIME #**4**/President James Madison `-TOOK the `-OFFICE of `-PRESIDENCY!!!!!~'

#**3**/FIRST LADY MARTHA JEFFERSON RANDOLPH at the `-START of being `-FIRST `-LADY was at the `-AGE of `-**28** `-YEARS / `-**158** `-DAYS!!!!!~'

`-**158** = (58 x 1) = `-**58** = (8 + 5) = `-**13** = "A VERY PIVOTAL NUMBER"!!!!!~'

(158 (-) 28) = `-**130** = (13 + 0) = `-**13** = "A VERY PIVOTAL NUMBER"!!!!!~'

(158 + 28) = `-**186** = (86 (-) 1) = `-**85** = (8 + 5) = `-**13** = "A VERY PIVOTAL NUMBER"!!!!!~'

#**3**/FIRST LADY MARTHA JEFFERSON RANDOLPH HAD `-**DIED** at the `-AGE of `-**64** `-YEARS; and, `-**13** `-**DAYS**!!!!!~'

(64 + 13) = `-**77** = "Yin/Yang" = "Multiple of `-ELEVEN" = "The `-CYCLE of `-LIFE"!!!!!~'

#**4**/President Thomas Jefferson `-TOOK the `-OFFICE of `-PRESIDENCY at the `-AGE of `-**57** `-YEARS / `-**325** `-DAYS!!!!!~'

`-**57** = **RECIPROCAL** = `-**75**

(75 + 57) = `-**132** = (32 x 1) = `-**32** = -a Prophetic Number!!!!!~'

(325 (-) 57) = `-**268** = `-**2(68)** = (68 x 2) = `-**136** = (36 x 1) = `-**36** = `-**3(6's)** = `-**666** = (6 x 6 x 6) = `-**216** = (2 x 16) = `-**32** = -a Prophetic Number!!!!!~'

(325 + 57) = `-**382** = `-**(38)2** = (38 x 2) = `-**76** = **RECIPROCAL** = `-**67** = "The `-YEAR that the "PROPHET'S" BROTHER was `-BORN, the `-AVERAGE `-AGE of the United States Presidents 1 to 28 in "SUCCESSION" above; and, below `-ALL `-PRESIDENTS that `-DIED at `-AGES `-66, `-67; and, `-68; and, The `-AGE of `-DEATH of the #1/President of the United States of America #1/President George Washington"!!!!!~'

(325 + 57) = `-**382** = `-**(38)2** = (38 x 2) = `-**76** = (7 + 6) = `-**13** = "A VERY PIVOTAL NUMBER"!!!!!~'

(325 + 57) = `-**382** = `-**(38)2** = (38 (-) 2) = `-**36** = `-**3(6's)** = `-**666** = (6 x 6 x 6) = `-**216** = (2 x 16) = `-**32** = -a Prophetic Number!!!!!~'

MARTHA JEFFERSON; #**4**/President Thomas Jefferson's `-WIFE, `-**DIED** in `-HER `-**34**th `-YEAR of `-LIVING; at the `-AGE of (`-**33**)!!!!!~'

`-**33** = "Yin/Yang" = "Multiple of `-ELEVEN" = "The `-CYCLE of `-LIFE"!!!!!~'

`-**34** = **RECIPROCAL** = `-**43** = "The `-**PRESIDENTIAL** #'s `-**NUMBERS**"!!!!!~'

#**2**/FIRST LADY ABIGAIL ADAMS at the `-START of being `-FIRST `-LADY was at the `-AGE of `-**52** `-YEARS / `-**113** `-DAYS!!!!!~'

`-**113** = (13 x 1) = `-**13** = "A VERY PIVOTAL NUMBER"!!!!!~' / (113 (-) 52) = `-**61**

`-**61** = (6 x 1) = `-**6** = `-**2** x `-**3** = `-**23** = -a Prophetic Number!!!!!~'

`-**61** = (6 x 1) = `-**6** = `-**3** x `-**2** = `-**32** = -a Prophetic Number!!!!!~'

(113 + 52) = `-**165** = (65 x 1) = `-**65** = "YEAR of `-DEATH of #16/President Abraham Lincoln"!!!!!~'

#**2**/President John Adams `-TOOK the `-OFFICE of `-PRESIDENCY at the `-AGE of `-**61** `-YEARS / `-**125** `-DAYS!!!!!~'

`-**61** = (6 x 1) = `-**6** = `-**2** x `-**3** = `-**23** = -a Prophetic Number!!!!!~'

`-**61** = (6 x 1) = `-**6** = `-**3** x `-**2** = `-**32** = -a Prophetic Number!!!!!~'

`-**125** = `-**12.5** = ROUNDED = `-**13** = "A VERY PIVOTAL NUMBER"!!!!!~'

(125 (-) 61) = `-**64** = "AGE of `-DEATH of #**36**/President Lyndon B. Johnson; and, FIRST LADY JACQUELINE LEE KENNEDY"!!!!!~'

(125 + 62) = `-**187** = (87 + 1) = `-**88** = "AGE of `-DEATH of the "PROPHET'S" GRANDFATHER (**F**ATHER'S **F**ATHER)!!!!!~'

AMERICAN/ENGLISH `-**ALPHABET** `-to-` `-**NUMBERS** #'s:!!!!!~'

FF = `-**6**, `-**6** = "The "PROPHET'S" FATHER `-DIED at the `-AGE of (`-**66**)"!!!!!~'

#**2**/FIRST LADY ABIGAIL ADAMS was `-MARRIED to `-HER `-HUSBAND #**2**/President John Adams for some `-**54** `-YEARS!!!!!~'

`-54 = "EARTHQUAKES"!!!!!~'

`-54 = RECIPROCAL = `-45 = "CURRENT `-AGE of the "PROPHET"-"!!!!!~'

The `-AGE of `-DEATHS `-ADDED `-UP for #2/FIRST LADY ABIGAIL ADAMS (`-73) `-YEARS / `-351 `-DAYS; and, `-HER `-HUSBAND #2/ President John Adams (`-90) `-YEARS / `-247 `-DAYS = `-EQUALS = `-163 = (63 x 1) = `-63 = "The `-AGE of `-DEATH of the "PROPHET'S" MOTHER; the `-YEAR of `-ASSASSINATION for #35/President John F. Kennedy; and, the `-YEAR of #36/President Lyndon B. Johnson taking over the `-PRESIDENCY"!!!!!~'

`-351 = (3 x 51) = `-153 = (53 x 1) = `-53 = "WAR of the WORLDS"!!!!!~'

`-247 = (24 + 7) = `-31 = RECIPROCAL = `-13 = "A PIVOTAL NUMBER"!!!!!~'

`-247 = (47 + 2) = `-49 = RECIPROCAL = `-94 = "The `-DEATH `-NUMBERS"!!!!!~'

`-247 = (2 x 47) = `-94 = RECIPROCAL = `-49

(9 + 4) = `-13 = "A VERY PIVOTAL NUMBER"!!!!!~'

(351 + 247) = `-598 = `-(59)8 = (59 + 8) = `-67 = "The `-YEAR that the "PROPHET'S" BROTHER was `-BORN, the `-AVERAGE `-AGE of the United States Presidents 1 to 28 in "SUCCESSION" above; and, below `-ALL `-PRESIDENTS that `-DIED at `-AGES `-66, `-67; and, `-68; and, The `-AGE of `-DEATH of the #1/President of the United States of America #1/President George Washington"!!!!!~'

#2/FIRST LADY ABIGAIL ADAMS was `-BORN on (11/22/17/44); and, had `-DIED on (10/28/18/18)!!!!!~' `-Did `-YOU `-CATCH the `-NUMBERS"!!!!!~'?

#2/FIRST LADY ABIGAIL ADAMS was `-BORN on the `-ASSASSINATION `-DAY of #35/President John F. Kennedy (11/22)!!!!!~'

AMERICAN/ENGLISH `-ALPHABET '-to-' `-NUMBERS #'s:!!!!!~'

AA = `-1, `-1

#2/President John Adams = JA = `-10, `-1

`-11 = "Yin/Yang" = "Multiple of `-ELEVEN" = "The `-CYCLE of `-LIFE"!!!!!~'

#1/FIRST LADY MARTHA WASHINGTON at the `-START of being `-FIRST `-LADY was at the `-AGE of `-57 `-YEARS / `-332 `-DAYS!!!!!~'

`-57 = RECIPROCAL = `-75

(75 + 57) = **`-132** = (32 x 1) = **`-32** = -a Prophetic Number!!!!!~'

**`-332** = "EMPHATIC `-EMPHASIS to the # `-NUMBER of `-32 = -a Prophetic Number!!!!!~'

`-332** = **`-(33)2 = (33 x 2) = **`-66** = "AGE of `-DEATH of the "PROPHET'S" FATHER"!!!!!~'

`-332** = **`-3(32) = (32 x 3) = **`-96** = **RECIPROCAL** = **`-69** = "Yin/Yang" = "The `-CYCLE of `-LIFE"!!!!!~'

(332 (-) 57) = **`-275** = **`-(27)5** = (27 + 5) = **`-32** = -a Prophetic Number!!!!!~'

(332 + 57) = **`-389** = **`-3(89)** = (89 x 3) = **`-267** = (**67** + 2) = **`-69** = "Yin/Yang" = "The `-CYCLE of `-LIFE"!!!!!~'

`-DIFFERENCES in `-AGES = (332 (-) 67) = **`-265** = (65 + 2) = **`-67** = "The `-YEAR that the "PROPHET'S" BROTHER was `-BORN, the `-AVERAGE `-AGE of the United States Presidents 1 to 28 in "SUCCESSION" above; and, below `-ALL `-PRESIDENTS that `-DIED at `-AGES `-66, `-67; and, `-68; and, The `-AGE of `-DEATH of the #1/President of the United States of America #1/President George Washington"!!!!!~'

AMERICAN/ENGLISH `-ALPHABET '-to-' `-NUMBERS #'s:!!!!!~'

Martha Washington / MW = `-13, `-23

#1/President George Washington = GW = `-7, `-23

MWGW = Martha Washington/George Washington

(13 + 23) = `-**36** = **RECIPROCAL** = `-**63** = "AGE of `-DEATH of the "PROPHET'S" MOTHER"!!!!!~'

`-**1789** = (89 (-) 17) = `-**72** (/`-2) = `-**36** = `-**3(6's)** = `-**666** = (6 x 6 x 6) = `-**216** = (2 x 16) = `-**32** = -a Prophetic Number!!!!!~'

(1789 (-) 1776) = `-**13** = "A VERY PIVOTAL NUMBER"!!!!!~

(2015 (-) 1789) = `-**226** = `-**22.6** = ROUNDED = `-**23** = -a Prophetic Number!!!!!~'

Martha Washington = (57 (-) 13) = `-**44** `-YEARS of `-AGE!!!!!~'

George Washington = (57 (-) 13) = `-**44** `-YEARS of `-AGE!!!!!~'

(**13** x **2**) = `-**26** = `-**13** x `-**2** = `-**132** = (1 x 32) = `-**32** = -a Prophetic Number!!!!!~'

The "PROPHET'S" MOTHER was `-BORN in (`-19**44**)!!!!!~'

(13 + 23 + 7 + 23) = `-**66** = "AGE of `-DEATH of the "PROPHET'S" FATHER"!!!!!~'

MWG = **M**artha **W**ashington/**G**eorge

Or,

GMW = **G**eorge/**M**artha **W**ashington

(13 + 23 + 7) = `-**43** = **RECIPROCAL** = `-**34** = "The `-**PRESIDENTIAL** **#'s** `-**NUMBERS**"!!!!!~'

#1/President George Washington; and, #1/FIRST LADY MARTHA WASHINGTON took the `-FIRST `-OFFICE on **April 30**[th] in `-1789!!!!!~'

April 30[th] = 04/**30** = (**43** + 0 + 0) = `-**43** = **RECIPROCAL** = `-**34** = "The `-**PRESIDENTIAL** **#'s** `-**NUMBERS**"!!!!!~'

#**1**/President George Washington `-TOOK the `-OFFICE of `-PRESIDENCY at the `-AGE of `-**57** `-YEARS / `-**67** `-DAYS!!!!!~'

`-**57** = **RECIPROCAL** = `-**75**

(75 + 57) = `-**132** = (32 x 1) = `-**32** = -a Prophetic Number!!!!!~'

199

`-**67** = "The `-YEAR that the "PROPHET'S" BROTHER was `-BORN, the `-AVERAGE `-AGE of the United States Presidents 1 to 28 in "SUCCESSION" above; and, below `-ALL `-PRESIDENTS that `-DIED at `-AGES `-66, `-67; and, `-68; and, The `-AGE of `-DEATH of the #1/President of the United States of America #1/President George Washington"!!!!!~'

(67 + 57) = `-**124** = (24 (-) 1) = `-**23** = -a Prophetic Number!!!!!~'

(332 + 67) = `-**399** = "EMPHATIC `-EMPHASIS on the # `-NUMBER `-**99**; and, the # `-NUMBER being `-ASSIGNED to the `-DEATH; of the #1/President George Washington, in (`-17**99**)"!!!!!~'

`-**399** = `-**(39)9** = (39 x 9) = `-**351** = (35 x 1) = `-**35** = **RECIPROCAL** = `-**53** = "WAR of the WORLDS"!!!!!~'

#**1**/FIRST LADY MARTHA WASHINGTON was `-MARRIED to `-HER `-HUSBAND #**1**/President George Washington for some `-**40** `-YEARS!!!!!~'

#**1**/FIRST LADY MARTHA WASHINGTON; and, `-HER `-HUSBAND #**1**/President George Washington were `-MARRIED for the `-EXACT `-SAME `-AMOUNT of `-TIME; (`-**40**) `-YEARS, as with the (`-**40**) `-YEARS; `-LINKED `-TO, the #**32**/FIRST LADY ELEANOR ROOSEVELT; and, `-HER `-HUSBAND #**32**/President Franklin Delano Roosevelt"!!!!!~'

(**40**/**40**) = (44 + 0 + 0) = `-**44** = "#**1**/President **George** Washington was `-**44** `-YEARS of `-AGE in (`-17**76**) on the very `-FIRST `-INDEPENDENCE `-DAY of which `-HE `-DIED on the `-EXACT same `-DAY `-RECIPROCAL # `-NUMBER of which `-HE was at the `-AGE of (`-**67**)-'"!!!!!~'

ALEXANDER HAMILTON was `-**44** `-YEARS of `-AGE at the `-TIME of `-DEATH of #1/President George Washington!!!!!~' ALEXANDER HAMILTON was `-BORN in (`-17**55**) which was `-**23** `-YEARS after that of the `-BIRTH of #1/President George Washington!!!!!~'

`-**23** = **RECIPROCAL** = `-**32**

#1/President George Washington was `-BORN in (`-17**32**); and, `-**23** `-YEARS after `-17**76**; `-HE `-DIED at the `-AGE of `-**67**!!!!!~'

`-**67** = **RECIPROCAL** = `-**76**

The `-AGE of `-DEATHS `-ADDED `-UP for #**1**/FIRST LADY MARTHA WASHINGTON (`-**70**) `-YEARS / `-**354** `-DAYS; and, `-HER `-HUSBAND #**1**/President George Washington (`-**67**) `-YEARS / `-**295** `-DAYS = `-**EQUALS** = `-**137** = (37 x 1) = `-**37** = `-**3(7's)** = (777) = (7 x 7 x 7) = `-**343** = **R**eciprocal-**S**equencing-**N**umerology-**RSN** = "The `-**PRESIDENTIAL** #'s `-**NUMBERS**"!!!!!~'

`-**354** = `-3(54) = (54 x 3) = `-**162** = (62 + 1) = `-**63** = "The `-AGE of `-DEATH of the "PROPHET'S" MOTHER; the `-YEAR of `-**ASSASSINATION** for #**35**/President John F. Kennedy; and, the `-YEAR of #**36**/President Lyndon B. Johnson taking over the `-**PRESIDENCY**"!!!!!~'

`-**295** = "The `-AMOUNT of `-TIME `-LIVING after `-THEIR `-BIRTHDAYS in the `-YEAR of `-THEIR `-DEATHS for the following FIRST LADYS just as well: #**35**/FIRST LADY JACQUELINE LEE KENNEDY; AND, "#**10**/FIRST LADY JULIA GARDINER TYLER"!!!!!~'

(70 + 67) = `-**137** = (37 x 1) = `-**37** = `-**3(7's)** = (777) = (7 x 7 x 7) = `-**343** = **R**eciprocal-**S**equencing-**N**umerology-**RSN** = "The `-**PRESIDENTIAL** #'s `-**NUMBERS**"!!!!!~'

Heavyweight Champion (-) Wladimir Klitschko; and, the #'s `-NUMBERS!!!!!~'-"

(11/28/2015) = (11 + 28) = `-**39** = **RECIPROCAL** = `-**93** = UFC `-193

Tyson Fury ends Wladimir Klitschko's Heavyweight Reign this past `-SATURDAY!!!!!~'

Wladimir Klitschko was `-BORN on March 25th in `-1976!!!!!~' Wladimir Klitschko is `-CURRENTLY `-39 `-YEARS of `-AGE!!!!!~'

`-**39** = `-**3(9's)** = `-**999** = (9 x 9 x 9) = `-**729** = `-7(29) = (7 x 29) = `-**203** = (23 + 0) = `-**23** = -a Prophetic Number!!!!!~'

Wladimir Klitschko's `-HEIGHT = 6' 6"

`-**66** = "The `-AGE of `-DEATH of the "PROPHET'S" FATHER"!!!!!~'

Wladimir Klitschko's `-WEIGHT = `-246 lbs.

`-**246** = `-(24)6 = (24 x 6) = `-**144** = (44 x 1) = `-**44** = "The `-YEAR of the "PROPHET'S" MOTHER'S `-BIRTH (`-19**44**)"!!!!!~'

Wladimir Klitschko's `-BIRTHDAY # `-NUMBER is = (03 + 25 + 19 + 76) = `-**123** = "Prophetic-Linear-Progression-PLP"!!!!!~'

(03 + 25 + 19) = `-**47** / `-**47** = RECIPROCAL = `-**74**

(11/28/2015) = (11 + 28 + 20 + 15) = `-**74** = `-**NIGHT** of the `-**FIGHT**; and, `-**LOSS!!!!!~'**

This `-HAPPENS all `-THROUGHOUT my `-BOOK!!!!!~ This `-STATEMENT is `-NOW `-ON; `-PAGE `-1**74**!!!!!~'

`-**76** = (7 + 6) = `-**13** = "A VERY PIVOTAL NUMBER"!!!!!~'

`-**76** = RECIPROCAL = `-**67** = "The `-YEAR that the "PROPHET'S" BROTHER was `-BORN, the `-AVERAGE `-AGE of the United States Presidents 1 to 28 in "SUCCESSION" above; and, below `-ALL `-PRESIDENTS that `-DIED at `-AGES `-66, `-67; and, `-68; and, The `-AGE of `-DEATH of the #1/President of the United States of America #1/President George Washington"!!!!!~'

AMERICAN/ENGLISH `-**ALPHABET** '-to-' `-**NUMBERS** #'s:!!!!!~'

WLADIMIR KLITSCHKO / WK = `-**23**, `-**11**

(23 + 11) = `-**34** = RECIPROCAL = `-**43** = "The `-**PRESIDENTIAL** #'s `-**NUMBERS**"!!!!!~'

Heavyweight Champion (-) Wladimir Klitschko; and, the #'s `-**NUMBERS!!!!!~'-**"

The `-**PRESIDENTS**: Abraham Lincoln, John F. Kennedy; and, Lyndon B. Johnson!!!!!~'

#16/President Abraham Lincoln was `-BORN on **February 12**[th] (**212**); and, was `-SHOT in being `-ASSASSINATED on **April 14**[th] (**414**)!!!!!~' `-**24** = **RECIPROCAL** = `-**42** = Reciprocal-Sequencing-Numerology-RSN!!!!!~'

(414 + 212) = `-**626** / `-**62** = RECIPROCAL = `-**26**

(62 (-) 26) = `-**36** = <u>**RECIPROCAL**</u> = `-**63** = "The `-YEAR #35/President John F. Kennedy was `-ASSASSINATED (`-19**63**); and, President John F. Kennedy's FUNERAL by `-HIS `-WIFE'S `-REQUEST (FIRST LADY JACQUELINE LEE KENNEDY) was `-PATTERNED after the #16/President Abraham Lincoln's `-FUNERAL; and, (#**63**) being the `-AGE of `-DEATH of the "PROPHET'S" MOTHER; and, the #16/President Abraham Lincoln's `-WIFE / FIRST LADY MARY TODD LINCOLN (#**63**)!!!!!~'

#35/President John F. Kennedy was `-<u>**ASSASSINATED**</u> at the `-AGE of `-**46**; while, FIRST LADY MARY TODD LINCOLN was at the `-<u>**AGE**</u> of `-**46** for when #16/President Abraham Lincoln was `-<u>**ASSASSINATED**</u>!!!!!~'

`-**46** = `-**23** x `-**2** = `-**232** = <u>**Reciprocal-Sequencing-Numerology-RSN**</u>!!!!!~'

`-**414** = (44 x 1) = `-**44** = "The "PROPHET'S" MOTHER was `-BORN in (`-19**44**)"!!!!!~'

(24 + 42) = `-**66** = "AGE of `-DEATH of the "PROPHET'S" FATHER"!!!!!~'

`-**212** = (21 + 2) = `-**23** = -a Prophetic Number!!!!!~' / `-**46** = <u>**RECIPROCAL**</u> = `-**64**

#36/President Lyndon B. Johnson `-<u>**DIED**</u> at the `-<u>**RECIPROCAL**</u> `-<u>**AGE**</u> of `-**64**; and, being **6' 4**" in `-HEIGHT just like #16/President Abraham Lincoln (**6' 4**")!!!!!~' The `-TWO `-TALLEST `-PRESIDENTS as of `-THIS `-DATE (1**2/03**/2015)!!!!!~'

#36/President Lyndon B. Johnson was `-<u>**BORN**</u> on **August 27**th **in** `-**1908** (08/27/**1908**); and, had `-<u>**DIED**</u> on **January 22**nd in `-1973 (01/22/1973)!!!!!~'

`-**BIRTHDAY # `-NUMBER** = (8 + 27 + 19 + 08) = `-**62**

(8 + 27) = `-**35** = <u>**RECIPROCAL**</u> = `-**53** = "WAR of the WORLDS"!!!!!~'

`-**DEATH/DAY # `-NUMBER** = (1 + 22 + 19 + 73) = `-**115**

(1 + 22) = `-**23** = -a Prophetic Number!!!!!~'

(115 (-) 62) = `-**53** = "WAR of the WORLDS"!!!!!~'

January 22nd = (**122**) = **#16/President Abraham Lincoln** = (**212**) = "Swipe 1"...(...)...-'~'

#16/President Abraham Lincoln was `-**BORN** in `-1**8**0**9**; while, #36/President Lyndon B. Johnson was `-**BORN** in `-1**9**0**8**!!!!!~'

`-1**809** = **RECIPROCAL** = `-1**908**

`-**89** = **RECIPROCAL** = `-**98**

`-**414** = (414 x 2) = `-**828** = `-BIRTH of #36/President Lyndon B. Johnson (**827**)…(…)…-"~'

AMERICAN/ENGLISH `-**ALPHABET** '-**to**-' `-**NUMBERS** #'s:!!!!!~'

BORN/BORN / BB = `-**2**, `-**2**

(414 (-) 212) = `-**202** = (22 + 0) = `-**22** = "Yin/Yang" = "Multiple of `-ELEVEN" = "The `-CYCLE of `-LIFE"!!!!!~'

#35/President John F. Kennedy was `-**ASSASSINATED** on (**11/22**)…(…)…-"~'

`-THIS `-DATE (1**2**/0**3**/2015) = (12 + 3 + 20 + 15) = `-**50**

(12 + 3 + 20) = `-**35** = **RECIPROCAL** = `-**53** = "WAR of the WORLDS"!!!!!~'

(19**6**3 + **50**) = `-**2013** = (23 + 0 x 1) = `-**23** = -a Prophetic Number!!!!!~'

#35/President John F. Kennedy was `-**BORN** on **May 29**[th] in `-**1917** (**05/29/1917**); and, had `-**DIED** on **November 22**[nd] in `-**1963** (**11/22/1963**)!!!!!~'

(5 + 29 + 19) = `-**53** = "**WAR of the WORLDS**"!!!!!~'

`-**BIRTHDAY** # `-**NUMBER** = (5 + 29 + 19 + 17) = `-**70**

`-**70** = "The `-YEAR of `-BIRTH of the "PROPHET" (`-19**70**)"!!!!!~'

The `-SAME `-BIRTHDAY # `-NUMBER as the "PROPHET'S" FATHER (`-**70**)!!!!!~'

`-**DEATH/DAY** # `-**NUMBER** = (11 + 22 + 19 + 63) = `-**115**

#35/President John F. Kennedy; and, #36/President Lyndon B. Johnson `-**BOTH** have the `-**EXACT** / `-**DEATH/DAY** # `-**NUMBER** of `-**115**!!!!!~'

(115 + 115) = `-**230** = (23 + 0) = `-**23** = -a Prophetic Number!!!!!~'

(November (-) May) = (11 (-) 5) = `-**6** / (29 (-) 22) = `-**7**

`-AGES of `-DEATH = (<u>46</u> + <u>56</u> + <u>64</u>) = `-**166** = (66 + 1) = `-**67**

`-**67** = "The `-YEAR that the "PROPHET'S" BROTHER was `-BORN, the `-AVERAGE `-AGE of the United States Presidents 1 to 28 in "SUCCESSION" above; and, below `-ALL `-PRESIDENTS that `-DIED at `-AGES `-66, `-67; and, `-68; and, The `-AGE of `-DEATH of the #1/President of the United States of America #1/President George Washington"!!!!!~'

`-AGES of `-DEATH = (<u>46</u> + <u>56</u> + <u>64</u>) = `-**166** = (66 x 1) = `-**66** = "The `-AGE of `-DEATH of the "PROPHET'S" FATHER"!!!!!~'

`-**AVERAGE** = (166 / 3) = `-**55.33** = `-**35** = **RECIPROCAL** = `-**53** = "WAR of the WORLDS"!!!!!~'

#36/President Lyndon B. Johnson `-**DIED** with a `-**10** `-**MONTH** `-**SEPARATION**; and, `-**10** `-**YEAR** `-**SEPARATION** in `-**DEATH** `-**DATES** with #35/President John F. Kennedy `-**DYING** on the `-SAME `-**DAY** of the **22**nd of the `-**MONTH!!!!!~'**

#35/President John F. Kennedy's `-WIFE / FIRST LADY JACQUELINE LEE KENNEDY was `-**34** `-**YEARS** of `-**AGE** at the `-TIME of `-HER `-HUSBAND'S #35/President John F. Kennedy's `-**ASSASSINATION**!!!!!~' FIRST LADY LADY BIRD JOHNSON had lived `-**34** `-**YEARS** beyond the `-**DEATH of** `-**HER** `-**HUSBAND** #36/President Lyndon B. Johnson**;** **and,** #36/President Lyndon B. Johnson `-**MARRIED** `-HIS `-WIFE / FIRST LADY LADY BIRD JOHNSON in the `-**CALENDAR** `-**YEAR** of `-**1934!!!!!~'**

`-**35** = **RECIPROCAL** = `-**53**

#**35**/President John F. Kennedy was `-**MARRIED** in `-19**53**!!!!!~' #35/President John F. Kennedy was `-**MARRIED** to `-HIS `-WIFE JACQUELINE LEE KENNEDY for `-**10** `-**YEARS**!!!!!~' #36/President Lyndon B. Johnson was `-**MARRIED** to `-HIS `-WIFE LADY BIRD JOHNSON for `-**39** `-**YEARS!!!!!~'**

(39 + 10) = `-**49** = **RECIPROCAL** = `-**94** = "LADY BIRD JOHNSON `-**DIED** at the `-**AGE** of `-**94**; while, JACQUELINE LEE KENNEDY `-**DIED** in (`-19**94**) the `-**EXACT** `-**SAME** `-**AGE** as FIRST LADY LADY BIRD JOHNSON'S `-HUSBAND #36/President Lyndon B. Johnson at `-**AGE** `-**64**; the **very** `-**RECIPROCAL** `-**AGE** of `-HER `-HUSBAND'S `-AGE of `-DEATH / #35/President John F. Kennedy (`-**46**) / `-**13** `-**YEARS** before FIRST LADY LADY BIRD JOHNSON'S `-DEATH!!!!!~'

`-**39** = `-**3(9's)** = `-**999** = (9 x 9 x 9) = `-**729** = `-7(29) = (7 x 29) = `-**203** = (23 + 0) = `-**23** = -a **Prophetic Number!!!!!~'**

`-**56** = **RECIPROCAL** = `-**65**

#16/President Abraham Lincoln `-**DIED** at the `-AGE of (`-**56**); in the `-**CALENDAR** `-**YEAR of** (`-18**65**)!!!!!~'

#16/President Abraham Lincoln was `-**MARRIED** to `-HIS `-WIFE / FIRST LADY MARY TODD LINCOLN / for `-**23** `-**YEARS!!!!!~'**

`-**23** = **RECIPROCAL** = `-**32** / `-**13** = "A VERY PIVOTAL NUMBER"!!!!!~'

`-**13**, `-**23**; &, `-**32** = "A `-**PARADIGM** `-**SHIFT** within `-**PENDULUM** `-**FLOW**"!!!!!~'

Lee Harvey Oswald was `-**BORN** on October 18th in `-19**39**; and, had `-**DIED** on November 24th in `-19**63**!!!!!~' Lee Harvey Oswald `-**DIED** at the `-**AGE** of `-**24**!!!!!~' There are `-**35** `-**DAYS** = **RECIPROCAL** = `-**53** = "WAR of the WORLDS" = that lie in between `-HIS 23rd & 24th `-**BIRTHDAY!!!!!~'** Lee Harvey Oswald `-**DIED** `-**22** `-**YEARS** `-**YOUNGER than** #35/President John F. Kennedy!!!!!~'

Lee Harvey Oswald's Birthday # `-NUMBER = (10 + 18 + 19 + 39) = `-**86**

Lee Harvey Oswald's Death/Day # `-NUMBER = (11 + 24 + 19 + 63) = `-**117**

(117 (-) 86) = `-**31** = **RECIPROCAL** = `-**13** = "A VERY PIVOTAL NUMBER"!!!!!~'

(117 + 86) = `-**203** = (23 + 0) = `-**23** = -a **Prophetic Number!!!!!~'**

I've `-CREATED a NEW TYPE of PHILOSOPHY (Reciprocal-Sequencing-Numerology) that `-PROVES without `-QUESTION the `-PRESENCE of GOD'S EXISTENCE in our DAILY AFFAIRS!!!!!~'

The `-PRESIDENTS: Abraham Lincoln, John F. Kennedy; and, Lyndon B. Johnson!!!!!~'

`-'THE -VICE-PRESIDENTS'!!!!!~'

#22/Vice-President Levi Parsons Morton `-TOOK the `-OFFICE of `-VICE-PRESIDENT at the `-AGE of `-64 `-YEARS / `-292 `-DAYS!!!!!~'

`-64 = "The `-AGE of `-DEATH of #36/President Lyndon B. Johnson; and, FIRST LADY JACQUELINE LEE KENNEDY"!!!!!~'

`-292 = Reciprocal-Sequenced-Numerology-RSN!!!!!~'

#22/Vice-President Levi Parsons Morton `-LIVED for (`-96 `-YEARS; and, `-0 `-DAYS / `-35,063 `-TOTAL `-DAYS); and, had `-SERVED in `-OFFICE; and, had `-DIED on May 16th of `-1920!!!!!~' #22/Vice-President Levi Parsons Morton was `-BORN on May 16th in `-1824!!!!!~'

May 16th = (5/16) = (56 x 1) = `-56 = "AGE of `-DEATH of #16/President Abraham Lincoln"!!!!!~'

(16 + 16) = `-32 = -a Prophetic Number!!!!!~'

(516 + 516) = `-1032 = (32 x 1 + 0) = `-32 = -a Prophetic Number!!!!!~'

`-23 = RECIPROCAL = `-32

#10/President John Tyler `-DIED at the `-AGE of `-71, #22/President Grover Cleveland; and, the `-SAME #24/President Grover Cleveland `-DIED at the `-AGE of `-71!!!!!~'

(10 + 22 + 24) = `-56

(71 + 71 + 71) = `-213 = (23 x 1) = `-23 = -a Prophetic Number!!!!!~'

'-**16**/President Abraham Lincoln '-**DIED** at the '-AGE of ('-**56**)-'; while, '-HIS '-WIFE FIRST LADY MARY TODD LINCOLN '-**DIED** at the '-AGE of ('-**63**)!!!!!~'

'-**56** = **RECIPROCAL** = '-**65**

#**12**/President Zachary Taylor '-**DIED** at the '-AGE of ('-**65**)-'; while, '-HIS '-WIFE FIRST LADY MARGARET TAYLOR '-**DIED** at the '-AGE of ('-**63**)!!!!!~'

(63 + 63) = '-**126** = (26 x 1) = '-**26** = '-**13** x '-**2** = '-**132** = (1 x 32) = '-**32** = -a **Prophetic Number!!!!!~'**

(#**12**ᵗʰ **President** / ('-4)|) = '-**3** (#**16**ᵗʰ **President** / ('-4)|) = '-**4**

'-**34** = **RECIPROCAL** = '-**43** = "The '-**PRESIDENTIAL** #'s '-**NUMBERS**"!!!!!~'

'-**BIRTHDAY** # '-**NUMBER** '-**EQUALS** = (5 + 16 + 18 + 24) = '-**63**

'-**DEATH/DAY** # '-**NUMBER** '-**EQUALS** = (5 + 16 + 19 + 20) = '-**60**

#**26**/President Theodore Roosevelt '-**DIED** at '-AGE ('-**60**) /|\ FIRST LADY EDITH KERMIT ROOSEVELT '-**DIED** at '-AGE ('-**87**)-'!!!!!~'

'-**26** = '-**13** x '-**2** = '-**132** = (1 x 32) = '-**32** = -a Prophetic Number!!!!!~'

(87 (-) 60) = '-**27** = "The ROMAN EMPIRE"!!!!!~'

'-**BIRTHDAY** # '-**NUMBER** (+) '-**DEATH/DAY** # '-**NUMBER** = (63 + 60) = '-**123** = "**P**rophetic-**L**inear-**P**rogression-**PLP**"!!!!!~'

'-**35,063** = '-**35** = **RECIPROCAL** = '-**53** = "WAR of the WORLDS"!!!!!~'

#**22**/Vice-President Levi Parsons Morton is the '-**ONLY** '-**CURRENT VICE-PRESIDENT to '-DIE on '-HIS '-OWN '-BIRTHDAY!!!!!~**

'-**96** = **RECIPROCAL** = '-**69**

'-**96** = '-**32** x '-**3** = '-**323** = **R**eciprocal-**S**equenced-**N**umerology-**RSN**!!!!!~'

'-**69** = '-**3** x '-**23** = '-**323** = **R**eciprocal-**S**equenced-**N**umerology-**RSN**!!!!!~'

'-**96** = **RECIPROCAL** = '-**69** = "Yin/Yang" = "The '-CYCLE of '-LIFE"!!!!!~'

#**22**/Vice-President Levi Parsons Morton also `-**SERVED** later as the `-**31**ˢᵗ **GOVERNOR of NEW YORK!!!!!**~'

`-**22** = (+**1**) = `-**23** = -a Prophetic Number!!!!!~'

`-**31** = (+**1**) = `-**32** = -a Prophetic Number!!!!!~'

#**14**/President Franklin Pierce; and, FIRST LADY JANE MEANS PIERCE are the `-**EXACT** `-**OPPOSITE** `-**RECIPROCALS** of #**16**/President Abraham Lincoln; and, FIRST LADY MARY TODD LINCOLN `-**PLUS** ± (+1)!!!!!~'

(1**4**/1**6**) = `-**46** = **RECIPROCAL** = `-**64**

The `-AGE of `-DEATHS for #**14**/President Franklin Pierce (`-**64**); and, `-HIS `-WIFE FIRST LADY JANE MEANS PIERCE (`-**57**) = `-**EQUALS** = `-**121** = **R**eciprocal-**S**equencing-**N**umerology-**RSN**!!!!!~'

FIRST LADY SARAH POLK `-DIED at `-AGE (`-87)-'!!!!!~' /|\ FIRST LADY EDITH KERMIT ROOSEVELT `-DIED at `-AGE (`-87)-'!!!!!~'

(87 + 87) = `-**174** = (74 x 1) = `-**74** = **RECIPROCAL** = `-**47** = "The `-DEATH/DAY; and, `-BIRTHDAY #'s of the FIRST LADYS"!!!!!~'

`-**87** = **RECIPROCAL** = `-**78** = "AGE of `-DEATH of #**23**/Vice-President Adlai Stevenson (I) (`-**78**)"!!!!!~'

#**32**/President Franklin Delano Roosevelt `-**DIED** at the `-AGE of (`-**63**); while, `-HIS `-WIFE FIRST LADY ELEANOR ROOSEVELT `-**DIED** at the `-AGE of (`-**78**)!!!!!~'

(78 + 78) = `-**156** = (56 x 1) = `-**56** = "AGE of `-DEATH of #**16**/President Abraham Lincoln"!!!!!~'

#**23**/Vice-President Adlai Stevenson (I) `-TOOK the `-OFFICE of `-VICE-PRESIDENT at the `-AGE of `-**57** `-YEARS / `-**132** `-DAYS!!!!!~'

`-**132** = (32 x 1) = `-**32** = -a Prophetic Number!!!!!~'

(365 (-) 132) = `-**233** = `-**23.3** = **ROUNDED** = `-**23** = -a Prophetic Number!!!!!~'

`-**57** = <u>**RECIPROCAL**</u> = `-**75**

(75 + 57) = `-**132** = (32 x 1) = `-**32** = -a Prophetic Number!!!!!~'

#**23**/Vice-President Adlai Stevenson (I) `-<u>**LIVED**</u> for (`-**78** `-YEARS; and, `-**234** `-DAYS / `-**28,723** `-TOTAL `-DAYS); and, had `-SERVED in `-OFFICE; and, had `-DIED on <u>**June 14**</u>th of `-**1914**!!!!!~' #**23**/Vice-President Adlai Stevenson (I) was `-BORN on <u>**October 23**</u>rd in `-**1835**!!!!!~'

#**23**/Vice-President Adlai Stevenson (I) was `-<u>**BORN**</u> on the `-**23**rd **of the** `-**MONTH**!!!!!~'

`-**234** = "**Prophetic-<u>L</u>inear-<u>P</u>rogression-<u>PLP</u>**" = `-**EMPHATIC** `-**WITNESS to the #** `-**NUMBER** = `-**34** = <u>**RECIPROCAL**</u> = `-**43** = "**The** `-**PRESIDENTIAL #'s** `-**NUMBERS**"!!!!!~'

{(<u>**365**</u> (-) <u>**234**</u>)} = `-**131** = (31 + 1) = `-**32** = -a Prophetic Number!!!!!~'

<u>**June 14**</u>th = (6/14) = (64 x 1) = `-**64** = "**The** `-**AGE of** `-**DEATH of #36/ President Lyndon B. Johnson; and, FIRST LADY JACQUELINE LEE KENNEDY**"!!!!!~'

`-**BIRTHDAY #** `-**NUMBER** `-**EQUALS** = (10 + 23 + 18 + 35) = `-**86**

`-**DEATH/DAY #** `-**NUMBER** `-**EQUALS** = (6 + 14 + 19 + 14) = `-**53**

#**11**/President James K. Polk `-<u>**DIED**</u> at `-AGE (`-**53**) /|\ FIRST LADY SARAH POLK `-DIED at `-AGE (`-**87**)-`!!!!!~'

`-**11** = "**Yin/Yang**" = "**Multiple of** `-**ELEVEN**" = "**The** `-**CYCLE of** `-**LIFE**"!!!!!~'

(87 (-) 53) = `-**34** = <u>**RECIPROCAL**</u> = `-**43** = "**The** `-**PRESIDENTIAL #'s** `-**NUMBERS**"!!!!!~'

`-**BIRTHDAY #** `-**NUMBER** (<u>+</u>) `-**DEATH/DAY #** `-**NUMBER** = (86 + 53) = `-**139** = (39 x 1) = `-**39** = `-**3(9's)** = `-**999** = (9 x 9 x 9) = `-**729** = `-7(29) = (7 x 29) = `-**203** = (23 + 0) = `-**23** = -a Prophetic Number!!!!!~'

`-**BIRTHDAY #** `-**NUMBER** (<u>-</u>) `-**DEATH/DAY #** `-**NUMBER** = (86 (-) 53) = `-**33** = "**Yin/Yang**" = "**Multiple of** `-**ELEVEN**" = "**The** `-**CYCLE of** `-**LIFE**"!!!!!~'

`-**1835** = (35 + 18) = `-**53** = "WAR of the WORLDS"!!!!!~'

#**23**/Vice-President Adlai Stevenson (I) `-**DIED** in the `-YEAR; of the `-START, of the `-FIRST `-WORLD `-WAR (`-1914)!!!!!~'

`-**1914** = (19 + 14) = `-**33** = "Yin/Yang" = "Multiple of `-ELEVEN" = "The `-CYCLE of `-LIFE"!!!!!~'

#**23**/Vice-President Adlai Stevenson's (I) `-**DEATH/DAY** # `-NUMBER (`-**53**) is the `-**RECIPROCAL** / of `-HIS `-BIRTH `-YEAR (`-18**35**)!!!!!~'

`-**35** = **RECIPROCAL** = `-**53** = "WAR of the WORLDS"!!!!!~'

`-'THE -VICE-PRESIDENTS, `-too!!!!!~'

`-The `-WHITE `-BLOOD `-CELLS!!!!!~'-"

`-NEUTROPHILS make `-UP **55%** to `-**70%** of the `-TOTAL `-AMOUNT of `-WHITE `-BLOOD `-CELLS within the `-BLOOD!!!!!~'

`-NEUTROPHILS are the `-CHIEF `-PHAGOCYTIC `-WHITE `-BLOOD `-CELLS of the `-BLOOD; which, stand `-WATCH as the `-CHIEF `-PATROLLERS; and, `-SENTINELS; of the `-IMMUNE `-SYSTEM!!!!!~' They `-ENGULF; and, `-CONSUME `-FOREIGN `-MATERIALS such as `-BACTERIA/VIRUS `-INFECTIONS, `-MICRO-ORGANISMS; and, `-DEBRIS; lysing `-THEM, via a `-PROCESS of `-DISINTEGERATION within; and, `-DISSOLUTION of these particular `-CELLS; within the `-CELL of the `-PHAGOCYTIC NEUTROPHIL!!!!!~'

`-**55** = `-**23** + `-**32**

`-**70** = (`-**2**) x (`-**35**) = **RECIPROCAL** = `-**53** = "WAR of the WORLDS"!!!!!~'

(70 + 55) = `-**125** = `-**12.5** = ROUNDED = `-**13** = "A VERY PIVOTAL NUMBER"!!!!!~'

Within these `-**White Blood Cells** – a `-**Special** `-**Class** of `-**Granulocyte** – **These** `-**Mature Neutrophils** are released into the blood system to where they circulate for **3** to 1**2** hours; and, then move to other tissues where they survive for only **2** to **3** days!!!!!~'

211

`-23 = RECIPROCAL = `-32

The `-LIFESPAN of other `-WHITE `-BLOOD `-CELLS can range from `-13 to `-20 `-DAYS, to where; after this time, `-THEY are `-DESTROYED by the `-LYMPHATIC `-SYSTEM!!!!!~'

`-13 = "A VERY PIVOTAL NUMBER"!!!!!~'

`-LYMPHOCYTES – WHITE BLOOD CELLS – (B-Cells) = antigen-binding antibody molecules that comprise the antibody-secreting plasma cells for when mature; and (&), (T-Cells) = which consist of highly specific cell-surface antigen receptors, to where some exude regulation of other immune cells; and, to where others directly attack; and, are used; to lyse antigen-bearing cells/tumors – they constitute `-20% to %30% of the `-WHITE BLOOD CELLS within the `-NORMAL `-HUMAN `-BLOOD!!!!!~'

`-HUMAN `-BLOOD `-PRESSURE `-READINGS:...(...)...-'"~'

`-120mmHg  =  `-2.3326984psi ("Pounds-Per-Square-Inch")... (...)...-'-'!!!!!~'

`-80mmHg  =  `-1.5469473684psi ("Pounds-Per-Square-Inch")... (...)...-'-'!!!!!~'

`-NORMAL `-HUMAN `-BLOOD `-PRESSURE `-READINGS:...(...)...-'"~'

`-WHOLE BLOOD is the `-BLOOD that runs through the `-ARTERIES, `-CAPILLARIES; and, the `-VEINS!!!!!~' `-IT'S a `-MIXTURE of about `-55% `-PLASMA; and, `-45% `-ACTUAL `-BLOOD `-CELLS!!!!!~' Known for their `-OXYGENATED `-RED `-COLOR, the `-RED `-BLOOD `-CELLS are the `-MOST `-ABUNDANT `-CELL in the `-BLOOD; which, `-THEY account for about `-40%-`-45% of the `-BLOOD'S `-TOTAL `-VOLUME!!!!!~'

`-RED `-BLOOD `-CELLS typically `-LIVE for about `-120 `-DAYS; or, `-4 `-MONTHS; within the `-BODY!!!!!~'

(120 + 120 + 80) = `-320 = (32 + 0) = `-32 = -a Prophetic Number!!!!!~'

(120/4) = (24 (-) 1 + 0) = `-23 = -a Prophetic Number!!!!!~'

(45 + 40) = `-**85** = (8 + 5) = `-**13** = "A VERY PIVOTAL NUMBER"!!!!!~'

`-WHITE `-BLOOD `-CELLS `-ACCOUNT for about `-LESS than `-**1**% of the `-BLOOD'S `-TOTAL `-VOLUME!!!!!~'

`-The `-WHITE `-BLOOD `-CELLS!!!!!~'-"

The `-BASKETBALL `-TEAMS; `-just as `-WELL!!!!!~'

(12/08/2015) – GOLDEN STATE WARRIORS Continue THEIR `-RECORD of `-ENTERTAINMENT in `-**Non-Stop** `-WINNING with a `-RECORD of – (`-**23-0**)!!!!!~'

`-WARRIORS `-SCORE a `-TOTAL of `-POINTS of (`-**131**) = Reciprocal-**S**equencing-**N**umerology-RSN!!!!!~'!!!!!~'

(31 + 1) = `-**32** = -a Prophetic Number!!!!!~'

`-PACERS `-SCORE a `-TOTAL of `-POINTS of (`-**123**)!!!!!~'

(23 x 1) = `-**23** = -a Prophetic Number!!!!!~'

`-**23** = **RECIPROCAL** = `-**32** / (12 + 8 + 20 + 15) = `-**55** = `-**23** + `-**32**

The `-BASKETBALL `-TEAMS; `-just as `-WELL!!!!!~'

`-MOM & `-A `-VICE-PRESIDENT'!!!!!~'

#**24**/Vice-President Garret Hobart `-TOOK the `-OFFICE of `-VICE-PRESIDENT at the `-AGE of `-**52** `-YEARS / `-**274** `-DAYS!!!!!~'

`-**52** = **RECIPROCAL** = `-**25** / (52 (-) 25) = `-**27** = "The ROMAN EMPIRE"!!!!!~'

`-**274** = (74 + 2) = `-**76** = **RECIPROCAL** = `-**67** = "The `-YEAR that the "PROPHET'S" BROTHER was `-BORN, the `-AVERAGE `-AGE of the United States Presidents 1 to 28 in "SUCCESSION" above; and, below `-ALL `-PRESIDENTS that `-DIED at `-AGES `-66, `-67; and, `-68;

and, The `-AGE of `-DEATH of the #1/President of the United States of America #1/President George Washington"!!!!!~'

`-274 = (74 x 2) = `-148 = (48 x 1) = `-48 = RECIPROCAL = `-84

(84 + 48) = `-132 = (32 x 1) = `-32 = -a Prophetic Number!!!!!~'

`-48 = "The `-AMOUNT of `-DAYS between the `-DEATH of the "PROPHET'S" MOTHER (04/16/2008); and, the `-BIRTH of #24/Vice-President Garret Hobart (06/03/1844)"!!!!!~'

DEATH/DAY # `-NUMBER = (04/16/2008) = (4 + 16 + 20 + 8) = `-48

(04/06) = `-46 = "AGE of `-DEATH of #35/President John F. Kennedy"!!!!!!~'

`-46 = RECIPROCAL = `-64 / (2008 (-) 1844) = `-164

`-6 = "The `-AMOUNT of `-DAYS between the `-BIRTH of the "PROPHET'S" MOTHER (11/15/1944); and, the `-DEATH of #24/Vice-President Garret Hobart (11/21/1899)"!!!!!~'

(48 (-) 6) = `-42 = RECIPROCAL = `-24 = #24/Vice-President Garret Hobart!!!!!~'

(11/11) = (11 + 11) = `-22 = "The `-ASSASSINATION of #35/President John F. Kennedy in the `-MONTH of `-NOVEMBER; and, on the `-22nd of the `-MONTH"!!!!!~'

(15/21) = (21 + 15) = `-36 = RECIPROCAL = `-63 = "The `-YEAR of `-DEATH of #35/President John F. Kennedy (`-1963)"!!!!!~'

(1944 (-) 1899) = `-45 = "CURRENT `-AGE of the "PROPHET"-"!!!!!~'

(149 (-) 6) = `-143 = (43 x 1) = `-43 = RECIPROCAL = `-34 = "The `-PRESIDENTIAL #'s `-NUMBERS"!!!!!~'

#24/Vice-President Garret Hobart `-LIVED for (`-55 `-YEARS; and, `-171 `-DAYS / `-20,259 `-TOTAL `-DAYS); and, had `-SERVED in `-OFFICE; and, had `-DIED on November 21st of `-1899!!!!!~' #24/Vice-President Garret Hobart was `-BORN on June 3rd in `-1844!!!!!~'

June 3rd in `-1844 = (6/3/44) = "The "PROPHET'S" MOTHER `-DIED at the `-AGE of (`-63); and, was `-BORN in (`-1944)!!!!!~'

`-**1844** = (44 (-) 18) = `-**26** = "AGE of the "PROPHET'S" MOTHER for when the "PROPHET" was `-BORN"!!!!!~'

`-**1899** = (89 (-) 19) = `-**70** = "The `-YEAR the "PROPHET" was `-BORN in (`-19**70**)"!!!!!~'

(**63** (-) **24**/Vice-President Garret Hobart) = `-**39** = `-**3(9's)** = `-**999** = (9 x 9 x 9) = `-**729** = `-7(29) = (7 x 29) = `-**203** = (23 + 0) = `-**23** = -a Prophetic Number!!!!!~'

`-**55** = `-**23** + `-**32** / `-**23** = **RECIPROCAL** = `-**32**

`-**171** = (71 x 1) = `-**71** = #**10**/President John Tyler `-**DIED** at the `-AGE of `-**71**, #**22**/President Grover Cleveland; and, the `-SAME #**24**/President Grover Cleveland `-**DIED** at the `-AGE of `-**71**!!!!!~'

(10 + 22 + 24) = `-**56** = "AGE of `-DEATH of #16/President Abraham Lincoln"!!!!!~'

(71 + 71 + 71) = `-**213** = (23 x 1) = `-**23** = -a Prophetic Number!!!!!~'

`-BIRTHDAY # `-NUMBER `-EQUALS = (6 + 3 + 18 + 44) = `-**71**

(365 (-) **171**) = `-**194** / `-**94** = **RECIPROCAL** = `-**49**

`-DEATH/DAY # `-NUMBER `-EQUALS = (11 + 21 + 18 + 99) = `-**149**

(11 + 21) = `-**32** = -a Prophetic Number!!!!!~'

(149 (-) 71) = `-**78** / `-**78** = **RECIPROCAL** = `-**87**

#**26**/President Theodore Roosevelt `-**DIED** at `-AGE (`-**60**) /|\ FIRST LADY EDITH KERMIT ROOSEVELT `-**DIED** at `-AGE (`-**87**)-'!!!!!~'

`-**26** = `-**13** x `-**2** = `-**132** = (1 x 32) = `-**32** = -a Prophetic Number!!!!!~'

(87 (-) 60) = `-**27** = "The ROMAN EMPIRE"!!!!!~'

`-BIRTHDAY # `-NUMBER (**+**) `-DEATH/DAY # `-NUMBER = (71 + 149) = `-**220** = (22 + 0) = `-**22** = "Yin/Yang" = "Multiple of `-ELEVEN" = "The `-CYCLE of `-LIFE"!!!!!~'

215

#**24**/Vice-President Garret Hobart was the `-**6**<sup></sup> `-U.S. AMERICAN `-VICE-PRESIDENT to `-DIE in `-OFFICE!!!!!~

FIRST LADY SARAH POLK `-DIED at `-AGE (`-**87**)-'!!!!!~' /|\ FIRST LADY EDITH KERMIT ROOSEVELT `-DIED at `-AGE (`-**87**)-'!!!!!~'

(87 + 87) = `-**174** = (74 x 1) = `-**74** = RECIPROCAL = `-**47** = "The `-DEATH/DAY; and, `-BIRTHDAY #'s of the FIRST LADYS"!!!!!~'

`-**87** = RECIPROCAL = `-**78** = "AGE of `-DEATH of #**23**/Vice-President Adlai Stevenson (I) (`-**78**)"!!!!!~'

#**32**/President Franklin Delano Roosevelt `-DIED at the `-AGE of (`-**63**); while, `-HIS `-WIFE FIRST LADY ELEANOR ROOSEVELT `-DIED at the `-AGE of (`-**78**)!!!!!~'

(78 + 78) = `-**156** = (56 x 1) = `-**56** = "AGE of `-DEATH of #**16**/President Abraham Lincoln"!!!!!~'

(56 + 56) = `-**112** = "The `-BIRTHDAY # `-NUMBER of the "PROPHET" (Dwayne W. Anderson) (0**3**/**20**/**1970**)!!!!!~'

`-**97** = RECIPROCAL = `-**79** = "AGE of `-DEATH of Mr. H. G. Wells for "WAR of the WORLDS"-'"!!!!!~'

(97 + 79) = `-**176** = (76 x 1) = `-**76** = RECIPROCAL = `-**67** = "The `-YEAR that the "PROPHET'S" BROTHER was `-BORN, the `-AVERAGE `-AGE of the United States Presidents 1 to 28 in "SUCCESSION" above; and, below `-ALL `-PRESIDENTS that `-DIED at `-AGES `-**66**, `-**67**; and, `-**68**; and, The `-AGE of `-DEATH of the #**1**/President of the United States of America #**1**/President George Washington"!!!!!~'

`-MOM & `-A `-VICE-PRESIDENT'!!!!!~'

`-BUILT FOR BUSINESS in `-WIN `-STREAKS!!!!!~'

`-MOST `-CONSECUTIVE `-GAMES `-WON in `-NBA `-HISTORY!!!!!~'

`-GUARD #**44** = JERRY WEST = "The `-YEAR that the "PROPHET'S" MOTHER was `-BORN (`-19**44**)"!!!!!~'

216

`-LOS ANGELES LAKERS = `-*33 STRAIGHT WINS* (-) __11/5/71__ – __1/7/72__

`-__33__ = "Yin/Yang" = "Multiple of `-ELEVEN" = "The `-CYCLE of `-LIFE"!!!!!~'

`-__71__ = __RECIPROCAL__ = `-__17__

(11 x 5) = `-__55__ = `-__23__ + `-__32__

`-GUARD #__30__ = STEPHEN CURRY!!!!!~'

`-GOLDEN STATE WARRIORS = `-__27__ *STRAIGHT WINS* (-) __4/9/15__ – ACTIVE

`-__27__ = __RECIPROCAL__ = `-__72__

(72 (-) 27) = `-__45__ = "The `-AGE of the "PROPHET"-'"!!!!!~'

`-__49__ = __RECIPROCAL__ = `-__94__

(94 (-) 49) = `-__45__ = "The `-AGE of the "PROPHET"-'"!!!!!~'

(94 + 49) = `-__143__ = (43 x 1) = `-__43__ = __RECIPROCAL__ = `-__34__ = "The `-__PRESIDENTIAL #'s__ `-__NUMBERS__"!!!!!__~__'

`-__4/9/15__ = (49 (-) 15) = `-__34__ = __RECIPROCAL__ = `-__43__ = "The `-__PRESIDENTIAL #'s__ `-__NUMBERS__"!!!!!__~__'

`-__4/9/15__ = (49 + 15) = `-__64__ = __RECIPROCAL__ = `-__46__ = "AGE of `-DEATH of #35/President John F. Kennedy"!!!!!!~'

(94 (-) 15) = `-__79__ = "AGE of `-DEATH of Mr. H. G. Wells for "WAR of the WORLDS"-'"!!!!!~'

`-__35__ = __RECIPROCAL__ = `-__53__ = "WAR of the WORLDS"!!!!!~'

`-FORWARD #__23__ = LEBRON JAMES!!!!!~'

`-MIAMI HEAT = `-__27__ *STRAIGHT WINS* (-) 02/03/__13__ – __3/25/13__

`-__23__ = __RECIPROCAL__ = `-__32__ / `-__13__ = "A VERY PIVOTAL NUMBER"!!!!!~'

(__3__25 (-) __20__3) = `-__122__ = (22 + 1) = `-__23__ = -a Prophetic Number!!!!!~'

`-TODAY'S `-DATE = (12/11/2015) = (12 + 11 + 20 + 15) = `-<u>58</u>

(12 + 11) = `-<u>23</u> = -a Prophetic Number!!!!!~'

(12 + 11 + 20) = `-<u>43</u> = <u>RECIPROCAL</u> = `-<u>34</u> = "The `-<u>PRESIDENTIAL</u> #'s `-<u>NUMBERS</u>"!!!!!~'

`-<u>58</u> = (8 + 5) = `-<u>13</u> = "A VERY PIVOTAL NUMBER"!!!!!~'

<u>G</u>OLDEN <u>S</u>TATE <u>W</u>ARRIORS &-`-HALFTIME-& <u>B</u>OSTON <u>C</u>ELTICS

(<u>GSW</u>) <u>33</u>% 1ST QTR FGS (<u>BC</u>) <u>46</u>%

(<u>GSW</u>) <u>52</u>% 2nd QTR FGS (<u>BC</u>) <u>57</u>%

(<u>GSW</u>) <u>5/17</u> 3-PT FGS (<u>BC</u>) <u>5/12</u>

(<u>GSW</u>) <u>12/17</u> FREE THROWS (<u>BC</u>) <u>2/7</u>

(<u>GSW</u>) <u>27</u> BENCH SCORING (<u>BC</u>) <u>21</u>

(<u>GSW</u>) <u>57</u> SCORING POINTS (<u>BC</u>) <u>53</u>

`-FINISHING the `-GAME!!!!!~'

(<u>GSW</u>) #<u>30</u> STEPHEN <u>C</u>URRY (=) <u>G</u>OLDEN <u>S</u>TATE <u>W</u>ARRIORS

(<u>SC</u>) NOVEMBER 14th vs. BROOKLYN: `-<u>13/31</u> FIELD GOALS

(<u>SC</u>) TONIGHT: `-<u>7/22</u> FIELD GOALS

`-<u>2:22</u> `-LEFT in the `-GAME!!!!!~'

(<u>SC</u>) `-<u>32</u> PTS (3-PT FGS) = <u>6/11</u> / FT: <u>10/10</u> / :<u>46</u>.8 `-LEFT in the `-GAME

`-OVERTIME at (GSW) `-<u>103</u> -to- (BC) `-<u>103</u> `-TOTAL `-POINTS!!!!!~'

`-<u>103</u> = (13 + 0) = `-<u>13</u> = "A VERY PIVOTAL NUMBER"!!!!!~'

(<u>STEPHEN CURRY</u>) TONIGHT: `-<u>9/27</u> FIELD GOALS

`-DOUBLE `-OVERTIME at (GSW) `-<u>110</u> -to- (BC) `-<u>110</u> `-TOTAL `-POINTS!!!!!~'

`-11 = "Yin/Yang" = "Multiple of `-ELEVEN" = "The `-CYCLE of `-LIFE"!!!!!~'

`-2:43 `-LEFT in the `-GAME!!!!!~'

(GSW) `-114 -to- (BC) `-113 `-TOTAL `-POINTS!!!!!~'

`-:51.5 `-LEFT in the `-GAME!!!!!~'

(GSW) `-118 -to- (BC) `-115 `-TOTAL `-POINTS!!!!!~'

(8 + 5) = `-13 = "A VERY PIVOTAL NUMBER"!!!!!~'

`-:17.8 `-LEFT in the `-GAME!!!!!~'

(GSW) `-118 -to- (BC) `-117 `-TOTAL `-POINTS!!!!!~'

`-78 = RECIPROCAL = `-87

(STEPHEN CURRY) #30 = TONIGHT: `-36 PTS / FT: 12/12

`-:13.4 `-LEFT in the `-GAME!!!!!~'

(GSW) `-122 -to- (BC) `-119 `-TOTAL `-POINTS!!!!!~'

`-122 = (22 + 1) = `-23 = -a Prophetic Number!!!!!~'

(GSW) `-124 -to- (BC) `-119 `-TOTAL `-POINTS!!!!!~'

GOLDEN STATE WARRIORS `-WIN; and, `-KEEP `-WIN `-STREAK `-ALIVE!!!!!~'

`-NOW 2nd `-MOST `-WINS in `-NBA `-HISTORY: at, `-28; and, `-0!!!!!~'

(STEPHEN CURRY) #30 = TONIGHT: `-38 PTS = `-38 = 3(8's) = `-888 = (8 x 8 x 8) = `-512 = (5 (1 + 2)) = `-53 = "WAR of the WORLDS"!!!!!~

`-124 = (24 x 1) = `-24 = `-24th `-WIN `-STREAK stays `-ALIVE = #24/ Vice-President Garret Hobart!!!!!~'

(124 + 119) = `-243 = `-2(43) = "EMPHATIC `-WITNESS to the # `-NUMBER `-43 = RECIPROCAL = `-34 = "The `-PRESIDENTIAL #'s `-NUMBERS"!!!!!~'

'-243 = '-(24)3 = "EMPHATIC '-EMPHASIS to the # '-NUMBER '-24 = "The '-24ᵗʰ '-WIN '-STREAK stays '-ALIVE; &, the #24/Vice-President Garret Hobart"!!!!!~'

'-243 = (43 + 2) = '-45 = "The '-CURRENT '-AGE of the "PROPHET"-"!!!!!~'

'-243 = '-(24)3 = '-72 = The '-LOS ANGELES LAKERS = '-33 *STRAIGHT WINS* (-) 11/5/71 – 1/7/72

11/05/71 – 01/07/72 = {(11 + 5 + 71) + (1 + 7 + 72)} = {(87) + (80)} = '-167 = (67 x 1) = '-67 = "The '-YEAR that the "PROPHET'S" BROTHER was '-BORN, the '-AVERAGE '-AGE of the United States Presidents 1 to 28 in "SUCCESSION" above; and, below '-ALL '-PRESIDENTS that '-DIED at '-AGES '-66, '-67; and, '-68; and, The '-AGE of '-DEATH of the #1/President of the United States of America #1/President George Washington"!!!!!~'

The '-GOLDEN '-STATE '-WARRIORS have '-SOLD '-OUT their '-NEXT '-144 '-HOME '-GAMES!!!!!~'

'-144 = (44 x 1) = '-44 = '-GUARD #44 = JERRY WEST = LOS ANGELES LAKERS!!!!!~'

The '-AVERAGE '-RESALE for a '-HOME '-GAME '-TICKET is '-AVERAGING '-AROUND ('-$344.00)!!!!!~'

'-$344.00 = '-3(44) = "EMPHATIC '-EMPHASIS for the # '-NUMBER '-44 = "#1/President George Washington was '-44 '-YEARS of '-AGE in ('-1776) on the very '-FIRST '-INDEPENDENCE '-DAY of which '-HE '-DIED on the '-EXACT same '-DAY '-RECIPROCAL # '-NUMBER of which '-HE was at the '-AGE of ('-67)-'; and, the '-BIRTHYEAR of the "PROPHET'S" MOTHER ('-1944)"!!!!!~'

'-$344.00 = '-(34)4 = (34 x 4) = '-136 = (36 x 1) = '-36 = RECIPROCAL = '-63 = "The '-YEAR #35/President John F. Kennedy was '-ASSASSINATED ('-1963); and, President John F. Kennedy's FUNERAL by '-HIS '-WIFE'S '-REQUEST (FIRST LADY JACQUELINE LEE KENNEDY) was '-PATTERNED after the #16/President Abraham Lincoln's '-FUNERAL; and, (#63) being the '-AGE of '-DEATH of the "PROPHET'S" MOTHER;

and, the #16/President Abraham Lincoln's `-WIFE / FIRST LADY MARY TODD LINCOLN (#**63**)!!!!!~'

`-$344.00 = `-(34)4 = (34 x 4) = `-**136** = (36 + 1) = `-**37** = `-3(7's) = (777) = (7 x 7 x 7) = `-**343** = Reciprocal-Sequencing-Numerology-RSN = "The `-PRESIDENTIAL #'s `-NUMBERS"!!!!!~'

`-IT `-TOOK `-A `-FULL `-**58** `-MINUTES to get `-IT `-DONE!!!!!~'

`-**58** = (8 + 5) = `-**13** = "A VERY PIVOTAL NUMBER"!!!!!~'

I've `-CREATED a NEW TYPE of PHILOSOPHY (Reciprocal-Sequencing-Numerology) that `-PROVES without `-QUESTION the `-PRESENCE of GOD'S EXISTENCE in our DAILY AFFAIRS!!!!!~'

`-*BUILT FOR BUSINESS* in `-REAL `-WIN `-STREAKS!!!!!~'

`-*THE* `-*WORLD* `-*WARS*!!!!!~'

`-**1881** = Reciprocal-Sequencing-Numerology-RSN = began the `-REPORTING of `-MASS `-VIOLENCE; and, `-TERRORISM; within this `-WORLD!!!!!~'

`-**18** = RECIPROCAL = `-**81**

`-NEW `-MILLENNIUM (`-1900's)!!!!!~'

(1900 (-) 1881) = `-**19** / (1914 (-) 1900) = `-**14**

(19/14) = `-**1914** = "The `-OUTBREAK of WORLD WAR (I)"!!!!!~'

(`-19**14**) …(…)…"Swipe 1"…(…)…-'-' (`-19**41**)

(`-**1941**) = "The `-OUTBREAK of WORLD WAR (II) <u>to include</u> `-AMERICA"!!!!!~'

`-**49** = RECIPROCAL = `-**94** = "THE `-LIFE; and, `-DEATH # `-NUMBERS"!!!!!~'

(`-19**14**) / (`-19**41**)…(…)…-'-'""

$(94 + 49)$ = `-**143** = $(43 \times 1)$ = `-**43**

`-**43** = **RECIPROCAL** = `-**34** = "The `-**PRESIDENTIAL** #'s `-**NUMBERS**"!!!!!~'

Micah 4:3 (-) "(3) and he shall judge between many peoples, and shall reprove strong nations afar off; and they shall beat their swords into plowshares, and their spears into pruninghooks: nation shall not lift up sword against nation, neither shall they learn war any more." -(**ENGLISH REVISED EDITION - 1885**)-

$(1914 (-) 1881)$ = `-**33** = "Yin/Yang" = "Multiple of `-**ELEVEN**" = "The `-**CYCLE of `-LIFE**"!!!!!~'

$(1941 (-) 1881)$ = `-**60** = "`-**PLEASE** `-**SEE** `-**BELOW** for the `-**HAND** of `-**GOD**"!!!!!~'

(`-**1914**) = $(19 + 14)$ = `-**33** = "Yin/Yang" = "Multiple of `-**ELEVEN**" = "The `-**CYCLE of `-LIFE**"!!!!!~'

(`-**1941**) = $(19 + 41)$ = `-**60** = $(6 + 0)$ = `-**6** = `-**2** x `-**3** = `-**23** = -a Prophetic Number!!!!!~'

(`-**1941**) = $(19 + 41)$ = `-**60** = $(6 + 0)$ = `-**6** = `-**3** x `-**2** = `-**32** = -a Prophetic Number!!!!!~'

`-**55** = "**EMPHATIC** `-**WITNESS** to being in the `-**GOOD** `-**HANDS** of the `-**HANDS** (`-5#) of `-**GOD** = "**SAVES LIVES**"!!!!!~'

`-**55** = `-**23** + `-**32**

$(55 (-) **41**)$ = `-**14** = (`-**1914**) --- **WORLD WAR (I)**!!!!!~'

$(55 (-) **14**)$ = `-**41** = (`-**1941**) --- **WORLD WAR (II)**!!!!!~'

$(55 + 55)$ = `-**110** = $(11 + 0)$ = `-**11** = "Yin/Yang" = "Multiple of `-**ELEVEN**" = "The `-**CYCLE of `-LIFE**"!!!!!~'

$(60 (-) 33)$ = `-**27** = "The ROMAN EMPIRE"!!!!!~'

$(19**41** (-) 19**14**)$ = `-**27** = "The ROMAN EMPIRE"!!!!!~'

`-14 = **RECIPROCAL** = `-41

`-35 = **RECIPROCAL** = `-53 = "WAR of the WORLDS"!!!!!~'

(14 + 35) = (`-49) = **RECIPROCAL** = (41 + 53) = (`-94)

1st **Thessalonians** 5:3 (-) "(3) When they are saying, Peace and safety, then sudden destruction cometh upon them, as travail upon a woman with child; and they shall in no wise escape." -(ENGLISH REVISED EDITION - 1885)-

1st **Thessalonians** 5:2 (-) "(2) For yourselves know perfectly that the day of the Lord so cometh as a thief in the night." -(**ENGLISH REVISED EDITION - 1885**)-

`-32 = **RECIPROCAL** = `-23

Isaiah 2:3 (-) "(3) And many peoples shall go and say, come ye, and let us go up to the mountain of the LORD, to the house of the God of Jacob; and he will teach us of his ways, and we will walk in his paths: for out of Zion shall go forth the law, and the word of the LORD from Jerusalem."
-(**ENGLISH REVISED EDITION - 1885**)-

Isaiah 2:4 (-) "(4) And he shall judge between the nations, and shall reprove many peoples: and they shall beat their swords into plowshares, and their spears into pruninghooks: nation shall not lift up sword against nation, neither shall they learn war any more." -(**ENGLISH REVISED EDITION - 1885**)-

`-THE `-GREAT `-WORLD `-WARS/A `-BIBLICAL `-PERSPECTIVE!!!!!~'

`-The `-**RESURRECTION**!!!!!~'

As "The Real Prophet of Doom (Kismet) – Introduction – Pendulum Flow –" used the "DEATH CIPHERS" to `-CALCULATE `-ANYONES `-AGE, `-DAY; and, `-EVERY `-CONCEIVABLE `-POSSIBILITY of `-DEATH, the `-NEXT `-LOGICAL `-STEP is `-ONLY; the `-RESURRECTION; or, the `-REVIVAL!!!!!~'

`-NOW, that `-IT is `-CLEARLY `-SEEN, that `-ALL of `-OUR `-LIVES; and, `-DEATHS; are `-ALREADY `-SET in `-PLACE by `-GOD, clearly;

a `-RESURRECTION in the `-PLANS, is `-NOW `-EASY; for `-GOD `-TO `-DO!!!!!~'

'NOW; let's `-TAKE a `-LOOK at what the `-BIBLE has to `-SAY on the `-SUBJECT of `-DEATH; and, the `-RESURRECTION `-Using `-Reciprocal-Sequencing-Numerology-RSN!!!!!~'

Ezekiel 32:23,32 (-) "(23) whose graves are set in the uttermost parts of the pit, and her company is round about her grave: all of them slain, fallen by the sword, which caused terror in the land of the living. (32) For I have put his terror in the land of the living: and he shall be laid in the midst of the uncircumcised, with them that are slain by the sword, even Pharaoh and all his multitude, saith the Lord GOD." -(ENGLISH REVISED EDITION - 1885)-

Revelation 20:13 (-) "(13) And the sea gave up the dead which were in it; and death and Hades gave up the dead which were in them: and they were judged every man according to their works." -(ENGLISH REVISED EDITION - 1885)-

`-34 = RECIPROCAL = `-43 = "The `-PRESIDENTIAL #'s `-NUMBERS"!!!!!~'

Hosea 13:14 (-) "(14) I will ransom them from the power of the grave; I will redeem them from death: O death, where are thy plagues? O grave, where is thy destruction? repentance shall be hid from mine eyes." -(ENGLISH REVISED EDITION - 1885)-

`-35 = RECIPROCAL = `-53

`-53, `-54, `-55 = "Prophetic-Linear-Progression-PLP"!!!!!~'

1st Corinthians 15:35,53,54,55 (-) "(35) But some one will say, How are the dead raised? and with what manner of body do they come? (53) For this corruptible must put on incorruption, and this mortal must put on immortality. (54) But when this corruptible shall have put on incorruption, and this mortal shall have put on immortality, then shall come to pass the saying that is written, Death is swallowed up in victory. (55) O death, where is thy victory? O death, where is thy sting?" -(ENGLISH REVISED EDITION - 1885)-

`-12 = <u>RECIPROCAL</u> = `-21

1ˢᵗ Corinthians <u>15:12-21</u> (-) **"(12)** Now if Christ is preached that he hath been raised from the dead, how say some among you that there is no resurrection of the dead? **(13)** But if there is no resurrection of the dead, neither hath Christ been raised: **(14)** and if Christ hath not been raised, then is our preaching vain, your faith also is vain. **(15)** Yea, and we are found false witnesses of God; because we witnessed of God that he raised up Christ: whom he raised not up, if so be that the dead are not raised. **(16)** For if the dead are not raised, neither hath Christ been raised: **(17)** and if Christ hath not been raised, your faith is vain; ye are yet in your sins. **(18)** Then they also which are fallen asleep in Christ have perished. **(19)** If in this life only we have hoped in Christ, we are of all men most pitiable. **(20)** But now hath Christ been raised from the dead, the firstfruits of them that are asleep. **(21)** For since by man came death, by man came also the resurrection of the dead." **-(ENGLISH REVISED EDITION - 1885)-**

`-A `-RESURRECTION; `-ALREADY, by `-CHRIST `-JESUS!!!!!~'

John <u>11:38-44</u> (-) **"(38)** Jesus therefore again groaning in himself cometh to the tomb. Now it was a cave, and a stone lay against it. **(39)** Jesus saith, Take ye away the stone. Martha, the sister of him that was dead, saith unto him, Lord, by this time he stinketh: for he hath been dead four days. **(40)** Jesus saith unto her, Said I not unto thee, that, if thou believedst, thou shouldest see the glory of God? **(41)** So they took away the stone. And Jesus lifted up his eyes, and said, Father, I thank thee that thou heardest me. **(42)** And I knew that thou hearest me always: but because of the multitude which standeth around I said it, that they may believe that thou didst send me. **(43)** And when he had thus spoken, he cried with a loud voice, Lazarus, come forth. **(44)** He that was dead came forth, bound hand and foot with grave-clothes; and his face was bound about with a napkin. Jesus saith unto them, Loose him, and let him go." **-(ENGLISH REVISED EDITION - 1885)-**

`-GOD, by `-HIS `-POWER; makes `-ALIVE!!!!!~'

Matthew 22:<u>23</u>,31,<u>32</u>,33 (-) **"(23)** On that day there came to him Sadducees, which say that there is no resurrection: and they asked him, (31) But as touching the resurrection of the dead, have ye not read that which was spoken unto you by God, saying, **(32)** I am the God of Abraham, and the God of Isaac, and the God of Jacob? God is not the God of the dead, but of the living. (33) And when the multitudes heard it, they were astonished at his teaching." -(ENGLISH REVISED EDITION - 1885)-

(17 (-) 4) = `-13 = "A VERY PIVOTAL NUMBER"!!!!!~'

Romans 4:17 (-) "(17) (as it is written, A father of many nations have I made thee) before him whom he believed, even God, who quickeneth the dead, and calleth the things that are not, as though they were." -(ENGLISH REVISED EDITION - 1885)-

`-BASIS for `-FAITH via `-JOB; though, `-NOW; a `-REALITY!!!!!~'

Job 14:13-15 (-) "(13) Oh that thou wouldest hide me in Sheol, that thou wouldest keep me secret, until thy wrath be past, that thou wouldest appoint me a set time, and remember me! (14) If a man die, shall he live again? all the days of my warfare would I wait, till my release should come. (15) Thou shouldest call, and I would answer thee: thou wouldest have a desire to the work of thine hands." -(ENGLISH REVISED EDITION - 1885)-

`-A `-HEAVENLY `-REVIVAL; or, that of; `-A `-HEAVENLY `-RESURRECTION!!!!!~'

`-35 = RECIPROCAL = `-53 = "WAR of the WORLDS"!!!!!~'

Acts 3:15 (-) "(15) and killed the Prince of life; whom God raised from the dead; whereof we are witnesses" -(ENGLISH REVISED EDITION - 1885)-

Acts 5:30 (-) "(30) The God of our fathers raised up Jesus, whom ye slew, hanging him on a tree." -(ENGLISH REVISED EDITION - 1885)-

`-424 = Reciprocal-Sequencing-Numerology-RSN!!!!!~'

Romans 4:24 (-) "(24) but for our sake also, unto whom it shall be reckoned, who believe on him that raised Jesus our Lord from the dead," -(ENGLISH REVISED EDITION - 1885)-

`-424 = (42 + 4) = `-46 = `-23 x `-2 = `-232 = Reciprocal-Sequencing-Numerology-RSN!!!!!~'

`-RESURRECTION for the `-BROTHERS of `-CHRIST that will `-RESIDE as `-KINGS, `-PRIESTS; and, `-JUDGES; in `-HEAVEN `-ITSELF!!!!!~'

`-34 = RECIPROCAL = `-43 = "The `-PRESIDENTIAL #'s `-NUMBERS"!!!!!~'

1st **Peter 1:3,4** (-) "(3) Blessed be the God and Father of our Lord Jesus Christ, who according to his great mercy begat us again unto a living hope by the resurrection of Jesus Christ from the dead, (4) unto an inheritance incorruptible, and undefiled, and that fadeth not away, reserved in heaven for you," -(ENGLISH REVISED EDITION - 1885)-

Romans 6:3-5 (-) "(3) Or are ye ignorant that all we who were baptized into Christ Jesus were baptized into his death? (4) We were buried therefore with him through baptism into death: that like as Christ was raised from the dead through the glory of the Father, so we also might walk in newness of life. (5) For if we have become united with him by the likeness of his death, we shall be also by the likeness of his resurrection;" -(ENGLISH REVISED EDITION - 1885)-

2nd **Corinthians 5:1-3** (-) "(1) For we know that if the earthly house of our tabernacle be dissolved, we have a building from God, a house not made with hands, eternal, in the heavens. (2) For verily in this we groan, longing to be clothed upon with our habitation which is from heaven: (3) if so be that being clothed we shall not be found naked." -(ENGLISH REVISED EDITION - 1885)-

1st **Corinthians 15:35** (-) "(35) But some one will say, How are the dead raised? and with what manner of body do they come?" -(ENGLISH REVISED EDITION - 1885)-

Hebrews 1:3,4 (-) "(3) who being the effulgence of his glory, and the very image of his substance, and upholding all things by the word of his power, when he had made purification of sins, sat down on the right hand of the Majesty on high; (4) having become by so much better than the angels, as he hath inherited a more excellent name than they." -(ENGLISH REVISED EDITION - 1885)-

Hebrews 10:12,13 (-) "(12) but he, when he had offered one sacrifice for sins for ever, sat down on the right hand of God; (13) from henceforth expecting till his enemies be made the footstool of his feet." -(ENGLISH REVISED EDITION - 1885)-

Philippians 3:20,21 (-) "(20) For our citizenship is in heaven; from whence also we wait for a Saviour, the Lord Jesus Christ: (21) who shall fashion anew the body of our humiliation, that it may be conformed to the body of his glory, according to the working whereby he is able even to subject all things unto himself." -(ENGLISH REVISED EDITION - 1885)-

1ˢᵗ **Corinthians** 15:20,23 (-) "(20) But now hath Christ been raised from the dead, the firstfruits of them that are asleep. (23) But each in his own order: Christ the firstfruits; then they that are Christ's, at his coming." -(ENGLISH REVISED EDITION - 1885)-

Revelation 14:4 (-) "(4) These are they which were not defiled with women; for they are virgins. These are they which follow the Lamb whithersoever he goeth. These were purchased from among men, to be the firstfruits unto God and unto the Lamb." -(ENGLISH REVISED EDITION - 1885)-

1ˢᵗ **Corinthians** 15:51,52,53 (-) "(51) Behold, I tell you a mystery: We shall not all sleep, but we shall all be changed, (52) in a moment, in the twinkling of an eye, at the last trump: for the trumpet shall sound, and the dead shall be raised incorruptible, and we shall be changed. (53) For this corruptible must put on incorruption, and this mortal must put on immortality." -(ENGLISH REVISED EDITION - 1885)-

Luke 22:30 (-) "(30) that ye may eat and drink at my table in my kingdom; and ye shall sit on thrones judging the twelve tribes of Israel." -(ENGLISH REVISED EDITION - 1885)-

`-46 = `-23 x `-2 = `-232 = **Reciprocal-Sequencing-Numerology-RSN!!!!!~'**

Revelation 20:4,6 (-) "(4) And I saw thrones, and they sat upon them, and judgment was given unto them: and I saw the souls of them that had been beheaded for the testimony of Jesus, and for the word of God, and such as worshipped not the beast, neither his image, and received not the mark upon their forehead and upon their hand; and they lived, and reigned with Christ a thousand years. (6) Blessed and holy is he that hath part in the first resurrection: over these the second death hath no power; but they shall be priests of God and of Christ, and shall reign with him a thousand years." -(ENGLISH REVISED EDITION - 1885)-

`-A `-RESURRECTION for the `-EARTHLY `-SUBJECTS of `-CHRIST that will `-RESIDE on `-EARTH `-ITSELF!!!!!~'

With a `-REASONING `-MIND; `-IF, "you" have `-KINGS, `-PRIESTS; and, `-JUDGES in `-HEAVEN; who, do `-THEY `-RESIDE/`-PRESIDE `-OVER!!!!!~' There has to be `-SOMEONE on `-EARTH!!!!!~'

Luke 23:42,43 (-) "(42) And he said, Jesus, remember me when thou comest in thy **kingdom**. (43) And he said unto him, Verily I say unto thee, Today shalt thou be with me in **Paradise**." -(ENGLISH REVISED EDITION - 1885)-

`-27 = "The ROMAN EMPIRE"!!!!!~'

Revelation 2:7 (-) "(7) He that hath an ear, let him hear what the Spirit saith to the churches. To him that overcometh, to him will I give to eat of the tree of life, which is in the Paradise of God." -(ENGLISH REVISED EDITION - 1885)-

`-77 = `-2(7's)

Revelation 7:17 (-) "(17) for the Lamb which is in the midst of the throne shall be their shepherd, and shall guide them unto fountains of waters of life: and God shall wipe away every tear from their eyes" -(ENGLISH REVISED EDITION - 1885)-

Revelation 20:12,13 (-) "(12) And I saw the dead, the great and the small, standing before the throne; and books were opened: and another book was opened, which is the book of life: and the dead were judged out of the things which were written in the books, according to their works. (13) And the sea gave up the dead which were in it; and death and Hades gave up the dead which were in them: and they were judged every man according to their works." -(ENGLISH REVISED EDITION - 1885)-

Romans 6:23 (-) "(23) For the wages of sin is death; but the free gift of God is eternal life in Christ Jesus our Lord." -(ENGLISH REVISED EDITION - 1885)-

John 5:25 (-) "(25) Verily, verily, I say unto you, The hour cometh, and now is, when the dead shall hear the voice of the Son of God; and they that hear shall live." -(ENGLISH REVISED EDITION - 1885)-

John 5:27,28,29 (-) "(27) and he gave him authority to execute judgment, because he is the Son of man. (28) Marvel not at this: for the hour cometh, in which all that are in the tombs shall hear his voice, (29) And shall come forth; they that have done good, unto the resurrection of life; and they that have done ill, unto the resurrection of judgment." -(**ENGLISH REVISED EDITION - 1885**)-

(5 + 7 + 8 + 9) = `-29 / (44 (-) 15) = `-29

(29 + 29) = `-58 = (5 + 8) = `-13 = "**A VERY PIVOTAL NUMBER**"!!!!!~'

1ˢᵗ Corinthians 15:44 (-) "(44) it is sown a natural body; it is raised a spiritual body. If there is a natural body, there is also a spiritual body." -(**ENGLISH REVISED EDITION - 1885**)-

1ˢᵗ Peter 4:3-6 (-) "(3) For the time past may suffice to have wrought the desire of the Gentiles, and to have walked in lasciviousness, lusts, winebibbings, revellings, carousings, and abominable idolatries: (4) wherein they think it strange that ye run not with them into the same excess of riot, speaking evil of you: (5) who shall give account to him that is ready to judge the quick and the dead. (6) For unto this end was the gospel preached even to the dead, that they might be judged according to men in the flesh, but live according to God in the spirit." -(**ENGLISH REVISED EDITION - 1885**)-

1ˢᵗ John 3:13,14 (-) "(13) Marvel not, brethren, if the world hateth you. (14) We know that we have passed out of death into life, because we love the brethren. He that loveth not abideth in death." -(**ENGLISH REVISED EDITION - 1885**)-

John 3:16 (-) "(16) For God so loved the world, that he gave his only begotten Son, that whosoever believeth on him should not perish, but have eternal life." -(**ENGLISH REVISED EDITION - 1885**)-

1ˢᵗ Thessalonians 4:13,14 (-) "(13) But we would not have you ignorant, brethren, concerning them that fall asleep; that ye sorrow not, even as the rest, which have no hope. (14) For if we believe that Jesus died and rose again, even so them also that are fallen asleep in Jesus will God bring with him." -(**ENGLISH REVISED EDITION - 1885**)-

Matthew 12:31,32 (-) "(31) Therefore I say unto you, Every sin and blasphemy shall be forgiven unto men; but the blasphemy against the Spirit shall not be forgiven. (32) And whosoever shall speak a word against the Son of man, it shall be forgiven him; but whosoever shall speak against the Holy Spirit, it shall not be forgiven him, neither in this world, nor in that which is to come." -(ENGLISH REVISED EDITION - 1885)-

"The Real Prophet of Doom – Volumes 1,2,3"; and, "The Real Prophet of Doom (Kismet) – Introduction – Pendulum Flow – "I"; and, "II"-'" have `-CLEARLY `-DEMONSTRATED the `-EFFECTS of; `-GOD'S `-HOLY `-SPIRIT, in `-ACTION!!!!!~'

Revelation 7:9,14 (-) "(9) After these things I saw, and behold, a great multitude, which no man could number, out of every nation and of all tribes and peoples and tongues, standing before the throne and before the Lamb, arrayed in white robes, and palms in their hands; (14) And I say unto him, My lord, thou knowest. And he said to me, These are they which come out of the great tribulation, and they washed their robes, and made them white in the blood of the Lamb." -(ENGLISH REVISED EDITION - 1885)-

`-79 = "The `-AGE of `-DEATH for Mr. H. G. Wells for the "WAR of the WORLDS" `-CREATION-'"!!!!!~'

`-49 = RECIPROCAL = `-94 = "The `-DEATH `-NUMBERS"!!!!!~'

Revelation 16:16 (-) "(16) And they gathered them together into the place which is called in Hebrew Har-Magedon." -(ENGLISH REVISED EDITION - 1885)-

(16 + 16) = `-32 = -a Prophetic Number!!!!!~'

`-HAR-MAGEDON = `-ARMAGEDDON = "The `-ONLY `-PLACE `-MENTIONED in the `-BIBLE"!!!!!~' (8 + 1 + 18) – (13 + 1 + 7 + 5 + 4 + 15 + 14) = (27)-(59) = {(59 (-) 27)} = `-32 = -a Prophetic Number!!!!!~' {(`-59 = "AGE of `-JESUS `-CHRIST'S MOTHER `-MARY'S DEATH"|}!!!!!~' {(`-27 = "The ROMAN EMPIRE")|}!!!!!~'

{(27)/(59 = (9 + 5) = `-14 = (2 x 7) = `-2(7's) = `-27)|}

`-27 + `-27 = `-54 = "EARTHQUAKES" = RECIPROCAL = `-45 = "CURRENT `-AGE of the "PROPHET"!!!!!~'

(86 + 86) = `-172 = (72 x 1) = `-72 = RECIPROCAL = `-27

`-**HAR**-**MAGEDON** = (27 + 59) = `-**86** = "PIANO KEY # `-NUMBER = A 7 / B 7 = AB(2(7's)) = "(1/2/KNOCK/OUT) `-The ROMAN EMPIRE"!!!!!~' (7 x 7 = `-**49**)!!!!!~'

`-**ARMAGEDDON** = (1 + 18 + 13 + 1 + 7 + 5 + 4 + 4 + 15 + 14) = `-**82** = **RECIPROCAL** = `-**28** = `-**2(8's)** = `-**88** = "PIANO KEYS"!!!!!~' `-**PIANO** = (16 + 9 + 1 + 14 + 15) = `-**55** = `-**23** + `-**32** = "SAVES LIVES"!!!!!!~'

`-**ARMAGEDDON** = (1 + 18 + 13 + 1 + 7 + 5 + 4 + 4) (+) (15 + 14) = (53)+(29) = (53)+(2(9's)) = (53)+(99) = `-**152** = (52 + 1) = `-**53** = "WAR of the WORLDS"!!!!!~'

`-**ARMAGEDDON** = `-**ARM** = **RECIPROCAL** = `-**MRA**

`-**MR. A** = `-**AGE** = `-**D** = `-**DON**

`-**MR. ANDERSON** = The `-**AGE** of `-**DEATH** # `-**NUMBERS** = `-**THE** = `-**GODFATHER** of `-**SOUL**!!!!!~'

`-The `-**PROFESSOR** of `-**SOUL** = `-**101**-'" = Reciprocal-Sequencing-Numerology-RSN!!!!!~'

`-The `-**RESURRECTION** `-**COMETH** `-**SOON**!!!!!~'

`-*BUILT FOR BUSINESS* in `-**REAL** `-**WIN** `-**STREAKS**!!!!!~'

`-**24**th `-**WIN** `-**STREAK** `-**DATE** = (12/11/2015) = (12 + 11 + 20 + 15) = `-**58**

(12 + 11) = `-**23** = -a Prophetic Number!!!!!~'

(12 + 11 + 20) = `-**43** = **RECIPROCAL** = `-**34** = "The `-**PRESIDENTIAL** #'s `-**NUMBERS**"!!!!!~'

`-**58** = (8 + 5) = `-**13** = "A VERY PIVOTAL NUMBER"!!!!!~'

`-**IT** `-**TOOK** `-**A** `-**FULL** `-**58** `-**MINUTES** to get `-**IT** `-**DONE** / **DOUBLE** **OVERTIME**!!!!!~'

`-**58** = (8 + 5) = `-**13** = "A VERY PIVOTAL NUMBER"!!!!!~'

I've `-CREATED a NEW TYPE of PHILOSOPHY (Reciprocal-Sequencing-Numerology) that `-PROVES without `-QUESTION the `-PRESENCE of GOD'S EXISTENCE in our DAILY AFFAIRS!!!!!~'

`-TODAY'S `-DATE = (12/12/2015) = (12 + 12 + 20 + 15) = `-59

`-59 = "The `-AGE of `-DEATH of "MARY"; `-JESUS `-CHRIST'S; `-MOTHER"!!!!!~'

`-59 = RECIPROCAL = `-95

The `-WIN `-STREAK `-ENDS at `-24!!!!!~' Future `-LOOK (121/112) – + – `-233!!!!!~' `-12 = RECIPROCAL = `-21

ENGLISH ALPHABET = GSW = `-7/19/23 / MB = `-13/2 / (7 + 19 + 23) = `-49 = `-GOLDEN STATE WARRIORS = `-27 STRAIGHT WINS (-) 4/9/15 = 4 + 9 + 15 = `-28-'

(GOLDEN STATE WARRIORS (`-95) –TO- (`-108) MILWAUKEE BUCKS)

(108 (-) 95) = `-13 = "A VERY PIVOTAL NUMBER"!!!!!~'

(108 + 95) = `-203 = (23 + 0) = `-23 = -a Prophetic Number!!!!!~'

`-BUILT FOR BUSINESS in `-REAL `-WIN `-STREAKS!!!!!~'

`-A `-PENDULUM `-SHIFT!!!!!~' / `-(UFC 194)-'"

`-A/ANOTHER `-NEW `-CHAMPION!!!!!~'

`-CONNER MCGREGOR `-DEFEATS `-JOSE ALDO in just `-13 `-SECONDS for the `-UFC `-CHAMPIONSHIP!!!!!~'

`-13 = "A VERY PIVOTAL NUMBER"!!!!!~'

AMERICAN/ENGLISH `-ALPHABET '-to-' `-NUMBERS #'s:!!!!!~'

CM = `-3, `-13 / JA = `-10, `-1

`-313 = Reciprocal-Sequencing-Numerology-RSN!!!!!-'

`-31 = RECIPROCAL = `-13

`-101 = Reciprocal-Sequencing-Numerology-RSN!!!!!-'

`-10 = RECIPROCAL = `-01

(313 (-) 101) = `-212 = "BIRTH of #16/President Abraham Lincoln"!!!!!-'

`-CONNER MCGREGOR is `-NOW the UNDISPUTED `-UFC `-FEATHERWEIGHT `-CHAMPION!!!!!-'

`-FORMER `-CHAMPION `-JOSE ALDO hadn't `-LOST in `-TEN (`-10) `-YEARS!!!!!-'

(13 + 10) = `-23 = -a Prophetic Number!!!!!-' / `-23 = RECIPROCAL = `-32

`-A/ANOTHER `-NEW `-CHAMPION!!!!!-'

`-LUKE ROCKHOLD `-DEFEATS `-CHRIS WEIDMAN for the `-UFC `-MIDDLEWEIGHT `-CHAMPIONSHIP!!!!!-'

`-LUKE ROCKHOLD is `-CURRENTLY `-AGE `-31!!!!!-' / UFC RECORD: 5-1

`-CHRIS WEIDMAN is `-CURRENTLY `-AGE `-31!!!!!-' / UFC RECORD: 9-1

`-31 = RECIPROCAL = `-13 = "A VERY PIVOTAL NUMBER"!!!!!-'

`-TODAY'S `-BIRTHDAY # `-NUMBER = `-59 = RECIPROCAL = `-95

(95 + 59) = `-154 = (54 + 1) = `-55 = `-23 + `-32

`-LUKE ROCKHOLD'S `-WEIGHT is `-CURRENTLY `-185lbs.!!!!!-'

`-CHRIS WEIDMAN'S `-WEIGHT is `-CURRENTLY `-185lbs.!!!!!-'

`-185 = (8 + 5 x 1) = `-13 = "A VERY PIVOTAL NUMBER"!!!!!-'

TKO: in ROUND 4 / (3:12) / 3 (minutes) :12 (seconds)…(…)…-'-'"

`-4321 = "Prophetic-Linear-Progression-PLP"!!!!!~'

`-312 = (32 x 1) = `-32 = -a Prophetic Number!!!!!~'

AMERICAN/ENGLISH `-ALPHABET `-to-` `-NUMBERS #'s:!!!!!~'

LR = `-12, `-18 / CW = `-3, `-23

`-1218 = (1 + 2 + 1 + 8) = `-12 = "ONE (`-1), TWO (`-2) `-KNOCK `-OUT"!!!!!~'

(81 + 12) = `-93 = UFC-193!!!!!~'

`-323 = Reciprocal-Sequencing-Numerology-RSN!!!!!~'

`-32 = RECIPROCAL = `-23

(1218 + 323) = `-1541 = (41 + 15) = `-56 = "AGE of `-DEATH of #16/ President Abraham Lincoln"!!!!!~'

(1218 (-) 323) = `-895 = (89 + 5) = `-94 = UFC-194!!!!!~'

(1218 (-) 323) = `-895 = (95 + 8) = `-103 = (13 + 0) = `-13 = "A VERY PIVOTAL NUMBER"!!!!!~'

(GOLDEN STATE WARRIORS (`-95) –TO- (`-108) MILWAUKEE BUCKS)

`-TODAY'S `-DATE = (12/12/2015) = (12 + 12 + 20 + 15) = `-59

`-13, `-23; &, `-32 = "A `-PARADIGM `-SHIFT; within, `-PENDULUM `-FLOW"!!!!!~'

`-LUKE ROCKHOLD is `-NOW the UNDISPUTED `-UFC `-MIDDLEWEIGHT `-CHAMPION!!!!!~'

#3 YOEL ROMERO (`-SON of `-GOD) `-DEFEATS #2 JACARE SOUZA

#2 JACARE SOUZA `-LANDED `-8 out of `-11 `-PUNCHES; while,

#3 YOEL ROMERO (`-SON of `-GOD) `-LANDED `-3 out of `-13 `-PUNCHES!!!!!~'

`-<u>811</u> = (11 x 8) = `-<u>88</u> = "Yin/Yang" = "Multiple of `-ELEVEN" = "The `-CYCLE of `-LIFE"!!!!!~'

`-<u>313</u> = Reciprocal-<u>S</u>equencing-<u>N</u>umerology-<u>RSN</u>!!!!!~'

(811 (-) 313) = `-<u>498</u> = (98 (-) 4) = `-<u>94</u> = UFC-194!!!!!~'

(811 + 313) = `-<u>1124</u> = (24 + 11) = `-<u>35</u> = <u>RECIPROCAL</u> = `-<u>53</u> = "WAR of the WORLDS"!!!!!~'

<u>AMERICAN/ENGLISH</u> `-<u>ALPHABET</u> `-<u>to</u>-' `-<u>NUMBERS</u> #'s:!!!!!~'

<u>YR</u> = `-<u>25</u>, `-<u>18</u> / <u>JS</u> = `-<u>10</u>, `-<u>19</u>

(2518 (-) 1019) = `-<u>1499</u> = (99 + 14) = `-<u>113</u> = (13 x 1) = `-<u>13</u> = "A VERY PIVOTAL NUMBER"!!!!!~'

(2518 (-) 1019) = `-<u>1499</u> = (99 (-) 14) = `-<u>85</u> = (8 + 5) = `-<u>13</u> = "A VERY PIVOTAL NUMBER"!!!!!~'

(2518 + 1019) = `-<u>3537</u> = (37 + 35) = `-<u>72</u> = <u>RECIPROCAL</u> = `-<u>27</u> = "The ROMAN EMPIRE"!!!!!~'

(25 + 18) = `-<u>43</u> = <u>RECIPROCAL</u> = `-<u>34</u> = "The `-<u>PRESIDENTIAL</u> #'s `-<u>NUMBERS</u>"!!!!!~' = "For the very `-FIRST `-TIME the UFC went `-<u>34</u> `-FIGHTS `-Back-to-Back-to-Back"!!!!!~'

(25 + 18 + 10) = `-<u>53</u> = "WAR of the WORLDS"!!!!!~'

(25 + 18 + 10 + 19) = `-<u>72</u> = <u>RECIPROCAL</u> = `-<u>27</u> = "The ROMAN EMPIRE"!!!!!~'

`-<u>A</u> `-<u>PENDULUM</u> `-<u>FLOW</u> `-<u>SHIFT</u>!!!!!~' / `-(UFC <u>194</u>)-'"

`-<u>QUANTUM</u> `-<u>PHYSICS</u>!!!!!~'

`-E=`-mc² = "When an `-ATOM `-SPLITS; the `-ENERGY `-RELEASED = `-EQUALS the `-LOSS of its `-PARTICULAR `-MASS (x) `-TIMES the `-SPEED of `-LIGHT / `-SQUARED"!!!!!~'

The `-SPEED of `-LIGHT = `-EQUALS = `-186,282 `-MILES-PER-SECOND!!!!!~'

`-186 = (86 (-) 1) = `-85 = (8 + 5) = `-13 = "A VERY PIVOTAL NUMBER"!!!!!~'

`-282 = Reciprocal-Sequencing-Numerology-RSN!!!!!~'

(186,282 (X) 186,282) = `-34,700,983,524

`-34 = RECIPROCAL = `-43 = "The `-PRESIDENTIAL #'s `-

The `-SPEED of `-LIGHT has `-ALSO been `-AGGREGATED at a `-SPEED of: `-186,282 `-MILES, `-698 `-YARDS, `-2 `-FEET; and, `-5 `-21/127 `-INCHES per `-SECOND!!!!!~'

`-698 = `-(69)8 = (69 x 8) = `-552 = "EMPHATIC `-WITNESS for the # `-NUMBER `-55 = `-23 + `-32

`-698 = `-6(98) = (98 x 6) = `-588 = "The `-AMOUNT of `-PAGES within "The Real Prophet Of Doom (Kismet) – Introduction – Pendulum Flow – "-""

`-5 `-21/127 `-INCHES = (127 + 21 + 5) = `-153 = (53 x 1) = `-53 = "WAR of the WORLDS"!!!!!~'

`-A LOT of `-ENERGY can be `-CREATED from a small `-AMOUNT of `-MASS!!!!!~'

The `-AMOUNT of `-ENERGY `-RELEASED in a `-CHEMICAL `-REACTION can be `-COMPARABLE to an `-EXAMPLE of say `-1lb.; which = `-EQUALS = `-450 grams of any `-SUBSTANCE being completely `-CONVERTED into `-EQUAL `-PORTIONS of `-COMPARATIVE `-ENERGY; which, could; and, would be; about, `-11 `-BILLION `-KILOWATT `-HOURS!!!!!~'

`-11 = "Yin/Yang" = "Multiple of `-ELEVEN" = "The `-CYCLE of `-LIFE"!!!!!~'

`-450 = (45 + 0) = `-45 = "CURRENT `-AGE of the "PROPHET" at the `-TIME of `-THIS `-WRITING"!!!!!~'

KILO/RENIN = `-KYLO REN!!!!!~'

`-RENIN = "THE `-RELEASE of `-ANGIOTENSIN VIA this `-PROTEOLYTIC `-ENZYME of the `-KIDNEYS"!!!!!~' The `-FIRST `-KNOWN `-USE of this `-WORD was in `-1906!!!!!~'

`-1906 = `-96 = RECIPROCAL = `-69 = "Yin/Yang" = "The `-CYCLE of `-LIFE"!!!!!~'

ANGEL = (1 + 14 + 7 + 5 + 12) = `-39 = `-3(9's) = `-999 = (9 x 9 x 9) = `-729 = `-7(29) = (7 x 29) = `-203 = (23 + 0) = `-23 = -a Prophetic Number!!!!!~'

`-A `-PROPHECY; `-LOOK for `-ABRAHAM `-LINCOLN'S # `-NUMBERS; in the # `-NUMBERS of `-SATAN for a `-TIME of `-BOTH `-WAR in `-HEAVEN, `-WAR on `-EARTH; and, for the "WAR against the `-WICKED in `-HAR-MAGEDON; which, will be an `-ESTIMATION of "WORLD WAR (III)"!!!!!~' The # `-NUMBERS will be `-ACCENTUATED by an `-APPROXIMATION of the `-*TIME of the `-END of the `-THOUSAND `-YEAR `-REIGN by* `-CHRIST `-JESUS with the # `-NUMBERS: `-35 = RECIPROCAL = `-53 = "The *"WAR of the WORLDS"*; in, `-*ITS `-ENTIRETY*"!!!!!~'

(19 + 14) = "WORLD WAR I"!!!!!~' (19 + 14) = `-33 = "Yin/Yang" = "Multiple of Eleven" = "The `-CYCLE of `-LIFE"!!!!!~'

`-14 = RECIPROCAL = `-41

(19 + 41) = "WORLD WAR II"!!!!!~' (19 + 41) = `-60!!!!!~'

(60 (-) 33) = `-27 = "The ROMAN EMPIRE"!!!!!~'

(`-1941) = (19 + 41) = `-60 = (6 + 0) = `-6 = `-2 x `-3 = `-23 = -a Prophetic Number!!!!!~'

(`-1941) = (19 + 41) = `-60 = (6 + 0) = `-6 = `-3 x `-2 = `-32 = -a Prophetic Number!!!!!~'

ONE `-1 `-FULL `-AVERAGE `-YEAR (`-365 / `-3.2) = `-114 / (365 (-) 114) = `-251 = (51 + 2) = `-53 = "WAR of the WORLDS" = `-1 WEEK after the `-START of WW2!!!!!~'

THE REAL PROPHET OF DOOM (KISMET) - INTRODUCTION - PENDULUM FLOW – II –

ONE `-1 `-FULL `-AVERAGE `-YEAR (`-365 / `-2.3) = `-158 / (365 (-) 158 = `-207 = (27 + 0) = `-27 = "The ROMAN EMPIRE" = `-1 DAY before the `-START of WW1!!!!!~'

WW1 / Started-July 28th-1914 -to- November 11th-1918-Ended / {1111 (-) 728} = `-383 = Reciprocal-Sequenced-Numerology-RSN = `-38 = RECIPROCAL = `-83!!!!!~'

WW2 / Started-September 1st-1939 -to- September 2nd-1945-Ended / {91 + 92} = `-183 = (83 x 1) = `-83!!!!!~'

(19 + 14 + 19 + 18) = `-70 = "YEAR the "PROPHET" was `-BORN (`-1970)"!!!!!~'

(19 + 39 + 19 + 45) = `-122 = (22 + 1) = `-23 = -a Prophetic Number!!!!!~'

December 7th `-1941 = `-DAY `-343 in a `-CALENDAR `-LEAP `-YEAR = `-343 = Reciprocal-Sequencing-Numerology-RSN = "The `-PRESIDENTIAL #'s `-NUMBERS"!!!!!~'!!!!!~'

`-366 (-) `-343 = `-23 = -a Prophetic Number!!!!!~'

December 7th `-1941 = (12 + 7 + 19 + 41) = `-79 = "WAR of the WORLDS"!!!!!~'

PSALM 83:18 (-) "(18) That *men* may know that thou, whose name alone *is* JEHOVAH, *art* the most high over all the earth." – KING JAMES –

JEH-*OVAH* = (10 + 5 + 8 + 15 + 22 + 1 + 8) = `-69 = "The `-CYCLE of `-LIFE"!!!!!~'

(19 + 20 + 14) = `-53 = "WAR of the WORLDS" in "HEAVEN"!!!!!~'

SATAN = (19 + 1 + 20 + 1 + 14) = `-55 = `-23 + `-32 = "CAN `-TAKE a `-LIFE"!!!!!~'

THE `-DEVIL = (20 + 8 + 5) + (4 + 5 + 22 + 9 + 12) = (33)+(52) = `-85 = (8 + 5) = `-13 = "A VERY PIVOTAL NUMBER"!!!!!~'

(55 + 85) = `-140 = (14 + 0) = `-14 = (2 x 7) = `-2(7's) = `-27 = "The ROMAN EMPIRE"!!!!!~'

`-The `-ATOM!!!!!~' (=) (GENE = (7/5/14/5) = (7 + 5 + 14 + 5) = `-31 = RECIPROCAL = `-13 = "A VERY PIVOTAL NUMBER")!!!!!~'

ATOM = (1 + 20 + 15 + 13) = `-49 = (7 x 7) = GALILEO GALILEI = `-UNIVERSE!!!!!~'

MOLECULE = (13 + 15 + 12 + 5 + 3 + 21 + 12 + 5) = `-86 = `-HAR-MAGEDON = (8 + 6) = `-14 = (2 x 7) = `-2(7's) = `-27 = "The ROMAN EMPIRE"!!!!!~'

CELL = (3 + 5 + 12 + 12) = `-32 = -a Prophetic Number!!!!!~'

PARTICLE = (16 + 1 + 18 + 20 + 9 + 3 + 12 + 5) = `-84 = RECIPROCAL = `-48

(84 + 48) = `-132 = (32 x 1) = `-32 = -a Prophetic Number!!!!!~'

AN `-ANCIENT `-GREEK `-PHILOSOPHER by the `-NAME of `-DEMOCRITUS formulated an `-IDEA of the `-ATOM!!!!!~' `-DEMOCRITUS `-LIVED from `-460B.C./B.C.E -to- `-370B.C./B.C.E!!!!!~' `-HE `-DIED at the `-AGE of `-90!!!!!~'

`-460 = (46 + 0) = `-46 = `-23 x `-2 = `-232 = Reciprocal-Sequencing-Numerology-RSN!!!!!~'

`-370 = (37 + 0) = `-37 = `-3(7's) = (777) = (7 x 7 x 7) = `-343 = Reciprocal-Sequencing-Numerology-RSN = "The `-PRESIDENTIAL #'s `-NUMBERS"!!!!!~'

(46 + 37) = `-83 = RECIPROCAL = `-38 = 3(8's) = `-888 = (8 x 8 x 8) = `-512 = (5 (1 + 2)) = `-53 = "WAR of the WORLDS"!!!!!~

`-J.J. ABRAMS – "STAR WARS – THE FORCE AWAKENS –"-'"

`-J.J. `-THOMPSON `-DISCOVERED the `-ELECTRON in `-1897!!!!!~'

`-97 = RECIPROCAL = `-79

`-1897 = (97 (-) `-18) = `-79 = "AGE of `-DEATH of Mr. H. G. WELLS for the "WAR of the WORLDS" -introduction- `-INTO the `-WORLD"!!!!!~'

`-ERNEST `-RUTHERFORD `-DISCOVERED the `-PROTON (`-A `-POSITIVELY `-CHARGED `-PARTICAL within the `-NUCLEUS of an `-ATOM) in `-1919!!!!!~'

`-1919 = Reciprocal-Sequencing-Numerology-RSN!!!!!~'

`-JAMES `-CHADWICK `-DISCOVERED the `-NEUTRON `-PARTICLE within the `-NUCLEUS of an `-ATOM in `-1932!!!!!~'

`-1932 = `-32 = -a Prophetic Number!!!!!~'

`-1932 = (32 (-) 19) = `-13 = "A VERY PIVOTAL NUMBER"!!!!!~'

`-AVERAGE = (1897 + 1919 + 1932) = `-5748/`-3 = `-1916 = (19 + 16) = `-35 = RECIPROCAL = `-53 = "WAR of the WORLDS"!!!!!~'

GENESIS 3:5 (-) "(5) for God doth know that in the day ye eat thereof, then your eyes shall be opened, and ye shall be as God, knowing good and evil." -(ENGLISH REVISED EDITION - 1885)- (SIS = 19/09/19 = 91 + 90 + 91 = `-272 = RSN)!!!!!~'

GENESIS 3:15 (-) "(15) and I will put enmity between thee and the woman, and between thy seed and her seed: it shall bruise thy head, and thou shalt bruise his heel." -(ENGLISH REVISED EDITION - 1885)- The `-HEAVENLY `-BATTLE between `-CHRIST; and, `-SATAN; `-FORETOLD!!!!!~'

1st JOHN 3:15 (-) "(15) Whosoever hateth his brother is a murderer: and ye know that no murderer hath eternal life abiding in him." -(ENGLISH REVISED EDITION - 1885)-

JOHN = (10 + 15 + 8 + 14) = `-47 = RECIPROCAL = `-74 = "JULY 4th" = "INDEPENDENCE `-DAY" = "WAR of the WORLDS"!!!!!~'

`-74 = (7 x 4) = `-28 = RECIPROCAL = `-82 = `-ARMAGEDDON!!!!!~'

`-POSITIVE; and, `-NEGATIVE `-ELECTRIC `-CHARGES…(…)…-'"

`-MR. LEONHARD EULER was a `-SWISS `-PHYSICIST, `-MATHEMATICIAN, `-ENGINEER, `-ASTRONOMER; and, just to `-NAME a `-FEW…(…)…-'"

LEONHARD EULER was `-BORN on `-APRIL 15th in `-1707; and, had `-DIED on `-SEPTEMBER 18th in `-1783!!!!!~'

`-BIRTHDAY # `-NUMBER = `-EQUALS = (4 + 15 + 17 + 7) = `-43

`-43 = <u>RECIPROCAL</u> = `-34 = "The `-<u>PRESIDENTIAL</u> #'s `-

(43 + 34) = `-<u>77</u> / `-<u>1707</u> = (77 x 1 + 0) = `-<u>77</u>

`-DEATH/DAY # `-NUMBER = `-EQUALS = (9 + 18 + 17 + 83) = `-<u>127</u>

`-<u>127</u> = (1 x 27) = `-<u>27</u> = `-<u>2(7's)</u> = `-<u>77</u>

(77 x 3) = `-<u>231</u> = (23 x 1) = `-<u>23</u> = -a Prophetic Number!!!!!~'

`-J.J. ABRAMS – "STAR WARS – THE FORCE AWAKENS –"-'" was `-BORN on the `-<u>27</u><sup>th</sup> of `-JUNE in `-19<u>66</u>!!!!!~'

`-<u>1783</u> = (83 (-) 17) = `-<u>66</u>

(66 + 66) = `-<u>132</u> = (32 x 1) = `-<u>32</u> = -a Prophetic Number!!!!!~'

`-<u>66</u> = "AGE of `-DEATH of the "PROPHET'S" FATHER"!!!!!~'

`-<u>1783</u> = {(7 = 3 + 4) 8) x 1} = `-EMPHASIZED in `-SCRIPTURE (`-3)!!!!!~'

PSALM 8:<u>3,4</u> (-) "(<u>3</u>) When I consider thy heavens, the work of thy fingers, the moon and the stars, which thou hast ordained; (<u>4</u>) What is man, that thou art mindful of him? and the son of man, that thou visitest him?" -(ENGLISH REVISED EDITION - 1885)-

`-SEPTEMBER(`-9)/`-JUNE(`-6) = `-<u>96</u> = <u>RECIPROCAL</u> = `-<u>69</u> = "Yin/ Yang" = "The `-CYCLE of `-LIFE"!!!!!~'

LEONHARD EULER `-<u>DIED</u> at the `-<u>AGE</u> of `-<u>76</u> = RECIPROCAL = `-<u>67</u> = "The `-YEAR that the "PROPHET'S" BROTHER was `-BORN, the `-AVERAGE `-AGE of the United States Presidents 1 to 28 in "SUCCESSION" above; and, below `-ALL `-PRESIDENTS that `-DIED at `-AGES `-66, `-67; and, `-68; and, The `-AGE of `-DEATH of the #1/President of the United States of America #1/President George Washington"!!!!!~'

`-DARK `-ENERGY is `-POSTULATED to `-MAKE `-UP `-<u>76</u>% of the `-UNIVERSE!!!!!~'

`-DARK `-MATTER is `-POSTULATED to `-MAKE `-UP `-<u>23</u>% of the `-MASS of the `-UNIVERSE!!!!!~'

(127 + 43) = `-170 = (70 x 1) = `-70 = "The `-YEAR that the "PROPHET" was `-BORN (`-1970)"!!!!!~'

(76 + 70) = `-146 = (46 x 1) = `-46 = `-23 x `-2 = `-232 = Reciprocal-Sequencing-Numerology-RSN!!!!!~'

At the `-TIME of `-THIS `-WRITING; `-IT `-MARKS the `-406th `-YEAR; since, a `-SCIENTIST `-UTILIZED; and, had the `-FIRST `-USE of an `-ASTRONOMICAL `-TELESCOPE; of which, it was none other than; that of `-GALILEO `-GALILEI!!!!!~'

`-406 = (46 + 0) = `-46 = `-23 x `-2 = `-232 = Reciprocal-Sequencing-Numerology-RSN!!!!!~'

`-46 = RECIPROCAL = `-64

AMERICAN/ENGLISH `-ALPHABET `-to-` `-NUMBERS #'s:!!!!!~'

GALILEO GALILEI = `-7, `-7 / `-77 = `-2(7's) = `-27 = "The ROMAN EMPIRE"!!!!!~'

GALILEO GALILEI `-DIED at the `-AGE of `-77!!!!!~'

GALILEO GALILEI was `-BORN on `-FEBRUARY 15th in `-1564; and, had `-DIED on `-JANUARY 8th in `-1642!!!!!~'

GALILEO GALILEI'S `-BIRTHDAY # `-NUMBER = `-EQUALS = (2 + 15 + 15 + 64) = `-96

`-96 = RECIPROCAL = `-69 = "Yin/Yang" = "The `-CYCLE of `-LIFE"!!!!!~'

(4/15 + 2/15) = `-630 = (63 + 0) = `-63 = "AGE of `-DEATH of the "PROPHET'S" MOTHER"!!!!!~'

LEONHARD EULER was `-BORN on `-APRIL 15th in `-1707!!!!!~'

(1707 (-) 1564) = `-143 = (43 x 1) = `-43

`-43 = RECIPROCAL = `-34 = "The `-PRESIDENTIAL #'s `-

(43 + 34) = `-77 / `-1707 = (77 x 1 + 0) = `-77

(17<u>83</u> (-) 1<u>642</u>) = `-<u>141</u> = <u>R</u>eciprocal-<u>S</u>equencing-<u>N</u>umerology-<u>RSN</u>!!!!!`-'

(141 (-) 77) = `-<u>64</u> = "BIRTH/YEAR of GALILEO GALILEI"!!!!!`-'

GALILEO GALILEI'S `-DEATH/DAY # `-NUMBER = `-EQUALS = (1 + 8 + 16 + 42) = `-<u>67</u>

LEONHARD EULER `-<u>DIED</u> at the `-<u>AGE</u> of `-<u>76</u> = <u>RECIPROCAL</u> = `-<u>67</u> = "The `-YEAR that the "PROPHET'S" BROTHER was `-BORN, the `-AVERAGE `-AGE of the United States Presidents 1 to 28 in "SUCCESSION" above; and, below `-ALL `-PRESIDENTS that `-DIED at `-AGES `-66, `-67; and, `-68; and, The `-AGE of `-DEATH of the #1/President of the United States of America #1/President George Washington"!!!!!`-'

`-<u>83</u> = <u>RECIPROCAL</u> = `-<u>38</u> = 3(8's) = `-<u>888</u> = (8 x 8 x 8) = `-<u>512</u> = (5 (1 + 2)) = `-<u>53</u> = "WAR of the WORLDS"!!!!!`-

GALILEO GALILEI `-DIED `-<u>38</u> `-DAYS before `-HIS `-NEXT `-BIRTHDAY!!!!!`-'

(365 (-) 38) = `-<u>327</u> = "EMPHATIC `-EMPHASIS on the # `-NUMBER `-<u>27</u> = "The `-HOLY-` ROMAN EMPIRE"; and, the `-AGE of `-DEATH OF MR. GALILEO GALILEI = `-<u>2(7's)</u> = `<u>77</u> `-YEARS of `-AGE-`"!!!!!`-'

`-MORE `-CHRIST = `-EQUALS = `-CHRISTMAS!!!!!`-' The `-LAST `-FULL `-MOON on `-CHRISTMAS `-DAY occurred in `-<u>1977</u>; and, the `-NEXT `-FULL `-MOON will be in the `-YEAR of `-20<u>34</u>!!!!!`-' (77 (-) 19 = `-<u>58</u>) / (34 (-) 20 = `-<u>14</u>) / (`-58 + `-14 = `-<u>72</u>) / `-<u>38</u> `-YEARS; since, the `-LAST OCCURRENCE of a `-FULL `-MOON on `-CHRISTMAS!!!!!`-'

(`-20<u>15</u> + `-<u>38</u> `-Years-` = `-20<u>53</u>)/|\(`-20<u>34</u> + `-<u>38</u> `-Years-` = `-20<u>72</u>)/|\!!!!!`-'

TODAY'S DATE = (12/25/2015) = (12 + 25 + 20 + 15) = `-<u>72</u> = <u>RECIPROCAL</u> = `-<u>27</u>-`"-

`-NEW `-YEARS = (01/01/2016) = (1 + 1 + 20 + 16) = `-<u>38</u> = `-EQUALS = "YEAR of the WAR of the WORLDS"!!!!!`-'

At the `-TIME of `-THE `-NEW `-YEAR; `-IT `-MARKS the `-<u>407</u>th `-YEAR; since, a `-SCIENTIST `-UTILIZED; and, had the `-FIRST

`-USE of an `-ASTRONOMICAL `-TELESCOPE; of which, it was none other than; that of `-GALILEO `-GALILEI!!!!!~'

`-GALILE (O/I) = ($7 + 1 + 12 + 9 + 12 + 5$) = `-46 = `-23 x `-2 = `-232 = Reciprocal-Sequencing-Numerology-RSN!!!!!~'

(O/I) = "INPUT/OUTPUT" = (15/9) = (59 x 1) = `-59 = "AGE of `-DEATH of JESUS CHRIST'S MOTHER MARY"!!!!!~' `-M = `-13 = "A VERY PIVOTAL NUMBER"!!!!!~'

There is the "CROWN PRINCE"; which, is the "PRINCE of `-PEACE"/ JESUS CHRIST; and, there is the "CLOWN `-PRINCE"; that is, of "BASKETBALL"!!!!!~'

The `-HARLEM `-GLOBETROTTER'S `-MEADOWLARK `-LEMON (MEADOW LEMON "III") `-DIES on the `-27th of `-DECEMBER (`-2015) at the `-AGE of `-83 = RECIPROCAL = `-38 = 3(8's) = `-888 = (8 x 8 x 8) = `-512 = (5 (1 + 2)) = `-53 = "WAR of the WORLDS"!!!!!~

`-MEADOWLARK `-LEMON = ML = (13 + 12) = (32 x 1 x 1) = `-32 = -a Prophetic Number!!!!!~'

`-MEADOWLARK `-LEMON was `-BORN in `-1932!!!!!~'

`-23 = RECIPROCAL = `-32 / SUPERBOWL `-50 (02/07) in `-2016!!!!!~' `-38 `-DAYS from the `-START of the `-NEW `-YEAR!!!!!~'

`-MEADOWLARK `-LEMON was `-ASSOCIATED with the `-GLOBETROTTER'S for some `-23 `-YEARS after an `-OPENING becoming `-VACANT in `-1953!!!!!~'

`-AGE of `-DEATH = (83 (-) 38) = `-45 = RECIPROCAL = `-54 = `-MEADOWLARK `-LEMON got `-STARTED in (`-1954)!!!!!~'

(54 (-) 19) = `-35 = RECIPROCAL = `-53 = "WAR of the WORLDS"!!!!!~'

(54 + 19) = `-73 = RECIPROCAL = `-37 / (73 (-) 37) = `-36 = RECIPROCAL = `-63 = "AGE of `-DEATH of the "PROPHET'S" MOTHER"!!!!!~'

`-MEADOWLARK `-LEMON soon `-STARTED with the `-HARLEM `-GLOBETROTTERS just beneath the tender `-AGE of `-23 `-YEARS of `-AGE!!!!!~'

`-<u>M</u>EADOWLARK `-<u>L</u>EMON left the `-TEAM in `-<u>1978</u>!!!!!~'

(78 (-) 19) = `-<u>59</u> = "<u>AGE</u> of `-<u>DEATH</u> of JESUS CHRIST'S <u>M</u>OTHER <u>M</u>ARY"!!!!!~'

(78 + 19) = `-<u>97</u> = <u>RECIPROCAL</u> = `-<u>79</u> = "WAR of the WORLDS"!!!!!~'

`-TWO (`-<u>2</u>) `-<u>DAYS</u> after `-<u>CHRISTMAS</u> = (12 + (<u>27</u>th) + 20 + 15) = `-<u>74</u>

`-<u>47</u> = <u>RECIPROCAL</u> = `-<u>74</u> = "<u>JULY</u> 4th" = "<u>INDEPENDENCE</u> `-<u>DAY</u>" = "WAR of the WORLDS"!!!!!~'

`-<u>47</u> = (4 x 7) = `-<u>28</u> = <u>RECIPROCAL</u> = `-<u>82</u> = `-<u>ARMAGEDDON</u>!!!!!~'

<u>J</u>ESUS = (10 + 5 + 19 + 21 + 19) = `-<u>74</u> = "INDEPENDENCE `-DAY" = "WAR of the WORLDS"!!!!!~'

<u>C</u>HRIST = (3 + 8 + 18 + 9 + 19 + 20) = `-<u>77</u> = `-<u>2(7's)</u> = "The ROMAN EMPIRE"!!!!!~'

<u>J</u>C = (10 + 3) = `-<u>13</u> = (`-M) for `-<u>M</u>ARY; `-JESUS `-CHRIST'S, `-MOTHER!!!!!~'

MARY = (13 + 1 + 18 + 25) = `-<u>57</u> = <u>RECIPROCAL</u> = `-<u>75</u>

(75 + 57) = `-<u>132</u> = (32 x 1) = `-<u>32</u> = -a Prophetic Number!!!!!~'

LUKE 1:<u>27</u> (-) "(27) to a virgin betrothed to a man whose name was Joseph, of the house of David; and the virgin's name was Mary." -(ENGLISH REVISED EDITION - 1885)-

LUKE 2:<u>27</u> (-) "(27) And he came in the Spirit into the temple: and when the parents brought in the child Jesus, that they might do concerning him after the custom of the law," -(ENGLISH REVISED EDITION - 1885)-

LUKE = (12 + 21 + 11 + 5) = `-<u>49</u> = (<u>7</u> x <u>7</u>) = `-<u>2(7's)</u> = `-<u>27</u> = "The ROMAN EMPIRE"!!!!!~'

JOHN <u>7</u>:<u>27</u> (-) "(27) Howbeit we know this man whence he is: but when the Christ cometh, no one knoweth whence he is." -(ENGLISH REVISED EDITION - 1885)-

`-APOSTLE = (1 + 16 + 15 + 19 + 20 + 12 + 5) = `-**88** = **2(8's)** = **RECIPROCAL** = `-**82** = `-**ARMAGEDDON!!!!!**~'

`-AGAIN, (JOHN) = (10 + 15 + 8 + 14) = `-**47** = **RECIPROCAL** = `-**74** = "**JULY 4**th" = "**INDEPENDENCE** `-**DAY**" = "**WAR of the WORLDS**"!!!!!~'

`-APOSTLE `-JOHN-` = (88 + 47) = `-**135** = (35 x 1) = `-**35** = **RECIPROCAL** = `-**53** = "**WAR of the WORLDS**"!!!!!~'

REVELATION 2:7 (-) "(**7**) He that hath an ear, let him hear what the Spirit saith to the churches. To him that overcometh, to him will I give to eat of the tree of life, which is in the Paradise of God." -(**ENGLISH REVISED EDITION - 1885**)-

REVELATION 7:2 (-) "(**2**) And I saw another angel ascend from the sunrising, having the seal of the living God: and he cried with a great voice to the four angels, to whom it was given to hurt the earth and the sea," -(**ENGLISH REVISED EDITION - 1885**)-

`-**ADAM** = (1 + 4 + 1 + 13) = `-**19**

`-**EVE** = (5 + 22 + 5) = `-**32** = -**a Prophetic Number!!!!!**~'

`-**EDEN** = (5 + 4 + 5 + 14) = `-**28** = **RECIPROCAL** = `-**82** = `-**ARMAGEDDON** = `-**AND the** `-**PARADISE** `-**to** `-**COME** `-**Afterward!!!!!**~'

(19 + 32 + 28) = `-**79** = "**WAR of the WORLDS**"!!!!!~'

A	B	C	D	E	F	G	H	I	J	K	L	M	N	O	P	Q	R	S	T	U	V	W	X	Y	Z
1	2	3	4	5	6	7	8	9	10	11	12	13	14	15	16	17	18	19	20	21	22	23	24	25	26

DWAYNE = (4 + 23 + 1 + 25 + 14 + 5) = `-**72** = "**The ROMAN EMPIRE**"!!!!!~'

WARREN = (23 + 1 + 18 + 18 + 5 + 14) = `-**79** = "**WAR of the WORLDS**"!!!!!~'

ANDERSON = (1 + 14 + 4 + 5 + 18 + 19 + 15 + 14) = `-**90** = "**W**INSTON **C**HURCHILL" = "**WORLD WAR /|\ (III) /|**"!!!!!~' **WC/MC** = "**M**ASTER of **C**EREMONY"!!!!!~'

`-**AUTHOR**: `-**MONOGRAM**/`-**INSIGNIA/|** = The "**PROPHET'S**" INITIALS for = **D**WAYNE **W.** **A**NDERSON = /|\ **MEDIATOR/ ARBITRATOR /|**

247

$\underline{D}$ = `-4 / $\underline{W}$ = `-23 / $\underline{A}$ = `-1 = `-$\underline{28}$ = RECIPROCAL = `-$\underline{82}$ = `-ARMAGEDDON!!!!!~'

`-The `-ATOM!!!!!~' (-within-) `-$\underline{QUANTUM}$ `-$\underline{PHYSICS}$!!!!!~'

The `-$\underline{EARTHQUAKES}$!!!!!~'

LOMA PRIETA `-EARTHQUAKE was a `-$\underline{6.9}$ MAGNITUDE at `-$\underline{5}$:0$\underline{4}$PM = (69 + 54) = `-$\underline{123}$ = "Prophetic-Linear-Progression-PLP"!!!!!~'

LOMA PRIETA `-OCCURRED on (10/$\underline{17}$/1989) = (10 + 17 + 19 + 89) = `-$\underline{135}$ = (35 x 1) = `-$\underline{35}$ = RECIPROCAL = `-$\underline{53}$ = "WAR of the WORLDS"!!!!!~'

NORTHRIDGE `-EARTHQUAKE was a `-6.7 MAGNITUDE at `-4:30:55AM = {(67 (-) 43 (-) (5/5 = `-1)} = `-$\underline{23}$ = -a Prophetic Number!!!!~'

`-$\underline{23}$ = RECIPROCAL = `-$\underline{32}$

NORTHRIDGE `-OCCURRED on (1/$\underline{17}$/1994) = (1 + 17 + 19 + 94) = `-$\underline{131}$ = Reciprocal-Sequencing-Numerology-RSN = `-$\underline{13}$ = RECIPROCAL = `-$\underline{31}$ = `-$\underline{131}$ = (31 + 1) = `-$\underline{32}$ = -a Prophetic Number!!!!~'

EARTHQUAKES `-$\underline{17}$[th] + `-$\underline{17}$[th] = `-$\underline{34}$ = RECIPROCAL = `-$\underline{43}$ = "The `-PRESIDENTIAL # `-NUMBERS"!!!!!~'

(34 + 43) = `-$\underline{77}$

$\underline{CHRIST}$ = (3 + 8 + 18 + 9 + 19 + 20) = `-$\underline{77}$ = `-$\underline{2(7's)}$ = "The ROMAN EMPIRE"!!!!!~'

`-APOSTLE = (1 + 16 + 15 + 19 + 20 + 12 + 5) = `-$\underline{88}$ = 2(8's) = RECIPROCAL = `-$\underline{82}$ = `-$\underline{ARMAGEDDON}$!!!!!~'

`-AGAIN, (JOHN) = (10 + 15 + 8 + 14) = `-$\underline{47}$ = RECIPROCAL = `-$\underline{74}$ = "JULY 4[th]" = "$\underline{INDEPENDENCE}$ `-$\underline{DAY}$" = "WAR of the WORLDS"!!!!!~'

`-APOSTLE `-JOHN-` = (88 + 47) = `-$\underline{135}$ = (35 x 1) = `-$\underline{35}$ = RECIPROCAL = `-$\underline{53}$ = "WAR of the WORLDS"!!!!!~'

SAN JOSE `-EARTHQUAKE `-TODAY (01/05/2016) at 6:30AM; a `-2.8 `-MAGNITUDE = (63 (-) 28) = `-35 = RECIPROCAL = `-53 = "WAR of the WORLDS"!!!!!~'

`-13, `-23; &, `-32 = "A `-PARADIGM `-SHIFT; `-within, `-PENDULUM `-FLOW"!!!!!~'

The `-EARTHQUAKES; `-TOO!!!!!~'

`-WEDDING `-PLAYLIST:

`-For the `-EARTHLY `-WEDDING `-CEREMONY of `-GOD!!!!!~'

The `-WORD (+) JESUS = `-EQUALS = (10 + 5 + 19 + 21 + 19) = `-74 = `-7(4) = July 4th = "INDEPENDENCE `-DAY" = RECIPROCAL = `-47 = "SONGS of ARTISTS"!!!!!~'

`-HAVE the `-BENEFIT `-CONCERT for the `-SICK; and, `-POOR on an `-INDEPENDENCE `-DAY with `-47 `-SONGS of `-35 "WAR of the WORLDS" `-ARTISTS!!!!!~'

The U. S. Presidents with the `-NUMBER `-53+_!!!!!~' AND; Russia's Vladimir Lenin died at the `-AGE of `-53; and, Russia's Joseph Stalin died in `-1953 on its `-RECIPROCAL `-DAY of \/ 03/05/1953 / `-35 = RECIPROCAL = `-53 = "WAR of the WORLDS"!!!!!~'

`-79 (`-WAR) (+) `-53 (`-WAR) = `-132 = (32 x 1) = `-32 = -a Prophetic Number!!!!!~'

The `-RECIPROCAL(S)!!!!!~'

`-97 (`-WAR) (+) `-35 (`-WAR) = `-132 = (32 x 1) = `-32 = -a Prophetic Number!!!!!~'

`-WORLD = (23 + 15 + 18 + 12 + 4) = `-72 = RECIPROCAL = `-27 = "The ROMAN EMPIRE"!!!!!~'

`-WORLD `-WAR = (`-72) + (23 + 1 + 18) = (`-72 + `-42) = `-114 = `-AN = `-ANOTHER `-NOTE!!!!!~'

249

`-WORLD `-WAR `-(I) = (`-114) + (`-9) = `-<u>123</u> = "<u>P</u>rophetic-<u>L</u>inear-<u>P</u>rogression-PLP"!!!!!~'

`-WORLD `-WAR `-(II) = (`-114) + (`-18) = `-<u>132</u> = (32 x 1) = `-<u>32</u> = -a Prophetic Number!!!!!~'

`-WORLD `-WAR `-(III) = (`-114) + (`-27) = `-<u>141</u> = "<u>R</u>eciprocal-<u>S</u>equencing-<u>N</u>umerology-RSN"!!!!!~'

`-<u>SONGS</u> that the "<u>PROPHET</u>" has `-<u>LISTENED</u> `-to; and, `-<u>CONFIRMED</u>-'"!!!!!~'

`-WEDDING `-PLAYLIST for the `-EARTHLY `-WEDDING `-CEREMONY of `-GOD!!!!!~'

1) Randy Travis – "Forever And Ever, Amen"!!!!!~'
2) Randy Travis – "Deeper Than The Holler"!!!!!~'
3) Garth Brooks – "The River"
4) Garth Brooks – "The Dance"

"The `-RIVER `-DANCE"!!!!!~'

5) Rascal Flatts – "Bless The Broken Road"!!!!!~'
6) Rascal Flatts – "Life Is A Highway"!!!!!~'
7) Rascal Flatts – "I Melt"!!!!!~'

`-SONGS for the `-EARTHLY `-TRANSITION!!!!!~'

8) Miranda Lambert – "Somethin Bad ft. Carrie Underwood"!!!!!~'
9) Miranda Lambert – "Little White Liar"!!!!!~'
10) Miranda Lambert – "Little Red Wagon"!!!!!~'
11) Carrie Underwood – "Smoke Break"!!!!!~'
12) Carrie Underwood – "Jesus Take The Wheel"!!!!!~'

`-SONGS of the `-HEAVENLY `-CROSSING!!!!!~'

13) The JACKSONS – "CAN YOU FEEL IT" – from the `-ALBUM `-TRIUMPH!!!!!!~'
14) The BEATLES – "LET IT BE"!!!!!~'
15) The BEATLES – "ELEANOR RIGBY"!!!!!~'
16) The BEATLES – "A DAY in the LIFE"!!!!!~'

17) The BEATLES – "WITH a LITTLE HELP from MY FRIENDS"!!!!!~'

18) CALVIN HARRIS – "PRAY to GOD ft. HAIM

19) CALVIN HARRIS & DISCIPLES – "HOW DEEP is YOUR LOVE"

20) CALVIN HARRIS – "BLAME" ft. JOHN NEWMAN!!!!!~'

21) LEONA LEWIS – "THUNDER"!!!!!~'

22) LULU – "TO SIR with LOVE"!!!!!~'

23) ROBIN THICKE – "An ANGEL on EACH ARM"!!!!!~'

24) QUEEN LATIFAH – "FIX ME JESUS"!!!!!~'

25) EVELYN HEARD/EUGENE MARZETTE – (AUNT & UNCLE)!!!!!~'
"PRECIOUS LORD – TAKE MY HAND"

26) AUDRA MCDONALD/FRANK BYRDWELL – (COUSIN & UNCLE)!!!!!~'
"I THINK IT'S GOING TO RAIN TODAY" -(BUILD A BRIDGE)!!!!!~'

27) AUDRA MCDONALD/PHYLLIS BYRDWELL – (COUSIN & AUNTIE)!!!!!~'
"LAY DOWN YOUR HEAD" –(HOW GLORY GOES)!!!!!~'

28) PRINCE – "CONTROVERSY"!!!!!~'

29) PRINCE – "DIAMONDS & PEARLS"!!!!!~'

30) KELLY CLARKSON – "STRONGER (WHAT DOESN'T KILL YOU)"

31) KELLY CLARKSON – "BREAKAWAY"!!!!!~'

32) INGRID MICHAELSON – "TIME MACHINE"!!!!!~'

33) JOHN LEGEND – "GLORY"!!!!!~'

34) LIFE OF DILLON – "OVERLOAD"!!!!!~'

35) LORDE – "ROYALS"!!!!!~'

36) MAJOR LAZER/DJ SNAKE – "LEAN ON" ft. MØ

37) NICO/VINZ – "AM I WRONG"!!!!!~'

38) SAINT MOTEL – "MY TYPE"!!!!!~'

39) YEARS & YEARS – "KING"!!!!!~'

40) TV on the RADIO – "HAPPY IDIOT"!!!!!~'

41) ALICE in CHAINS – "MAN in the BOX"!!!!!~'

42) CHRIS CORNELL – "NEARLY FORGOT MY BROKEN HEART"!!!!!~'

43) SOUNDGARDEN – "BURDEN in MY HAND"!!!!!~'
(THE MAX `-FREEZING DEGREES `-FAHRENHEIT)!!!!!~'

44) TEMPLE of the DOG – "HUNGER STRIKE"!!!!!~'
45) DAVE MATTHEWS BAND – "ANTS MARCHING"!!!!!~'
46) HOOTIE & THE BLOWFISH – "HOLD MY HAND"!!!!!!~'
47) EDDIE MURPHY – "OH JAH JAH"!!!!!~'

`-JAH is the `-ABBREVIATION for that of `-GOD'S `-NAME `-JEHOVAH!!!!!~'

(68 + 4) = `-72 = `"WORLD" of `-CREATION-'"!!!!!~' WAR x 4 = `-168 = (68 x 1) = `-68

PSALMS 68:4 (-) "(4) Sing unto God, sing praises to his name: cast up a highway for him that rideth through the deserts; his name is **JAH**; and exult ye before him." -(ENGLISH REVISED EDITION - 1885)-

(68 + 18) = `-86 = "HAR-MAGEDON"!!!!!~'

PSALMS 68:18 (-) "(18) Thou hast ascended on high, Thou hast taken captive captivity, Thou hast taken gifts for men, That even the refractory may rest, O **Jah God**." –Young's Literal Translation–

JEH-*OVAH* = (10 + 5 + 8 + 15 + 22 + 1 + 8) = `-69 = RECIPROCAL = `-96 = "The `-CYCLE of `-LIFE"!!!!!~' {"I AM + I AM + I AM" = (23 + 23 + 23) = `-69 = The Name of `-JEHOVAH} = `-VIA-'" = "The TRANSITIVE `-PROPERTY of `-EQUALITY"!!!!!~'

JAH = (10 + 1 + 8) = `-19

REVELATION 19:6 (-) "(6) And I heard as it were the voice of a great multitude, and as the voice of many waters, and as the voice of mighty thunders, saying, **Hallelujah**: for the Lord our God, the Almighty, reigneth." -(ENGLISH REVISED EDITION - 1885)-

HALLELUJAH = "PRAISE `-JAH" = (8 + 1 + 12 + 12 + 5 + 12 + 21 + 10 + 1 + 8) = `-90 = "MASTER of CEREMONY"!!!!!~'

EXODUS 3:14 (-) "(14) And God said unto Moses, **I AM** THAT **I AM**: and he said, Thus shalt thou say unto the children of Israel, **I AM** hath sent me unto you." -(ENGLISH REVISED EDITION - 1885)- (`-68 / `-2 = `-34)!!!!!~' (3 x 14 = `-42 = `-WAR)!!!!!~'

I **AM** / I **AM** = (9 + 1 + 13) = `-23 x `-2 = `-232 = Reciprocal-Sequenced-Numerology-**RSN!!!!!**-' Praise be to the `-**GOD** in `-**HEAVEN** /|\ **JEHOVAH!!!!!**-'

`"- **(Kismet)** - **INTRODUCTION** - `-**PENDULUM** `-**FLOW** - **II** -"`

`-GOD'S

`-INSIDE `-<u>SECRET</u>

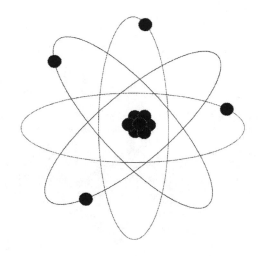

`-<u>RSN</u>-*Reciprocals* – The `-<u>ATOM</u>!!!!!~'

"The Real Prophet Of Doom (Kismet) – Introduction – Pendulum Flow –"

`-SEE; how `-IT `-ALL got `-STARTED!!!!!~'

The `-TONIGHT `-SHOW `-GANG for the `-YEAR of `-2016!!!!!~'

The `-TONIGHT `-SHOW with `-JIMMY `-FALLON = <u>S1/EP/394</u>

The `-LATE `-LATE `-SHOW with `-JAMES `-CORDEN = <u>S1/EP/127</u>

The `-LATE `-SHOW with `-STEPHEN COLBERT = <u>S1/EP/64</u>

(394 (-) 127 (-) `-64) = `-<u>203</u> = (23 + 0) = `-<u>23</u> = -a Prophetic Number!!!!!~'

(64 + 64 = `-<u>128</u> = `-<u>ENCAPSULATION</u>-'")!!!!!~'

The `-LATE `-NIGHT with `-SETH `-MEYERS = <u>S1/EP/306</u>

(306 (-) 203) = `-<u>103</u> = (13 + 0) = `-<u>13</u> = "A VERY PIVOTAL NUMBER"!!!!!~'

(394 + 127 + 64) = `-<u>585</u> = "<u>R</u>eciprocal-<u>S</u>equenced-<u>N</u>umerology-<u>RSN</u>"!!!!!~'

(585 + 306) = `-<u>891</u> = (89 + 1) = `-<u>90</u> = "MASTERS of <u>C</u>EREMONIES"!!!!!~'

(585) = (5 + 8 + 5) = `-<u>18</u> / (891) = (8 + 9 + 1) = `-<u>18</u>

(18 + 18) = `-<u>36</u> = `-<u>3(6's)</u> = `-<u>666</u> = (6 x 6 x 6) = `-<u>216</u> = (`-<u>2016</u>) = (16 x 2) = `-<u>32</u> = -a Prophetic Number!!!!!~'

(585 (-) 306) = `-<u>279</u> = "EFFECTIVE `-WITNESS to the # `-NUMBER `-<u>79</u> being the "WAR of the WORLDS" of Mr. H. G. WELLS"!!!!!~'

YESTERDAY'S `-DATE = (01/05/20/16) = (1 + 5 + 20 + 16) = `-<u>42</u> = "<u>WAR</u>"!!!!!~'

TODAY'S `-DATE = (01/06/20/16) = (1 + 6 + 20 + 16) = `-<u>43</u> = <u>RECIPROCAL</u> = `-<u>34</u> = "The `-PRESIDENTIAL # `-NUMBERS"!!!!!~'

WAR<u>REN</u> = (23 + 1 + 18 + 18 + 5 + 14) = `-<u>79</u> = "WAR of the WORLDS"!!!!!~'

<u>REN</u> = (18 + 5 + 14) = `-<u>37</u> = `-<u>3(7's)</u> = `-<u>777</u> = (7 x 7 x 7) = `-<u>343</u> = "The `-PRESIDENTIAL # `-NUMBERS"!!!!!~'

The `-TONIGHT `-SHOW `-GANG for the `-YEAR of `-2016!!!!!~'

`-PAT `-HARRINGTON Jr. `-DIES at the `-AGE of `-86-'"!!!!!~'

`-HAR-MAGEDON = `-86-'" / "ONE – DAY – AT – A – TIME" – !!!!!~'

`-26 `-FAMILIES touched IN **`-NEWTOWN** because of **`-26 `-DEATHS**
on **`-DECEMBER 14ᵗʰ, in `-2012!!!!!~'**

(12 + 14 + 20 + 12) = **`-58** = (5 + 8) = **`-13** = **"A VERY PIVOTAL
NUMBER"!!!!!~'**

(58 (-) 26) = **`-32** = **-a Prophetic Number!!!!!~'** / **`-32** = **RECIPROCAL** =
`-23

According to a report from the Stockholm International Peace Research
Institute (SIPRI), **nine** nations — the United States, Russia, United
Kingdom, France, China, India, Pakistan, Israel and North Korea — possess
approximately **16,300 nuclear weapons** in total. **(Information Dated at:
June 17ᵗʰ, `-2014)!!!!!~'** (Who is `-THIS)!!!!!~'

1) Tracy Bonham - Mother Mother
2) Tracy Bonham - Behind Every Good Woman
3) Tracy Bonham - The One
4) Republica - Ready to Go
5) Luscious Jackson - Naked Eye
6) Luscious Jackson - Under Your Skin
7) Fiona Apple - Criminal
8) Fiona Apple - Sleep To Dream
9) Fiona Apple - Never Is A Promise
10) Johnny Cash and Fiona Apple - Bridge Over Troubled Waters
11) Johnny Cash and Fiona Apple - Father and Son
12) Fiona Apple - "Across The Universe"
13) Fiona Apple - Fast As You Can
14) Liz Phair - Supernova
15) Liz Phair - Why Can't I?
16) Sneaker Pimps - Spin Spin Sugar
17) Sneaker Pimps - 6 Underground
18) Tori Amos - "Crucify"
19) Tori Kelly - Nobody Love

20) Kelly Clarkson - Heartbeat Song
21) Kelly Clarkson - Walk Away
22) Kelly Clarkson - Invincible
23) Janet Jackson – Every Time

(1/2/2016) Golden State Warriors (**30/2**) = `-**32**; and, Denver Nuggets (**12/21**) = `-**12** = **RECIPROCAL** = `-**21** / `-At (`-**3**:18) (**1ˢᵗ QTR**) the `-**SCORE** was (**27/2**) = `-**272**-'"!!!!!~'

`-BRUSHES with `-GREATNESS!!!!!~' (Here are a `-FEW)!!!!!~'

1) Cousin BRIAN WILLIAMS/BISON DELE played with the `-GREAT `-MICHAEL `-JORDAN!!!!!~'
2) Cousin LEE HARRIS played with the `-GREAT `-JOE `-MONTANA on the Kansas City Chiefs!!!!!~'
3) Cousin REVELL MARZETTE was in a `-DRUG `-DIVERSION `-PROGRAM with Young and the Restless `-STAR `-KRISTOFF `-SAINT `-JOHN!!!!!~'
4) CURLY from the `-HARLEM `-GLOBETROTTER'S `-DROPPED `-DOWN an `-AUTOGRAPHED `-PICTURE of the `-TEAM from `-HIS `-TEAM `-BUS for when `-THEY were `-LEAVING a `-PERFORMANCE to `-ME!!!!!~'
5) When `-DANCING with `-FRIENDS at a `-NIGHT `-CLUB in Los Angeles on `-VACATION; the `-MUSICIAN "DMX", walked right by `-ME at the `-ENTRANCE to the `-BUILDING as `-I was `-LEAVING!!!!!~'
6) I was at a `-NIGHT `-CLUB; and, met `-CLARENCE `-WEATHERSPOON from the then `-GOLDEN `-STATE `-WARRIORS who had said that my `COUSIN `-BISON `-DELE from the `-CHICAGO `-BULLS, `-LOS `-ANGELES `-CLIPPERS; and, `-DETROIT `-PISTONS was a `-VERY `-GOOD `-PLAYER!!!!!~'
7) I met `-SACRAMENTO `-KINGS `-PLAYER; and, `-MAYOR of `-SACRAMENTO `-CALIFORNIA; `-KEVIN `-JOHNSON; on an `-AMERICAN `-WEST `-AIRLINER, as `-WE `-BOTH `-HEADED off to `-PHOENIX, ARIZONA, to where `-HE had `-SAID that `-I looked like "MUHAMMAD ALI"!!!!!~'
8) My `-LITTLE `-BROTHER `-OTIS `-ODDIE met "MUHAMMAD ALI"!!!!!~'

9) NAUGHTY by NATURES "VINNY"; walked into the `-BATHROOM as `-I was `-LEAVING the `-BATHROOM at `-WATCHTOWER `-FARMS!!!!!~'

10) LARK VOORHIES sat `-DIRECTLY `-ACROSS the `-ROOM at `-LUNCHTIME from `-ME at `-WATCHTOWER `-FARMS for when "VINNY" from `-NAUGHTY-BY-NATURE was by `-HER `-SIDE!!!!!~'

11) I `-MET; `-TALKED; and, `-JOKED with `-COMEDIAN (`-BILL `-BELLAMY) at the `-AIRPORT for when `-I was `-23-YEARS-OF-AGE; and, was `-LEAVING `-WATCHTOWER `-FARMS!!!!!~'

12) When `-I was taking a `-BREAK; and, going on my way to the `-BATHROOM at U C Berkeley (Certification in Mediation & Arbitration); John Cho from "HAROLD AND KUMAR", who was `-SINGING with `-HIS `-BAND `-OUTSIDE said `-HELLO to `-ME; and, `-I to `-HIM; as `-WE were `-BOTH `-WALKING `-DOWN the `-HALLWAY!!!!!~'

13) I had bought `-TICKETS to the "HORDE FESTIVAL" at the "SHORELINE AMPHITHEATER" in the `-SEATS; when, a `-GUEST of my `-EX-GIRLFRIENDS / `-BABY `-SISTER / had a `-FRIEND that `-KNEW the `-WIFE of `-STEVE `-WOZNIAK!!!!!~' HE approached; and, `-STEVE `-WOZNIAK allowed us in `-HIS `-BOX `-SEATS to where `-HE was `-PLAYING `-**TETRIS**!!!!!~' We sat there all the `-WAY up `-FRONT; and, `-DIRECTLY to `-HIS `-LEFT!!!!!~' OTHERS began to `-ENTER; and, these were the `-STARS of a `-MOVIE that `-I had seen about the `-WAR of the `-NERDS between `-APPLE `-COMPUTERS; and, `-MICROSOFT!!!!!~' The `-CEO, `-CHIEF `-SCIENTIST; and, `-CHIEF `-ENGINEER of `-APPLE `-COMPUTERS came in as well!!!!!!~' I `-TALKED with their `-HOUSE `-KEEPER as `-SHE was in the `-BOX `-SEATS with `-THEM, `-too!!!!!~' We stayed `-ALL the `-WAY; until, the `-END of the `-CONCERT; to where, `-STEVE `-WOZNIAK walked `-OUT of the `-BOXED `-SEATS; right `-PAST my `-LEFT `-SHOULDER!!!!!~'

14) I had a `-JOB at `-ONE `-TIME to `-WHERE `-I installed `-MODULARS; and, had done so for `-GEORGE `-LUCAS on his `-RANCH to where some of the `-SCENES from `-STAR `-WARS had been `-SHOT!!!!!~' I ate `-LUNCH there at `-EITHER the `-WHITEHOUSE; or, the `-REDHOUSE!!!!!~'

15) I had a `-JOB at `-ONE `-TIME to `-WHERE `-I installed `-MODULARS on the U. S. S. Abraham Lincoln Air Craft

Carrier!!!!!~' I had to carry my own `-GENERATORS; and, `-TOOLS; on by `-MYSELF for their `-RADIOACTIVE `-COURSE!!!!!~'

16) I made a "BEEF in WINE SAUCE" for my `-COUSIN `-GENE "GENO" WILLIAMS from the LEGENDARY GROUP the "PLATTERS"; and, `-HIS `-GIRLFRIEND; at my `-MOTHER'S `-HOME that `-I HAD `-BOUGHT for `-HER, before `-HIS `-UNTIMELY `-DEATH!!!!!~'

17) I met my `-COUSIN-BY-MARRIAGE `-AUDRA MCDONALD at `-HER `-FATHER'S `-FUNERAL in `-FRESNO, CALIFORNIA!!!!!~' HER `-FATHER `-DIED at the `-AGE of `-62, the "PROPHET'S" MOTHER at the `-AGE of `-63; and, `-GENE "GENO" WILLIAMS at the `-AGE of `-64!!!!!~'

`-AGE of `-DEATHS = `-(62,63,64)-'" = Prophetic-Linear-Progression-PLP!!!!!~'

**What's the `-WEATHER `-LIKE / `-THERE?????~'** What's the `-DEW `-POINT; and, `-RELATIVE `-HUMIDITY?????~' `-LOOK within the `-EQUATION `-(25/9) = (`-2.77)!!!~' / `-(77/2) = `-(38.5)!!!!!~' `-DIVIDE any `-PAGE that you're `-READING by `-(1.38) to `-SEE the `-EXACT `-PAGE that the "PROPHET" was `-WORKING `-ON!~'

$$T_{dp\,:\,f} = T_f\,(-)\,9/25\,(100\,(-)\,RH);$$
$$-IN\text{-}WEATHER\text{-}RECIPROCAL-$$
$$RH = 100\,(-)\,25/9\,(T_f\,(-)\,T_{dp\,:\,f});$$

T = Temperature / dp = Dew Point
f = Fahrenheit / RH = Relative Humidity

Go `-FIGURE!!!!!~' / By the `-WAY, `-HOW do `-YOU `-FEEL `-THERE!!!!!~'

The "PROPHET" Dwayne W. Anderson...(...)...-'"-"

1) Kelly Clarkson - Anytime
2) Enya - The Celts
3) Enya - Storms In Africa
4) Enya - Only Time
5) Enya - Caribbean Blue
6) Enya - Orinoco Flow
7) Enya - On My Way Home

DAVID BOWIE `-DIES on (01/10/20/16) = `-47; and, was `-BORN in `-1947!!!!!~' DAVID BOWIE `-DIED within `-47 `-DAYS of `-BASEBALL `-GREAT `-MONTE `-IRVIN'S `-NEXT `-BIRTHDAY!!!!!~' DAVID BOWIE `-DIED at the `-AGE of `-69 = RECIPROCAL = `-96!!!!!~' MR. MONTE IRVIN `-DIED at the `-AGE of `-96 the `-VERY `-NEXT `-DAY!!!!!~'

MONTE IRVIN was `-BORN on (02/25/19/19); and, had `-DIED on (01/11/20/16)!!!!!~' `-HIS `-BIRTHDAY # `-NUMBER (`-65) (+) `-HIS `-DEATH/DAY # `-NUMBER (`-48) = `-113 = (13 x 1) = `-13 = "A VERY PIVOTAL NUMBER"!!!!!~' #20 on the SAN FRANCISCO GIANTS; and, `-HIS EDUCATION: `-LINCOLN `-UNIVERSITY!!!!!~'

DAVID BOWIE was `-MARRIED to `-IMAN for some `-23 `-YEARS from `-JUNE `-6th, in `-1992 to `-2016!!!!!~' SWITCH `-EVERY (`-A) to an (`-I); and, `-EVERY (`-E) to an (`-O); and, (`-IMAN) = (`-AMIN) = (`-AMEN)!!!!!~'

`-IMAN was `-BORN on (07/25/19/55)!!!!!~' `-HER `-BIRTHDAY # `-NUMBER is `-106 = (16 + 0) = `-16 = "YEAR of the `-DEATH of `-HER `-HUSBAND (`-2016)-"!!!!!~' (2 x 16) = `-32 / (25 + 7) = `-32 = -a Prophetic Number!!!!!~' / `-55 = `-23 + `-32

DAVID BOWIE was `-BORN on (01/08/19/47); and, with that `-HIS `-BIRTHDAY # `-NUMBER = `-75!!!!!~' `-BIRTHDAY # `-NUMBER (`-75) (+) `-DEATH/DAY # `-NUMBER (`-47) = `-122 = (22 + 1) = `-23 = -a Prophetic Number!!!!!~' `-BIRTHDAY # `-NUMBER (`-75) (-) `-DEATH/DAY # `-NUMBER (`-47) = `-28 = RECIPROCAL = `-82 = `-ARMAGEDDON!!!!!~'

ALAN RICKMAN `-DIES on (01/14/20/16) at the `-AGE of `-69 /`-just as well!!!!!~' (69 + 69 = `-138 = (38 x 1) = `-38 = 3(8's) = `-888 = (8 x 8 x 8) = `-512 = (5 (1 + 2)) = `-53 = "WAR of the WORLDS"!!!!!~' (69 + 69 + 96) = `-234 = Prophetic-Linear-Progression-PLP!!!!!~'

ALAN RICKMAN was `-BORN on (02/21/19/46); and, `-HIS `-BIRTHDAY # `-NUMBER = `-88 = `-2(8's) = `-28 = RECIPROCAL = `-82 = `-ARMAGEDDON!!!!!~'

ALAN RICKMAN `-DIED `-38 `-DAYS before `-HIS `-NEXT `-BIRTHDAY just like`-GALILEO `-GALILEI!!!!!~' (38 + 38) = `-76 = (7

+ 6) = `-<u>13</u> = "A VERY PIVOTAL NUMBER"!!!!!~' ALAN RICKMAN `-DIED on a `-<u>14</u>th; and, was `-BORN on a `-<u>21</u>st!!!!!~' (`-14/`-<u>7</u> = `-<u>2</u>) / (`-21/`-<u>7</u> = `-<u>3</u>) / (<u>=</u>) `-<u>23</u> = -a Prophetic Number!!!!!~' GALILEO `-GALILEI `-<u>DIED</u> at the `-AGE of `-<u>77</u> = `-<u>2(7's)</u> = `-<u>27</u> = "The ROMAN EMPIRE"!!!!!~'

Legendary KCBS RADIO ANCHOR (AL HART = "<u>ALL</u> <u>HEART</u>") `-<u>DIES</u> at the `-AGE of `-<u>88</u>!!!!!~' AL HART `-JOINED KCBS in `-19<u>66</u>!!!!!~' (88 x 2) = `-<u>176</u> = (76 x 1) = `-<u>76</u> = (7 + 6) = `-<u>13</u> = "A VERY PIVOTAL NUMBER"!!!!!~' (66 (-) 19) = `-<u>47</u>!!!!!~'

René Angélil `-<u>DIES</u> (`-<u>2</u>) `-DAYS before `-HIS `-BIRTHDAY in `-TURNING `-<u>74</u> (01/<u>16</u>/<u>19</u>/<u>42</u>)!!!!!~' DAVID BOWIE `-DIED (`-<u>2</u>) `-DAYS after `-HIS `-BIRTHDAY!!!!!~' (01/<u>14</u>/<u>20</u>/<u>16</u>) `-BIRTHDAY (-) `-DEATH/DAY = (78 (-) 51) = `-<u>27</u> = `-<u>2(7's)</u> = `-<u>77</u>!!!!!~'

Dan Haggerty "Grizzly Adams" `-<u>DIES</u> at the `-AGE of `-<u>74</u> (01/<u>15</u>/<u>20</u>/<u>16</u>)!!!!!~' `-BIRTHDAY # `-NUMBER (11/<u>19</u>/<u>19</u>/<u>41</u>) = `-<u>90</u>!!!!!~' BIRTHDAY # `-NUMBER (-) DEATH/DAY # `-NUMBER (`-<u>52</u>) = `-<u>38</u>!!!!!~' DEATH `-<u>57</u> `-DAYS after <u>BIRTHDAY</u>!~' (`-<u>365</u>-Calendar Year (-) `-<u>57</u>) = `-<u>308</u> = (38 + 0) = `-<u>38</u> = 3(8's) = `-<u>888</u>!!!!!~'

René Angélil's Brother-In-Law (Daniel Dion) Celine Dion's Brother `-<u>DIES</u> at the tender `-AGE of `-<u>59</u> (`-Mary-'" (Jesus Christ's Mother's `-AGE of `-DEATH (`-59))) (`-<u>2</u>) `-DAYS after the `-DEATH of René Angélil (Celine Dion's Husband)!!!!!~' Daniel Dion's BIRTHDAY # `-NUMBER is (11/<u>29</u>/<u>19</u>/<u>56</u>) = `-<u>115</u>; and, `-HIS DEATH/DAY # `-NUMBER is (01/<u>16</u>/<u>20</u>/<u>16</u>) = `-<u>53</u> = "WAR of the WORLDS"!!!!!~' (`-<u>115</u> = (15 x 1) = `-<u>15</u>) = {(53 (-) 15) = `-<u>38</u>}!!!!!~' There are `-<u>47</u> `-DAYS that `-LIE in-between-in-between- the `-BIRTHDAY; and, `-DEATH/DAY of Mr. DANIEL DION!!!!!~' (`-<u>365</u>-Calendar Year (-) `-<u>47</u>) = `-<u>318</u> = (38 x 1) = `-<u>38</u> = 3(8's) = `-<u>888</u> = (8 x 8 x 8) = `-<u>512</u> = (5 (1 + 2)) = `-<u>53</u> = "WAR of the WORLDS"!!!!!~'!!!!!~'

DANIEL DION'S BIRTHDAY # `-NUMBER (11 + 29 + 19) = `-<u>59</u> = "AGE" of "DEATH"!!!!!~' Celine Dion's Husband `-DIED `-<u>74</u> DAYS before `-HER NEXT `-BIRTHDAY; and, Celine Dion is `-CURRENTLY `-<u>47</u> YEARS of `-AGE!!!!!~'

`-<u>47</u> = <u>RECIPROCAL</u> = `-<u>74</u> / `-<u>38</u> = <u>RECIPROCAL</u> = `-<u>83</u> = (WWI & WWII)

Glenn Lewis Frey `-DIES at the `-AGE of `-67 = RECIPROCAL = `-76 on (01/18/20/16)!!!!!~' `-BIRTHDAY # `-NUMBER (11/06/19/48) = `-84!!!!!~' BIRTHDAY # `-NUMBER (+) DEATH/DAY # `-NUMBER (`-55) = `-139 = (39 (-) 1) = `-38 = 3(8's) = `-888 = (8 x 8 x 8) = `-512 = (5 (1 + 2)) = `-53 = "WAR of the WORLDS"!!!!!~'!!!!!~'!!!!!~' GLENN LEWIS FREY'S `-DEATH is `-74 `-DAYS after `-HIS BIRTHDAY!!!!!~' `-48 = RECIPROCAL = `-84 / (84 + 48) = `-132 = (32 x 1) = `-32 = -a Prophetic Number!!!!!~' Martin Luther King, Jr. `-DIED at the tender `-AGE of `-39; just as well as, Mr. Malcolm X; a tender -(`-39)-!!!!!~'

GLENN LEWIS FREY'S BIRTHDAY # `-NUMBER (11 + 06 + 19) = `-36 = RECIPROCAL = `-63 = {+4 from (`-48)} = `-67 = "AGE" of "DEATH"!!!!!~'

Daniel Dion BIRTHDAY # `-NUMBER (-) DEATH/DAY # `-NUMBER = (115 (-) 53) = `-62!!!!!~' Glenn Lewis Frey was `-BORN on 11/06 = RECIPROCAL = 06/11 / (11 = 1 +
1) = `-2 = `-06/02 = `-62!!!!!~' Glenn Lewis Frey BIRTHDAY # `-NUMBER (-) DEATH/DAY # `-NUMBER = (84 (-) 55) = `-29!!!!!~' Daniel Dion was `-BORN on the `-29th!!!!!~' Glenn Lewis Frey's `-BIRTHDAY/YEAR = `-1948 = (48 (-) 19) = `-29!!!!!~' `-29 = RECIPROCAL = `-92

(92 + 62) = `-154 = (54 (-) 1) = `-53 = "WAR of the WORLDS"!!!!!~'

(29 + 26) = `-55 = `-23 + `-32-'"!!!!!~' / `-23 = RECIPROCAL = `-32

(67 + 59) = `-126 = (26 x 1) = `-26 = `-13 x `-2 = `-132 = (32 x 1) = `-32 = -a Prophetic Number!!!!!~' The `-YEAR; and, `-LIVES; of `-38's!!!!!~'

DANIEL DION (29th); and, GLENN LEWIS FREY (6th); `-both, `-BORN within the `-MONTH of `-NOVEMBER!!!!!~' (29 (-) 6) = `-23 = -a Prophetic Number!!!!!~' (29 + 6) = `-35 = RECIPROCAL = `-53 = "WAR of the WORLDS"!!!!!~'

Clarence Henry Reid "Blowfly" `-DIED on (01/17/20/16); and, `-HIS DEATH/DAY # `-NUMBER is = `-54!!!!!~'

01 + 17 + 20 = `-38!!!!!~' `-38 = 3(8's) = `-888 = (8 x 8 x 8) = `-512 = (5 (1 + 2)) = `-53 = "WAR of the WORLDS"!!!!!~'

Clarence Henry Reid "Blowfly" was `-BORN on (02/14/19/39); and, `-HIS BIRTHDAY # `-NUMBER is = `-74!!!!!~'

02 + 14 + 19 = `-35!!!!!~' `-35 = RECIPROCAL = `-53 = "WAR of the WORLDS"!!!!!~'

February 1<u>4</u> / January 1<u>7</u> = (1<u>4</u>/1<u>7</u>) = (47 x 1 x 1) = `-<u>47</u> = RECIPROCAL = `-<u>74</u> = "Joseph Stalin `-<u>DIED</u> at the `-AGE of `-<u>74</u>!!!!!~' January 31st (-) January 17th = `-<u>14</u>!!!!!~' (14 + 14) = `-<u>28</u> = "Clarence Henry Reid "Blowfly" `-<u>DIED</u> `-<u>28</u> DAYS before `-HIS `-NEXT `-BIRTHDAY"!!!!!~' (74 + 54) = `-<u>128</u> = (28 x 1) = `-<u>28</u> DAYS!!!!!~'

The Presidents with the `-NUMBER `-53+_!!!!!~' Russia's Vladimir Lenin died at the `-AGE of `-53; and, Russia's Joseph Stalin died in `-19<u>53</u> on its `-RECIPROCAL `-DAY / 0<u>3</u>/05/19<u>53</u> / `-<u>35</u> = RECIPROCAL = `-<u>53</u>/|_!!!!!~'

Clarence Henry Reid "Blowfly" `-<u>DIED</u> at the `-AGE of `-<u>76</u> = RECIPROCAL = `-<u>67</u>!!!!!~' Glenn Lewis Frey `-<u>DIES</u> at the `-AGE of `-<u>67</u> the very `-NEXT `-DAY on the `-<u>18</u>th!!!!!~' (17th + 18th = `-<u>35</u> = RECIPROCAL = `-<u>53</u> = "WAR of the WORLDS"!!!!!~'

Terence Dale "Buffin" Griffin `-<u>DIED</u> on (01/1<u>7</u>/20/16); and, `-HIS DEATH/DAY # `-NUMBER is = `-<u>54</u>!!!!!~' `-HE `-DIED at the tender `-AGE of `-<u>67</u> = RECIPROCAL = `-<u>76</u>; and, the very `-SAME `-DAY as Clarence Henry Reid "Blowfly" who was `-<u>76</u> "YEARS of AGE" at the `-"TIME of `-HIS `-DEATH"!!!!!~'

01 + 17 + 20 = `-<u>38</u>!!!!!~' `-<u>38</u> = <u>3(8's)</u> = `-<u>888</u> = (8 x 8 x 8) = `-<u>512</u> = (5 (1 + 2)) = `-<u>53</u> = "WAR of the WORLDS"!!!!!~'

Terence Dale "Buffin" Griffin was `-<u>BORN</u> on (10/2<u>4</u>/1<u>9</u>/4<u>8</u>); and, `-HIS BIRTHDAY # `-NUMBER is = `-<u>101</u>!!!!!~'

10 + 24 + 19 = `-<u>53</u>!!!!!~' `-<u>53</u> = "WAR of the WORLDS"!!!!!~'

BIRTHDAY # `-NUMBER (`-<u>101</u>) (-) DEATH/DAY # `-NUMBER (`-<u>54</u>) = `-<u>47</u> = RECIPROCAL = `-<u>74</u>!!!!!~'

October 2<u>4</u> / January 1<u>7</u> = (2<u>4</u>/17) = (47 x 1 x 2) = `-<u>94</u> = RECIPROCAL = `-<u>49</u> = "The `-DEATH # `-NUMBERS!!!!!~' René Angélil; and, Celine Dion were `-<u>MARRIED</u> in (`-19<u>94</u>)!!!!!~'

Terence Dale "Buffin" Griffin `-<u>DIED</u> (`-<u>85</u>) DAYS after `-HIS `-LAST `-BIRTHDAY!!!!!~' (`-<u>365</u>-Calendar Year (-) `-<u>85</u>) = `-<u>280</u> = (28 + 0) = `-<u>28</u>

= "Clarence Henry Reid "Blowfly"-'"!!!!!~' (1024 (+) 214) = `-1238 = (38 x 1 x 2) = `-76!!!!!~'

"MotorHead's" Ian Fraser Kilmister "LEMMY" `-DIED at the `-AGE of `-70!!!!!~' `-HE `-DIED (`-4) DAYS after `-HIS `-BIRTHDAY!!!!!~' (70 + 4) = `-74!!!!!~'

"MotorHead's" Ian Fraser Kilmister "LEMMY" `-DIED on (12/28/20/15); and, `-HIS DEATH/DAY # `-NUMBER is = `-75!!!!!~'

"MotorHead's" Ian Fraser Kilmister "LEMMY" was `-BORN on (12/24/19/45); and, `-HIS BIRTHDAY # `-NUMBER is = `-100!!!!!~'

Terence Dale "Buffin" Griffin `-BIRTHDAY # `-NUMBER (`-101) (+) Clarence Henry Reid "Blowfly" `-BIRTHDAY # `-NUMBER (`-74) = `-175!!!!!~'

"MotorHead's" Ian Fraser Kilmister "LEMMY" `-BIRTHDAY # `-NUMBER (`-100) (+) `-DEATH/DAY # `-NUMBER (`-75) = `-175!!!!!~' `-175 = (75 (-) 1) = (`-74)-!!!!!~'

The `-TELEVISION `-SHOW = `-("MASH")-/ = (13 + 1 + 19 + 8) = `-41 = WAYNE ROGERS & NATALIE COLE = "FIGURE OUT THE `-EQUATIONS"!!!!!~'

Natalie Maria Cole `-DIED on (12/31/20/15); and, `-HER `-DEATH/DAY # `-NUMBER is = `-78!!!!!~' (78 (+) 78) = `-156 = (56 x 1) = `-56 = RECIPROCAL = `-65!!!!!~'

Natalie Maria Cole was `-BORN on (02/06/19/50); and, `-HER `-BIRTHDAY # `-NUMBER is = `-77!!!!!~'

`-HER `-BIRTHDAY; and, `-DEATH/DAY are `-ONLY `-OFF by (`-1) `-NUMBER!!!!!~' (78 + 77) = `-155 = (55 x 1) = `-55 = `-23 + `-32!!!!!~' `-SHE `-DIED `-38 DAYS before `-HER `-NEXT `-BIRTHDAY!!!!!~' `-SHE `-DIED at the `-AGE of `-65!!!!!~'

William Wayne McMillan Rogers (III) `-DIED on (12/31/20/15) at (`-82); and, `-HIS `-DEATH/DAY # `-NUMBER is = `-78!!!!!~' (78 x 2) = "for Natalie Maria Cole"!!!!!~'

12 + 31 + 20 = `-<u>63</u> = `-BIRTHDAY # `-NUMBER!!!!!~' / `-<u>47</u> = RECIPROCAL = `-<u>74</u>

William Wayne McMillan Rogers (III) was `-BORN on (0<u>4</u>/0<u>7</u>/<u>19</u>/<u>33</u>); and, `-HIS `-BIRTHDAY # `-NUMBER is = `-<u>63</u>!!!!!~' (33 (-) 19) = `-<u>14</u>!!!!!~' (82 + 65) = `-<u>147</u>!!!!!~'

`-HIS `-BIRTHDAY; and, `-DEATH/DAY are `-ONLY `-OFF by a `-NUMBER of (`-15) = "The `-YEAR of `-HIS `-DEATH"!!!!!~' (78 + 63) = `-<u>141</u> = Reciprocal-<u>S</u>equenced-<u>N</u>umerology-<u>RSN</u> = `-<u>14</u> = RECIPROCAL = `-<u>41</u> = "WORLD WAR (I); and, (II)"!!!!!~'

William Wayne McMillan Rogers (III) -("MASH")- `-<u>DIED</u> `-<u>97</u> DAYS before `-HIS `-NEXT `-BIRTHDAY!!!!!~' `-<u>97</u> = RECIPROCAL = `-<u>79</u> = "WAR of the WORLDS"!!!!!~'

<u>JESUS</u> = `-<u>74</u> = "INDEPENDENCE `-DAY" = RECIPROCAL = `-<u>47</u> = (0<u>7</u>/04/<u>20</u>/<u>16</u>)!!!~'

<u>CHRIST</u> = `-<u>77</u> = `-<u>2(7's)</u> = "The ROMAN EMPIRE" = RECIPROCAL = `-<u>72</u> = The "<u>WORLD</u>"!!!!!~'

<u>MARY</u> = (13 + 1 + 18 + 25) = `-<u>57</u>!!!!!~' (/|\) (74 + 77 + 57 + 69) = `-<u>277</u>!!!!!~'

<u>JEH</u>-*OVAH* = (<u>10</u> + <u>5</u> + <u>8</u> + *15* + *22* + *1* + *8*) = `-<u>69</u> = "The `-CYCLE of `-LIFE"!!!!!~'

(74 + 72 + 57 + 69) = `-<u>272</u> = "<u>R</u>eciprocal-<u>S</u>equencing-<u>N</u>umerology-<u>RSN</u>"-'"!!!!!~'

PLANET = (16 + 12 + 1 + 14 + 5 + 20) = `-<u>68</u> = (WAR x 4)-!!!!!~'

`-<u>272</u> = (68 x 4) = <u>4</u>th `-<u>PLANET</u> = `-<u>MARS</u>!!!!!~' MAR = `-<u>32</u> = -a Prophetic Number!!!!!~' MAR/S = (32 / 19) = `-<u>1.68</u> = WAR x 4-!!!!!~'

(277 + 68) = `-<u>345</u> = "<u>P</u>rophetic-<u>L</u>inear-<u>P</u>rogression-<u>PLP</u>"-'"!!!!!~'

Travel the `-BREADTH of `-ONE (`-1) `-DIRECTION, reverse back-in-time; and, travel the `-BREADTH of the `-OPPOSITE `-DIRECTION!!!!!~' Now, `-TURN 90 `-degrees `-PERPENDICULAR; and, `-REPEAT the `-COURSE; until, the `-UNIVERSE runs `-OUT; on, `-EACH; and, `-EVERY `-TRAJECTORY!!!!!~' Now; `-REPEAT for `-EVERY `-ANGLE

of `-360 `-DEGREES; until, `-YOU have a `-FULL `-CIRCLE `-SPHERE of the `-EARTH!!!!!~' NOW; `-GOD is `-EVERYWHERE!!!!!~' `-HE'S all `-THROUGHOUT those `-JOURNEYS you've been `-TAKING!!!!!~' `-HE'S been `-SEEN `-ALL THROUGHOUT; while, `-CONTROLLING; `-EVERYTHING!!!!!~' Down to the `-ATOMS; and, `-WITHIN `-EVERYTHING!!!!!~' `-HE'S been `-DOING `-IT /|\ PRECISELY /|\ `-ALL of `-IT `-SIMULTANEOUSLY /|\ FOREVER!!!!!~' `-EVEN, what `-WE/`-I/`-YOU'LL; never, `-SEE /|\ `-EVER!!!!!~' For `-ALL that `-GOD has `-
PROMISED; `-HE will `-SURELY `-FULFILL!!!!!~' `-AMEN, `-AMEN; `-AMEN!!!!!~'

<u>Dwayne</u> <u>Warren</u> <u>Anderson</u> is a `-<u>MONK</u>!!!!!~' (<u>M</u>-13 / <u>O</u>-15 / <u>N</u>-14 / <u>K</u>-11) = (13 + 15 + 14 + 11) = `-<u>53</u> = "WAR of the WORLDS"!!!!!~'

`-<u>38</u> = <u>RECIPROCAL</u> = `-<u>83</u> / (32 + 44) = `-<u>76</u> = <u>RECIPROCAL</u> = `-<u>67</u>!!!!!~'

`-<u>2016</u> is the `-YEAR of the `-MONKEY according to the "Chinese Calendar"; and, with the "Chinese New Year" which = `-<u>46</u>!!!!!~' The "PROPHET'S" MOTHER was `-BORN in the `-YEAR of the `-MONKEY in (`-19<u>44</u>)!!!!!~' "A WOOD MONKEY"!!!!!~' Uncle CAL; Aunt SANDRA'S Husband, was `-BORN in the `-YEAR of the `-MONKEY just as `-WELL in (`-19<u>32</u>) – "A WATER MONKEY"!!!!!~' `-HE is `-NOW, `-<u>83</u> YEARS-of-AGE!!!!!~' His `-DAUGHTER is `-<u>38</u> YEARS-of-AGE right `-NOW!!!!!~'

`-<u>MONKEY</u> = (<u>M</u>-13 / <u>O</u>-15 / <u>N</u>-14 / <u>K</u>-11 / <u>E</u>-5 / <u>Y</u>-25) = (13 + 15 + 14 + 11 + 5 + 25) = `-<u>83</u> = "WORLD WARS (I) & (II)"!!!!!~'

ONE `-1 `-FULL `-AVERAGE `-YEAR (`-365 / `-3.2) = `-<u>114</u> / (365 (-) 114) = `-<u>251</u> = (51 + 2) = `-<u>53</u> = "WAR of the WORLDS" = `-1 WEEK after the `-START of WW2!!!!!~'

ONE `-1 `-FULL `-AVERAGE `-YEAR (`-365 / `-2.3) = `-<u>158</u> / (365 (-) 158 = `-<u>207</u> = (27 + 0) = `-<u>27</u> = "The ROMAN EMPIRE" = `-1 DAY before the `-START of WW1!!!!!~'

WW1 / Started-July 28th-1914 -to- November 11th-1918-Ended / {1111 (-) 728} = `-<u>383</u> = <u>R</u>eciprocal-<u>S</u>equenced-<u>N</u>umerology-<u>RSN</u>~ = `-<u>38</u> = <u>RECIPROCAL</u> = `-<u>83</u>!!!!!~'

WW2 / Started-September 1ˢᵗ-1939 -to- September 2ⁿᵈ-1945-Ended / {91 + 92} = `-183 = (83 x 1) = `-83!!!!!~'

WATER = (W-23 / A-1 / T-20 / E-5 / R-18) = (23 + 1 + 20 + 5 + 18) = `-67 = "The `-YEAR that the "PROPHET'S" BROTHER was `-BORN, the `-AVERAGE `-AGE of the United States Presidents 1 to 28 in "SUCCESSION" above; and, below `-ALL `-PRESIDENTS that `-DIED at `-AGES `-66, `-67; and, `-68; and, The `-AGE of `-DEATH of the #1/President of the United States of America #1/President George Washington"!!!!!~'

WOOD = (W-23 / O-15 / O-15 / D-4) = (23 + 15 + 15 + 4) = `-57 = "MARY" & "WARREN G. HARDING"!!!!!~' M = RECIPROCAL = W!!!!!~'

WOO = \'wü\ = (W-23 / O-15 / O-15) = "to try to make (someone) love you : to try to have a romantic relationship with (someone)" (Webster's Dictionary)…(…)…-'-' = (23 + 15 + 15) = `-53 = "WAR of the WORLDS"!!!!!~'

WO = (W-23 / O-15) = "WARRANT OFFICER" = (23 + 15) = `-38 = WARREN!!!!!~'

(67 + 57) = `-124 = (24 x 1) = `-24 = RECIPROCAL = `-42 = "WAR"!!!!!~'

`-2016 is the `-YEAR of the `-FIRE `-MONKEY!!!!!~' (83 (-) 16) = `-67!!!!!~'

FIRE = (F-6 / I-9 / R-18 / E-5) = (6 + 9 + 18 + 5) = `-38 = RECIPROCAL = `-83 = "MONKEY"!!!!!~'

`-MON = (M-13 / O-15 / N-14) = `-42 = "WAR"!!!!!~'

`-KEY = (K-11 / E-5 / Y-25) = (11 + 5 + 25) = `-41 = RECIPROCAL = `-14 = "WORLD WAR (II); and, WORLD WAR (I)"!!!!!~'

`-KING = (K-11 / I-9 / N-14 / G-7) = (11 + 9 + 14 + 7) = `-41 = RECIPROCAL = `-14 = "WORLD WAR (II); and, WORLD WAR (I)"!!!!!~'

"KEY KING" = (41 + 41) = `-82 = `-"ARMAGEDDON"!!!!!~'

"<u>WHAT</u>" are the "<u>KEYS</u> <u>of</u> <u>the</u> <u>KINGDOM</u>"!!!!!~' (60 + 21 + 33 + 73) = `-<u>187</u> = (87 + 1) = `-<u>88</u> PIANO KEYS = (87 (-1) = `-<u>86</u> = "<u>HAR</u>-<u>MAGEDON</u>"!!!!!~'

`-<u>KEYS</u> = (<u>K</u>-11 / <u>E</u>-5 / <u>Y</u>-25 / <u>S</u>-19) = (11 + 5 + 25 + 19) = `-<u>60</u>

`-<u>OF</u> = (<u>O</u>-15 / <u>F</u>-6) = (15 + 6) = `-<u>21</u>

`-<u>THE</u> = (<u>T</u>-20 / <u>H</u>-8 / <u>E</u>-5) = (20 + 8 + 5) = `-<u>33</u>

`-<u>KINGDOM</u> = (<u>K</u>-11 / <u>I</u>-9 / <u>N</u>-14 / <u>G</u>-7 / <u>D</u>-4 / <u>O</u>-15 / <u>M</u>-13) = (11 + 9 + 14 + 7 + 4 + 15 + 13) = `-<u>73</u>

`-<u>11</u> = "Yin/Yang" = "Multiple of `-ELEVEN" = "The `-CYCLE of `-LIFE"!!!!!~'

MATTHEW 16:<u>19</u> (-) "(<u>19</u>) I will give unto thee the keys of the kingdom of heaven: and whatsoever thou shalt bind on earth shall be bound in heaven: and whatsoever thou shalt loose on earth shall be loosed in heaven." -(ENGLISH REVISED EDITION - 1885)- {The `-WORLD (+/-) (`-72 + `-11 = `-<u>83</u>)}!!!!!~'

<u>JEH</u>-*OVAH* = (<u>10</u> + <u>5</u> + <u>8</u> + *15* + *22* + *1* + *8*) = `-<u>69</u> = "The `-CYCLE of `-LIFE"!!!!!~'

REVELATION 9:<u>1</u> (-) "(<u>1</u>) And the fifth angel sounded, and I saw a star from heaven fallen unto the earth: and there was given to him the key of the pit of the abyss." -(ENGLISH REVISED EDITION - 1885)- (<u>91</u> = RECIPROCAL = <u>19</u>) = (91 - 19) = `-<u>72</u>!~'

The `-<u>WORD</u> (-) `-<u>LUCIFER</u> = (<u>L</u>-12 / <u>U</u>-21 / <u>C</u>-3 / <u>I</u>-9 / <u>F</u>-6 / <u>E</u>-5 / <u>R</u>-18) = (12 + 21 + 3 + 9 + 6 + 5 + 18) = `-<u>74</u> = "INDEPENDENCE DAY"!!!!!~'

The `-<u>WORD</u> (+) <u>JESUS</u> = `-<u>EQUALS</u> = (<u>J</u>-10 / <u>E</u>-5 / <u>S</u>-19 / <u>U</u>-21 / <u>S</u>-19) = `-<u>74</u> = "INDEPENDENCE `-DAY" from `-<u>LUCIFER</u>!!!!!~'

`-<u>MONDAY</u> = (<u>M</u>-13 / <u>O</u>-15 / <u>N</u>-14 / <u>D</u>-4 / <u>A</u>-1 / <u>Y</u>-25) = `-<u>72</u> = The "<u>WORLD</u>"!!!!!~'

`-ABE `-VIGODA has `-<u>DIED</u> at the `-AGE of `-<u>94</u> `-TODAY!!!!!~'

`-ABE `-VIGODA'S DEATH/DAY # `-NUMBER = (01/26/2016) = (1 + 26 + 20 + 16) = `-<u>63</u> = "AGE of `-DEATH of #16/President Abraham

Lincoln's `-WIFE / FIRST LADY MARY TODD LINCOLN"!!!!!~' (1 + 26 + 20) = `-47 = RECIPROCAL = `-74 / `-1865 = (65 (-) 18) = `-47!!!!!~'

`-ABE `-VIGODA lived `-38 `-YEARS LONGER than `-ABRAHAM LINCOLN!!!!!~' ABRAHAM LINCOLN `-DIED at the `-AGE of `-56!!!!!~' `-ABE `-VIGODA was `-BORN `-56 YEARS LATER; after, the `-DEATH of Mr. ABRAHAM LINCOLN in (`-1865)!!!!!~' `-ABE `-VIGODA `-DIED `-150 `-YEARS after the `-DEATH of `-PRESIDENT ABRAHAM LINCOLN!!!!!~' `-ABE `-VIGODA `-DIED `-206 `-YEARS after the `-BIRTH of PRESIDENT ABRAHAM LINCOLN!!!!!~' `-ABE `-VIGODA `-DIED on the `-26th of the `-MONTH!!!!!~' (94 (-) 56) = `-38 = RECIPROCAL = `-83 = "The `-YEAR of the "FIRE MONKEY"-'"!!!!!~'

`-ABE `-VIGODA `-MARRIED `-HIS `-WIFE `-BEATRICE `-SCHY in the `-YEAR of the "EARTH MONKEY" in (`-1968); and, `-HIS `-WIFE `-ENDED their `-MARRIAGE by `-DEATH `-24 `-YEARS `-LATER in the `-YEAR of the "WATER MONKEY) in (`-1992)!!!!!~'

`-1968 = (68 (-) 19) = `-49 = RECIPROCAL = `-94 = "AGE of `-DEATH of Mr. `-ABE `-VIGODA!!!!!~' (68 + 19) = `-87!!!!!~' `-ABE `-VIGODA `-DIED `-94 `-DAYS before `-HIS `-WIFE'S `-DEATH `-ANNIVERSARY -on- (04/30/19/92); which occurred `-23 `-YEARS `-AGO; as, `-ABE LINCOLN was `-MARRIED to HIS WIFE for `-23 YEARS!~'

`-1992 = (99 (-) 12) = `-87 / (87 + 87) = `-174 = (74 x 1) = `-74!!!!!~'

`-ABE `-VIGODA `-DIED `-29 `-DAYS before `-HIS `-NEXT `-BIRTHDAY; and, `-30 `-DAYS before `-HIS `-NEXT `-WEDDING `-ANNIVERSARY that had occurred `-47 `-YEARS `-AGO!!!!!~' (47 + 30) = `-77 = The "CHRIST"!!!!!~' `-

`-ABE `-VIGODA'S `-BIRTHDAY # `-NUMBER (`-66) (+) `-HIS `-DEATH/DAY # `-NUMBER (`-63) = (66 + 63) = `-129 = (29 x 1) = `-29 = `-ABE `-VIGODA had `-DIED `-29 `-DAYS before `-HIS `-NEXT `-BIRTHDAY!!!!!~'

ABRAHAM LINCOLN was `-BORN on the `-12th of FEBRUARY; while, `-ABE `-VIGODA was `-BORN on the `-24th of FEBRUARY!!!!!~' (24 + 12) = `-36 = RECIPROCAL = `-63 = "AGE of `-DEATH of the "PROPHET'S" MOTHER"!!!!!~'

`-ABE `-VIGODA'S BIRTHDAY # `-NUMBER = (02/24/19/21) = (2 + 24 + 19 + 21) = `-66 = "AGE of `-DEATH of the "PROPHET'S" FATHER"!!!!!~' ABE VIGODA `-DIED `-53 `-DAYS before "The REAL "PROPHET" of "DOOM'S"-'" `-BIRTHDAY / Dwayne Warren Anderson's -(03/20/2016)- who will be `-46 `-YEARS- of-AGE = The `-BIRTHDAY # `-NUMBER for the `-YEAR of the `-FIRE MONKEY!!!!!~'

BUDDY CIANCI `-DIES `-TODAY on (01/28/2016) at the `-AGE of `-74!!!!!~' `-HE was `-BORN on the DEATH/DAY of `-ABE `-VIGODA'S `-WIFE (04/30/19/41)!!!!!~' `-HIS BIRTHDAY # `-NUMBER `-94 (-) DEATH/DAY = (94 (-) 65) = `-29 = `-ABE `-VIGODA `-DYING `-29 `-DAYS before `-HIS `-NEXT `-BIRTHDAY!!!!!~'

`-PAUL `-LORIN `-KANTNER; CO-FOUNDER, of JEFFERSON AIRPLANE; and, `-VOCALIST and AMERICAN GUITARIST `-DIES `-TODAY at the `-AGE of `-74 with = RECIPROCAL = `-47 `-DAYS `-LYING in-between-in-between `-HIS `-DEATH/DAY; and, `-HIS `-NEXT `-BIRTHDAY!!!!!~' (365 (-) 47) = `-318 = (38 x 1) = `-38 = RECIPROCAL = `-83 = "The `-YEAR of the `-FIRE `-MONKEY"!!!!!~'

THERE are `-49 `-DAYS from `-DAY-to-DAY from `-PAUL `-LORIN `-KANTNER'S `-DEATH/DAY to `-HIS BIRTHDAY = RECIPROCAL = `-94 = `-ABE VIGODA!!!!!~'

`-PAUL `-LORIN `-KANTNER was `-BORN on (03/17/19/41) with a `-BIRTHDAY # `-NUMBER of = (3 + 17 + 19 + 41) = `-80!!!!!~' `-PAUL `-LORIN `-KANTNER `-DIED on (01/28/20/16) with a `-DEATH/DAY # `-NUMBER of = (1 + 28 + 20 + 16) = `-65!!!!!~' #16/President `-ABE `-LINCOLN `-DIED in (`-1865)!!!!!~' (65 (-) 18) = `-47!!!!!~'

(80 + 65) = `-145 = (45 x 1) = `-45 = "CURRENT `-AGE of the "PROPHET" at the `-TIME of `-PAUL `-LORIN `-KANTNER'S `-DEATH"!!!!!~'

`-PAUL `-LORIN `-KANTNER'S (MUSIC GROUPS) = "JEFFERSON AIRPLANE (1965-1996) / JEFFERSON STARSHIP (1974-2016)"!!!!!~'

(1996 (-) 1965) = `-31 = RECIPROCAL = `-13 = "A VERY PIVOTAL NUMBER"!!!!!~'

(2016 (-) 1974) = `-42 = "WAR"!!!!!~' (38 + 83) = `-121 / (47 + 74) = `-121 / (121 + 121) = `-242 = `-24 = RECIPROCAL = `-42 = `-WAR = (23 + 1 +

18) = (W-23 / A-1 / R-18)!!!!!~' '-ABE '-LINCOLN '-(ONE) '-(C-3 / E-5 / N-14 / T-20) = '-42 = '-WAR!!!!!~'

In the '-LAST '-THREE '-WEEKS; how '-MANY '-CELEBRITIES have '-DIED '-38, '-47; or, '-74 '-DAYS before '-THEIR '-NEXT; or, '-LAST '-BIRTHDAY!!!!!~'

The '-ANSWER = '-EQUALS = '-38 = '-LIVES with '-DEATH!!!!!~'

'-UPDATE: '-EARTH, '-WIND; and, '-FIRE!!!!!~'

'-EARTH, '-WIND; and, '-FIRE'S / '-MAURICE '-WHITE '-DIES '-TODAY (02/04/20/16) at the '-AGE of '-74 = RECIPROCAL = '-47 '-DAYS after '-HIS '-LAST '-BIRTHDAY!!!!!~'

'-MAURICE '-WHITE'S '-BIRTHDAY # '-NUMBER = (12/19/19/41) = (12 + 19 + 19 + 41) = '-91!!!!!~'

'-MAURICE '-WHITE'S '-DEATH/DAY # '-NUMBER = (02/04/20/16) = (2 + 4 + 20 + 16) = '-42!!!!!~'

(91 (-) 42) = '-49 = RECIPROCAL = '-94 = "The '-DEATH # '-NUMBERS"!!!!!~'

'-ACTOR '-DAVID MARGULIES '-DIES at the '-AGE of '-78 on (01/11/20/16) = '-DEATH/DAY # '-NUMBER = (1 + 11 + 20 + 16) = '-48!!!!!~'

'-ACTOR '-DAVID MARGULIES '-BIRTHDAY # '-NUMBER = (02/19/19/37) = (2 + 19 + 19 + 37) = '-77!!!!!~' (77 (-) 48) = '-29 = '-ABE '-VIGODA; and, '-BOB '-ELLIOTT!!!!!~'

'-ACTOR '-DAVID MARGULIES '-DIED '-38 '-DAYS before '-HIS '-NEXT '-BIRTHDAY!!!!!~'

'-ACTOR '-DAVID MARGULIES (02/19); and, '-EARTH, '-WIND; and, '-FIRE'S / '-MAURICE '-WHITE (12/19) = '-212 = "BOILING '-POINT of '-WATER through the '-EYES of '-FAHRENHEIT = '-MEN '-BOTH '-BORN on the '-19th OF the '-MONTH = (19 + 19) = '-38 = "The '-YEAR of the '-FIRE '-MONKEY"!!!!!~'

`-29 = RECIPROCAL = `-92 = `-COMEDIAN `-BOB `-ELLIOTT `-DIES on (02/02/20/16) at the `-AGE of `-92!!!!!~' `-COMEDIAN `-BOB `-ELLIOTT'S `-DEATH/DAY # `-NUMBER = (2 + 2 + 20 + 16) = `-40!!!!!~' `-HE `-DIES `-53 DAYS before `-HIS `-NEXT `-BIRTHDAY = "WAR of the WORLDS"!!!!!~'

(38 + 47 + 53) = `-138 = (38 x 1) = `-38 = "The `-YEAR of the `-FIRE `-MONKEY"!!!!!~'

`-COMEDIAN `-BOB `-ELLIOTT'S `-BIRTHDAY # `-NUMBER = (03/26/19/23) = (3 + 26 + 19 + 23) = `-71!!!!!~'

(3 + 26) = `-29 / (3 + 26 + 19) = `-48 / (48 + 29) = `-77 = `-ACTOR `-DAVID MARGULIES!!!!!~'

(71 (-) 40) = `-31 = RECIPROCAL = `-13 = "A VERY PIVOTAL NUMBER"!!!!!~'

SUPERBOWL `-50 = "The `-HOTTEST `-DAY this `-WINTER `-SEASON in SAN FRANCISCO/EARTHQUAKE = `-IT will be a `-SPRING `-TIME `-72 `-DEGREES!!!!!~'

The `-YEAR of the `-FIRE `-MONKEY starts on a `-WAR/DAY of `-MONDAY = (M-13 / O-15 / N-14 / D-4 / A-1 / Y-25) = `-72 = The `-CREATIVE-' "WORLD"!!!!!~'

The `-YEAR of the `-FIRE (`-38) `-MONKEY (`-83)!!!!!~'

The `-YEAR; and, `-LIVES; of `-38's!!!!!~'

The `-YEAR; and, `-LIVES; of `-38's in `-DEATH!!!!!~'

`-ANTONIN `-SCALIA (-) ASSOCIATE JUSTICE of the `-SUPREME `-COURT of the `-UNITED `-STATES of `-AMERICA `-DIES at the `-AGE of `-79 = "WAR of the WORLDS" = on (02/13/20/16)!!!!!~' `-ANTONIN `-SCALIA'S `-DEATH/DAY # `-NUMBER is = (2 + 13 + 20 + 16) = `-51!!!!!~' `-51 = RECIPROCAL = `-15 / (51 + 15) = `-66 = "FATHER-"!!!!!~' (2 + 13 + 20) = `-35 = RECIPROCAL = `-53 = "WAR of the WORLDS"!!!!!~' (53 + 16) = `-69 = `-BIRTHDAY # `-NUMBER of the `-JUDGE!!!!!~'

'-JUDGE '-ANTONIN '-SCALIA'S '-BIRTHDAY # '-NUMBER (03/11/19/36) = (3 + 11 + 19 + 36) = '-<u>69</u> = '-<u>SUPREME</u>-'"!!!!!~' ('-<u>888</u>) = (88 x 8) = '-<u>704</u> = (74 + 0) = '-<u>74</u>!!!!!~'

(19<u>36</u>/20<u>16</u>) = '-<u>36</u> = <u>RECIPROCAL</u> = '-<u>63</u> / (63 + 16) = '-<u>79</u> = "AGE of '-DEATH of '-SUPREME '-COURT '-JUDGE '-ANTONIN '-SCALIA"!!!!!~' (63 (-) 16) = '-<u>47</u>!!!!!~'

(36 + 61) = '-<u>97</u> = <u>RECIPROCAL</u> = '-<u>79</u> = "WAR of the WORLDS"!!!!!~'

There are some '-<u>338</u> '-DAYS that '-LIE '-IN-BETWEEN '-JUDGE '-ANTONIN '-SCALIA'S '-<u>BIRTHDAY</u>; and, '-<u>DEATH/\DAY</u>!!!!!~' '-<u>74</u> = <u>RECIPROCAL</u> = '-<u>47</u>!!!!!~'

VANITY (-) '-DENISE '-KATRINA '-MATTHEWS '-<u>DIED</u> at the '-AGE of '-<u>57</u> on (02/15/20/16)!!!!!~' VANITY'S '-DEATH/DAY # '-NUMBER is (2 + 15 + 20 + 16) = '-<u>53</u> = "WAR of the WORLDS" = on "PRESIDENT'S '-DAY"-'"!!!!!~'

VANITY (-) '-DENISE '-KATRINA '-MATTHEWS '-BIRTHDAY # '-NUMBER is = (01/04/19/59) = (1 + 4 + 19 + 59) = '-<u>83</u> = "The '-YEAR of the '-<u>MONKEY</u>"-'"!!!!!~'

'-BIRTHDAY # '-NUMBER (+) '-DEATH/DAY # '-NUMBER = (83 + <u>53</u>) = '-<u>136</u> = (36 x 1) = '-<u>36</u> = "YEAR of '-BIRTH of the '-SUPREME '-COURT '-JUDGE '-ANTONIN '-SCALIA of the '-UNITED '-STATES of '-AMERICA '-SUPREME '-COURT"!!!!!~'

(19<u>59</u>/20<u>16</u>) = '-<u>59</u> = <u>RECIPROCAL</u> = '-<u>95</u> / (95 (-) 16 = '-<u>79</u> = "AGE of '-DEATH of '-SUPREME '-COURT '-JUDGE '-ANTONIN '-SCALIA"!!!!!~'

(59 + 16) = '-<u>75</u> = <u>RECIPROCAL</u> = '-<u>57</u> = "AGE of '-DEATH of VANITY (-) '-DENISE '-KATRINA '-MATTHEWS"!!!!!~'

VANITY (-) '-DENISE '-KATRINA '-MATTHEWS '-<u>DIED</u> '-<u>42</u> = '-<u>WAR</u>-'" = '-<u>DAYS</u> after '-<u>HER</u> '-<u>BIRTHDAY</u>!!!!!~' '-SUPREME '-COURT '-JUDGE '-ANTONIN '-SCALIA '-<u>DIED</u> '-<u>27</u> '-<u>DAYS</u> before '-<u>HIS</u> '-<u>NEXT</u> '-<u>BIRTHDAY</u>!!!!!~' (42 + 27) = '-<u>69</u> = '-<u>SUPREME</u>-'" <u>JUDGE</u>-'"!!!!!~'

`-JUDGE `-ANTONIN `-SCALIA'S `-BIRTHDAY # `-NUMBER (+)`-DEATH/DAY # `-NUMBER = (69 + 51) = `-120!!!!!~' `-DENISE (`-136) (-) `-ANTONIN (`-120) = `-16 = "YEAR (`-2016) of `-DEATH for `-BOTH (MALE; and, FEMALE) = (20 + 16) = `-36 = 3(6's) = `-666 = (6 x 6 x 6) = `-216 = "FEBRUARY 16th = "DAY of the `-FINAL `-ENTRY of this `-BOOK"!!!!!~' The `-MARK of the `-BEAST = `-EQUALS = `-666!!!!!~'

`-A /VANITY (-) `-DENISE `-KATRINA `-MATTHEWS (`-PARALLEL) is the `-ACTOR `-GEORGE GAYNES who had `-DIED on the `-VERY `-EXACT `-SAME `-DAY!!!!!~' `-ACTOR `-GEORGE GAYNES is like GALILEO `-GALILEI who had `-DIED at the `-AGE of `-77!!!!!~' (`-GG) of GEORGE GAYNES; and, GALILEO `-GALILEI = `-77 = "ACCORDING to the `-AMERICAN `-ENGLISH `-ALPHABET = (`-G) = (`-7)!!!!!~'

GEORGE GAYNES `-BIRTHDAY # `-NUMBER (05/16/19/17) = (5 + 16 + 19 + 17) = `-57 = "The `-DEATH `-AGE of VANITY (-) `-DENISE `-KATRINA `-MATTHEWS!!!!!~'

GEORGE GAYNES `-DIED (`-77) `-DAYS after `-HIS `-WIFE'S `-BIRTHDAY!!!!!~' GEORGE GAYNES WIFE (ALLYN ANN McLERIE) is (`-89) YEARS of `-AGE `-CURRENTLY!!!!!~' GEORGE GAYNES `-DIED on the `-RECIPROCAL `-AGE of `-HIS `-WIFE at the `-AGE of (`-98)!!!!!~' GEORGE GAYNES MARRIED `-HIS `-WIFE in (`-1953)!!!!!~' GEORGE GAYNES had `-DIED with a `-DEATH/DAY # `-NUMBER of (`-53) on (02/15/20/16) = (2 + 15 + 20 + 16) = `-53!!!!!~' GEORGE GAYNES; and, `-HIS `-WIFE; ALLYN ANN McLERIE, were `-MARRIED for `-63 `-YEARS = RECIPROCAL = `-36 = `-JUDGE `-ANTONIN `-SCALIA'S `-BIRTH/YEAR!!!!!~'

ALLYN ANN McLERIE was `-BORN on (12/01/19/26) = a `-BIRTHDAY # `-NUMBER of = (12 + 1 + 19 + 26) = `-58 = (5 + 8) = `-13 = "A VERY PIVOTAL NUMBER"!!!!!~' (98 (-) 26) = `-72 = RECIPROCAL = `-27 = `-2(7's) = `-77!!!!!~' (89 (-) 26) = `-63!!!!!~'

Former `-UNITED `-NATIONS `-SIXTH `-SECRETARY `-GENERAL `-BOUTROS BOUTROS-GHALI `-DIED at the `-AGE of `-93 on (02/16/20/16) = (2 + 16 + 20 + 16) = `-54 = "EARTHQUAKES"!!!!!~' (2 + 16 + 20) = `-38 = 3(8's) = `-888 = (8 x 8 x 8) = `-512 = (5 (1 + 2)) = `-53 = "WAR of the WORLDS"!!!!!~' (93 + 93) = `-186 = (86 x 1) = `-86

275

= "HAR-MAGEDON"!!!!!~' `-93 = <u>RECIPROCAL</u> = `-<u>39</u> / (93 + 39) = `-<u>132</u> = (32 x 1) = `-<u>32</u> = -a Prophetic Number!!!!!~' / `-<u>32</u> = <u>RECIPROCAL</u> = `-<u>23</u> \

`-BOUTROS BOUTROS-GHALI `-<u>DIED</u> (`-<u>93</u>) `-DAYS after `-HIS (`-<u>93</u>rd) `-BIRTHDAY on = (11/14/19/22) = (11 + 14 + 19 + 22) = `-<u>66</u> = "<u>FATHER</u>"-'"!!!!!~' "<u>F</u>" = (`-<u>6</u>)!!!!!~'

`-BOUTROS BOUTROS-GHALI was `-SUCCEEDED `-BY `-KOFI ANNAN who has a `-BIRTHDAY # `-NUMBER of = (04/08/19/<u>38</u>) = (4 + 8 + 19 + <u>38</u>) = `-<u>69</u> = `-<u>SUPREME-</u>'" JUDGE-'"!!!!!~' `-KOFI ANNAN is `-CURRENTLY (`-<u>77</u>) `-YEARS of `-AGE!!!!!~'

`-KOFI ANNAN was `-SUCCEEDED `-BY `-BAN KI-MOON who has a `-BIRTHDAY # `-NUMBER of = (06/13/19/<u>44</u>) = (6 + 13 + 19 + 44) = `-<u>82</u> = "ARMAGEDDON"!!!!!~' (6 + 13 + 19) = `-<u>38</u> = 3(8's) = `-<u>888</u> = (8 x 8 x 8) = `-<u>512</u> = (5 (1 + 2)) = `-<u>53</u> = "WAR of the WORLDS"!!!!!~' (06/13) = (63 x 1 + 0) = `-<u>63</u> = "MOTHER"-'"!!!!!~' `-BAN KI-MOON is `-CURRENTLY (`-<u>71</u>) `-YEARS of `-AGE; and, `-SOON to be; (`-<u>72</u>)!!!!!~'

`-READ `-BETWEEN the `-LINES!!!!!~' (`-ALL) are (`-TIED) /|\ (`-TOGETHER)!!!!!~'

THERE ARE `-<u>88</u> `-MODERN `-CONSTELLATIONS `-TODAY!!!!!~'

The "PROPHET" `-SEES `-ARMAGEDDON; coming from, /|\ `-<u>GEMINI</u>-'"!!!!!~

Alphabetical Listing of Constellations

1) <u>Andromeda</u>
2) <u>Antlia</u>
3) <u>Apus</u>
4) <u>Aquarius</u>
5) <u>Aquila</u>
6) <u>Ara</u>
7) <u>Aries</u>
8) <u>Auriga</u>
9) <u>Boötes</u>
10) <u>Caelum</u>
11) <u>Camelopardalis</u>
12) <u>Cancer</u>

13) Canes Venatici
14) Canis Major
15) Canis Minor
16) Capricornus
17) Carina
18) Cassiopeia
19) Centaurus
20) Cepheus
21) Cetus
22) Chamaeleon
23) Circinus
24) Columba
25) Coma Berenices
26) Corona Austrina
27) Corona Borealis
28) Corvus
29) Crater
30) Crux
31) Cygnus
32) Delphinus
33) Dorado
34) Draco
35) Equuleus
36) Eridanus
37) Fornax
38) Gemini
39) Grus
40) Hercules
41) Horologium
42) Hydra
43) Hydrus
44) Indus
45) Lacerta
46) Leo
47) Leo Minor
48) Lepus
49) Libra
50) Lupus
51) Lynx
52) Lyra

53) <u>Mensa</u>
54) <u>Microscopium</u>
55) <u>Monoceros</u>
56) <u>Musca</u>
57) <u>Norma</u>
58) <u>Octans</u>
59) <u>Ophiuchus</u>
60) <u>Orion</u>
61) <u>Pavo</u>
62) <u>Pegasus</u>
63) <u>Perseus</u>
64) <u>Phoenix</u>
65) <u>Pictor</u>
66) <u>Pisces</u>
67) <u>Piscis Austrinus</u>
68) <u>Puppis</u>
69) <u>Pyxis</u>
70) <u>Reticulum</u>
71) <u>Sagitta</u>
72) <u>Sagittarius</u>
73) <u>Scorpius</u>
74) <u>Sculptor</u>
75) <u>Scutum</u>
76) <u>Serpens</u>
77) <u>Sextans</u>
78) <u>Taurus</u>
79) <u>Telescopium</u>
80) <u>Triangulum</u>
81) <u>Triangulum Australe</u>
82) <u>Tucana</u>
83) <u>Ursa Major</u>
84) <u>Ursa Minor</u>
85) <u>Vela</u>
86) <u>Virgo</u>
87) <u>Volans</u>
88) <u>Vulpecula</u>

JOB 38:7 (-) "(<u>7</u>) When the morning stars sang together, and all the sons of God shouted for joy?" -(**ENGLISH REVISED EDITION - 1885**)-

JOB 38:4-7 (-) "(**4**) Where wast thou when I laid the foundations of the earth? declare, if thou hast understanding. (**5**) Who determined the measures thereof, if thou knowest? or who stretched the line upon it? (**6**) Whereupon were the foundations thereof fastened? or who laid the corner stone thereof; (**7**) When the morning stars sang together, and all the sons of God shouted for joy?" -(**ENGLISH REVISED EDITION - 1885**)-

`-**38** = **RECIPROCAL** = `-**83**

PROVERBS 8:30 (-) "(**30**) Then I was by him, as a master workman: and I was daily his delight, rejoicing always before him;" -(**ENGLISH REVISED EDITION - 1885**)-

HEBREWS 1:7,14 (-) "(**7**) And of the angels he saith, Who maketh his angels winds, And his ministers a flame of fire: (**14**) Are they not all ministering spirits, sent forth to do service for the sake of them that shall inherit salvation?" -(**ENGLISH REVISED EDITION - 1885**)-

`-**74** = **RECIPROCAL** = `-**47**

PSALM 34:7 (-) "(**7**) The angel of the LORD encampeth round about them that fear him, and delivereth them." -(**ENGLISH REVISED EDITION - 1885**)-

HEBREWS 11:4,7 (-) "(**4**) By faith Abel offered unto God a more excellent sacrifice than Cain, through which he had witness borne to him that he was righteous, God bearing witness in respect of his gifts: and through it he being dead yet speaketh. (**7**) By faith Noah, being warned of God concerning things not seen as yet, moved with godly fear, prepared an ark to the saving of his house; through which he condemned the world, and became heir of the righteousness which is according to faith." -(**ENGLISH REVISED EDITION - 1885**)-

GENESIS 7:23 (-) "(**23**) And every living thing was destroyed which was upon the face of the ground, both man, and cattle, and creeping thing, and fowl of the heaven; and they were destroyed from the earth: and Noah only was left, and they that were with him in the ark." -(**ENGLISH REVISED EDITION - 1885**)-

DEUTERONOMY 18:10,11 (-) "(**10**) There shall not be found with thee any one that maketh his son or his daughter to pass through the fire, one that useth divination, one that practiseth augury, or an enchanter, or a sorcerer,

(11) or a charmer, or a consulter with a familiar spirit, or a wizard, or a necromancer." -(ENGLISH REVISED EDITION - 1885)- (7 + 23 + 18 + 10 + 11) = `-69 = `"Je·ho'vah"'`!!!!!~'

PROVERBS 18:10 (-) "**(10)** The name of the LORD is a strong tower: the righteous runneth into it, and is safe." -(ENGLISH REVISED EDITION - 1885)- /|(=) `-38|\

JOEL 2:32 (-) "**(32)** And it shall come to pass, that whosoever shall call on the name of the LORD shall be delivered: for in mount Zion and in Jerusalem there shall be those that escape, as the LORD hath said, and among the remnant those whom the LORD doth call." -(ENGLISH REVISED EDITION - 1885)-

`-23 = RECIPROCAL = `-32 / `-35 = RECIPROCAL = `-53 = "WAR of the WORLDS"!~

EXODUS 3:15 (-) "**(15)** And God said moreover unto Moses, Thus shalt thou say unto the children of Israel, The LORD, the God of your fathers, the God of Abraham, the God of Isaac, and the God of Jacob, hath sent me unto you: this is my name for ever, and this is my memorial unto all generations." -(ENGLISH REVISED EDITION - 1885)-

(32 + 15) = `-47 / `-47 = RECIPROCAL = `-74 / `-27 = RECIPROCAL = `-72

PSALM 47:2 (-) "**(2)** For **Jehovah** Most High is **fearful**, A great king over all the earth." –Young's Literal Translation–

PSALM 72:4 (-) "**(4)** He shall judge the poor of the people, he shall save the children of the needy, and shall break in pieces the oppressor." -(ENGLISH REVISED EDITION - 1885)-

PSALM 27:4 (-) "**(4)** One thing have I asked of the LORD, that will I seek after; that I may dwell in the house of the LORD all the days of my life, to behold the beauty of the LORD, and to inquire in his temple." -(ENGLISH REVISED EDITION - 1885)-

HEBREWS 4:13 (-) "**(13)** And there is no creature that is not manifest in his sight: but all things are naked and laid open before the eyes of him with whom we have to do." -(ENGLISH REVISED EDITION - 1885)-

`-SCRIPTURE `-VERSES = (2 + 4 + 4 + 13) = `-23 = -a Prophetic Number!!!!!~' `-The `-SACRED `-WRITINGS of `-JEHOVAH `-GOD!!!!!~' `-GOD; our, `-FATHER!!!~'

REVELATION 5:3 (-) "(3) And no one in the heaven, or on the earth, or under the earth, was able to open the book, or to look thereon." -(ENGLISH REVISED EDITION - 1885)-

REVELATION 5:13 (-) "(13) And every created thing which is in the heaven, and on the earth, and under the earth, and on the sea, and all things that are in them, heard I saying, Unto him that sitteth on the throne, and unto the Lamb, be the blessing, and the honour, and the glory, and the dominion, for ever and ever." -(ENGLISH REVISED EDITION - 1885)-

REVELATION 3:5 (-) "(5) He that overcometh shall thus be arrayed in white garments; and I will in no wise blot his name out of the book of life, and I will confess his name before my Father, and before his angels." -(ENGLISH REVISED EDITION - 1885)-

`-313 = Reciprocal-Sequenced-Numerology = (313 + 5) = `-318 = (38 x 1) = `-38/|\

HEAVEN = (H-8 / E-5 / A-1 / V-22 / E-5 / N-14) = (8 + 5 + 1 + 22 + 5 + 14) = `-55 = `-23 + `-32!!!!!~'

HADES = (H-8 / A-1 / D-4 / E-5 / S-19) = (8 + 1 + 4 + 5 + 19) = `-37!!!!!~'

HELL = (H-8 / E-5 / L-12 / L-12) = (8 + 5 + 12 + 12) = `-37!!!!!~' / (37 + 37) = `-74!!!!!~'

`-HEAVEN, `-HADES; and, `-HELL = (HHH) = (888) = 3(8's) = `-38 = `-888 = (8 x 8 x 8) = `-512 = (5 (1 + 2)) = `-53 = "WAR of the WORLDS"!!!!!~'

(55 + 37) = `-92 / (55 + 74) = `-129 / `-29 = RECIPROCAL = `-92 / (129 + 92) = `-221 = "SWIPE `-1" = `-212 = `-BOILING `-POINT of `-FAHRENHEIT!!!!!~'

(221 + 212) = `-433 = (`-43) + (`-33) = (`-76) = DIVIDED by `-2 = `-38 = `-888 = (8 x 8 x 8) = `-512 = (5 (1 + 2)) = `-53 = "WAR of the WORLDS"!!!!!~'

EARTHQUAKES = (E-5 / A-1 / R-18 / T-20 / H-8 / Q-17 / U-21 / A-1 / K-11 / E-5 / S-19) = (5 + 1 + 18 + 20 + 8 + 17 + 21 + 1 + 11 + 5 + 19) = `-126 = (26 x 1) = `-26!!!!!~'

PESTILENCES = (P-16 / E-5 / S-19 / T-20 / I-9 / L-12 / E-5 / N-14 / C-3 / E-5 / S-19) = (16 + 5 + 19 + 20 + 9 + 12 + 5 + 14 + 3 + 5 + 19) = `-127 = (27 x 1) = `-27!!!!!~'

PESTILENCES & EARTHQUAKES = (27 + 26) = `-53 = "WAR of the WORLDS"!!!!!~'

PESTILENCES = `-ELEVEN (`-11) `-LETTERS = EARTHQUAKES = `-22 = "Yin/Yang" = "Multiple of `-ELEVEN" = "The `-CYCLE of `-LIFE"!!!!!~'

HURRICANE = (H-8 / U-21 / R-18 / R-18 / I-9 / C-3 / A-1 / N-14 / E-5) = (8 +21 + 18 + 18 + 9 + 3 + 1 + 14 + 5) = `-97 = "WAR of the WORLDS"!!!!!~'

`-79 = RECIPROCAL = `-97 / (97 + 97) = `-194 = (94 x 1) = `-94 = RECIPROCAL = `-49 = "The `-DEATH # `-NUMBERS"!!!!!~'

TORNADO = (T-20 / O-15 / R-18 / N-14 / A-1 / D-4 / O-15) = (20 + 15 + 18 + 14 + 1 + 4 + 15) = `-87!!!!!~' (87 + 87) = `-174 = (74 x 1) = `-74% of the `-UNIVERSE is `-POSTULATED to be `-DARK `-ENERGY!!!!!~' The `-DEAD `-SEA `-SCROLLS were `-Discovered in `-1947!!!!!~' `-74 = RECIPROCAL = `-47 / (47 + 19) = `-66!!!!!~'

What are the `-END of `-TIMES!!!!!~' What will `-ARMAGEDDON be `-LIKE!!!!!~'

`-END = (E-5 / N-14 / D-4) = (5 + 14 + 4) = `-23 = -a Prophetic Number!!!!!~'

`-TIMES = (T-20 / I-9 / M-13 / E-5 / S-19) = (20 + 9 + 13 + 5 + 19) = `-66 = "Yin/Yang" = "Multiple of `-ELEVEN" = "The `-CYCLE of `-LIFE"!!!!!~'

`-LIKE = (L-12 / I-9 / K-11/ E-5) = (12 + 9 + 11 + 5) = `-37 = `-HADES; or, `-HELL!!!!!~'

The `-KING; and, `-HIS `-KINGDOM!!!!!~' A `-MESSIANIC `-MESSAGE of `-HOPE!~'

CHRIST = (_3_ + _8_ + 18 + _9_ + 19 + 20) = `-77 = `-2(7's) = "The ROMAN EMPIRE"!!!!!-'

The `-**WORD** (-) `-**LUCIFER** = (**L**-12 / **U**-21 / **C**-3 / **I**-9 / **F**-6 / **E**-5 / R-18) = (12 + 21 + 3 + 9 + 6 + 5 + 18) = `-74 = "INDEPENDENCE DAY"!!!!!-'

The `-**WORD** (+) **JESUS** = `-**EQUALS** = (**J**-10 / **E**-5 / **S**-19 / **U**-21 / **S**-19) = `-74 = "INDEPENDENCE `-DAY" from `-**LUCIFER**!!!!!-'

A	B	C	D	E	F	G	H	I	J	K	L	M	N	O	P	Q	R	S	T	U	V	W	X	Y	Z
1	2	3	4	5	6	7	8	9	10	11	12	13	14	15	16	17	18	19	20	21	22	23	24	25	26

JEH-_OVAH_ = (10 + _5_ + _8_ + _15_ + _22_ + _1_ + 8) = `-69 = "The `-CYCLE of `-LIFE"!!!!!-'

DARK = (D-4 / A-1 / R-18 / K-11) = (4 + 1 + 18 + 11) = `-34!!!!!-'

ENERGY = (E-5 / N-14 / E-5 / R-18 / G-7 / Y-25) = (5 + 14 + 5 + 18 + 7 + 25) = `-74!!!!!-'

DARK = (D-4 / A-1 / R-18 / K-11) = (4 + 1 + 18 + 11) = `-34!!!!!-'

MATTER = (M-13 / A-1 / T-20 / T-20 / E-5 / R-18) = (13 + 1 + 20 + 20 + 5 + 18) = `-77!!!!!-'

LIGHT = (L-12 / I-9 / G-7 / H-8 / T-20) = (12 + 9 + 7 + 8 + 20) = `-56!!!!!-'

(69 x 2) = `-138 = (38 x 1) = `-38 = 3(8's) = `-888 = (8 x 8 x 8) = `-512 = (5 (1 + 2)) = `-53 = "WAR of the WORLDS"!!!!!-' PLANET = (16 + 12 + 1 + 14 + 5 + 20) = `-68-'"

(69 x 3) = `-207 = "Three `-TIMES for `-EMPHASIS"!!!!!-'

`-**GOD** is `-**NOT** `-**DARK** `-**ENERGY** `-**MATTER;** but, `-**HE** is; `-**LIGHT** `-**ENERGY** `-**MATTER** (`-**RECIPROCALS**-`)-'!!!!!-' OMNIPRESENT/ OMNISCIENT/OMNIPOTENT/|\

(56 + 74 + 77) = `-207 = "Three `-TIMES for `-EMPHASIS"!!!!!-'

`-13, `-23; &, `-32 = "ARE / A `-PARADIGM `-SHIFT within THE PHENOMENON of `-PENDULUM `-FLOW"!!!!!-' (69 (-) 13) = `-56!!!!!-'

(13 + 23 + 32) = `-68 = "**DARK** x `-2"!!!!!-'

A = 1 / QUANTUM = (Q-17 + U-21 + A-1 + N-14 + T-20 + U-21 + M-13) = `-107 / PHYSICS = (P-16 / H-8 / Y-25 / S-19 / I-9 / C-3 / S-19) = `-99 / (1 + 107 + 99) = `-207 =

"Three `-TIMES for `-EMPHASIS"!!!!!~' `-GOD is "`-A `-QUANTUM `-PHYSICS"!!!!!~'

`-SCIENTIFIC `-LAWS have a SCIENTIFIC MESSAGE LEFT WITHIN THE COSMIC CODE!!!!!~'

`-EXPLORE in a `-HIDDEN `-LEVEL the `-HIDDEN `-ORDER of `-NATURE within the – (`-RECIPROCALS-"")!!!!!~'

With a `-360 `-DEGREE `-VIEW, within this `-SPHERICAL `-STRUCTURE; `-VIEW, the `-UNIVERSE of `-THINGS!!!!!~'

There are `-ALTERNATE `-DIMENSIONS that are `-INFINITE; and, not like the `-11 `-DIMENSIONS of `-STRING `-THEORY!!!!!~'

With `-QUANTUM `-THEORY; only, a `-UNIVERSAL `-CREATOR; could have `-EXISTED; and, `-CREATED `-EVERYTHING!!!!!~'

The `-MULTIVERSE has `-11 `-DIMENSIONS; and, with an `-ULTIMATE `-ASSORTMENT; of an `-ENORMOUS amount, of; `-INFINITE `-UNIVERSES, this `-too; seems, `-EXTREMELY `-UNLIKELY; and, `-LACKING!!!!!~'

`-3.14159 = `-PI = (P-16 / I-9) = (16/9) = (169) = (69 x 1) = `-69 = JEH-OVAH!!!!!~'

π = `-3.14159 = (3 + 1 + 4 + 1 + 5 + 9) = `-23 = -a Prophetic Number!!!!!~'

(360 x 3.14159) = `-1130.9724 = (1 + 1 + 3 + 0 + 9 + 7 + 2 + 4) = `-27 = "The Roman Empire"/`-ALL ENCOMPASSING!!!!!~'

(360 x 3.14159) = `-1130.9724 = ROUNDED UP = `-1131 = (1 + 1 + 3 + 1) = `-6!!!!!~'

`-2 x `-3 = `-6 / `-3 x `-2 = `-6 / `-23 = RECIPROCAL = `-32 / `-23 + `-32 = `-55-'

(1131 / `-13) = `-87 / `-87 + `-87 = `-174 / 87 = RECIPROCAL = 78 / `-78 + `-78 = `-156-'

(174 + 156) = `-330 = (33 + 0) = `-33 = "Yin/Yang" = "Multiple of `-ELEVEN" = "The `-CYCLE of `-LIFE"!!!!!~' `-DEAD `-SEA `-SCROLLS `-Discovered (1947-1956)!!!!!~'

`-74 = RECIPROCAL = `-47 / `-56 = RECIPROCAL = `-65 / (74 + 47 + 56 + 65) = `-242'

`-LIGHT = `-56 / (56 x 2) = `-112 = 47 + 65 = `-112 = (112 + 112) = `-224 = "SWIPE `-1"

(242 + 224) = `-466 / (466 / `-2) = `-233 = (`-23) (`-33) = (23 + 33) = `-56 = LIGHT!!!!!~'

The `-ALTERNATE `-DIMENSIONS can be; AND, have been `-USED, for `-TIME `-TRAVEL!!!!!~' A `-MIND of `-GOD that can `-SEPARATE `-REALITY from any of these `-ALTERNATE `-DIMENSIONS; and, to `-INSERT these `-ALTERNATE `-DIMENSIONS into `-REALITY within `-OUR `-CURRENT `-STREAM of `-TIME!!!!!~'
This `-STATE of `-AFFAIRS-'"; with `-JEHOVAH `-GOD, is `-MAGNANIMOUS!!!!!~'

Where is `-JEHOVAH `-GOD'S `-HOME!!!!!~' I've `-TOLD `-YOU!!!!!~'

MATTHEW 6:9 (-) "(9) After this manner therefore pray ye: Our Father which art in heaven, Hallowed be thy name." -(ENGLISH REVISED EDITION - 1885)- (`-69) = `-JEHOVAH)!~

DWAYNE'S `-FORMULA!!!!!~'

"Compound interest is the eighth wonder of the world. He who understands it, earns it … he who doesn't … pays it."

`-ALBERT `-EINSTEIN'S `-QUOTE"!~'

A= 300,000 (1+0.03517)^30

A= 300,000 (1+0.04)^30

A= 300,000 (1+0.04017)^30

A= 300,000 (1+0.04517)^30

A= 300,000 (1+0.05017)^30

$A = P (1+R)^\wedge T$

A = `-*TOTAL* `-*AMOUNT* `-*PAID!!!!!~*'

P = `-*PRINCIPAL!!!!!~*'

R = `-*INTEREST* `-*RATE!!!!!~*'

T = `-*TIME in* `-*YEARS!!!!!~*'

^ = `-*TO* `-*THE* `-*POWER* `-*OF!!!!!~*'

DWAYNE W. ANDERSON'S `-**RULE of** `-**THUMB;** `-*NOW* `-*DIVIDE* `-*BY,* (`-1.74/3.517%), (`-1.88/4%), (`-1.905/4.017%), (`-2.07/4.517%), (`-2.235/5%), (`-2.235/5.017%)...(`-***ADD*** -(`-**0.165**)/`-***Abraham Lincoln's # *** `-***NUMBER***)- **to** `-**EVERY** (`-1/2% `-*PERCENTAGE* `-*POINT to be* `-*ADDED);* `-**DIVIDE** `-**BY** (`-30); **and,** `-**NOW** `-**DIVIDE** `-**BY** (`-12); `-**FOR A** `-**NEW** `-**MONTHLY** `-**PAYMENT** `-**AMOUNT on a** `-**NEW** `-**MORTGAGE!!!!!~**'

ISAIAH 42:8 (-) "(8) I am Jehovah, that is my name; and my glory will I not give to another, neither my praise unto graven images." -(*AMERICAN STANDARD VERSION*)-

`-**545** = **Reciprocal-Sequencing-Numerology-RSN!~** `-**234** = **Prophetic-Linear-Progression-PLP!~**

ISAIAH 54:5 (-) "(5) For thy Maker is thy husband; Jehovah of hosts is his name: and the Holy One of Israel is thy Redeemer; the God of the whole earth shall he be called." -(*AMERICAN STANDARD VERSION*)-

`-GOLDEN `-STATE `-WARRIORS `-WIN for the `-RECORD of `-**53** `-WINS; and, `-**5** `-LOSSES against the `-OKLAHOMA `-CITY `-THUNDER `-**41** `-WINS; and, `-**18** `-LOSSES (`-**121** (+) `-**118**) = (121 + 118) = `-**239** = (23 + 9) = `-**32** = **-a Prophetic Number!!!!!~**'

(41 (-) 18) = `-**23** = **-a PROPHETIC NUMBER!!!!!~**' / `-**32** = **RECIPROCAL** = `-**23** / `-**35** = **RECIPROCAL** = `-**53**

`-GAME = `-EQUALED = `-SATURDAY (FEBRUARY **27**[h]) at `-**5:30**PM at the `-CHESAPEAKE `-ENERGY `-ARENA!!!!!~'

`-**35** = `-KEVIN `-DURANT / `-OKLAHOMA `-CITY `-THUNDER / `-ALMOST `-WINS the `-GAME for the `-OKLAHOMA `-CITY `-THUNDER!!!!!-' `-KEVIN `-DURANT is `-CURRENTLY `-**27** `-YEARS of `-AGE; and, was `-BORN on (**9/29/1988**)!!!!!-' (9 + 29) = `-**38**!!!!!-' (9 + 29 + 19 + 88) = `-**145**!!!!!-'

`-GOLDEN `-STATE `-WARRIORS `-WIN for the `-RECORD of `-**55** `-WINS; and, `-**5** `-LOSSES against the `-OKLAHOMA `-CITY `-THUNDER `-**42** `-WINS; and, `-**20** `-LOSSES (`-**121** (+) `-**106**) = (121 + 106) = `-**227** = `-EMPHATIC `-WITNESS to the `-# `-NUMBER `-**27**!!!!!-' (42 + 20) = `-**62** / (55 + 5) = `-**60** / (62 + 60) = `-**122** = (22 + 1) = `-**23** = -a **PROPHETIC NUMBER!!!!!-'**

(121 (-) 118) = `-**3** / (121 (-) 106) = `-**15** / (`-**315**) = (35 x 1) = `-**35** = **RECIPROCAL** = `-**53**!!!!!-'

(118 (-) 106) = `-**12** = **RECIPROCAL** = `-**21** = `-**121** = Reciprocal-Sequenced-Numerology-**RSN**!!!!!-'

`-GAME = `-EQUALED = `-THURSDAY (MARCH **3**rd) at `-**7:30**PM at the `-**ORACLE** `-**ARENA**!!!!!-'

`-DATE (**3/5**/2016) – UFC **196** = `-**96** = **RECIPROCAL** = `-**69** = `-**JEHOVAH**!!!!!-' `-MIESHA `-TATE at `-1**35** lbs. `-WINS the `-BANTANWEIGHT `-CHAMPIONSHIP over `-**HOLLY** `-**HOLM**!!!!!-'

`-**135** lb.= `-**MIESHA** `-**TATE** is `-CURRENTLY `-**29** `-YEARS of `-AGE; and, was `-BORN on (**8/18/1986**)!!!!!-' (8 + 18 + 19 + 86) = `-**131** = (31 + 1) = `-**32** = -a **PROPHETIC NUMBER** !!!!!-'

(**8** + **18** + 19) = `-**45** = "CURRENT `-AGE of the `-PROPHET" = `-DWAYNE `-W. `-ANDERSON-!!!!!-'

`-**REMEMBER** (`-**818**) = `-**RONDA** `-**ROUSEY** & `-**HOLLY** `-**HOLM**!!!!!- `-**UFC** `-**CHAMPIONS**!!!!!-'

(`-**818**) & (`-**929**) = `-**BOTH** = `-**EQUAL** = Reciprocal-Sequencing-Numerology-**RSN**!!!!!-' (929 (-) 818) = `-**111** / (929 + 818) = `-**1747** = (`-747 x 1) = `-**747** = **RSN**!!!!!-' (747 (-) 111) = `-**EQUALS** = `-**636** = Reciprocal-Sequencing-Numerology-**RSN**!!!!!-'

FIRST LADY `-NANCY `-REAGAN `-<u>DIES</u> on (<u>3</u>/<u>6</u>/<u>2016</u>) = (20 + 16) = `-<u>36</u> = `-<u>3(6's)</u> = (`-<u>666</u>)-!!!!!~'

(36 x 2) = `-<u>72</u> = <u>RECIPROCAL</u> = `-<u>27</u> = "The ROMAN EMPIRE"!!!!!~'

FIRST LADY `-NANCY `-REAGAN; and, FIRST LADY `-LADY `-BIRD `-JOHNSON `-BOTH `-<u>DIE</u> at the `-AGE of `-<u>94</u>!!!!!~' `-NANCY `-<u>DIED</u> on the <u>6</u><sup>th</sup>; and, was `-BURIED `-<u>5</u> `-DAYS `-LATER!!!!!~'

FIRST LADY `-LADY `-BIRD `-JOHNSON `-<u>DIED</u> on (7/11/2007) = (20 + 07) = `-<u>27</u> = "The ROMAN EMPIRE"!!!!!~' (7 + 11 + 20) = `-<u>38</u> / (7 + 11 + 20 + 7) = `-<u>45</u> = "CURRENT `-AGE of the `-PROPHET"!~' (94 / 2) = `-<u>47</u> / (94 x 2) = `-<u>188</u> = (88 x 1) = `-<u>88</u> = **"The `-PIANO `-KEYS"!!!!!~'**

FIRST LADY `-LADY `-BIRD `-JOHNSON was `-BORN on (<u>12</u>/<u>22</u>/19<u>12</u>) = (`-<u>122</u>) / (12 + 22 + 19) = `-<u>53</u> = "WAR of the WORLDS"!!!!!~' (12 + 22 + 19 + 12) = `-<u>65</u> = "ABRAHAM LINCOLN"!!!!!~'

`-<u>12</u> = <u>RECIPROCAL</u> = `-<u>21</u> / `-<u>56</u> = <u>RECIPROCAL</u> = `-<u>65</u> / `-<u>67</u> = <u>RECIPROCAL</u> = `-<u>76</u>

FIRST LADY `-NANCY `-REAGAN was `-BORN on (<u>7</u>/<u>6</u>/19<u>21</u>) = (7 + 6 + 19 + 21) = `-<u>53</u> = "WAR of the `-WORLDS"!!!!!~' FIRST LADY `-NANCY `-REAGAN `-<u>DIED</u> on (<u>3</u>/<u>6</u>/2016) = (3 + 6 + 20 + 16) = `-<u>45</u> = "CURRENT `-AGE of the `-PROPHET" = `-DWAYNE `-W. `-ANDERSON-!!!!!~'

FIRST LADY `-NANCY `-REAGAN `-<u>DIED</u> (`-<u>74</u>) `-<u>DAYS</u> after the `-<u>BIRTHDAY</u> of FIRST LADY `-LADY `-BIRD `-JOHNSON!!!!!~' FIRST LADY `-NANCY `-REAGAN `-<u>DIED</u> (`-<u>122</u>) `-<u>DAYS</u> before `-HER `-<u>NEXT</u> `-<u>BIRTHDAY</u>!!!!!~' (`-<u>122</u>) = (22 + 1) = `-<u>23</u> = -a PROPHETIC NUMBER!!!!!~'

#40/PRESIDENT RONALD REAGAN `-<u>DIED</u> on (<u>6</u>/<u>5</u>/2004) = (6 + 5 + 20 + 4) = `-<u>35</u> = <u>RECIPROCAL</u> = `-<u>53</u> = "WAR of the WORLDS"!!!!!~' #40/PRESIDENT RONALD REAGAN was `-BORN on (2/6/1911) = (2 + 6 + 19 + 11) = `-<u>38</u> = <u>3(8's)</u> = `-<u>888</u> = (8 x 8 x 8) = `-<u>512</u> = (5 (1 + 2)) = `-<u>53</u> = "WAR of the WORLDS"!!!!!~' #36/PRESIDENT LYNDON B. JOHNSON `-<u>DIED</u> on (`-<u>122</u>)!!!!!~'

#40 + #36 = `-<u>76</u> = `-PRESIDENT RONALD REAGAN & PRESIDENT LYNDON B. JOHNSON!!!!!~' `-DEATH = `-200<u>7</u> = LADY BIRD

JOHNSON / `-DEATH = `-201<u>6</u> = NANCY REAGAN / = `-<u>76</u>!!!!!~' `-16 + `-7 = `-<u>23</u> = a Prophetic Number!!!!!~'

#40/PRESIDENT RONALD REAGAN & FIRST LADY `-NANCY `-REAGAN were `-MARRIED for (`-<u>52</u>) `-YEARS; `-ENCAPSULATED, by the `-# (`-<u>53</u>)!!!!!~' (34 + 37 + 52) = `-<u>123</u> = <u>P</u>rophetic-<u>L</u>inear-<u>P</u>rogression-<u>PLP</u>!~!!!!!~' (34 + 37 + 40) = `-<u>111</u>-!!!!!~'

#34/President Dwight D. Eisenhower was `-MARRIED to `-HIS `-WIFE FIRST LADY MAMIE GENEVA DOUD EISENHOWER for `-<u>53</u> `-YEARS = "WAR of the WORLDS"!!!!!~' #34/President Dwight D. Eisenhower's Vice-**President Richard M. Nixon** was `-MARRIED to `-HIS `-WIFE FIRST LADY THELMA "PAT" NIXON for `-<u>53</u> `-YEARS = "WAR of the WORLDS"!!!!!~' #<u>34</u>/President Dwight D. Eisenhower /|\ #<u>37</u>/President Richard M. Nixon!!!!!~' **#2/FIRST LADY ABIGAIL ADAMS** was `-MARRIED to `-HER `-HUSBAND #2/President John Adams for some `-<u>54</u> `-YEARS!!!!!~' (54 + 52 / `-2) = `-<u>53</u> / (#40 (-) #2) = `-#<u>38</u> President Gerald Ford who was `-BORN on (<u>7</u>/1<u>4</u>/19<u>13</u>) = (7 + 14 + 19 + 13) = `-<u>53</u> = "WAR of the WORLDS"!!!~'

George Martin (Beatles Producer) `-DIES on (3/<u>8</u>) of `-201<u>6</u>; (`-<u>65</u>) `-DAYS after `-HIS `-LAST `-BIRTHDAY!!!!!~' `-HE was `-BORN on (1/3/1926); and, `-DIED at the `-AGE of `-90!!!!!~'

Joe Santos (The Rockford Files) `-DIES on (3/18) of `-201<u>6</u>; (`-<u>83</u>) `-DAYS before `-HIS `-NEXT `-BIRTHDAY!!!!!~' `-HE was `-BORN on (6/9/1931); and, `-DIED at the `-AGE of `-84!!!!!~'

`-George Martin & Joe Santos `-ADDED `-UP = (84 + 90) = `-<u>174</u> = (74 x 1) = `-<u>74</u>!!!!!~' `-DEATH/DAY # `-NUMBER = (0<u>3</u>/1<u>8</u>/2016) = (3 + 18 + 20 + 16) = `-<u>57</u>!!!!!~' `-BIRTHDAY # `-NUMBER = (0<u>6</u>/0<u>9</u>/19<u>31</u>) = (6 + 9 + 19 + 31) = `-<u>65</u>!!!!!~' (65 + 57) = `-<u>122</u> = (22 + 1) = `-<u>23</u> = -a Prophetic Number!!!!!~'

(`-<u>122</u>) FIRST LADY `-NANCY REAGAN, (`-<u>122</u>) #<u>40</u>/PRESIDENT `-RONALD REAGAN, (`-<u>1/22</u>) FIRST LADY `-LADY BIRD JOHNSON; and, (`-<u>1/22</u>) #<u>36</u>/PRESIDENT `-LYNDON B. JOHNSON!!!!!~'

Joe Garagiola Sr. (Legendary Baseball Announcer) `-DIES on (3/<u>23</u>) of `-201<u>6</u>; (`-<u>38</u>) `-DAYS that `-LAY in `-BETWEEN `-HIS `-LAST

`-BIRTHDAY; and, `-HIS `-DEATH/DAY!!!!!~' `-HE was `-BORN on (2/12/1926); and, `-DIED at the `-AGE of `-90!!!!!~'

`-323 = (32 x 3); or, (3 x 23) = (96; or, `-69) = Reciprocal-Sequenced-Numerology-RSN!!!!!~'

`-3/23/2016 = "The `-MEMORIAL `-CELEBRATION of `-JESUS `-CHRIST'S `-DEATH"!!!!!~'

Joe Garagiola Sr. was `-BORN on the `-BIRTHDAY of #16/President Abraham Lincoln (`-212) = "SWIPE 1" = (`-122)!!!!!~' `-Joe Garagiola Sr. `-DIED (`-23) `-DAYS before the `-DEATH/DAY of #16/President Abraham Lincoln (4/15/1865)!!!!!~'

Joe Garagiola Sr. `-BIRTHDAY # `-NUMBER = (2 + 12 + 19 + 26) = `-59 = "AGE of `-DEATH of `-MARY (JESUS `-CHRIST'S MOTHER)!!!!!~'

Joe Garagiola Sr. `-DEATH/DAY # `-NUMBER = (3 + 23 + 20 + 16) = `-62 = (100 (-) 62) = `-38 = 3(8's) = `-888 = (8 x 8 x 8) = `-512 = (5 (1 + 2)) = `-53 = "WAR of the WORLDS"!!!!!~'

(59 + 62) = `-121 = `-12 = RECIPROCAL = `-21!!!!!~'

Kenneth Joseph Howard Jr. (An American Actor that `-PLAYED the Basketball Coach Ken Reeves in the Television `-HIT `-SHOW - "The White Shadow" - of which the "PROPHET" both `-LIKED; and, `-WATCHED) – (He also `-PLAYED - "THOMAS JEFFERSON" - in `-1776) `-DIES on (3/23) of `-2016; (`-5) `-DAYS before `-HIS `-NEXT `-BIRTHDAY!!!!!~' `-HE was `-BORN on (3/28/1944); and, `-DIED at the `-AGE of `-71!!!!!~'

Kenneth Joseph Howard Jr. `-BIRTHDAY # `-NUMBER = (3 + 28 + 19 + 44) = `-94 = "AGE of `-DEATH `-# `-NUMBERS = "If the "PROPHET'S" MOTHER were `-ALIVE, `-THEY; would be the `-VERY `-SAME `-AGE" = (`-71)!!!!!~'

Kenneth Joseph Howard Jr. `-DEATH/DAY # `-NUMBER = (3 + 23 + 20 + 16) = `-62 = (100 (-) 62) = `-38 = 3(8's) = `-888 = (8 x 8 x 8) = `-512 = (5 (1 + 2)) = `-53 = "WAR of the WORLDS"!!!!!~'

(94 + 62) = `-156 = (56 x 1) = `-56 = "AGE of `-DEATH of #16/President Abraham Lincoln"!!!!!~' Golden State Warriors `-BEAT the LA Clippers

(`-114/`-98) = (114 + 98) = `-212 = `-Joe & `-Abe's `-BIRTHDAY = "SWIPE 1" = `-122!!!!!~' The `-CURRENT `-RECORD of the `-GOLDEN `-STATE `-WARRIORS is (64-7) = (64 + 7) = `-71 = "Joseph"!!!!!~' Stephen Curry (`-33) `-Points / Klay Thompson (`-32) `-Points = (33 + 32) = `-65 = "YEAR of `-DEATH of #16/President Abraham Lincoln"!!!!!~'

(`-5) `-DAYS in the `-MONTH of (`-3) `-MARCH = `-53 = "WAR of the WORLDS"!!!!!~' (GEO (`-90), JOE (`-84), JOE (`-90); and, JOSEPH (`-71) = (90 + 84 + 90 + 71) = `-335 = "EMPHATIC `-EMPHASIS for the `-# `-NUMBER `-35 = RECIPROCAL = `-53 = "WAR of the WORLDS"!!!!!~'

The `-AMERICAN `-ENGLISH `-ALPHABET = Joseph (`-73), Joe (`-30), Joe (`-30); and, Geo (`-27) = `-160 = `-2016 = `-YEAR of `-DEATH for `-ALL of `-THEM_-'" = `-REVIEW the "CIPHERS of DEATH"; or, the "DEATH CIPHERS" within the `-INITIAL `-BOOK = "The REAL PROPHET of DOOM (KISMET) – INTRODUCTION – PENDULUM FLOW –"!!!!!~'

The `-PRESIDENTIAL `-PARALLELS /|\ in `-TIME-'"!!!!!~'

`-The

`-EYE-"

In the

`-SKY-'"!!!~'

The "PROPHET" `-DECLARES `-GOD'S NAME `-IS:

-(GOD'S NAME)-

=

-(יהוה)-

=

YHWH; or, JHVH

=

JEHOVAH!~'

-(`-THANKING `-GOD for the `-TRUE `-PURITY
of `-THOUGHT - Dwayne W. Anderson-'")-

ABOUT THE AUTHOR

Dwayne W. Anderson, retired Site Infrastructure Senior Engineer. Former California licensed LIFE, HEALTH; AND, DISABILITY INSURANCE AGENT. A retired FOREMAN in CONSTRUCTION. Certified in MEDIATION/ARBITRATION from the UNIVERSITY of BERKELEY, in CALIFORNIA. Singer, Songwriter, Musician; and, Author.

THE REAL PROPHET OF DOOM

(KISMET) - INTRODUCTION - PENDULUM FLOW -

Dwayne W. Anderson

iUniverse

The
REAL PROPHET
OF DOOM

(KISMET) - INTRODUCTION
- PENDULUM FLOW -
II

Dwayne W. Anderson

Printed in the United States
By Bookmasters